The Political Economy
of Globalization

RECENT ECONOMIC THOUGHT SERIES

Editors:

Warren J. Samuels
Michigan State University
East Lansing, Michigan, USA

William Darity, Jr.
University of North Carolina
Chapel Hill, North Carolina, USA

Other books in the series:

The Political Economy of Globalization

Edited by

Satya Dev Gupta
St. Thomas University,
Fredericton, New Brunswick
Canada

Kluwer Academic Publishers
Boston / Dordrecht / London

Distributors for North America:
Kluwer Academic Publishers
101 Philip Drive
Assinippi Park
Norwell, Massachusetts 02061 USA

Distributors for all other countries:
Kluwer Academic Publishers Group
Distribution Centre
Post Office Box 322
3300 AH Dordrecht, THE NETHERLANDS

Library of Congress Cataloging-in-Publication Data

A C.I.P. Catalogue record for this book is available from
the Library of Congress.

Copyright © 1997 by Kluwer Academic Publishers

Printed on acid-free paper

Printed in the United States of America

To Hansa and Santosh

Contents

Preface

Globalization is transforming the world at an accelerated pace. Integration of the world continues, widening and intensifying international linkages in economic, political and social relations. Liberalization of trade and finance, lubricated by revolutionary changes in information technology, has resulted in significant economic growth at the global level. On the other hand, the process of globalization is changing the nature of production relations, threatening the traditional roles of the nation-state, and carrying with it far-reaching implications for sustainable growth, development and the environment.

Although both developed and developing countries are actively participating in this saga of globalization, nearly ninety countries, as the United Nations' *Human Development Report, 1996* indicates, are worse off economically than they were ten years ago, leading to "global polarization" between haves and have nots. The report further indicates that the gap between the per capita incomes of the industrialized world and the developing countries, far from narrowing, has more than tripled during the last thirty years. Further, a majority of the countries benefitting from this globalization drive have seen a rise in inequality and poverty. This failure of market driven globalization to reward the benefits equitably led the United Nations to proclaim 1996 as the International Year for the Eradication of Poverty (IYEP) and the decade of 1997-2006 as the international decade for the eradication of poverty, and to promote "people-centered sustainable development".

It is against this backdrop that nearly seventy leading scholars world wide have come together to explore and analyze a variety of challenges facing this "global village". Their research work is contained in a set of three volumes. One volume, entitled *Globalization, Growth and Sustainability*, focuses on the implications of both regional and global trade liberalization on growth, equity, sustainability and the environment. Another volume, entitled *Dynamics of Globalization and Development*, examines the impact of liberalization in the fields of aid, finance, capital, technology and management policies both at the micro and macro levels.

This volume focuses on the issues arising from a political economy perspective on globalization. Contributors to this volume have addressed such issues as erosion of national sovereignty, strained relations between capital and labor, gender equity, increasing tensions between North and South, and changes in the roles of international institutions, labor organizations, nation-states and non-governmental organizations. Although authors disagree over details, they all recognize an urgent need for refinements in the dominant capitalist paradigm, and a need for strong leadership to implement the changes in a way that would enable all people to achieve their full potential, both as individuals and as members of the global family. This anthology will provide valuable insights and important background analysis for scholars working in the field of globalization as well as senior undergraduate and graduate students in a variety of curricula, including economics, development studies, political science, international relations and international business.

A project of this nature, obviously, can not be carried out without substantial help from others. Nearly two years ago, Sandy Darity Jr. invited me to edit one volume on a current topic for the *Recent Economic Thought Series*. However, the response on the subject matter of this project was so overwhelming that I could not accommodate nearly thirty proposals . I therefore first thank all the scholars who expressed an interest in contributing to the project and apologize to those who, in spite of their excellent proposals, could not be included. Second, I owe a special sense of gratitude to Nanda Choudhry who provided help for this volume in the initial stages of the project and to Francis Adams who helped me in a number of ways in the final stages of the project, including co-authoring the introductory chapter for this volume . Third, I am thankful to the anonymous reviewers whose comments, though invisible, are well reflected in the chapters of this book. Fourth, I wish to thank St. Thomas University for research grants and a number of colleagues including Stan Atherton, Roger Barnsley, Ian Fraser, Tom Good, John Jennings, Santosh Kabadi, Joan McFarland, Richard Myers and Andrew Secord for their help and encouragement. Preparing manuscripts in a camera-ready format, as I learned from this experience, can become a tedious and an extremely time consuming job for an academic. I owe special thanks to a number of assistants who helped me in this venture. Fifth, I wish to thank Sandy Darity Jr. and Warren Samuels, co-editors of the *Recent Economic Thought Series* and Zachry Rolnick and his staff at Kluwer for providing this opportunity and, in particular, for their help, encouragement and understanding in publishing three oversized volumes on the subject. Finally, I owe a special sense of appreciation to my wife Sarita and children Hansa and Santosh who were often deprived of usual family and social discourse for nearly two years. They also deserve special thanks for their labor of love on a number of tasks associated with this project.

Dev Gupta
December 1996

1

THE POLITICAL ECONOMY OF GLOBALIZATION: *An Introduction*

Francis Adams
Old Dominion University, USA
Satya Dev Gupta
St. Thomas University, Canada

Since the dawn of the modern era, nations have carefully guarded their sovereignty and independence. National governments emerged as the primary arbiters of economic and political affairs within clearly delineated territorial boundaries. These governments gradually assumed broad responsibilities for stimulating economic growth, maintaining political stability, and promoting societal welfare.

As the twentieth century comes to a close, the modern system of independent states is being transformed. National governments are gradually losing control over domestic economic and political affairs. Separate national economies are being replaced by a single, integrated global economy and basic political functions, which have traditionally been the province of national authorities, are being delegated to international institutions including transnational corporations. The twin processes of economic and political integration have fundamentally altered our world order.

The term *"globalization"* has come to signify this transition to a single *transnational* political-economy. This volume examines the process of globalization in considerable detail. Focus is placed on the extent to which globalization jeopardizes continued international economic development and sustainability. As the world community hurtles toward economic and political unity, will we be able to effectively respond to the challenges of future generations? Can we move toward a world in which economic expansion helps meet the basic needs of all people? A world in which the vast inequalities between and within nations are reduced? A world in which our natural environments are preserved and protected? Development within the context of globalization must balance these objectives of growth, equity, and sustainability. Finding an effective balance is one of the central themes of this book.

Economic and Political Integration

Economic integration is proceeding at a breathtaking pace. There is, of course, nothing new to the movement of goods and services across national boundaries. However, the rapid increase in international trade in recent years is unprecedented. Foreign trade has quadrupled during the past generation and is now valued at three *trillion* dollars per year. Economic integration is also reflected in the internationalization of production. Since the mid-1970s there has been a truly spectacular growth in the number and size of transnational corporations. Production is now organized on a global basis as corporations routinely shift operations from one venue to the next in search of the most profitable investments. Capital flows have also expanded exponentially. International capital markets currently transfer hundreds of billions of dollars *every day* in response to the slightest change in corporate earnings, currency values, or interest rates. Economic integration is also reflected in the rapid dissemination of new technologies which replicate production facilities in distant corners of the world. Finally, integration can be seen in the movement of people across national boundaries in the insatiable quest for a better standard of living.

The emergence of a single global economy is the product of multiple forces. Clearly the "technological revolution" has contributed to the permeability of national boundaries. Advances in transportation have made it much easier for transnational corporations to produce and market their products around the world. Advances in communications and information systems have had a similar effect. Computers, satellites, lasers, fiber optics and micro chip technologies allow corporations to maintain direct and near instantaneous contact with affiliates virtually anywhere in the world. Economic integration is also a product of governmental reforms. During the past two decades most of the world's governments have adopted neo-liberal reforms to liberalize trade, deregulate production, and integrate domestic economies in global markets.

Economic integration shows little sign of slowing down. One of the central issues addressed in this book is the relationship between economic integration and political sovereignty. While the world continues to be divided territorially, and national governments are vested with substantial powers, economic integration has clearly eroded political sovereignty. National governments have lost effective control over much of the economic activity which takes place within their territories. This includes controlling the money supply, setting interest rates, establishing wages rates, and enhancing social welfare. Governments appear to have a difficult time stimulating their domestic economies. Expansionary fiscal and monetary policies often result in capital flight and a devaluation of the local currency. Attempts to raise taxes or increase controls on private corporations only encourage a shift in production to some other parts of the world.

The erosion of national sovereignty also undermines democratic processes. As a number of the contributors to this volume point out, there has been a noticeable shift in political power away from national governments and toward unelected corporate bodies and unaccountable international institutions. Economic integration propels political integration. As national interests are subordinated to the logic of global markets, heretofore domestic political responsibilities are subsumed by supranational institutions.

Uneven Development

While economic and political integration is transforming the modern world system, this transformation is by no means uniform. The benefits of globalization are unequally distributed, with some nations and groups advancing at the expense of other nations and groups. The uneven nature of development is also a consistent theme of this volume.

The most profound and intractable division today lies between the industrialized nations of the North and the developing nations of the South. The industrialized nations have been the primary beneficiaries of globalization. Economic and political power is concentrated in the transnational corporations, capital markets, and financial institutions of the North. In many respects, globalization has widened the gap between the world's rich and poor nations. Latin American, African, and Asian countries continue to occupy a subordinate position in the global economy. Approximately three quarters of the world's people live in the developing world, yet they possess just one-seventh of the world's wealth.

The integration of developing economies into the global system has proceeded at a rapid pace. This has been especially true since the crisis years of the 1980s. The accumulation of large foreign debts, coupled with a reduction of export earnings, led to chronic foreign exchange shortages throughout the South. In order to continue purchasing vital imports, developing nations turned to international financial institutions, particularly the International Monetary Fund. Foreign exchange support and debt rescheduling were contingent on the integration of domestic economies into global markets. Governments were pressured to ease restrictions on foreign trade by slashing protectionist tariffs and non-tariff barriers. Governments were also required to lessen restrictions on foreign investment. Past requirements, such as local equity participation, employment creation, capital reinvestment, the use of local resources, or the transfer of technology, were replaced by generous incentives to attract foreign capital. Moreover, the privatization of state-owned industries allowed foreign inventors to acquire local productive assets at substantial discounts.

The integration of developing nations into global markets has produced mixed results. The expansion of exports has increased economic growth rates while the influx of new foreign investment has introduced much needed capital and advanced technology. A number of our contributors highlight the potential benefits of economic integration for developing countries. However, most of these economies remain extremely vulnerable to capital flight, currency manipulation, changes in international interest rates, and the fluctuation of global commodity prices.

The benefits of globalization have also been unevenly distributed *within* the world's nations. This is readily apparent in the North. While corporations and professionals have gained, many segments of the workforce, especially unskilled laborers, have been adversely affected. Capital mobility has led to a reduction in the number of manufacturing jobs and a decrease in basic wage rates. Companies are also in a much stronger position to subcontract work out to non-union shops or buy foreign inputs. This results in lower wages, the loss of job security, and a more unequal distribution of income. The adverse effects of globalization also go beyond the immediate workplace. Globalization has undermined entire communities. In the past corporations cultivated ties with the communities in which they operated, often contributing to local infrastructure, education, training, and health care. Today's high level of capital mobility has weakened these community ties. Corporations are less willing to make positive contributions to local communities yet demand tax breaks and reduced health, safety, and environmental regulations. Should local communities resist, these firms threaten to shift production elsewhere.

Unequal distribution is even more apparent in the South. Up to this point, the benefits of globalization have flowed to a fairly narrow segment of the population. Large landowners and export-oriented entrepreneurs have gained wider markets for their products, local businesspeople have benefited from joint venture arrangements with foreign investors, and professionals have found expanded employment opportunities with transnational corporations. Poor and working class people, on the other hand, have seen their fortunes decline. Small landowners have been displaced by local and foreign exporters and small scale artisans have been overwhelmed by an influx of mass-produced foreign products. Although foreign direct investment has produced some manufacturing jobs, these positions are generally characterized by low wage rates, poor health and safety conditions, long working hours, and forced overtime. Overall working conditions have actually deteriorated throughout the South as nations compete with one another to attract foreign investment.

Policy Reform and Popular Organization

Economic and political integration is clearly transforming the lives of people around the world. While some have registered substantial gains in income and wealth, the benefits of globalization have been unevenly distributed both between and within the world's nations. As outlined above, northern nations have benefited to a much greater extent than their southern counterparts while entrepreneurs and professionals in both the North and South have gained at the expense of the poor and working class.

How can the globalization process be structured to promote a more equitable distribution of the world's resources? International institutions, such as the World Bank, International Monetary Fund, and World Trade Organization, are likely to continue to play a central role in the management of international economic relations. While these institutions have helped stimulate global economic growth, they have been less successful in promoting equity, sustainability, and participatory development. One proposal highlighted in this volume is to develop a set of coordinated rules to control capital flows. This would include international standards for labor rights and environmental protections. A code of conduct for multinational corporations could be enacted to require advanced notification of plant closing, mandatory corporate funding for retraining workers, and the prohibition of child labor.

Labor unions and non-governmental organizations must also play a central role in promoting growth, equity, and sustainability. Popular organizations will be critical to establishing universal health and safety standards, and pressuring transnational corporations and international financial institutions to be more accountable and democratic. As a number of our contributors note, the success of labor unions and nongovernmental organizations rests on their ability to operate cross-nationally. Popular organizations need to extend beyond their national frontiers to operate at regional and global levels. Networks of activists from both the North and South must work together to raise living standards, achieve a more equitable distribution of the world's income, protect our natural environments, and preserve democratic rights.

A Brief Review of the Chapters

This books examines the above issues in considerable detail. We have included contributions from some of the leading scholars in their field. The articles are grouped into four broad areas The first part includes those articles which describe the broad process of globalization and examine implications of the shift in power from national to transnational entities. The second and third parts mirror the North-South division in the world. While the articles in the second part focus primarily on the industrialized nations, the articles in the third part turn to the developing nations of Latin America, Africa, and Asia. The book concludes with a set of policy-oriented papers which advance specific proposals for reform.

Globalization and National Sovereignty

The articles in Part One of this anthology examine the overall process of globalization. Each contribution outlines the basic nature of globalization and considers the extent to which globalization is eroding national autonomy. While there is some overlap in the arguments of all three authors, there are also important areas of disagreement.

The first two chapters by Deepak Nayyar and Cyrus Bina provide a broad introduction to the globalization process. Nayyar's primary objective is to place the current period of globalization within a wider historical context. The author points to important similarities between the economic order of the late nineteenth century and today's global economy. For Nayyar, the most significant difference between the two periods is the role played by nation states. While the nineteenth century system largely revolved around nation states, the current period is marked by the rise of multinational corporations and international financial institutions. The autonomy of the nation state is being eroded by international industrial and finance capital. The game of globalization in a world of unequal partners and asymmetrical rules, the author argues, will lead to uneven development unless appropriate corrective policies are undertaken by the concerned nation states in a timely manner.

Bina also links globalization with a decline of national autonomy. He offers a detailed analysis of the dynamic elements of the process of globalization in terms of the globalization of social relations of capital and corresponding transnationalization of the labor process. The global hegemony of social capital, an organic manifold beyond the challenge of any one nation-state or region, the author argues, is rendering the traditional geographic, legal, and cultural barriers irrelevant, if not obsolete. The current phase of globalization, as a unified structure, the author notes, is the outcome of the simultaneous (internal) transformation of both the third world and the advanced capitalist societies. This transformation, however, has not proceeded at an uneven pace. While the third world economies have become an organic part of the global economy, they remain in a subordinate position and realize few of the benefits of globalization.

Tim Koechlin's contribution departs from the earlier two chapters in a number of important respects and thus provides a forum for continued debate. Koechlin provides a contrast of mainstream and heterodox versions of economic openness. While the author agrees with the critique of the mainstream theory by the heterodox economists, he questions the degree of mobility of productive capital in the heterodox literature. Based on an examination of the aggregative data for several countries, the author finds that investment is overwhelmingly undertaken by domestic firms responding to domestic economic conditions thus leaving considerable autonomy and flexibility for nation states in undertaking appropriate policies.

Industrialized Nations of the North

The second part of this volume includes articles which focus more specifically on the industrialized nations of the North. Globalization is clearly having a profound impact on the industrialized world. The authors consider the political, economic, and social changes which these societies are experiencing.

This section begins with a piece by Beth V. Yarbrough and Robert M. Yarbrough. The authors present alternative measurements for international trade which go beyond simply measuring the total volume of trade to also consider changes in the kinds of trade and the patterns of participation. Their analysis suggests that while the patterns of both imports and exports remain virtually untouched in their allocation between industrial and developing trading partners, and while international trade remains overwhelmingly dominated by the industrialized nations, there is a significant change in the *kinds* of trade and in the patterns of *participation*, especially by the developing countries. The authors in turn examine the relative roles of policy-induced and non-policy-induced factors in the process of globalization.

Globalization or internationalization does not imply convergence, nor does it lead to convergence. Brigitte Unger, in the next chapter, argues that the forces towards convergence and towards divergence exist and interact within the same time frame. The author emphasizes convergence as an interdisciplinary issue and analyzes the forces behind convergence and divergence in the context of the European Union. She singles out four channels of convergence: imitation, market competition, state competition and enforcement and demonstrates how these channels have been 'clogged' by the institutional factors including political, social, and cultural differences among the member nations.

The following two contributions by S. Mansoob Murshed and by Dwight W. Adamson and Mark Partridge document a distinct decline in the bargaining power of northern labor unions. Murshed constructs an innovative theoretical macroeconomic model of North-South interaction to examine the impact of inter-regional trade on the wages of unskilled workers in the North. It is not the trade with the South, *per se*, Murshed argues, that undermines the position of unskilled labor in the North. Rather, other factors internal to the North such as the nature of labor market imperfections and the process of technological change inherent in the capitalist system, are responsible for a diminished competitiveness of unskilled workers in the North and the resulting lower wages. Furthermore, the author notes, it is highly implausible that the North, with its dominant political and economic power can, in an overall sense, be disadvantaged with its interactions with the South. Murshed also offers a variety of solutions for improving the conditions of the Northern workers.

Union opposition to free trade policies suggest that a freer trade damages labor movement and thereby increases income inequality. Adamson and Partridge document the negative correlation between changes in trade shares and the level of unionization. However, a better understanding of the influence of trade on unionization can not be gained without separating the effects of trade on workers' demand for unionization and the hiring decisions of the firms in the unionized sector. The authors construct empirical models to estimate the probability of workers joining the unions and the probability of union firms hiring these workers.

Results suggest that union employment is more sensitive to exports rather than imports and that the firms' hiring decisions are more sensitive than worker choice. Based on the evidence of differential impacts of trade on union employment in different sectors, the authors recommend some viable strategies for the unions.

Developing Nations of the South

The third part of this volume turns more specifically to the developing nations of the South. Clearly, globalization is having an even more dramatic impact on the political and economic fabric of these societies. The abject poverty of so many people throughout Latin America, Africa, and Asia only heightens their vulnerability to global economic and political change. Over one billion people survive on a dollar a day and do not have access to adequate nutrition, safe water, or basic health care.

The Uruguay Round of the General Agreement on Tariffs and Trade was a rather dramatic example of institutional change in response to globalization. The chapter by Francis Adams outlines the key components of this round of multilateral trade negotiations. Adams places particular emphasis on those elements of the Accord which expand market access, extend foreign investment rights, and liberalize trade in services. The remainder of this chapter considers the implications of Uruguay Round reforms for developing nations. Although the author points to some short term advantages for developing countries, he concludes that the Round as a whole jeopardizes long-term prospects for development. Adams also highlights the extent to which Uruguay Round reforms are likely to exacerbate inequalities within developing nations.

The following two chapters focus on specific regions within the developing world. Sandra J. MacLean and Timothy M. Shaw review recent economic and political changes in sub-Saharan Africa and consider the continent's prospects for both development and democracy. The authors outline how the accumulation of large external debts limited the economic policy options of African nations while structural adjustment programs undermined the position of popular sectors. MacLean and Shaw also review the region's recent political experience, which has often been characterized by corporatism, authoritarianism, and anarchy. The authors go on to link prospects for both development and democracy with the relative strength of civil societies and nongovernmental organizations.

Saud Choudhury provides an empirical analysis of the effects of globalization on the third world women. It is commonly argued that labor-intensive, export-oriented industrialization reduces the economic status of women as more jobs become insecure, low-paying and hold few prospects for advancement. On the basis of a detailed analysis of manufacturing industries in Hong Kong, Singapore, and South Korea, Choudhury refutes some of these basic assumptions. His analysis suggests that market forces are actually undermining gender-based discrimination and creating more opportunities for women. Paid formal sector employment, he concludes, has been the catalyst for significant social change in all three nations.

Promoting Growth with Equity: An Agenda for Reforms

The last section includes articles with a clear policy orientation. How can the globalization process be structured to promote growth, equity, and sustainability? The four chapters in this section offer reform proposals on a diverse set of issues.

The first two chapters call for reform of existing international economic institutions. Sylvia Ostry points to significant change in the sectoral composition of trade toward technologically-intensive manufacturing and services. She argues that the growing importance of intra-industry and intra-firm trade in these technologically sophisticated sectors has heightened the international rivalry of multinational corporations. At the same time, there has been surprisingly little response in the international policy sphere. She proposes a number of policy initiatives to offset increasing friction. Existing institutions such as the World Trade Organization and the Organization for Economic Cooperation and Development, need to be reformed to deal better with global technological change. The author's proposals for reform cover a number of trade policy issues including research and development subsidies, government procurement, intellectual property rights and strategic dumping in high tech sectors; investment policy initiatives such as R&D Consortia; and, finally, the promotion of basic research, an 'international public good', through international cooperation.

The piece by Kunibert Raffer focuses on the World Bank and the International Monetary Fund. Raffer contends that these two institutions were surprisingly ineffective in responding to the third world debt crisis when it first emerged in the 1970s. Once the Bank and the Fund did recognize the extent of the problem, the author contends, their policies actually intensified rather than lessened the crisis. Raffer concludes with some innovative ideas for long-term resolution of the crisis, including the establishment of international "chapter nine insolvency" for the largest debtor nations.

The next Chapter by Esmail Hossein-zadeh turns to the role of labor unions. For Esmail Hossein-zadeh the clear lesson to be learned from North American integration is the need for a coherent strategy to challenge the multinational corporations' free trade agenda. Such a strategy would replace the current downward competition between workers of different countries with coordinated bargaining and problem solving policies. Labor unions should also work toward reducing international labor rivalry by taking the necessary steps toward the establishment of wage parity within the same company and the same trade. For Hossein-zadeh, the globalization of production, technology, and information has created opportunities for a successful emergence of labor internationalism, as a balancing force in the process of globalization, in the quest for sustainable development.

The last chapter by Brigitte Levy brings home many of the concerns expressed in this volume. Sustainable development includes elements of economic, social and environmental sustainability as well as interactions among these elements. Globalization driven solely by the dominant capitalist paradigm poses serious threats to sustainable development. Globalization, she argues, is pressuring countries to harmonize downward a wide variety of laws and policies, including labor legislation and pollution standards. Her proposals incorporate concerns for a more equitable distribution of resources, poverty eradication, gender equality, and environmental protections. This can, however, be achieved within the context of globalization, the author concludes, by refining the current capitalist paradigm to include ethical principles under the stewardship of strong political leadership.

Concluding Remarks

Globalization is clearly a complex and multi-faceted process. Together the articles in this volume examine the central issues, questions, and problems which have arisen as a result of globalization. Although the authors disagree on details, they all recognize the inherent dangers in this process. The challenge in the years to come will be to structure the globalization process in such a way that it bridges the interests of both capital and labor, North and South, and present and future generations.

Development efforts must be structured toward broadening political participation and returning control over resources to local communities. This includes building local communities in both the North and South which are based on the principles of equity, popular empowerment, and democratic decision-making. By helping poor people gain effective control over their own lives and resources, and by challenging existing power structures, these communities will contribute to positive, long-term economic and political development.

Globalization has profound implications for development as we enter the twenty-first century. Our ability to promote growth, equity, and sustainability in both the North and South will be the central challenge facing humankind well into the future. Creating vibrant, equitable, and sustainable human communities will require fundamental transformation of international political and economic relations. Contributors to this volume have addressed a variety of issues including an erosion of national sovereignty, strained relations between the capital and labor, increasing tensions between the North and South, deteriorating conditions of the working class, environmental degradation, and the roles of the international institutions, labor organizations, nation states and the non-governmental organizations in relation to the present phase of globalization and its implications for our future generations. We all share a desire to refine the dominant capitalist paradigm in a way that enables all people to achieve their full potential, both as individuals and as members of the global family. By providing some insight into the issues and by raising some fundamental questions for further research, we hope to contribute to this transformation.

2

GLOBALIZATION:
The Game,the Players and the Rules
Deepak Nayyar[1]

Jawharlal Nehru University, India

There is a common perception that the dynamic forces and character of the world economy in the current phase of globalization are altogether new and represent a fundamental departure from the past. This chapter investigates the contours of this process of globalization at present and situates it in historical perspective with globalization process in the nineteenth century. The study provides a detailed picture of the similarities and differences in the nature of the game, the players and the rules in both phases of globalization in terms of the underlying factors. An examination of inequalities and asymmetries in a world of unequal partners leads the author to suggest corrective actions by nation states to avoid uneven development both within and between countries.

Globalization means different things to different people. It can be defined, simply, as the expansion of economic activities across political boundaries of nation states. More important, perhaps, it refers to a process of increasing economic openness, growing economic interdependence and deepening economic integration between countries in the world economy. It is associated not only with a phenomenal spread and volume of cross-border economic transactions, but also with an organization of economic activities which straddles national boundaries. This process is driven by the lure of profit and the threat of competition in the market.

The word globalization is used in two ways, which is a source of confusion and a cause of controversy. It is used in a positive sense to describe a process of increasing integration into the world economy : the characterization of this process is by no means uniform. It is used in a normative sense to prescribe a strategy of development based on a rapid integration with the world economy : some see this as salvation, while others see it as damnation.

There is a common presumption that the present conjuncture, when globalization is changing the character of the world economy, is altogether new and represents a fundamental departure from the past. But this presumption is not correct. Globalization is not new. Indeed, there was a similar phase of globalization which began a century earlier, circa 1870, and gathered momentum until 1914 when it came to an abrupt end with the outbreak of the First World War. I believe that this recognition is essential for an understanding.[2] And there is much that we can learn from history, for there is the past in our present.

The object of this essay is to sketch a picture of globalization, then and now, with a focus on the game, the players and the rules, to analyze the implications for the developing world.[3] The structure of the essay is as follows. Next section outlines the contours of the process of globalization in our times and situates it in historical perspective through a comparison with the late nineteenth century. In the following section, I explore the similarities and the differences in the game between these two phases of globalization by analyzing the underlying factors. The penultimate section examines the inequalities and the asymmetries in a world of unequal partners, common to both phases, to suggest that the game is similar but the players of the game are new and the rules of the game are different. The last section discusses the actual consequences in the past and the possible consequences in the future, to argue that globalization led to uneven development then and, without correctives, would lead to uneven development now.

A Historical Parallel: *The Late Nineteenth and Twentieth Centuries*

The world economy has experienced a progressive international economic integration since 1950. However, there has been a marked acceleration in this process of globalization during the last quarter of the twentieth century. The fundamental attribute of globalization is the increasing degree of openness in most countries. There are three dimensions of this phenomenon: international trade, international investment and international finance. It needs to be said that openness is not simply confined to trade flows, investment flows and financial flows. It also extends to flows of services, technology, information and ideas across national boundaries. But the cross-border movement of people is closely regulated and highly restricted. And, there can be no doubt that trade, investment and finance constitute the cutting edge of globalization.

In many ways, the world economy in the late twentieth century resembles the world economy in the late nineteenth century. The parallels between the two periods, in the spheres of trade, investment and finance, are striking and suggest that the historical origins of globalization need to be recognized.

Trade

The second half of the twentieth century has witnessed a phenomenal expansion in international trade flows. World exports increased from $61 billion in 1950 to $315 billion in 1970 and $3447 billion in 1990.[4] Throughout this period, the growth in world trade was significantly higher than the growth in world output, although the gap narrowed after the early 1970s.[5] Consequently, an increasing proportion of world output entered into world trade. The share of world exports in world GDP rose from about 6 per cent in 1950 to 12 per cent in 1973 and 16 per cent in 1992. For the industrialized countries, this proportion increased from 12 per cent in 1973 to 17 per cent in 1992. This experience is not anything new for the world economy. The period from 1870 to 1913 witnessed a similar expansion in international trade flows.[6] For 16 major industrialized countries, now in the OECD, the share of exports in GDP rose from 18.2 per cent in 1900 to 21.2 per cent in 1913.

The parallels between the two periods emerge more clearly if we consider available evidence for selected industrialized countries.[7] In the United Kingdom, the share of exports in GDP rose from 14.4 per cent in 1950 to 16.4 per cent in 1973 and 18.2 per cent in 1992, compared with 14.9 in 1900 and 20.9 per cent in 1913. In France, the share of exports in GDP rose from 10.6 per cent in 1950 to 14.4 per cent in 1973 and 17.5 per cent in 1992, compared with 12.5 per cent in 1900 and 13.9 per cent in 1913. In Germany, the share of exports in GDP rose from 8.5 in 1950 to 19.7 per cent in 1973 and 24 per cent in 1992, compared with 13.5 per cent in 1900 and 17.5 per cent in 1913. In Japan, the share of exports in GDP rose from 4.7 per cent in 1950 to 8.9 per cent in 1973 and 9 per cent in 1992, compared with 8.3 per cent in 1900 and 12.3 per cent in 1913. In the United States, the share of exports in GDP rose from 3.6 per cent in 1950 to 5 per cent in 1973 and 7.1 per cent in 1992 compared with 7.5 per cent in 1900 and 6.1 per cent in 1913. It would seem that the integration of the world economy through international trade at the turn of the last century was about the same as it is towards the end of this century.[8]

Investment

The story is almost the same for international investment flows. The stock of direct foreign investment in the world economy increased from $68 billion in 1960 to $502 billion in 1980 and $1948 billion in 1992. The flows of direct foreign investment in the world economy increased from less than $5 billion in 1960 to $52 billion in 1980 and $171 billion in 1992.[9] Consequently, the stock of direct foreign investment in the world as a proportion of world output increased from 4.4 per cent in 1960 to 4.8 per cent in 1980 and 8.4 per cent in 1992.[10] Over the same period, world direct foreign investment inflows as a proportion of world gross fixed capital formation rose from 1.1 per cent in 1960 to 2 per cent in 1980 and 3.7 per cent in 1992.[11] In the industrialized countries, this proportion increased from 2.3 per cent during 1981-1985 to 4.4 per cent during 1986-1990 but dropped to 2.9 per cent in 1992. In the developing countries, however, this proportion, increased slightly from 2.4 per cent during 1981-1985 to 2.7 per cent during 1986-1990 but jumped to 7.8 per cent in 1992.[12]

Any comparison with the period 1870-1913 cannot be complete because we do not have similar data. An estimate made by the United Nations suggests that the stock of direct foreign investment in the world economy as a proportion of world output was 9 per cent in 1913.[13] The total stock of long-term foreign investment in the world reached $44 billion by 1914, of which $14 billion, about one-third, was direct foreign investment.[14] At 1980 prices, total foreign investment in the world economy in 1914 was $ 347 billion compared with the actual stock of direct foreign investment in 1980 at $ 448 billion.[15] About one-half of foreign investment then was in a small group of newly industrializing countries in North America and Europe, as also in Australia. In some of these countries, it constituted as much as 50 per cent of gross domestic investment.[16] The stock of foreign investment in developing countries, direct and portfolio, rose from $5.3 billion in 1870 to $ 11.4 billion in 1900 and $22.7 billion in 1914.[17] Such foreign investment in the developing world was large in both relative and absolute terms. For one, it was probably equal to about one-fourth of the GDP of developing countries at the turn of the century.[18] For another, it was substantial even by contemporary standards. The stock of foreign investment in developing countries in 1914, at 1980 prices, was $179 billion which was almost double the stock of direct foreign investment in developing countries in 1980 at $ 96 billion.[19]

Finance

The past two decades have witnessed an explosive growth in international finance. The movement of finance across national boundaries is enormous. So much so that, in terms of magnitudes, trade and investment are now dwarfed by finance. This internationalization of financial markets has four dimensions: foreign exchange, bank lending, financial assets and government bonds. Consider each in turn.

In foreign exchange markets, trading was a modest $15 billion per day in 1973. It rose to $60 billion per day in 1983, and soared to $900 billion per day in 1992.[20] Consequently, the ratio of world-wide transactions in foreign exchange to world trade rose from 9:1 in 1973 to 12:1 in 1983 and 90:1 in 1992.[21] Some absolute numbers would help situate these magnitudes in perspective. In 1992, for example, world GDP was $64 billion per day while world exports were $10 billion per day, compared with global foreign exchange transactions of $900 billion per day.[22] It is also worth noting that daily foreign exchange transactions in the world economy were larger than the foreign exchange reserves of all central banks put together, which were $ 693 billion in 1992.[23]

The expansion of international banking is also phenomenal. As a proportion of world output, net international bank loans rose from 0.7 per cent in 1964 to 8.0 per cent in 1980 and 16.3 per cent in 1991. As a proportion of world trade, net international bank loans rose from 7.5 per cent in 1964 to 42.6 per cent in 1980 and 104.6 per cent in 1991. As a proportion of world gross fixed domestic investment net international bank loans rose from 6.2 per cent in 1964 to 51.1 per cent in 1980 and 131.4 per cent in 1991.[24] It is worth noting that the gross size of the international banking market was roughly twice that of net international bank lending. Cross-border inter-bank liabilities rose from a modest $ 455 billion in 1970 to $ 5560 billion in 1990.[25]

The international market for financial assets experienced a similar growth starting somewhat later. Between 1980 and 1993 gross sales and purchases of bonds and equities transacted between domestic and foreign residents rose from less than 10 per cent of GDP in the United States, Germany and Japan to 135 per cent of GDP in the United States, 170 per cent of GDP in Germany and 80 per cent of GDP in Japan.[26] In the UK, the value of such transactions was more than ten times that of the GDP in 1993. Similarly, between 1980 and 1993, the share of foreign bonds and equities in pension-fund assets rose from 10 per cent to 20 per cent in the UK, from 0.7 per cent to 6 per cent in the United States, and from 0.5

per cent to 9 per cent in Japan. IMF estimates suggest that total cross-border ownership of tradeable securities was $2500 billion in 1992.

Government debt has also become tradeable in the global market for financial assets. There is a growing international market for government bonds. Between 1980 and 1992, the proportion of government bonds held by foreigners rose from less than 1 per cent to 43 per cent in France, from 9 per cent to 17 per cent in the UK, from 10 per cent to 27 per cent in Germany, while it remained steady at about 20 per cent in the United States.[27]

These numbers are staggering but even the globalization of finance is not new. There was a significant integration of international financial markets in the late nineteenth century and early twentieth century. The only dimension missing was international transactions in foreign exchange which were determined entirely by trade flows and capital flows, given the regime of fixed exchange rates under the gold standard. The cross-national ownership of securities, including government bonds, reached very high levels during this period. In 1913, for example, foreign securities constituted 59 per cent of all securities traded in London. Similarly, in 1908, the corresponding proportion was 53 per cent in Paris.[28] It is worth noting that there was a correlation between interest rates, exchange rates and stock prices in the leading markets during this phase. There was also an established market for government bonds. In 1920, for instance, Moody's rated bonds issued by 50 governments. As late as 1985, only 15 governments were borrowing in the capital market of the United States. The number reached 50, once again, in the 1990s.[29] International bank lending was substantial. Both governments and private investors floated long-term bonds directly in the financial markets of London, Paris and New York. Merchant banks or investment banks were the intermediaries in facilitating these capital flows from private individuals and financial institutions, in these industrialised countries, in search of long-term investments on the one hand, to firms or governments, mostly in the newly industrialising countries or the underdeveloped countries, which issued long- term liabilities, on the other.[30] In relative terms, net international capital flows then were much bigger than now. During the period from 1880 to 1913, Britain ran an average current account surplus in its balance of payments which was the equivalent of 5 per cent of GDP.[31] And, in some years, this was as much as 8 per cent of GDP. In contrast, since 1950, the current account surplus of the United States to begin with, or Germany and Japan in subsequent years, did not exceed 3 per cent of GDP.

The Game: Similarities and Differences

It is clear that the internationalisation of trade, investment and finance during the last quarter of the twentieth century is not new. There was such an internationalisation of trade, investment and finance in the last quarter of the nineteenth century which continued until the onset of the First World War. There are both similarities and differences between these two phases of globalisation in the world economy. The similarities are in underlying factors which made globalisation possible then and now. The differences are in the form, the nature and the depth of globalisation during these two phases.

Similarities

There are four similarities that I would like to highlight: the absence or the dismantling of barriers to international economic transactions; the development of enabling technologies; emerging forms of industrial organisation; political hegemony or dominance.

Liberalization. The four decades from 1870 to 1913 were the age of laissez faire. There were almost no restrictions on the movement of goods, capital and labour across national boundaries. Government intervention in economic activity was minimal. The gold standard, strictly adhered to by most countries, imparted stability to the system. Keynes believed that a virtuous circle of rapid economic growth and international economic integration in this era created the core of a global economy.[32] This was followed by three decades of conflict and autarchy. The two World Wars and the Great Depression interspersed these troubled times. Economic growth was a casualty. International economic transactions were progressively constrained by barriers and regulations that were erected during this period of economic and political conflict. These barriers and regulations were dismantled step by step during the second half of the twentieth century. Globalisation has followed the sequence of deregulation. Trade liberalisation came first, which led to an unprecedented expansion of international trade between 1950 and 1970. The liberalisation of regimes for foreign investment came next. And there was a surge in international investment which began in the late 1960s. Financial liberalisation came last, starting in the early around 1980s. This had two dimensions: the de-regulation of the domestic financial sector in the industrialised countries and the introduction of convertibility on capital account in the balance of payments. The latter was not simultaneous. The United States, Canada, Germany and Switzerland removed restrictions on capital movements in 1973, Britain in 1979, Japan in 1980, while France and Italy made the transition as late as 1990. The globalisation of finance, at a scorching pace since the mid-1980s, is not unrelated to the dismantling of regulations and controls.

Technological Revolution. Both phases of globalisation coincided with a technological revolution in transport and communications, which brought about an enormous reduction in the time needed, as also the cost incurred, in traversing geographical distances. The second half of the nineteenth century saw the advent of the steamship, the railway and the telegraph. The substitution of steam for sails, and of iron for wooden hulls in ships, reduced ocean freight by two-thirds between 1870 and 1900.[33] The spread of the railways brought the hinterland of countries into the world economy. The arrival of the telegraph revolutionised communication and shrank the world. The second half of the twentieth century has witnessed the advent of jet aircraft, computers and satellites. The synthesis of communications technology, which is concerned with the transmission of information, and computer technology, which is concerned with the processing of information, has created information technology, which is remarkable in both reach and speed. These technological developments have had an even more dramatic impact on reducing geographical barriers. The time needed is a tiny fraction of what it was earlier. The cost incurred has come down sharply. Obviously, enabling technologies made the globalisation of economic activities that much easier both then and now.

Industrial Organization. Emerging forms of industrial organisation, in both phases, played a role in making globalisation possible. In the late nineteenth century, it was the advent of mass production which was characterised by a rigid compartmentalisation of functions and a high degree of mechanisation. The production of perfectly interchangeable parts, the introduction of the moving assembly line developed by Ford and methods of management evolved by Taylor provided the foundations for this new form of industrial organisation. Mass production realised economies of scale and led to huge cost reductions compared with craft manufacturing.[34] The accumulation and concentration of capital reinforced the process of globalisation. In the late twentieth century, the emerging flexible production system, shaped by the nature of the technical progress, the changing output mix and the organisational characteristics (based on Japanese management systems), is forcing firms to constantly choose between trade and investment in their drive to expand activities across borders. The declining share of wages in production costs, the increasing importance of proximity between producers and consumers, and the the growing externalisation of services, are bound to influence the strategies and the behaviour of firms in the process of globalisation.[35]

Politics of Hegemony. The politics of hegemony or dominance is conducive to the economics of globalisation. The first phase of globalisation from 1870 to 1913 coincided with what has described as `the age of empire', when Britain more or less ruled the world.[36] The second phase of globalisation beginning in the early 1970s coincided with the political dominance of the United States as the superpower. This poliltical dominance has grown stronger with the collapse of communism and the triumph of capitalism, which has been described as `the end of history'.[37] And the political conjuncture has transformed the concept of globalisation into a `virtual ideology' of our times. Apart from dominance in the realm of politics, there is another similarity in the sphere of economics between Pax Britannica and Pax Americana. That is the existence of a reserve currency which is the equivalent of international money: as a unit of account, a medium of exchange and a store of value. In the late nineteenth century and the early twentieth century, this role was performed by the pound sterling. In the late twentieth century, this role is being performed by the US dollar, ironically enough after the collapse of the Bretton Woods system when its statutory role as a reserve currency came to an end. It would seem that, in both phases, globalisation required a dominant economic power with a national currency that was, and is, acceptable as international money.

Differences

There are, also, important differences between the two phases of globalisation. I would like to highlight four such differences: in trade flows, in investment flows, in financial flows and most important, perhaps, in labour flows, across national boundaries.

Trade flows. Let me begin with trade flows, where there are differences in the composition of trade and in the channels of trade. During the period from 1870 to 1913, a large proportion of international trade was constituted by inter- sectoral trade, where primary commodities were exchanged for manufactured goods. This trade was, to a significant extent, based on absolute advantage derived from natural resources or climatic conditions. It is possible to discern two phases since 1950. During the period 1950-1970, inter-industry trade in manufactures, based on differences in factor endowments, labor productivity or technological leads and lags, constituted an increasing proportion of international trade.[38] During the period 1970-1990, intra-industry trade in manufactures, based on scale economies and product differentiation, constituted an increasing proportion of international trade. At first sight, it may seem that trade flows were in the domain of large international firms then as much as now. There are, however, two important differences. First, the large trading firms of the nineteenth century, such as the East India Company or the Royal African Company, "were like dinosaurs, large in bulk but small in brain, feeding on the lush vegetations of the new worlds".[39] The forerunners of what we now describe as transnational corporations were not these giant trading firms but the small workshops and the entrepreneurial firms of the late nineteenth century. Second, during the present phase of globalization, an increasing proportion of international trade is intra-firm trade, across national boundaries but between affiliates of the same firm. In the early 1970s, such intra-firm trade accounted for about one-fifth of world trade, but by the early 1990s, this proportion was one-third of world trade.[40] Even more important perhaps is the changed composition of intra-firm trade. The second half of the twentieth century has witnessed a steady decline in the importance of primary commodities, and a sharp increase in the importance of manufactured goods and intermediate products, in intra-firm trade.

Investment flows. Consider, next, investment flows, where there are differences in the geographical-destination, the sectoral- distribution and the risk-form of the investment. In 1914, the stock of long-term foreign investment in the world economy was distributed as follows: 55 per cent in the industrialized world (30 per cent in Europe, 25 per cent in the United States) and 45 per cent in the underdeveloped world (20 per cent in Latin America and 25 per cent in Asia and Africa).[41] In 1992, the stock of direct foreign investment in the world economy was distributed in a far more uneven manner: 78 per cent in the industrialized countries and 22 per cent in the developing countries.[42] We do not have comparable data for flows of foreign investment during the two periods. However, during the 1980s, industrialized countries absorbed 80 per cent of the inflows of direct foreign investment in the world economy whereas developing countries received only 20 per cent.[43] It is clear that developing countries are now far less central to the process. But the spatial web of direct foreign investment is almost certainly more extensive than it was at the beginning of this century. The principal recipients then were China, India and Indonesia in Asia, with Argentina, Brazil and Mexico in

Latin America. The number of recipients now is much larger and the sectoral distribution is also considerably different. In 1913, the primary sector accounted for 55 per cent of long-term foreign investment in the world, while transport, trade and distribution accounted for another 30 per cent; the manufacturing sector accounted for only 10 per cent and much of this was concentrated in North America or Europe.[44] In 1992, the primary sector accounted for less than 10 per cent of the stock of direct foreign investment in the world, while the manufacturing sector accounted for about 40 per cent and the services sector for the remaining 50 per cent.[45] The nature of the risk borne by foreign investors was discernibly different in two phases. In the early twentieth century, such investment was only long-term: two-thirds of it was portfolio while one-third of it was direct. In the late twentieth century, much of such long- term investment is direct, although portfolio investment has risen sharply in the 1990s.

Financial flows. Let me now turn to financial flows. The most striking difference is the size of international financial markets in absolute if not relative terms. There are, however, important differences in the destination, the object, the intermediaries and the instruments. In the last quarter of the nineteenth century, capital flows were a means of transferring investible resources to underdeveloped countries or newly industrializing countries with the most attractive growth opportunities. In the last quarter of the twentieth century, these capital flows are destined mostly for the industrialized countries which have high deficits and high interest rates to finance public consumption and transfer payments rather than productive investment.[46] During the first phase of globalization from 1870 to 1913, the object of financial flows was to find avenues for long- term investment in search of profit. During the second phase of globalization since the early 1970s, financial flows are constituted mostly by short-term capital movements, sensitive to exchange rates and interest rates, in search of capital gains.

The intermediaries, too, are different. In the late nineteenth century, banks were the only intermediaries between lenders and borrowers in the form of bonds with very long maturities. In the late twentieth century, institutional investors such as pension- funds and mutual-funds are more important than banks; the latter continue to act as intermediaries but now borrow short to lend long, thus resulting in a maturity mismatch. Consequently, the financial instruments need to be far more sophisticated and diversified than earlier. In the late nineteenth century, there were mostly long-term bonds with sovereign guarantees provided by the imperial powers or the governments in borrowing countries. In the late twentieth century, there has been an enormous amount of financial innovation through the introduction of derivatives (futures, swaps and options). These derivatives (which are also not entirely new to the world and are reported to have existed in the seventeenth and eighteenth centuries : options in the Amsterdam stock exchange and futures in the Osaka rice market) are a means of managing the financial risks associated with international investment. This is essential now because, unlike the earlier phase of globalization, there is a maturity mismatch and there is no effective securitization provided by nation states. International financial markets have simply developed the instruments to meet the needs of the times. It is paradoxical that such derivatives, which have been introduced to counter risk may, in fact, increase the risk associated with international financial flows by increasing the volatility of short-term capital movements.

Labor flows. The fundamental difference between the two phases of globalization is in the sphere of labor flows. In the late nineteenth century, there were no restrictions on the mobility of people across national boundaries. Passports were seldom needed. Immigrants were granted citizenship with ease. Between 1870 and 1914, international labor migration was enormous. During this period, about 50 million people left Europe, of whom two-thirds went to the United States while the remaining one-third went to Canada, Australia, New Zealand, South Africa, Argentina and Brazil.[47] This mass emigration from Europe amounted to one-eighth its population in 1900.[48] But that was not all. Beginning somewhat earlier, following the abolition of slavery in the British Empire, about 50 million people left India and China to work as indentured labor on mines, plantations and construction in Latin America, the Caribbean, Southern Africa, South East Asia and other distant lands.[49] The destinations were mostly British, Dutch, French and German colonies. In the second half of the twentieth century, there was a limited amount of international labor migration from the developing countries to the industrialized world during the period 1950-1970. This was largely attributable to the post-war labor shortages in Europe and the post-colonial ties embedded in a common language.[50] Since then, however, international migration has been reduced to a trickle because of draconian immigration laws and restrictive consular practices. The only significant evidence of labor mobility during the last quarter of the twentieth century is the temporary migration of workers to Europe, the Middle East and East Asia.

The present phase of globalization has found substitutes for labor mobility in the form of trade flows and investment flows. For one, industrialized countries now import manufactured goods that embody scarce labor: the share of developing countries in world manufactured exports rose from 5.5 per cent in 1970 to 15.9 per cent in 1990, while the share of manufactured exports in total exports of developing countries rose from 18.7 in 1970 to 54.7 per cent in 1990.[51] For another, industrialized countries export capital which employs scarce labor abroad to provide such goods. In 1992, for example, total employment in transnational corporations was 73 million, of which 44 million were employed in the home countries while 17 million were employed in affiliates in industrialized countries and 12 million were employed in affiliates in developing countries; the share of developing countries in such employment rose from one- tenth in 1985 to one-sixth in 1992.[52]

The first phase of globalization in the late nineteenth century was characterized by an integration of markets through an exchange of goods which was facilitated by the movement of capital and labor across national boundaries. This was associated with a simple vertical division of labor between countries in the world economy. The second phase of globalization during the late twentieth century is characterized by an integration of production with linkages that are wider and deeper. It is reflected not only in the movement of goods, services, capital, technology, information and ideas, but also in the organization of economic activities across national boundaries. This is associated with a more complex-part horizontal and part vertical - division of labor between the industrialized countries and a few developing countries in the world economy.

Unequal Partners and Asymmetrical Rules

A comparison of globalization in the late twentieth century with globalization in the late nineteenth century suggests that the game is similar though not quite the same. But the players of the game are new. And the rules of the game are very different.

The Players

The process of globalization then was dominated by imperial nation states not only in the realm of politics but also in the sphere of economics. There can be no doubt that these imperial nation states were the key players in the game. The process of globalization now has placed new players centre-stage. There are two main sets of players in this game: transnational corporations which dominate investment, production and trade in the world economy, and international banks or financial intermediaries which control the world of finance. It would seem that the present conjuncture represents the final frontier in the global reach of capitalism to organize production, trade, investment and finance on a world scale without any fetters except, of course, for tight controls on labor mobility.[53]

It is not surprising that the advent of international capital has meant significant political adjustments in the contemporary world. It has induced a strategic withdrawal on the part of the nation state in some important spheres. Thus, nation states are not the key players that they were in the late nineteenth century during the first incarnation of globalization. They remain the main political players but are no longer the main economic players. We live in an era where the old fashioned autonomy of the nation state is being eroded by international industrial capital and international finance capital everywhere, both in the industrialized world and in the developing world.[54] It needs to be stressed, however, that there is a qualitative difference in the relationship between international capital and the nation state, when we compare the industrialized world with the developing world. The nation state in the former has far more room for manoeuvre than the nation state in the latter. In the industrialised countries, the political interests of the nation state often coincide with the economic interests of international capital. This is not so for developing countries from which very few transnational corporations or international banks originate. In spite of the profound changes unleashed by the present phase of globalization, however, it would be naive write off the nation state, for it remains a crucial player in   political and strategic terms. Even today, only nation states have the authority to set rules of the game. The nation states in the industrialized world provide international capital with the means to set new rules for the game of globalization. The nation states in the developing world provide these countries and their people with the means of finding degrees of freedom vis-a- vis international capital in the pursuit of development.

The Rules: the Asymmetries

The process of globalization, then and now, has been characterized by inequalities and asymmetries - economic and political - between countries in the world. These inequalities and asymmetries were, and are, implicit in the rules of the game. The late nineteenth century was the age of empire. There were a few imperial nation states at one end and many colonies (de jure or de facto) at the other. The unequal political power meant dominance by the few and subservience of the many. The rules of the game were set by the military strength of the imperial powers. The unequal relationship was, so to speak, sustained by gunboat diplomacy. And the risks associated with trade, investment and finance across national boundaries were, in effect, underwritten by the imperial nation states.

The late twentieth century is a different world. It is not as if the use of military strength is ruled out. In exceptional situations, as in Iraq, it could still be used but only where strategic geo-political interests are involved. As a rule, this is neither feasible nor desirable in the present phase of globalization, in part because the nation state does not have the same strength and in part because international capital would prefer rules that can be invoked without muscle. For this purpose, transnational corporations and international banks or financial intermediaries wish to set new rules of the game which would enable them to manage the risks associated with globalization. In this task, the nation states of the industrialized world provide the much needed political clout and support. The multilateral framework of the WTO, the IMF and the World Bank is, perhaps, the most important medium.

The Uruguay Round of multilateral trade negotiations was launched in an attempt to resolve the crisis in the international trading system, but was different from its predecessor rounds in a fundamental sense. It was not concerned with conventional tariff reductions for trade liberalization. At one level, in the realm of traditional GATT issues, it was about the implementation of existing rules in the multilateral trading system which had been eroded, circumvented or flouted in the recent past. At another level, apropos new issues, it was about the formulation of new rules in vital spheres of international economic transactions, many of which had thus far been a matter for bilateral negotiations. It is necessary but not sufficient to recognize why and how the Uruguay Round was different from the earlier rounds of multilateral trade negotiations. The differences are much wider and deeper than its enlarged scope. GATT type rules and principles, with provision for dispute settlement, compensation and retaliation are sought to be extended beyond trade in goods to international flows of capital, technology, information, services and personnel. The multilateral regimes for trade-related investment measures, trade-related intellectual property rights and trade in services, now created in the WTO, coincide closely with the interests of transnational corporations which are capital-exporters, technology-leaders and service-providers in the world economy. The interests of transnational corporations provided the nation states of the industrialized countries with the political impetus to conclude the negotiations.

The international regime of discipline that is being created is asymmetrical in almost every dimension. The liberalization of international trade in goods is selective, for the discipline on non-tariff barriers is not binding just as there are important exclusions. In the sphere of textiles, the dismantling of the MFA remains a distant promise and in substantive terms trade liberalization would begin only after the onset of the twenty-first century. The pressure from the industrialized countries to introduce a 'social clause' and an `environment clause' on the agenda for the world trading system is simply a pretext for circumventing the rules of trade liberalization wherever necessary. In the General Agreement on Trade and Services, there is almost nothing on labor mobility which would allow developing countries to exploit their comparative advantage in services. In sharp contrast, it caters to the interest of the industrialized countries, which have a revealed comparative advantage in capital-intensive or technology-intensive services, even if this implies changes in investment laws or technology policies of developing countries. The Uruguay Round did not yield significant results on trade-related investment measures but, since then, the industrialized countries have mounted increasing pressure to create a multilateral framework for international investment in the WTO. Apart from the most favored nation (non- discrimination) rule, this initiative seeks free access and national treatment for foreign investors, combined with provisions to enforce   commitments and obligations to foreign investors. While   liberalization and guarantees are sought for investment flows,   the international regime of discipline for technology flows embodies protection with guarantees. The WTO regime for the protection of intellectual property rights is both restrictive and protective. The inequality is obvious. It seeks to protect the monopoly profits or the quasi-rents for transnational corporations but it ignores the implications for developing countries.[55]

It would seem that the institutional framework for globalization is characterized by a striking asymmetry. National boundaries should not matter for trade flows and capital flows but should be clearly demarcated for technology flows and labor flows.[56] It follows that the developing countries would provide access to their markets without a corresponding access to technology and would accept capital mobility without a corresponding provision for labor mobility. This asymmetry, particularly that between the free movement of capital and the unfree movement of labor across national boundaries, I must emphasize, lies at the heart of the inequality in the rules of the game for globalization in the late twentieth century. These new rules, which serve the interests of transnational corporations in the process of globalization, are explicit as an integral part of a multilateral regime of discipline.

The rules of the game, which would serve the interests of international banks or financial intermediaries in the process of globalization, are in part implicit and in part unwritten. Even here, there is an asymmetry as there are rules for some but not for others. There are no rules for surplus countries, or even deficit countries, in the industrialized world which do not borrow from the multilateral financial institutions. But the IMF and the World Bank set rules for borrowers in the developing world and the erstwhile socialist bloc. The conditionality is meant in principle to ensure repayment but in practice it imposes conditions or invokes rules to serve the interests of international banks which lend to the same countries. The Bretton Woods institutions, then, act as watchdogs for moneylenders in international capital markets. This has been so for some time. But there is more to it now. IMF programmes of stabilization and World Bank programmes of structural adjustment, in developing countries and in the erstwhile communist countries, impose conditions that stipulate a structural reform of policy regimes. The object is to increase the degree of openness of these economies and to reduce the role of the state, so that market forces shape economic decisions. In this manner, the Bretton Woods institutions seek to harmonize policies and institutions across countries which also meets the needs of globalization.

International financial markets are, perhaps, the exception in so far as they have enormous clout even vis-a-vis governments and central banks of industrialized countries. Globalization of finance has almost certainly eroded the ability of governments everywhere to tax, to print money and to borrow. Monetary policy and fiscal policy are blunted. Macro-economic management in the pursuit of internal and external balance is that much more difficult. But financial markets are erratic in their exercise of discipline. There are as yet no clear or set rules of the game. However, there is an asymmetry even here as international finance cannot exercise any discipline on the dominant economic power without risking the stability of international financial system. So long as the US dollar is the only national currency that can serve as international money, it is as good as gold and financial markets would stop and think before they undermine the keystone in the arch.

Uneven Development

Some ideologues believe that globalization led to rapid industrialization and economic convergence in the world economy during the late nineteenth century. In their view, the promise of the emerging global capitalist system was wasted for more than half a century, to begin with by three decades of conflict and autarchy that followed the First World War and subsequently, for another three decades, by the socialist path and a statist worldview. The return of globalization in the late twentieth century is thus seen as the road to salvation, particularly for the developing countries and the former communist countries where governments are urged or pushed into adopting a comprehensive agenda of privatization (to minimize the role of the state) and liberalization (of trade flows, investment flows and financial flows). It is suggested that such policy regimes would provide the foundations for a global economic system characterized by free trade, unrestricted capital mobility, open markets and harmonized institutions. The conclusion drawn is that globalization now - as much as then - promises economic prosperity for countries that join the system and economic deprivation for countries that do not.[57]

The Past

It needs to be stressed that this normative and prescriptive view of globalization is driven in part by ideology and in part by hope. It is not borne out by history. And facts tell a different story.

It should be obvious that the process of globalization will not reproduce or replicate the United States everywhere, just as it did not reproduce or replicate Britain everywhere a   century earlier.   It was associated with an uneven development then. In the absence of correctives, it is bound to produce uneven development now, not only between countries but also within countries.

This is a lesson that emerges from history. The economic consequences of globalization in the late nineteenth century were, to say the least, asymmetrical. Most of the gains from the international economic integration of this era accrued to the imperial countries which exported capital and imported commodities. There were a few countries such as the United States, Canada and Australia - new lands with temperate climates and white settlers - which also derived some benefits. In these countries, the pre-conditions for industrialization were already being created and international economic integration strengthened this process. Direct foreign investment in manufacturing activities stimulated by rising tariff barriers, combined with technological and managerial flows, reinforced the process.[58]   The outcome was industrialization and development. But this did not happen everywhere.

Development was uneven in the industrial world. Much of southern and eastern Europe lagged behind. This meant divergence rather than convergence in terms of industrialization and growth.[59]   Countries in Asia, Africa and Latin America, which were also a part of this process of globalization, were even less fortunate. Indeed, during the same period of rapid international economic integration, some of the most open economies in this phase of globalization - India, China and Indonesia - experienced de-industrialization and underdevelopment. We need to remind ourselves that, in the period from 1870 to 1914, these three countries practiced free trade as much as the United Kingdom and the Netherlands, where average tariff levels were close to negligible 3-5 per cent); in contrast, tariff levels in Germany, Japan and France were significantly higher (12-14 per cent), whereas tariff levels in the United States were very much higher (33 per cent).[60] What is more, these three countries were also among the largest recipients of foreign investment.[61] But their globalization did not lead to development. The outcome was similar elsewhere : in Asia, Africa and Latin America. So much so that, between 1860 and 1913, the share of developing countries in world manufacturing output declined from over one-third to under one-tenth.[62] Export-oriented production in mines, plantations and cash-crop agriculture created enclaves in these economies which were integrated with the world economy in a vertical division of labor. But there were almost no backward linkages. Productivity levels outside the export enclaves stagnated at low levels. They simply created dualist economic structures where the benefits of globalization accrued mostly to the outside world and in small part to local elites.

The Present

The process of globalization was uneven then. It is so uneven now. There are less than a dozen developing countries which are an integral part of globalization in the late twentieth century: Argentina, Brazil and Mexico in Latin America and Korea, Hong Kong, Taiwan, Singapore, China, Indonesia, Malaysia and Thailand in Asia. These eleven countries accounted for about 30 per cent of total exports from developing countries during the period 1970-1980. This share rose to 59 per cent in 1990 and 66 per cent in 1992.[63] The same countries, excluding Korea, were also the main recipients of direct foreign investment in the developing world accounting for 66 per cent of the average annual inflows during the period 1981-1991.[64] There are no firm data on the distribution of portfolio investment but it is almost certain that the same countries, described as `emerging markets', were the destination for an overwhelming proportion of portfolio investment flows to the developing world. This evidence suggests that globalization is most uneven in its spread and there is an exclusion in the process. Sub-Saharan Africa, West Africa, Central Asia and South Asia are simply not in the picture, apart from many countries in Latin America, Asia and the Pacific which are left out altogether.

The process of globalization has been uneven over time and across space. The inequalities and the asymmetries implicit in the process which led to uneven development in the late nineteenth century, mostly for political reasons, are bound to create uneven development in the late twentieth century, mostly for economic reasons. There is a real danger that some countries may experience an exclusion from this process of globalization, just as many people within these countries would experience an exclusion from prosperity. Such exclusion from the process of development would increase the economic distance between nations and widen the income disparities between peoples of the world. This would be difficult to sustain in a world where demonstration effects are strong and are reinforced by globalization which creates strong aspirations for consumption patterns or life styles. Economic deprivation could accentuate social divides and political alienation. If globalization turns into a secession of the successful, it could have an analogue in terms of a secession of the deprived.

Role of the State

The benefits of integration with the world economy, through globalization, would accrue only to those countries which have laid the requisite foundations for industrialization and development. This means investing in the development of human resources and the creation of a physical infrastructure. This means raising productivity in the agricultural sector. This means using strategic industrial policy for the development of technological and managerial capabilities at a micro-level. This means establishing institutions that would regulate, govern and facilitate the functioning of markets. In each of these pursuits, strategic forms of state intervention are essential. The countries which have not created these pre-conditions could end up globalizing prices without globalizing incomes. In the process, a narrow segment of their population may be integrated with the world economy, in terms of consumption patterns or living styles, but a large proportion of their population may be marginalized even further.

Globalization has reduced the autonomy of the nation state in matters economic, if not political, but there remain some degrees of freedom which must be exploited in the pursuit of industrialization and development. The object of any sensible strategy of development in a world of liberalization and globalization should be to create economic space for the pursuit of national interests and development objectives. In this task there is a strategic role for the nation state.

Clearly, it is necessary to redefine the economic role of the state vis-a-vis the market at the present conjuncture. Such a redefinition should be based on two basic propositions.[65] First, the state and the market cannot be substitutes for each other but must complement each other. Second, the relationship between the state and the market cannot be specified once and for all in any dogmatic manner for the two institutions must adapt to one another in a co-operative manner over time. The ideology of globalization seeks to harmonize not only policy regimes but also institutions, including the economic role of the state, across the world. This is a mistake because the role of he state in an economy depends on its level of income and stage of development. What is more, the state is the only institution that can create room for introducing correctives.

In fact, during the twentieth century, success at economic development is observed mostly in cases where the state has performed a strategic role vis-a-vis international capital as also created the pre-conditions for industrialization. This is evident if we consider, for example, the development experience of industrial capitalism in Japan after the Meiji Restoration in 1868 or the emergence of market socialism in China after the modernization and reform programme was launched in 1978. The economic role of the state has been just as crucial in South Korea, Taiwan and even Singapore.[66]

The pursuit of development in the context of globalization necessitates a role for the nation state in the domestic economic sphere and in economic or political interaction with the outside world. In the national context, the state must endeavor to create the pre-conditions for industrialization and development, bargain with international capital to improve the distribution of gains from cross-border economic transactions, practice prudence in the macro management of the economy so as to reduce vulnerability, and intervene to minimize the social costs associated with globalization. In the international context, the state should attempt to reduce the asymmetries and the inequalities in the rules of the game, build strategic alliances among developing countries for this purpose and, wherever possible, seek out areas of convergence with the state in industrialized countries in terms of realpolitik or geo-political interests.

Endnotes

1. I would like to thank Amit Bhaduri, Satish Jain and Shrirang Shukla for helpful comments.

2. This historical parallel was the theme of my Presidential Address to the Indian Economic Association in December 1995. At the time that it was written, I had not seen the article by Sachs and Warner (1995), which was published around the same time, or the work of Bairoch and Kozul-Wright (1996) which was published some months later. It is worth noting that both sets of authors make similar comparisons but from very different perspectives.

3. This essay draws upon the author's earlier work on globalization mentioned above (Nayyar, 1995).

4. United Nations, *Yearbook of International Trade Statistics*, various issues.

5. For a comparison of growth in world trade and world output, see Maddison (1991). The export-GDP ratios for 1950, 1973 and 1992 in this paragraph, however, are calculated from data on exports in UNCTAD, *Handbook of International Trade and Development Statistics* (various issues) and data on GDP in World Bank, *World Development Report* (various issues) and United Nations, *Yearbook of National Accounts Statistics* (various issues).

6. cf.. Maizels (1963) and Bairoch (1982). For estimates of the share of exports in GDP during this period, cited here, see Maddison (1989).

7. The data for 1950, 1973 and 1992 cited in this paragraph are reported in *World Investment Report 1994*, p. 127, while the estimates for 1900 and 1913 are obtained from Maddison (1989), p. 143.

8. It is striking that the average tariff rates on imports of manufactured goods in these industrialized countries, with the exception of the United Kingdom, at that time, were in the range of 20 to 40 per cent compared with an average tariff rate of about 5 per cent in 1990 (Bairoch, 1993). Tariffs were much higher then but non-tariff barriers are stronger now.

9. For data on stocks and flows of direct foreign investment in the world economy, cited here, see United Nations, *Transnational Corporations in World Development*, various surveys, UNCTAD, *World Investment Report*, various issues.

10. UNCTAD, *World Investment Report 1994*, p. 20 and p. 130.

11. *Ibid.*, p. 20 and p. 130.

12. For detailed evidence on the ratio of direct foreign investment inflows to gross fixed capital formation, see UNCTAD, *World Investment Report 1994*, pp. 421-426.

13. This estimate is reported in UNCTAD, *World Investment Report 1994*, p. 130.

14. *Ibid.*, pp. 120-121.

15. The stock of foreign investment in the world, at $ 44 billion in 1914, has been converted into 1980 prices by using the consumer price index in the United States as the deflator, while the figure for the actual stock of direct foreign investment in 1980 is obtained from UNCTAD, *World Investment Report 1993*, p. 248.

16. Cf.. Panic (1992), p. 101.

17. See Maddison (1989), p. 30.

18. *Ibid.*, p. 29.

19. The figure for the stock of direct foreign investment in developing countries in 1980 is obtained from UNCTAD, *World Investment Report 1993*, p. 248, while the estimate of the stock of foreign capital in developing countries in 1914, at 1980 prices, is obtained from Maddison (1989), p. 30.

20. Bank for International Settlements (BIS), *Survey of Foreign Exchange Market Activity*, Bosle, various issues.

21. Calculated from BIS data on trading in foreign exchange markets and United Nations data on world trade.

22. The value of world GDP and world exports in 1992, reported by the United nations, has been converted into an average daily figure for the purpose of this comparison.

23. International Monetary Fund (IMF), *Annual Report 1993*, p. 105.

24. The figures on the increasing significance of net international bank loans, cited in this paragraph, are obtained from UNCTAD, *World Investment Report 1994*, p. 128.

25. *Ibid.*

26. These proportions, as also the others cited in this paragraph, are estimated from data compiled by BIS and IMF, and are reported in `A Survey of the World Economy', *The Economist*, London, 7 October 1995.

27. *Ibid.*

28. For a discussion, as also the evidence, see Morgenstern (1959).

29. Cf. `A Survey of the World Economy', *The Economist*, London, 7 October 1995.

30. This intermediation is described and analysed in Kregel (1994).

31. For evidence, see Panic (1992).

32. Cf. Keynes (1921).

33. Freight costs began to decline from the mid-nineteenth century but the spectacular downturn came after 1870 (Lewis, 1977).

34. See Lewis (1978) and Chandler (1990).

35. For a detailed discussion on the relationship between forms of industrial organisation and the process of globalisation, see Oman (1994).

36. For a succinct and perceptive historical analysis of this period, see Hobsbawm (1987).

37. See Fukuyama (1989).

38. cf.. Glyn et al (1990).

39. Hymer (1972).

40. See UNCTAD, *World Investment Report 1994*, p. 143.

41. The total foreign investment of $44 billion was distributed as follows: $14 billion in Europe, $10.5 billion in the United States, $8.5 billion in Latin America, and $11 billion in Asia and Africa (UNCTAD, *World Investment Report 1994*, p. 158).

42. In 1992, the stock of direct foreign investment in the world economy was $1948 billion; of this, $1520 billion was in the industrialized countries, while the remaining $420 billion was in the developing countries (UNCTAD, *World Investment Report 1994*, p. 415).

43. Cf.. UNCTAD, *World Investment Report*, various issues. During the 1990s, however, the share of developing countries in these inflows has registered a steady increase.

44. See Dunning (1983).

45. UNCTAD, *World Investment Report 1994*, p. 18.

46. For a comparison of the destination of such financial flows, during the two phases, see Kregel (1994).

47. See Lewis (1977), p. 14.

48. For some countries such as Britain, Italy, Spain and Portugal, such migration constituted 20 to 40 per cent of their population (Stalker, 1994).

49. Cf.. Tinker (1974) and Lewis (1977).

50. For evidence on, and an analysis of such migration, see Nayyar (1994).

51. Calculated from data in UNCTAD *Handbook of International Trade and Development Statistics*, various issues.

52. UNCTAD,_199 *World Investment Report 4*, p. 175.

53. See Nayyar (1988).

54. For a more detailed treatment of this issue, see Bhaduri and Nayyar (1996).

55. For a discussion on the implications of the new intellectual property rights regime for developing countries, see Nayyar (1993).

56. This proposition, which follows from the preceding discussion on asymmetrical rules of the international trading system, is also developed, in a wider context and a different perspective, elsewhere (Nayyar, 1996).

57. See, for example, Sachs and Warner (1995), who provide the clearest articulation of the view set out in this paragraph.

58. Cf.Lewis (1978) and Panic (1992).

59. See Bairoch and Kozul-Wright (1996). The authors provide a lucid discussion of how globalization in the period 1870-1913 led to uneven development in the world economy, not simply between the colonizers and the colonized but also within Europe.

60. See Maddison (1989) and Bairoch (1993).

61. Maddison (1989).

62. Bairoch (1982).

63. These proportions have been calculated from UNCTAD, *Handbook of International Trade and Development Statistics*, various issues.

64. Calculated from data in UNCTAD, *World Investment Report 1994*, p. 14.

65. For a detailed discussion, see Bhaduri and Nayyar (1996).

66. See Amsden (1989) and Wade (1991).

References

Amsden, A. *Asia's Next Giant : South Korea and Late Industrialisation*, New York : Oxford University Press, 1989.

Bairoch, P. "International Industrialization Levels from 1750 to 1980," *Journal of European Economic History*, Vol.11, pp.269-310, 1982.

_____. *Economics and World History*, Brighton: Wheatsheaf, 1993.

_____ **and Kozul-Wright, R.** "Globalisation Myths: Some Historical Reflections on Integration, Industrialization and Growth in the World Economy," Geneva: UNCTAD, *Discussion Papers*, No. 13, March1996.

Bank for International Settlements (BIS). *Survey of Foreign Exchange Market Activity*, Basle, various issues.

Bhaduri, A. and Nayyar, D. *The Intelligent Person's Guide to Liberalization*, New Delhi: Penguin Books, 1996.

Chandler, A. *Economies of Scale and Scope*, Cambridge: Harvard University Press, 1990.

Dunning, J.H. "Changes in the Level and Structure of International Production : the last one hundred years," in M. Casson ed., *The Growth of International Business*, London : Allen and Unwin, pp. 84-139, 1983.

Fukuyama, F. "The End of History," *The National Interest*, Vol.16, pp.3-18, 1989 .

Glyn, A. et al. "The Rise and Fall of the Golden Age," in S. Marglin and J. Schor eds. *The Golden Age of Capitalism*, Oxford : Clarendon Press, pp. 39-125, 1990.

Hobsbawm, E. *The Age of Empire*, London : Weidenfeld and Nicolson, 1987.

Hymer, S. "The Multinational Corporation and the Law of Uneven Development," in J. Bhagwati ed., *Economics and World Order from the 1970s to the 1990s*, London : Macmillan, pp. 113-140, 1972.

International Monetary Fund. *International Financial Statistics and World Economic Outlook*, Washington DC, various issues.

Keynes, J.M. *The Economic Consequences of the Peace*, London : Macmillan, 1921.

Kregel, J. "Capital Flows : Globalisation of Production and Financing Development," *UNCTAD Review*, pp. 23-38, 1994.

Lewis, W.A. *The Evolution of the International Economic Order*, Princeton : Princeton University Press, 1977.

_____. *Growth and Fluctuations : 1870-1913*, London: Allen and Unwin, 1978.

Maddison, A. *The World Economy in the Twentieth Century,* Paris : OECD Development Centre, 1989.

_____. *Dynamic Forces in Capitalist Development,* New York: Oxford University Press, 1991.

Maizels, A. *Industrial Growth and World Trade,* Cambridge: Cambridge University Press, 1963.

Morgenstern, O. *International Financial Transactions and Business Cycles,* Princeton : Princeton University Press, 1959.

Nayyar, D. "Political Economy of International Trade in Services," *Cambridge Journal of Economics,* Vol.12, pp. 279-298, 1988.

_____. "National and International Approaches to Intellectual Property Rights," in M.B. Wallerstein et al eds., *Global Dimensions of Intellectual Property Rights in Science and Technology,* Washington DC : National Academy of Sciences, pp. 162-168, 1993.

_____. *Migration, Remittances and Capital Flows,* Delhi : Oxford University Press, 1994.

_____. "Globalisation: The Past in Our Present," Presidential Address to the Indian Economic Association, reprinted in *Indian Economic Journal,* January 1996, pp. 1-18, 1995.

_____. "Free Trade: Why, When and for Whom?," *Banco Nazionale del Lavoro Quarterly Review,* September 1996.

Oman, C. *Globalisation and Regionalisation : The Challenge for Developing Countries,* Paris : OECD Development Centre, 1994.

Panic, M. *European Monetary Union : Lessons from the Classical Gold Standard,* London : Macmillan, 1992.

Sachs, J. and Warner, A.. "Economic Reforms and the Process of Global Integration," *Brookings Papers on Economic Activity,* No. 1, 1995.

Stalker, P. *The Work of Strangers : A survey of international labour migration,* Geneva : International Labour Office, 1994.

Tinker, H. *A New System of Slavery : The Export of Indian Labour Overseas : 1830-1920,* Oxford : Oxford University Press, 1974.

United Nations Conference on Trade and Development (UNCTAD), *Trade and Development Report,* and *Handbook of International Trade and Development Statistics,* Geneva, various issues.

United Nations Centre on Transnational Corporations (UNCTC), *Transnational Corporations and World Development*, New York, various surveys, and UNCTAD, *World Investment Report*, Geneva, various issues.

Wade, R. *Governing the Market*, Princeton : Princeton University Press, 1991.

World Bank. *World Development Report*, Washington DC, various issues.

F02
510

3

GLOBALIZATION:
The Epochal Imperatives and Developmental Tendencies[1]
Cyrus Bina
University of Redlands, USA

In this essay, an attempt has been made to situate the meaning of the contemporary globalization in the context of transnationalization of social capital and spread of its circuits beyond the nation-state. The essay begins with the transnationalization of basic forms of capital--commodity, money, and productive capital--and the evolution of their corresponding global circuits. Globalization, so defined, is a tendency to the unified and worldwide cheapening of labor power, a macro phenomenon that is otherwise known as global technological change. This has led to worldwide hegemony of social capital and the emergence of global social relations beyond the nation-state.

Globalization, as has been intended in the earlier writings of the present author, refers to a macro socioeconomic concept that encompasses an intertwined, systematic, and stage-by-stage integration of world economy, polity, and social structure. It is a newly-emerged historical stage beyond the conventional international trade and transnational capital movements. Globalization is countering the existing local, regional, national, legal, and, presumably, cultural boundaries that have been seemingly blocking the material, ideological, and social transformation of our epoch under the hegemony of global social capital. This view of globalization, although not without controversy, combines the tendency to unification with a multitude of counter-tendencies that are both external and internal to the development of capitalism worldwide. The notion of social capital here is a key concept behind what Marx (1973: 729-30) called "the victory of the mode of production," and, as such, departs from methodological individualism and, consequently, differs from the conventional solutions that center on simple aggregation of individual capitals around the globe. Historically, this "victory" has led to an overall hegemonic transformation that resulted in systematic penetration and thus organic internalization of capital's social relations globally. Yet, the piece-by-piece implosion of the pre-capitalist socioeconomic structures has not remained immune from the manifold resistances that are brought to bear against the capitalist development and its polarizing ideological tendencies worldwide. It goes without saying that such a "victory" has also led to well recognized devastations for the environment today whose coverage clearly requires a separate and extensive space.

There has been a sweeping transformation within the world economy toward the globalization of social relations of capital and corresponding transnationalization of the labor process, particularly since the early 1970s. This transformation has been taking place both in the advanced capitalist countries (ACCs) and less developed countries (LDCs) at an uneven pace, thus leading to further polarization and complex mixture of global integration and disintegration. The integration is through the structure of global social capital against the traditional forces associated with the social fabric of immediate postwar era, including the economic, political, and ideological institutions of Pax Americana . Pax Americana is a shorthand reference to the post-Second World War political/economic global arrangement under the U.S. hegemony that played itself out as a transition from a hegemonic alliance (U. S.) to the hegemony of social capital. The U.S. hegemony lasted a little over a quarter of a century (see Bina, 1993, 1994, 1995). These forces and their corresponding institutional facade (e.g., the international monetary system, postwar international system of nation-states, etc.), which, at one time had led to the very cause of globalization, are now either being abolished, challenged, or transformed by the currents of globalization of the economy and polity. In this manner, hegemony of the Pax Americana has been lost to the global hegemony of social capital, an organic manifold beyond the challenge of any one nation or even any single region alone. Today's globalization is rendering the traditional, national, geographical, legal, and cultural barriers irrelevant, if not obsolete, as it tends to create new barriers of formidable magnitude that are particular to its internal development. Among these barriers are the schizophrenic transformation of technology, erratic devastation of workplace and, consequently, frightful class polarization of worldwide magnitude. Today, at the threshold of the next global century, it appears that, whether we like it or not, we are all in the same boat.

The arguments presented in this essay are based on my previous work on the transnationalization of capital during the last two decades or so. Yet, the reader in certain instances may come across concepts and issues that are not fully explored here. The objective of this chapter rather is to offer food for thought, so to speak, especially on the concept of social capital and its organic relationship with the process of globalization. In the first section the stage is set for the introduction of social capital, and its external and internal limits concerning the development of global capitalism. A brief survey of both orthodox and heterodox literature on the cause of transnationalization will be presented in the second section. The point here is to show the basic contrast between the theory of internationalization of capital and its counterpart in the transaction cost tradition. In addition, it will be argued that globalization, as a unified structure, is the outcome of the simultaneous (internal) transformation of the both Third world and advanced capitalist societies. The third section outlines the internationalization of circuits of social capital and globalization of social relations, followed by conclusion.

Globalization: A Prelude to an Integrated World Order

Today, despite the popular appeal of common-sense interpretation of globalism and the imposing global forces that, particularly since the 1970s, have been transforming the configuration of national boundaries and economies, the concept of globalization has acquired more than one meaning in the minds of economists, orthodox and heterodox alike. Despite this apparent diversity in orientation, however, scholars of all stripes strive for a common understanding of the significance of modern national economies in the face of epoch-making penetration of today's global accumulation. To be sure, the identification of actual forces surrounding the phenomenon of globalization is one thing, and their potential role in shaping the future of global economy and polity is quite another. One way to come to grips with the phenomenon of recent globalization is to keep track of the evolutionary and stage-by-stage development of social relations of capital beyond the nation-states. This, of course, is the focus of this chapter, in which we intend to give priority to the very basic forces behind the evolution of global capitalism. This evolution corresponds with the emerging stage-by-stage socioeconomic structures connected with economic/political institutions that have come to signify the qualitative transformation of the global landscape.

The manifold reality of globalization must be seen in terms of a set of specific, intertwined and hierarchical structures that have cumulatively contributed to the hegemony of global social capital. They have also, conceptually, provided us the recognition of the fact that the national economies can no longer constitute a self-contained unit of analysis. Running its course, capitalism, whose very birth was historically inaugurated within the cocoon of modern nation-state (e.g., in Europe), has already gone beyond such historical limits. Having gained its full potential throughout the twentieth century, social capital is presently accumulating globally by overcoming many of the external limits--e.g. in such domains as culture, environment, geography, legality, morality, nature, and nation--that were previously considered as total impediments to its worldwide expansion. The implication is that when it comes to its self-regulation, global social capital has been confined to its own internal limits that are bound up with the system's diminished capacity to restructure and resolve contradictions at the global level. Therefore, necessarily, any compelling concept of globalization requires a stage theory corresponding with social capital's evolution and self-limitation.

Theories of Global Orientation

There is vast literature on the issues of global integration that centers around the emergence of transnational corporations (TNCs). Two common questions exist in the mainstream literature, namely, "Why does the multinational company exist?" and "Why does this particular economic organization represent a viable coalition of economic resources?" (Caves, 1982: ix). These views can be divided according to their explicit and/or implicit methodology. *First* are the mainstream views of TNCs in which a tendency toward embracing what is known as methodological individualism is prevalent and, axiomatically, the idealization of efficient allocation of resources constitute its starting point (see Fine, 1981, Ch.1, Arrow, 1994). In this category, there are many differing strands: (1) the capital flow models associated with Leontief (1954, 1956), Mundell (1957), (Wilkins, 1970), Kindleberger (1969, 1984), Caves (1971, 1982), and Purvis (1972); (2) the product life-cycle models, originated in Vernon (1966), and expanded by Wells (1972), and Vernon (1971, 1977), among others; and (3) the so-called internalization or transaction cost models, founded on Coase (1937, 1960) by McManus (1972), Buckley and Casson (1976), Hood and Young (1979), Williamson (1975, 1981, 1985), Dunning (1981, 1989), Teece (1977, 1986), Hennart (1982), and Rugman (1980, 1986).

The *second* approach can be described as the global reach variety, having to do with the strategy of oligopolistic firms in search of the so-called "market power" and opportunity for transfer pricing. The main proponents of this view are Hymer (1976 [1960]), Knickerboker (1973), Barnnett and Muller (1974), Lall and Streetten (1977), Graham (1978), Cohen et al. (1979), Lall (1980), and Newfarmer (1980), among others.

The *third* view is associated with the theories of unequal exchange, surplus transfer and monopoly capitalism, having to do with dependency and dualistic concept of global development and underdevelopment. Among the proponents of this view are: Baran (1957), Baran and Sweezy (1966), Sweezy and Magdoff (1969), Emmanuel (1972), Frank(1967, 1979), Sunkel (1972, 1973), Amin (1974, 1976), and Cowling and Sugden (1987).

Finally, there is a view that is associated with the internationalization of capital that by and large tends to treat TNCs not only as a sui generis institution but also as the reflection of a new stage in the development of world economy and global capitalism. The basic features of this approach can be found in Warren (1975), Murray (1975), Poulantzas (1975), Palloix (1975, 1977), Radice (1975, 1984), Cypher (1979), Shaikh (1979, 1980), Jenkins (1987), Bina (1985, 1989), Bina and Yaghmaian (1988, 1991), Bryan (1995), and Bina and Davis (1996), among others.

Among the various conceptual frameworks identified above, the mainstream internalization (transaction cost) theory and the radical theory of internationalization of capital stand out as the most systematic and, perhaps, comprehensive views of globalization today; even though methodologically and ideologically both of these approaches are also diametrically opposed to each other. The so-called internalization theory maintains that the very existence of the TNCs is the result of market imperfections, including the costly market transactions across the boundaries of nation-states. Here the idealized non-hierarchical function of markets plays much like the premise of original sin in theology. Departing from idealism, associated with the first principle of the theory, for the sake of some realism may not be without negation of the entire concept. In such cases, even resorting to successive approximation may not prove adequate (for the critique of issues similar to this see Fine, 1981, Ch.1). Market, a perceived non-hierarchical entity, thus encounters costly transactions, which in turn demand appropriate hierarchies in order to internalize them for the sake of efficiency. But, for obvious reasons, presenting an argument by assumption about the "non-hierarchical" nature of capitalist markets is not enough.

In the case of TNCs, the transaction costs associated with exporting (or licensing) such intangible assets as the technical know-how, managerial expertise, and information, or those of the locational preferences and specific assets are said to be too costly to be efficient. Thus, "internalization" of such transactions in the face of existing transnational markets justifies the development of TNCs (see Pitelis, 1991: 19). The main argument here boils down to the conquest of non-hierarchical by the hierarchical institutions in the name of efficiency. This, of course, is beside the point that capitalist markets are sui generis hierarchies themselves. For the sake of argument, the development of hierarchies depends upon the prior existence of markets. Alchian and Demsetz (1972), however, propose that at the outset "there is no difference between the firm and the market, and that the firm is essentially a market: ... a privately owned market" (cited in Pitelis 1991: 19). Yet, as North (1981) indicates, hierarchies historically preceded the markets. To claim that the market precedes the firm or vice-versa is a matter that cannot be resolved by appealing to tautology (i.e., at the level of the transaction-cost hypothesis) alone. On the other hand, facts by themselves do not exhibit any significant meaning with their corresponding philosophical outlook.

For instance, the elimination of the distinction between the firm and the market would by no means resolve the question of why there is a tendency toward hierarchies in the first place. Therefore, far from solving the problem, we are back to square one again. Finally, and this is the most devastating, as the capitalist markets themselves have become the bastion of formidable hierarchies, they provide doubt that the entire doctrine of efficiency-seeking transaction cost (and, consequently, its application to the expansion of TNCs) may ever be able to stand on its own foundation (see Pitelis, 1991, Ch. 2).

The theory of internationalization of capital, on the other hand, holds no illusion about the hierarchical nature of capitalist markets. In this theory, the concept of transaction (i.e., the realm of exchange) is not separate from the concept of accumulation. A truly transnational market, therefore, must certainly be dependent upon a truly transnational production process. However, historically, the development of a full-fledged transnational production process is the result of a series of structural transformations within the global circuits of social capital, which receives its early stimulus from transnational mobility of capital. Such mobility, of course, must be defined in terms of all three primary forms of capital (i.e., in terms of commodity, money, and productive forms) so that there will be sufficient condition for truly global accumulation via the global circuits of social capital beyond the nation-states. Therefore, the theory of internationalization of capital, relying upon capital's transnational mobility (and, ultimately, the resultant transnational labor processes and transnational technological development), tends to make the classical as well as neoclassical versions of comparative advantage (costs) theory obsolete (see Bryan, 1995, Ch. 9).

The literature on transnationalization of capital is far from unified (For example, see Capital & Class, No. 43, Spring 1991). To be sure, there are many strands of "globalization theory," which would fall short of providing a consistent methodological framework within social relations of capital (see, for instance, Froebel et al., 1980, on the so-called international division of labor). In this brief chapter our task is to recapitulate the main points concerning the theory of transnationalization of capital that is based upon the globalization of social relations, thus looking at TNCs as a symptom rather than a cause of globalization (see Bina and Yaghmaian, 1988, Bina and Davis, 1996).

Let us, at the outset, define social capital as opposed to individual capital which is normally identified with the operation of a single TNC. We refer to social capital as the realm of macroeconomic activity and the accumulation process as a whole. It is an all-encompassing network of capital in its collectivity and undivided whole that provides a meaningful historical framework for the individual capital. Social capital here constitutes a body composed of the individual cells. However, the aggregation of all individual cells may not represent the body as a whole. This amounts to our first principle in the present argument. In other words, we reject the fallacy of composition and thus give priority to the realm of macroeconomics. We simply deny that any socioeconomic whole can be reduced to the relation of its component parts alone. In this sense, social capital must first be understood in its undifferentiated and undivided whole. Social capital represents the hierarchical structures of accumulation and the labor process in capitalism. It has hegemonic consequences for the reproduction of economy, polity, and society. Indeed, social capital is the body that would give meaning to its functioning cells. The most important task of social capital is the cheapening of labor power worldwide, that is, a tendency to constant technological revolution in order to devalue the realm of human activity. This is done through the application of technology and continuous innovations that play as a double-edged sword: the application of technology (in capitalism) creates new and more powerful means of production at the expense of the constant destruction of such means. This is what Schumpeter referred to as the process of "creative destruction" (see Schumpeter 1987: 83). Yet, in actuality, the process of technological change in advanced capitalism may be better explained as destructive creation par excellence. In other words, the majority of innovations today are to make the very functioning means of production, including the technical skills on the part of the workers, redundant at an ever-increasing pace.

On the other hand, individual capital, which is a microeconomic entity, strives to cut the cost of production, including search for cheap labor. Conceptually, there is a significant difference between the utilization of an already existing supply of cheap labor by a single transnational operation and the worldwide cheapening of labor power via endless transformation and revolution in technology. The former has no necessity for establishment of the capitalist social relations. A simple plunder and forceful submission of the local population often can do the job. The latter, however, is the reflection of the fact that capitalism, as a mode of production, has already taken roots. It amounts to internal revolution within the structure of the society in question. In order to show how global capitalism has emerged conceptually, we need a stage theory (corresponding with capital's global transformation) in order to keep track of its evolution.

It is rather insufficient to argue that since capital has been considered a global phenomenon from its birth, its accumulation must come under the immediate scope of transnational jurisdiction (as Bryan (1995) seems to have implied). Such an argument confuses the historical development of global capitalism with its developed form--it assumes global capitalism before the development of global capitalism. Use of the phrase "global capitalism" here refers to the establishment of social relations of capital globally. This is a relatively recent phenomenon associated with the worldwide production of relative surplus value. This amounts to what Marx calls the "victory of mode of production" at the global level (see Marx, 1973: 728-30). It is within this context that the transnationalization of three basic forms of capital provides us with a stage theory appropriate for evolution of globalization and, ultimately, the recognition of worldwide hegemony of social capital.

One of the fundamental developments, entwined with the post-Second World War sociopolitical division of the globe, has been the elimination of outright colonialism and the emergence of a great number of nation-states that collectively have become known as the Third World. The nominal independence of most of these nations, however, may not be understood in isolation from the post-Second World War division of the world economy and its corresponding division of labor and the accumulation process. As a result, given the U. S. postwar global hegemony, there remained a considerable number of post-colonial nations that have yet to improve practically their position far beyond the status of a neocolony.

Accepting that the development of capitalism emerges both intra-nationally (within the nation-state boundaries) and inter-nationally (beyond such boundaries), it would be instructive to study the nature and historical significance of such a contradictory process in terms of (1) the transformation of national social formations in the postwar period with dominant pre-capitalist relations, (2) the further development of social formations within advanced capitalist societies, and (3) the unified structure of global social relations (of capitalism) as a whole. These three interrelated trajectories are both conceptual and historical, and, as such, would constitute an appropriate framework for the analysis of today's global economy and global polity.

The post-Second World War transformation of the Third World via the primary and advanced stages of primitive accumulation indicates that qualitatively our modern global economy is already beyond the stage of what is known as the colonial world system--an order within which the politico-military dominance of "center" over the "periphery" has been the sine qua non of the global relations (Bina and Yaghmaian, 1988). Instead, in this modern global atmosphere the influence of economic relations has been predominant. Capitalism gradually but persistently tended to overcome the barriers of pre-capitalist social structures by restructuring the world according to its own image; yet in doing so created new barriers according to its own transitory nature and epochal imperatives. The complexity of this transformation is considerable, especially from the standpoint of the emerging network of global social relations in all four corners of the world today. It is within such a context that, for instance, one may easily recognize the significance of the past several decades of import-substitution industrialization (ISI) and/or export-led development aimed at the Third World (Bina and Yaghmaian, 1988).

An integral part of the above framework is necessarily the role of state in the social and economic reproduction. Moreover, the state in both ACCs and LDCs are part and parcel of the contradictory development of the nation-state itself. In the LDCs, both under the ISI and the export-led regimes, the very nation-state promoted the task of the internationalization of capital. Despite their nationalistic outlook, ISI development programs provided the initial stage for transnationalization of capital through the creation of internal market in many LDCs, before the implementation of export-led strategies. Yet, there were certain countries that due to their insignificant size (i.e., the lack of potential internal market) skipped the ISI programs altogether and moved toward export-led industrialization directly.

Nation-States and the Modern International Relations

Given the historical context associated with the rise of the modern nation-states, there has been a growing interdependence between the international economy and the emerging nation-states: especially in the case of a large group of nations that are better known as the Third World. With further development of capitalism, the existing national economies have become integrated into the global economy, however unevenly, as the mutual relationship of modern nation-states and their global counterpart has been further solidified. Historically, this has taken three stages through the internationalization of (1) commodity capital, (2) money or finance capital, and (3) productive capital.

The first stage in the internationalization of capital is the globalization of commodity trade (given the development of world market) which associates with the circuit of commodity capital (C'-M'-C. . .P'. . .C', where C' stands for commodity, M' for money capital, P' for production process and C'=C+c; here c represents surplus value in commodity form) at the international level, and which is historically prior to the development of finance or money capital on a global scale. This phase, from the standpoint of global development of capitalist social relations, has been coincided with the extraction of absolute surplus value in the vast majority of the regions of the world, even though there existed many nation-states (in Western Europe and elsewhere) whose accumulation process has already been in tune with the production of relative surplus value. Colonial trade--i.e., the import of raw materials from the pre-capitalist colonial regions of the world by the advanced (European, etc.) countries and the export of manufactured consumer goods to the colonies--is in fact the main feature of world trade that gradually diminished prior to the First World War.

The internationalization of finance capital. however, set the stage for the transition toward a fully integrated capitalist economy at the global level. With this, the circuit of money capital--i.e., M-C... P...C'-M' (where M' stands for money capital, given M'=M+m; and m is surplus value in money form)-- has been fully expanded internationally (Marx, 1981, Ch. 1). For social capital to become a de facto global entity there had to be a global circuit in all its social forms. This has been accomplished through the internationalization of productive capital, which completed the globalization of capital in all its social forms and resulted in the unfolding of colossal and integrated entities known as transnational corporations. Having direct control over many labor processes around the world, productive capital tends to exploit the labor power globally through the circuit of P. . .C'-M'-C ... P' (Marx, 1981, Ch.2; see also Palliox, 1975, 1977, Fine, 1981, Ch. 2).

The reader should be reminded that following the transnationalization of all circuits of social capital there has been a qualitative change in the role of finance capital in respect to global accumulation. In other words, the post-1970s globalization is not merely a quantitative extension of the transnationalization of the immediate postwar era. It goes without saying that all the above circuits manifest the organic unity of social capital globally with the last phase of globalization of productive capital. Once the study of accumulation and development of capitalist social relations are placed within the globe itself, it will become necessary to do away with the priority of traditional national economic categories and to recognize three distinct but interrelated tendencies.

First is the genesis of capitalist development as it evolved within the majority of predominantly pre-capitalist regions of the world known as the Third World; the second is the internal transformation of the capitalist mode of production itself, including its supranational features in the advanced regions of the world. Third is the recognition of overall global social relations. Such an analysis is already beyond the narrow limits of the nation-state. Such a socioeconomic structure must nevertheless interconnect with the contradictory structure of the modern state that is both global and national at the same time. In other words, going beyond the nation-state attempts to reflect the very contradictory reality that has already been manifested by the relationship of state and the global capital. If social capital (i.e., capital-in-general) will no longer remain a national entity (see Radice, 1984), the role of the state as an agent of social reproduction will have to be transformed in such a manner that it will be able to internalize additional contradictions that are particularly global in nature. If so, then the notion of nation-state is in need of reconceptualization in view of the emerging realities of today's economy and polity (see also Picciotto, 1991).

It is hard to understand, therefore, why there is so much emphasis on the exclusivity of the nation-state as a concept at the expense of disregarding the material basis of the global analysis (see, for instance, Gordon, 1988). A glance at the post-Second World War development and its corresponding regime of accumulation reveals that, indeed, the process of globalization of capitalist social relations has already been materializing through the institutional characteristics of the economy and polity of this period. For instance, almost all the land reform programs (throughout the 1950s, 1960s, and the 1970s) proposed and imposed by the United States in many Third World countries pointedly served the same global objective, namely to facilitate the process of "primitive accumulation" on a global scale (Bina and Yaghmaian, 1988). In addition to the role played by the United States and its many subordinate (and client) states within the Third World, there are a number of international institutions, such as the World Bank and IMF, that have diligently engaged in the implementation of an all-encompassing global program of (intended and unintended) social and economic reforms in the Third World. The role of the nation-states and the (supra-national) states in all these programs is clearly the promotion of global objectives, since the main beneficiaries were proved to be the transnational capitals. It is also understandable that the Third World import substitution industrialization programs could not have taken effect without such global land reform programs. The institution and implementation of the postwar land reform programs have almost universally led to proletarianization of the peasantry in the Third World, an immense and fresh source of surplus labor for the emerging import-substituting industries (Lewis, 1954, 1958).

It goes without saying that all these land reforms were supposed to be implemented in such a manner as to minimize the risk of social upheavals and political disturbances that have had a destabilizing effect upon the economy and the polity of the individual nations involved. That is why these reforms were almost universally accompanied with imposition from the above, and accomplished through repressive policies of notorious dictatorships that had the unconditional support of the United States and its hegemonic Pax Americana. In some respects, this is somewhat similar to the early development of capitalism in Europe where, for instance, the role of the state in the process of "primitive accumulation" was so crucial.

The British "enclosures" of commons are a remarkable example in this context. Nevertheless, one has to recognize the fundamental differences that may exist between this twentieth century phenomenon and its eighteenth century counterpart in Britain. First, almost all the Third World land reform programs were imposed by the historically backward states with the unconditional support of Western powers, at the forefront of which stood the United States. Second, the principal target of the postwar land reform programs was to uproot the existing pre-capitalist social relations in order to overrun the boundaries of the Third World through rapid spread of capitalism. This was accomplished on a global basis which facilitated a broad global "primitive accumulation". These programs, fully successful or not, provided the necessary socioeconomic preconditions that were to be utilized for the stages of import-substitution and export platform industrialization programs before all these newly-established modern nation-states became an organic part of the global economy.

Conclusion

It has been shown that the postwar global economy can be characterized as the unity and contradiction of manifold socioeconomic forces that transformed the fabric of social life everywhere. Its remarkable, but sadly devastating, outcome has been the disintegration of the old social relations by the direct imposition of the state and the penetrating forces of global social capital in the Third World. The role played by the all-embracing global land reform policies supported by the United States has been singled out in order to show that the internationalization of capital and globalization of capitalist social relations were manifested in the two interrelated socioeconomic transformations: (1) the integration of the Third World into the global economy, having to do with forced "primitive accumulation" and the subsequent import-substitution and export platform policies, and (2) the internal transformation of the capitalist mode of production in the advanced capitalist countries themselves.

Endnotes

1.This essay is a revised version of a university lecture delivered at the annual meeting of Omicron Delta Epsilon (chapter at Drew University, Madison, New Jersey), April 24, 1996. My thanks are due to Dev Gupta and an anonymous reviewer who have provided me with helpful and constructive criticism on the final draft of this chapter. I wish to express my appreciation to Nora Colton for the invitation to Drew University and her confidence in the project. I am also grateful to Fred Curtis and other members of the Economics Department at Drew University for their enthusiastic reception and helpful comments.

References

Alchian, A. A. and Demsetz H. "Production, Information Cost, and Economic Organization," *American Economic Review*, December 1972, 62 (5), pp. 777-95.

Amin, S. *Accumulation on a World Scale,* 2 Vols, New York: Monthly Review, 1974.

_____. Unequal Development, New York: Monthly Review, 1976.

Arrow, K. J. "Methodological Individualism and Social Knowledge," *American Economic Review*, May 1994, 84(2), pp. 1-9.

Baran, P. *The Political Economy of Growth*, New York: Monthly Review, 1957.

_____. and Sweezy P. M. *Monopoly Capital*, New York: Monthly Review, 1966.

Barnett, R. S. and Muller, R. E. Global Reach: *The Power of Multinational Corporations* New York: Simon and Schuster, 1974.

Bina, C. *The Economics of the Oil Crisis* New York: St. Martin's, 1985.

_____. "Competition, Control and Price Formation in the International Energy Industry," *Energy Economics*, July 1989,11(3), pp. 162-68.

_____.The Rhetoric of Oil and the Dilemma of War and American Hegemony," *Arab Studies Quarterly*, Summer 1993,15(3), pp. 1-20.

_____."Oil, Japan, and Globalization," *Challenge*, May/June 1994 ,37(3), pp. 41-48.

_____."On Sand Castles and Sand-Castle Conjectures: A Rejoinder," *Arab Studies Quarterly*, Winter/Spring 1995,17(1 & 2), pp. 167-71.

_____**and Davis, C.** "Wage Labor and Global Capital: Global Competition and Universalization of the Labor Movement," in Bina et al. (eds.) *Beyond Survival: Wage Labor in the Late Twentieth Century*, Armonk, New York: M. E. Sharpe, 1996.

_____**and Yaghmaian, B.**"Import Substitution and Export Promotion Within the Context of the Internationalization of Capital," *Review of Radical Political Economics*, 1988, 20(2 &3), pp. 234-40.

_____."Postwar Global Accumulation and the Transnationalization of Capital, *Capital & Class* (Joint Issue with the Review of Radical Political Economics), Spring 1991, No. 43, pp. 107-30.

Bryan, D. *The Chase Across the Globe*, Boulder, CO: Westview Press, 1995.

Buckley, P. J. and Casson, M. *The Future of Multinational Enterprise,* New York: Holmes & Meier, 1976.

Capital & Class/ Review of Radical Political Economics Joint Issue, (Beyond the Nation-State), *Capital & Class*, No. 43, Spring 1991.

Caves, R. E." International Corporations: The Industrial Economics of Foreign Investment," *Economica,* 1971 38(141), pp. 1-27.

_____.*Multinational Enterprise and Economic Analysis,* Cambridge, UK: Cambridge University Press, 1982.

Coase, R. H. "The Nature of the Firm," *Economica* , 1937 New Series, 4, pp. 386-405.

_____."The Problem of Social Cost," *Journal of Law and Economics,* 1960, 3(1), pp. 1-44.

Cohen, R. B.; Felton, N; Van Liere. J. and Nkosi M.(eds.) *The Multinational Corporations: A Radical Approach,* Papers by Stephen Herbert Hymer, Cambridge, UK: Cambridge University Press, 1979.

Cowling, K. and Sugden, R. *Transnational Monopoly Capitalism,* Brighton, UK: Wheatsheaf, 1987.

Cypher, J. "The Internationalization of Capital and the Transformation of Social Formations: A Critique of the 'Monthly Review School'," *Review of Radical Political Economics* Winter 1979, pp. 39-49.

Dunning, J. H. *International Production and the Multinational Enterprise* , London: Allen and Unwin, 1981.

_____.*Explaining International Production,* London: Unwin/Hyman, 1989.

Emmanuel, A. *Unequal Exchange,* New York: Monthly Review, 1972.

Fine, B. *Economic Theory and Ideology,* New York: Holmes & Meier, 1981.

Frank, A. G. *Capitalism and Underdevelopment in Latin America,* New York: Monthly Review, 1967.

Frank, A. G. *Dependent Accumulation and Underdevelopment,* New York: Monthly Review, 1979.

Frobel, F.; Heinrich, J. and Kreye, O. *The New International Division of Labor,* Cambridge, UK: Cambridge University Press, 1980.

Gordon, D. M. "The Global Economy: New Edifice or Crumbling Foundations?" *New Left Review,* No. 168.

Graham, E. M. "Transatlantic Investment by Multinational Firms: A Rivalistic Phenomenon?" *Journal of Post-Keynesian Economics,* Fall 1978, 1(1), pp. 82-99.

Hennart, J. F. *A Theory of Multinational Enterprise*, Ann Arbor, MI: The University of Michigan Press, 1982.

Hood, N. and Young, S. *The Economics of the Multinational Enterprise,* London: Longman, 1979.

Hymer, S. H. *The International Operation of National Firms: A Study of Direct Foreign Investment,* Cambridge, MA: MIT Press, 1976 [his Ph.D. dissertation 1960]).

Jenkins, R. *Transnational Corporations and Uneven Development*, New York: Methuen, 1987.

Kindleberger, C. P. *American Business Abroad*, New Haven, CT: Yale University Press, 1969.

_____. *Multinational Excursions* , Cambridge, MA: MIT Press, 1984.

Knickerbocker, F. T. *Oligopolistic Reaction and Multinational Enterprise* , Boston: Harvard Graduate School of Business Administration, 1973.

Lall, S. *The Multinational Corporations: Nine Essays*, London: Macmillan, 1980.

_____**and Streetten, P.** *Foreign Investment, Transnationals and Developing Countries*, Colorado: Westview, 1977.

Leontief, W. W. "Domestic Production and Foreign Trade: The American Capital Position Re-examined," *Economia Internazionale*, February 1954.

_____."Factor Proportions and the Structure of the American Trade: Further Theoretical and Empirical Analysis," *Review of Economics and Statistics*, November 1956.

Lewis, W. A. "Economic Development with Unlimited Supply of Labor," *The Manchester School*, May 1954, 139-91.

_____." Unlimited Labor: Further Notes," *The Manchester School*, January 1958, pp.1-32.

Marx, K. *Grundrisse,* New York: Vintage, 1973[1932].

Marx, K. *Capital, Vol. II* , New York: Vintage, 1981[1894].

McManus, J. C. "The Theory of the International Firm," in G. Paquet (ed.), *The Multinational Firm and the Nation-State,* Toronto: Collier-Macmillan, 1972.

Mundell, R. A. "International Trade and Factor Mobility," *American Economic Review,* June 1957.

Murray, R. "The Internationalization of Capital and the Nation-State," in H. Radice (ed.), *International Firm and Modern Imperialism,* Harmondsworth: Penguin, 1975.

Newfarmer, R. *Transnational Corporations and the Economics of Dependent Development.* Greenwich, CT: JAI Press, 1980.

North, D. C. *Structure and Change in Economic History,* New York: W. W. Norton, 1981.

Palloix, C. "The Internationalization of Capital and Circuit of Social Capital," in H. Radice (ed.), *International Firm and Modern Imperialism,* Harmonsworth: Penguin, 1975.

_____."The Self-Expansion of Capital on a World Scale," *Review of Radical Political Economics,,* Summer 1977, 9(2).

Picciotto, S. "The Internationalization of the State," *Capital and Class,* Spring 1991, 43, pp. 43-63.

Pitelis, C. *Market and Non-Market Hierarchies: Theory of Institutional Failure,* Cambridge, MA: Basil Blackwell, 1991.

Poulantzas, N. "Internationalization of Capitalist Relations and the Nation-State," *Economy and Society,* 1975, 3, pp. 145-79.

Purvis, D. D. "Technology, Trade, and Factor Mobility," *Economic Journal,* 1972, 82, pp. 991-99.

Radice, H. "The National Economy: A Keynesian Myth?" *Capital and Class,* 1984, 22.

_____ (ed.). *International Firm and Modern Imperialism ,* Harmondsworth: Penguin, 1975.

Rugman, A. M. " Internalization as a General Theory of Foreign Direct Investment: A Re-Appraisal of the Literature," *Weltwirtschaftliches Archiv,* 1980, 116, pp. 365-79.

_____. " New Theories of Multinational Enterprises: An Assessment of Internalization Theory," *Bulletin of Economic Research,* May 1986, 38(2), pp. 101-18.

Schumpeter, J. *Capitalism, Socialism and Democracy* 5th ed, (London: Unwin and Hyman, 1987.

Shaikh, A. "Foreign Trade and the Law of Value: Part I," *Science and Society,* Fall 1979, 63 (3), pp. 281-302.

_____. "Foreign Trade and the Law of Value: Part II," *Science and Society*, Spring 1980, 64(1), pp. 27-57.

Sunkel, O. "Big Business and 'Dependencia': A Latin American View," *Foreign Affairs*, 1972, pp. 517-31.

_____." Transnational Capitalism and National Disintegration in Latin America," *Social and Economic Studies*, 1973, 22(1).

Sweezy, P. M. and Magdoff, H. "Notes on the Multinational Corporations," *Monthly Review*, 1969, 21, (5 and 6).

Teece, D. J. "Technology Transfer by Multinational Firms: The Resource Cost of Transferring Technological Knowhow," *Economic Journal*, 1977, 87.

_____. "Transaction Cost Economics and the Multinational Enterprise: An Assessment," *Journal of Economic Behavior and Organization,* 1986, 7, pp. 21-45.

Vernon, R. "International Investment and International Trade in the Product Cycle," *Quarterly Journal of Economics*, May 1966, 80, pp.190-207.

_____.*Sovereignty at Bay: The Multinational Spread of U.S. Enterprises*, New York: Basic Books, 1971.

_____. *Storm Over the Multinationals: The Real Issues,* Cambridge, MA: Harvard University Press, 1977.

Warren, B. "How International is Capital?" in H. Radice (ed.), *International Firm and Modern Imperialism,*Harmondsworth: Penguin, 1975.

Wells, L. T. (ed.). *The Product Cycle and International Trade,* Boston: Harvard Business School, 1972.

Wilkins, M. *The Emergence of Multinational Enterprise: American Business Abroad from the Colonial Era to 1914,* Cambridge, MA: Harvard University Press, 1970.

Williamson, O. E. *Market and Hierarchies: Analysis and Antitrust Implications,* New York: Free Press, 1975.

_____. " The Modern Corporation: Origins, Evolution, Attributes," *Journal of Economic Literature*, December 1981, 19, pp. 1537-68.

_____.*The Economic Institutions of Capitalism: Firms, Markets, Relational Contracting,* New York: Free Press, 1985.

(global)

Fo 2
F21 519

4

THE LIMITS OF GLOBALIZATION:
An Assessment of the Extent and Consequences of the Mobility of Productive Capital

Tim Koechlin
Skidmore College, USA

This paper argues that the extent and consequences of the globalization of productive investment tend to be overstated. The evidence presented here indicates that the investment process, far from transcending the nation state, remains essentially a national phenomenon. Investment is largely undertaken by domestic firms responding to domestic economic conditions. The paper also provides a contrast of mainstream and heterodox visions of economic openness. It is argued that the heterodox critique of mainstream theory is well founded. A more realistic set of assumptions leads to less sanguine conclusions about the consequences of economic openness. The paper concludes that advances in capital mobility are indeed likely to undermine the bargaining power of workers, communities and nation states. But, on the other hand, capital is considerably less mobile than many heterodox thinkers claim.

The presumption that economic activity has become increasingly global in recent years is shared by economists from virtually every school of thought. Indeed, the idea that globalization is important and pervasive is typically treated as self-evident fact of economic life. US Secretary of Labor and political economist Robert B. Reich asserts that we live in a world of "global capital" in which "borders become ever more meaningless in economic terms" (1991, p.3). Business Week proclaims that "big global companies are effectively making decisions with little regard for national borders" (Holstein, 1990). And Charles Kindleberger argued nearly three decades ago that advances in the mobility of capital mean that "the nation state is just about through as an economic unit" (1969, p. 207). Declarations of this sort have become commonplace in policy debates, the popular press and in scholarly journals.

This simple and important premise has considerable intuitive appeal. Dramatic advances in the technologies of transportation and communication have indeed facilitated connections between and among once remote cultures and economies. National governments have consciously promoted globalization, most notably through international trade and investment agreements. And, of course, consumers confront evidence of globalization every day in shopping malls and car dealerships. By virtually any measure, international flows of goods, services, capital and people have grown steadily -- and in many cases dramatically -- over the past few decades.

Economists disagree, for sure, about the specific hazards and opportunities associated with globalization. But there is widespread agreement that advances in economic openness are real and consequential. Mainstream economists argue that economic integration tends to enhance economic welfare by compelling nations to specialize in the production of goods and services in which they enjoy a comparative advantage. Heterodox economists, in contrast, tend to highlight the potential dangers of globalization. In particular, globalization is likely to undermine the bargaining power of workers, communities and progressive governments vis a vis increasingly mobile multinational corporations (MNCs).[1] The consequences include declining living standards for working people and dim prospects for progressive economic, social and environmental policy.

I make two related arguments in this chapter. *First*, I argue that the concerns about globalization articulated by heterodox economists are well founded. Key assumptions underlying the mainstream case for free trade are questionable and this calls the optimistic conclusions of the classical theory of trade into question. A more reasonable set of assumptions, particularly those relating to the operation of labor markets and capital markets, leads to a less sanguine set of conclusions about the consequences of economic openness.

Second, this paper, unlike much of the heterodox literature on globalization, takes a skeptical view of the widely shared premise that globalization -- especially with regard to productive investment -- is an extensive and pervasive economic phenomenon. In particular, I argue that the mobility of productive capital, perhaps the most threatening and important aspect of globalization as envisioned by heterodox economists, is quite limited. The evidence presented here indicates that, even in the most open economies, investment is overwhelming undertaken by domestic firms responding to domestic economic conditions.

This conclusion is important for a few related reasons. Exaggerated claims about the extent of globalization provide an inadequate basis for understanding either the process of capital accumulation or the constraints and opportunities confronting workers and policy makers. The argument presented here calls into question the dramatic consequences often associated with globalization and, further, it suggests that the prospects for progressive economic and social policy are less constrained than they might be in a world of "hypermobile" capital.

This argument is however less than conclusive, most notably because it focuses on a particular aspect of globalization: the apparent internationalization of productive capital. This chapter says considerably less about the extent and consequences of international trade, and almost nothing about international financial flows and immigration, each of which are surely of interest and consequence. Still, the evidence presented here raises serious questions about the significance of international investment and this, in turn, raises questions about the nature of the accumulation process and the extent to which workers and progressive policy makers are constrained by globalization.

This essay is organized as follows. The next two sections provide brief critical discussions of the ways in which mainstream and heterodox economists have thought about the potential consequences of globalization. The penultimate section provides evidence suggesting that globalization is not be as extensive as is commonly presumed. The last section discusses some of the implications of the arguments presented in this chapter.

The Mainstream Case for Openness

While mainstream economists have dedicated considerable attention to trade, international capital flows and other aspects of openness, they tend to spend little energy fretting about its consequences.[2] Their faith that trade liberalization enhances welfare is not easily shaken. Mainstream studies of the North American Free Trade Agreement (NAFTA), for example, differed primarily in their assessments of how extensive the gains from trade were likely to be.[3] Paul R. Krugman writes: "If there were an Economist's Creed it would surely contain the affirmations 'I understand the Principle of Comparative Advantage' and 'I advocate Free Trade'"(1987, 131). Far from being a source of legitimate anxiety, mainstream economists contend that openness should be actively pursued and promoted.

The mainstream defense of openness is rooted in the classical theory of trade. Free trade, the argument goes, results in a more efficient international division of labor as nations are compelled to specialize in the production of goods and services in which they have a comparative advantage. The primary beneficiaries of free trade are consumers, who enjoy more choice, lower prices and, on average, higher real incomes. The gains from trade are still greater in models which assume increasing returns to scale and "dynamic gains from trade." Free trade, in short, provides a free lunch.

The conclusion that freer trade is welfare enhancing depends, of course, on a number of strong assumptions. Resources (including labor) are assumed to be fully employed before and after liberalization; goods markets and domestic factor markets are assumed to be perfectly competitive; all factors of production are assumed to be immobile internationally; and exports are assumed to equal exports for each country.[4]

Mainstream trade theorists acknowledge that even under these restrictive assumptions free trade does not benefit everyone. Indeed this is an explicit conclusion of the Heckscher-Ohlin-Samuelson (HOS) model of trade. The reallocation of resources that comes with trade liberalization means that some firms will be ruined by import competition and some workers will lose their jobs. But more than this, entire classes of income earners are likely to see their incomes decline; in particular, owners of a nation's relatively scarce factor of production will see the price of their factor decline as a consequence of trade liberalization. But while the HOS model of trade suggests that trade liberalization may affect the distribution of income in potentially troubling ways, this conclusion does not ultimately undermine the case for free trade.[5] Free trade enhances welfare in the aggregate. Those who lose their jobs will (by assumption) eventually find work and capital that is liberated in one industry will be employed more efficiently elsewhere. The income losses sustained by some may be an unpleasant and enduring fact of life, but we are reassured that the gains from trade are sufficiently large that liberalization's losers could, in principle, be fully compensated for their losses. And this is true for every country in a world of free trade; that is, while free trade does not improve the welfare of each individual, it does improve the collective welfare of each country.[6]

Some economists have made a stronger if less theoretically rigorous case for freer trade, particularly in the context of policy debates. For example, many proponents of the North American Free Trade Agreement (NAFTA) and the GATT argued that trade liberalization would create jobs -- an irrelevant issue in a world of full employment. Gary Hufbauer and Jeffrey Schott (1993), for example, argued that NAFTA would improve the US balance of trade with Mexico and create 170,000 new jobs in the US. Rudiger Dornbusch (1991), in testimony before a House subcommittee, argued that NAFTA would mean "more good jobs for American workers." Others have argued that trade liberalization is likely to promote capital accumulation and/or economic growth.

Mainstream economists acknowledge that free trade may not always be the optimal policy. Protection of an infant industry may be welfare enhancing in the long run. Similarly, protecting and/or subsidizing an industry characterized by economies of scale may be a country's best interest. Further, a country may choose to protect an industry for reasons having to do with national security, the preservation of its culture or some other non-economic consideration. But despite these (and other) exceptions to the rule, the mainstream view -- and the view articulated resoundingly in international trade textbooks and debates over trade policy -- is that the benefits of free trade outstrip its costs. After arguing that the traditional case for free trade is less universal than is typically presumed, Paul Krugman concludes that free trade should clearly be "a rule of thumb" (143).

The consideration of capital mobility -- which is ruled out by assumption in the classical model of trade -- complicates the case for openness considerably. Mobile capital creates the very real possibility that openness may enhance the welfare of one nation at the expense of another. In a world of full employment and competitive markets, capital movements will improve global welfare, but net capital flows from one country to another may well reduce productivity, output and incomes in the source country by reducing the size of its capital stock.

But this possibility has tended to provoke little concern among mainstream commentators. Many of the most influential models of NAFTA's effects, for example, simply assumed that liberalization would not lead to a relocation of productive capital, despite the centrality of this issue in the policy debate over NAFTA.[7] Others have assumed, asserted or argued that freer trade tends to accelerate the pace of capital accumulation, thus augmenting the gains from trade in the long run. In their influential book on NAFTA, Hufbauer and Schott argue that, despite the potential dangers of capital mobility, outward direct foreign investment is "good event" for the US which, on balance, creates jobs and enhances labor income (1993, p. 19). More generally, mainstream discussions of openness tend to focus on the (overwhelmingly positive) effects of trade while treating flows of productive investment as an afterthought. And so there is a clear consensus among mainstream economists that more openness is better. Concerns about unemployment, declining wages, deteriorating environmental standards and/or deindustrialization tend to be seen as reflecting either narrow self-interest, a misunderstanding of the indirect effects of trade, or both. Skepticism about free trade -- and the defense of "protectionism" that it is often presumed to imply -- is like arguing that the world is flat: both positions offer some intuitive appeal, but both are wrong, counter-productive and rooted in ignorance.

But despite its widespread acceptance among professional economists, the case for free trade is far from invulnerable. Its rosy conclusions about the benefits of trade depend fundamentally on a series of questionable assumptions. Heterodox economists reject several of these key assumptions, and the alternative vision that this implies suggests a very different set of conclusions about the consequences of openness. Heterodox economists see openness as a two-edged sword at best. Along with the efficiency gains highlighted by mainstream trade theory, trade and investment liberalization may destroy jobs, erode wages and limit the prospects for progressive economic policy.

A Critical Assessment of the Case for Free Trade

Classical and heterodox models of international trade and investment differ in a number of important ways.[8] I focus here on three areas in which these differences are especially consequential.

Mainstream models of trade assume that labor markets clear, both before and after liberalization. Heterodox models, in contrast, typically assume that unemployment is a regular -- even chronic -- feature of a capitalist economy.[9] The assumption of full employment contributes to the optimistic conclusions of the classical model in two particularly important ways. First, it allows defenders of free trade to dodge the fundamental question of whether trade and investment liberalization is likely to destroy jobs. By assumption it does not.[10] Second, the assumption of full employment all but ensures the conclusion that trade liberalization will improve national welfare. If liberalization shifts labor and other resources from relatively low to relatively high productivity industries, then the volume of goods and services produced by this still fully employed labor force is sure to increase. And so this central assumption at once allows defenders of free trade to dismiss concerns about job loss and demonstrate that trade improves aggregate welfare. The heterodox rejection of this assumption means that these two critical questions remain open.

The classical theory of trade assumes, further, that factors of production are immobile. Heterodox economists, in contrast, focus considerable attention on the consequences of mobile capital.[11] Like the assumption of full employment, the assumption that capital is immobile leads to an overly optimistic assessment of the consequences of openness. The very real possibility that net capital outflows might undermine the prosperity of a source country is ruled out by assumption.

Models that do not consider the consequences of capital mobility ignore an important dimension of globalization and thus provide a dubious basis for understanding its implications. This assumption is inappropriate for a number of reasons. Most obviously, international capital flows are substantial and growing, and so assuming that capital is immobile is absurdly unrealistic. Further, NAFTA, the GATT and most other important trade agreements liberalize investment as well as trade, so an assessment of these agreements demands a consideration of the effects of capital mobility. Finally, trade liberalization *per se* is likely to promote capital movements. In particular, freer trade may encourage a relocation of investment from high cost countries (e.g., the US, Germany, France and the UK) to low cost countries (e.g., Mexico, Greece, Ireland and Spain) as liberalization allows mobile firms to exploit lower production costs without surrendering access to rich consumers.[12]

Mainstream economists assume, finally, that the distribution of income is the result of an essentially asocial process. Workers and capital owners earn incomes based on the marginal revenue products of their respective inputs. Heterodox economists, in contrast, assume that the distribution of income -- along with the content of state policy -- depends critically upon the bargaining power of workers, multinational corporations, national governments, citizens' groups and other political-economic contenders. More specifically, globalization is likely to undermine the bargaining power of workers and nation states vis a vis increasingly footloose MNCs.

The heterodox model thus allows for the possibility that trade and investment liberalization may, on balance, benefit the typical citizen.[13] But it might not. Liberalization may result in some combination of unemployment, wage erosion, deindustrialization, environmental degradation and a declining social wage.[14]

Classical trade theory suggests that gains from trade tend to be distributed widely, as consumers enjoy small benefits in the form of lower prices and higher quality goods and services. In the aggregate these benefits may be large. The heterodox approach to trade suggests that workers may lose in an analogous way. Accelerating capital mobility and intensifying import competition may lead to net job loss. But further, globalization is likely to undermine the bargaining power and thus the wages of many employed workers. Each affected worker's living standard is eroded slightly. In the aggregate, however, these losses may be great.

The heterodox model clearly highlights the potentially dangerous consequences of globalization. But while it raises a series of threatening possibilities, it does not demonstrate that capital is highly mobile, nor does it provide an assessment of the extent to which capital mobility is likely to hurt workers and other potentially vulnerable parties. These are ultimately empirical questions.

Still, progressive commentators have tended to see the potential dangers of globalization as more than possibilities. Advances in the mobility of goods and capital, the argument goes, have altered the terms of class struggle quite dramatically in favor of international capital. Footloose MNCs now make location decisions in a "global market for production sites," (Frobel, et al., 1980) throwing workers, national governments and communities into a fierce, self-destructive competition for investment and jobs. The apparently inevitable consequence is lower wages, a declining social wage, less effective regulation of capital, greater economic insecurity, increasingly ineffective macroeconomic policy, and a "downward harmonization" of labor and environmental standards.[15] Accelerating capital mobility forces workers, communities and governments to limit their demands vis a vis investors, or watch capital and jobs disappear. In the words of Stephen Hymer transnational corporations are able to "create a world in their own image" (1975, p. 38).

The *prima facie* evidence suggests that there may be something to this disconcerting vision of globalization. The volume of DFI has grown more or less steadily during the post war period, and a growing share of global output is traded. Manufacturing employment has declined in the US while its imports of manufactures from the Third World have grown (Wood, 1994). In the meanwhile, wages in the US have eroded, and an assault on the welfare state is underway in virtually every developed country.

But the persuasiveness of this vision of globalization hinges, ultimately, on the answers to a few key questions. How mobile is productive capital? What sorts of investment climates tend to attract mobile capital? And, if capital is indeed mobile, to what extent does this undermine the bargaining power of workers, communities and nation states?

Globalization of Investment?

The mobility of productive capital is a defining feature of globalization and key mechanism by which globalization is presumed to undermine the bargaining power and living standards of workers. In this section I present evidence which strongly suggests that the mobility of productive capital is quite limited. Indeed, the data suggest that the process of capital accumulation remains an essentially national phenomenon. Investment is undertaken overwhelmingly by domestic firms responding to domestic economic conditions.

Stocks and annual flows of direct foreign investment (DFI) by every major source country have grown considerably over the past few decades. These impressive growth rates are often cited as evidence of advances in the globalization of investment.[16] But these data do not, in fact, tell us much about the globalization of the investment process. The fact that there is more DFI does not necessarily indicate that the mobility of MNCs has grown.

Table 1 shows the ratio of outward DFI flows to total investment by domestic firms for eight advanced capitalist countries, each a leading source of DFI. These eight countries accounted for 89% of the world stock of outward DFI in 1960 and 83% in 1993. On the one hand, these data indicate that DFI is a growing share of total investment; there is a positive and statistically significant time trend in this ratio for six of the eight countries (all but the US and Italy) and for the eight countries as a group (Koechlin, 1996). And so the impression that DFI is of growing importance is in fact correct. But perhaps more striking than this is the fact that the ratios are very small. DFI accounts for just four percent of total investment for the group as a whole over the entire period, and only seven percent between 1986 and 1992. Far from indicating that the investment process transcends the nation state, these data suggest that investors are remarkably reluctant to invest abroad.

Alternative measures of the globalization of investment and production are entirely consistent with the data presented in Table 1. Table 2 shows the ratio of capital expenditures (purchases of plant, equipment and structures) by US MNCs to US domestic investment.[17] While these ratios are slightly higher than those presented in Table 1, they also indicate that firms are not particularly eager to invest abroad. And like the data presented in Table 1, these data indicate that the share of outward foreign investment in total investment has not grown substantially in recent years. Similarly, the number of employees of US foreign affiliates declined slightly between 1982 and 1993, both in manufacturing and all industries.

Table 1: Outward Direct Foreign Investment as a Percentage of Total Investment by Domestic Firms for Eight Countries

Country	1960-1969	1970-1979	1980-1985	1986-1992	1960-1992
United States	4.5	5.6	2.4	5.3	4.6
US Manufacturing	8.2	9.8	4.7	7.4	7.8
United Kingdom	6.1	9.7	10.4	17.0	10.0
Netherlands	6.3	9.0	11.0	20.7	10.7
Germany	1.8	3.1	3.3	7.2	3.6
Canada	1.3	2.9	4.5	6.2	3.3
France	1.8	3.1	2.8	6.7	3.3
Italy	2.1	1.1	2.0	3.6	2.0
Japan	0.6	1.1	1.7	6.5	2.2
Average for Eight Countries	3.2	4.3	3.1	7.0	4.2
Average for the US, UK, Germany and Netherlands	4.2	5.8	3.8	8.0	5.3

Notes: Total investment is equal to gross fixed domestic non-residential investment plus outward DFI by domestic firms minus inward DFI. DFI figures for France, Italy, Canada and Japan do not include reinvested earnings by foreign affiliates, and thus understate the actual flow of DFI from these countries. The averages presented in the last two rows are weighted averages, where each national ratio is weighted in proportion to total investment by its firms.
Sources: Data on domestic investment are from OECD, various years. Data on DFI is from, UN Centre on Transnational Corporations (1983); OECD (1984, 1989, 1993) and; Rutter, 1992. This table also appears in Koechlin (1993).

A reasonable argument can be made that these data in fact overstate the extent to which DFI undermines the bargaining power of workers, because DFI is not necessarily at the expense of investment at home. DFI often allows a firm to serve a market in which its exports are not competitive. DFI may, under some circumstances, promote net exports and jobs at home.[18]

Table 2: Capital Expenditures by Foreign Affiliates of US Parents as a Percentage of US Capital Formation

	1985-1991	1977-1984
All Industries	8.9	9.0
LDCs	2.4	2.0
Manufacturing	10.2	10.6
LDCs	---	1.8

Sources: Capital expenditures of foreign affiliates is from Survey of Current Business, March 1987, March 1989 and March 1993. Gross fixed non-residential investment is from Economic Report of the President. Gross investment in manufacturing is from Census of Manufactures, Bureau of the Census, various years.

The claim that capital is likely to flee to greener pastures hinges on the assumption that domestic and foreign investment are close substitutes, that a more favorable investment climate abroad will motivate a substitution of foreign for domestic investment. Indeed this is why globalization is presumed to be a threat to workers and their living standards: if workers' demands are excessive by global standards, their employer can easily pick up and move. How responsive are firms to differences in national investment climates?

A number of studies indicate that investment is quite unresponsive to differences in international profit rates. In a separate paper, I estimated investment functions for the seven largest advanced capitalist countries (for 1960-1985) in an effort to assess the extent to which domestic and foreign investment are substitutes (Koechlin, 1992a). Virtually every estimate presented in this paper indicates that the rate of growth of the domestic capital stock is responsive to the domestic investment climate -- the rate of profit, the rate of income growth and (in some cases) the rate of interest.[19] But in all but a few cases, the pace of domestic investment is essentially unresponsive to foreign profit rates and the rate of growth of foreign income. That is, the investment climate abroad does not appear to affect significantly the pace of investment at home. Indeed, in virtually every case the explanatory power of the model is all but unaffected by the inclusion of foreign economic variables. And further, these estimates provide no evidence that the pace of domestic investment has become increasingly sensitive to foreign economic conditions over time. And so, at the risk of understatement, foreign and domestic investment are far from perfect substitutes.

Advances in capital mobility should lead to a more complete and rapid convergence of profit rates across countries, as mobile firms abandon unprofitable locations for profitable opportunities elsewhere.[20] But after-tax profits continue to vary widely across OECD countries (Weisskopf, 1988; Glyn, 1995), and David M. Gordon (1988) finds that between 1960 and 1985, manufacturing profit rates in the seven largest OECD countries did not converge. Similarly, Gerald Epstein (1996) finds that profit rates on US DFI across host countries have not tended to converge over time, nor has the responsiveness of US DFI to profit rate differentials increased over time.

Concern about the consequences of globalization for workers depends, further, on a presumption about where mobile capital is likely to go. Advances in the technologies of transportation and communication, the argument goes, increase the ability of footloose MNCs to relocate to once remote low cost investment sites. But the data suggest that the appeal of low cost production sites is quite limited. In 1994, just 25% of the world stock of DFI was located in the Third World, and this ratio is slightly lower than in it was in 1960 and in 1980 (UNCTAD, 1995). Between 1985 and 1993, US DFI flows to less developed countries represented less than two percent of all investment by US firms. And while this ratio is quite low, it likely overstates the extent to which US firms have used poor countries as export platforms. In 1991, about two thirds of the production of US foreign affiliates in the Third World was sold locally rather than being exported to the US or elsewhere. Further, affiliates of US MNCs in the Third World employed fewer people in 1993 than in 1982. Finally, Matthew Slaughter (1995) finds that the outsourcing of production by US firms to their affiliates in the Third World had no measurable impact on the wages of US workers.[21]

Statistical studies of the determinants of the location of DFI are consistent with the data presented above. While labor costs and tax rates are, in most studies, statistically significant in explaining the location of DFI, market size (GDP) and the market growth (the rate of growth of GDP) are the most important determinants of DFI flows.[22] MNCs are, in the aggregate, more concerned with finding customers than with finding low wage workers.

DFI is also quite meager from the point of view of poor host countries. Between 1980 and 1990 the ratio of inward DFI to domestic investment in developing countries was just over 3%. For most poor countries, this ratio is very close to zero (UNCTAD, 1995).

Finally, Eban Goodstein (1996) shows that because the costs of compliance with environmental regulations is typically a tiny share of a firm's total costs, firms rarely relocate in response to international differences in environmental standards.

Productive capital thus appears to be remarkably immobile internationally. But a few caveats are clearly in order. First, while the aggregate data suggest that productive capital is less than perfectly mobile, this is clearly not true for all industries. First World workers in some industries -- textiles for example -- have been hit very hard by the flight of capital and jobs to the Third World. Similarly, MNCs are clearly more willing and able to relocate than firms in the aggregate, and so the figures cited here clearly understate the risks faced by employees of large MNCs. Second, it may be that a little relocation -- or merely the threat of relocation -- can have a considerable impact on worker bargaining power. Third, integration among the developed countries may well undermine the bargaining power of workers.[23] Fourth, and perhaps most importantly, the DFI data do not measure the extent to which firms outsource production to unaffiliated firms overseas.[24]

Further, while the evidence suggests that the mobility of capital tends to be overstated, there has been a considerable increase in DFI flows over the past few years (see Table 1). And so concerns about the consequences of capital mobility are clearly warranted. Still, it is important, for both analytical and political purposes, to keep these developments in perspective: increases in DFI flows have been relatively undramatic, and they remain a small share of total investment.

The effects of trade on labor markets is a separate and complicated matter, but the evidence suggests a set of conclusions that are similar to those articulated above with regard to DFI flows.[25] On the one hand, the volume of trade is growing and its form is changing, and these changes pose threats to working people, especially in the rich countries of the North. But the trade data also indicate that the extent and consequences of globalization on labor market outcomes are limited.

The volume of international trade has grown steadily but modestly over the past few decades. The ratio of OECD exports to GDP for 1974-1979 was 16.3%; for 1990-93 it was 17.6% (Glyn, 1996). However these numbers clearly obscure some important developments. International competition in manufacturing has clearly intensified. Manufacturing import penetration of northern markets has grown much more quickly than has trade in general, and a growing share of manufacturing imports originate in the Third World (Wood, 1994).

The changing composition of Third World exports to the North -- away from primary products and toward manufactures -- has been a particularly striking development. Adrian Wood (1994) reports that the share of manufactures in non-fuel LDC exports to the developed countries increased from 23.4% in 1970 to 45.1% in 1980 and to 70.9% in 1989. But this growth of LDC exports of manufactures appears less dramatic from the perspective of the developed countries, however. In 1993, imports from low-wage countries were just over one percent of OECD GDP (Krugman, 1994). Imports of manufactures from the Third World relative to US manufacturing GDP increased from 5.3% in 1978 to 11.2% in 1990.

There is a large body of evidence suggesting that these changing trade patterns have had an effect on labor markets, particularly in manufacturing. Most studies conclude that manufacturing imports have contributed to declining manufacturing employment and increasing wage inequality in the North, although several conclude that these effects are quite small, even negligible.[26] Belman and Lee (1995) conclude that "the evidence is yet incomplete and more research remains to be done but...the balance of research supports the view the consequences of trade are real..." (1995, p. 99).[27]

Conclusion

The evidence presented here shows that the mobility of productive capital is clearly limited. Still, the ability of firms to relocate surely matters. Manufacturing employment has fallen in absolute terms in the US, and workers with a high school education or less have seen their wages fall by 13% since 1979. Relocation -- and the threat of flight -- have undoubtedly played a role.

But many heterodox students of international trade and investment have been unable to keep this admittedly important development in perspective. Despite considerable evidence to the contrary, many leftists are unable to resist overselling the importance of capital mobility. Globalization is often treated as a pervasive, alien force -- an apparently inevitable result of capitalism's essential driving force, accumulation. Globalization has become a fetish, to coin a phrase.

Excessive claims about globalization are problematic for a couple of reasons at least. First, these claims are inaccurate and so they provide an inadequate basis for understanding either the process of capital accumulation or the prospects for workers and other potential victims of globalization. Further, these claims tend to undermine the important and persuasive argument that globalization does indeed tend to undermine the living standards and political power of working people.

The heterodox critique of mainstream models of openness raises a series of important questions about the consequences of liberalization. This model shows that liberalization can, under plausible conditions, undermine the living standards of workers and limit the range of options available to policy makers. At the very least, this model indicates that the effects of liberalization are ambiguous, and so the aggressive pursuit of unregulated trade and investment (especially) is a questionable "rule of thumb." It can easily be shown that the advances in capital mobility may reduce the welfare of some countries and by intensifying the competition among national working classes and communities for capital and jobs, capital mobility may well redistribute income (and political influence) from labor to capital.

These potential effects of capital mobility indicate the need for a policy package designed to ensure that the benefits and costs of international trade and investment are distributed fairly. The relative immobility of productive capital suggests that a policy agenda of this sort is viable. The evidence strongly suggests that the trade-off between progressive, egalitarian policies and jobs is a false one.

A policy package of this sort should address trade and investment flows explicitly. Displaced workers should be compensated for their losses, and trade agreements should include provisions designed to prevent the erosion of labor and environmental standards. But, perhaps more importantly, national governments ought to pursue egalitarian domestic policies without worrying that a pro-worker policy agenda will scare off investors. An adequate social wage and more aggressive aggregate demand management is likely to affect the lot of workers in the industrialized countries more than the regulation of trade and DFI.

Third World workers may, under some circumstances, be among the beneficiaries of advances in the globalization of investment. But this does not imply that unregulated investment is in their best interest. The evidence presented here suggests that efforts by Third World governments to raise wages and environmental standards are unlikely to scare off multinational investors. A higher minimum wage in Mexico, for example, will not overwhelm the many advantages US MNCs in Mexico enjoy.

The focus here on DFI flows suggests that policy makers retain a considerable autonomy and flexibility. But there are a number of countries for which this is not true, in particular, countries that have been forced to turn to the International Monetary Fund (IMF) for help with their external debt problems. For many of these countries, relations with the IMF and foreign banks are (or have been) the most important determinant of domestic economic outcomes. But the outcomes that often come with reliance on the IMF -- an improving trade balance along with declining wages, rising unemployment, fewer social services, plummeting GDP growth and, often, social unrest -- are not the result of a set of abstract global economic/technological pressures (Pieper and Taylor, 1996). They are the result, rather, of a set of consciously chosen (or imposed) policies which embody excessive faith in the ability of markets to generate efficient and fair outcomes, and a prioritization of debt service over economic growth.

And so external factors clearly influence the trajectory of many national economies. But these external constraints are not the inevitable outcome of the globalization of capital *per se*. They reflect, rather, shortcomings of mainstream theory, of which the IMF is a staunch proponent, and the role of political and economic power in shaping political-economic outcomes.

Endnotes

1. See, for example, Bluestone and Harrison (1982); Frobel, Heinrichs and Kreye (1980) and Crotty (1993).

2. This and the next section of this chapter contrast the views of "Mainstream" and "Heterodox" visions of openness. While this bifurcation of the literature is clearly an oversimplification, it frames the issue in a useful way. Mainstream trade theory, as I use the phrase here, includes models that accept the essential principles and conclusions of the classical theory of trade. In particular, mainstream theorists share the view that comparative advantage is the key principle upon which an understanding of trade should be based. And so "mainstream" thinkers believe that trade liberalization will generally enhance welfare. I include Paul Krugman in this category, for example, even though his work has questioned some important aspects of classical trade theory. There are clearly important differences among mainstream thinkers. But for the purposes of this chapter, it is reasonable to categorize them based on their shared and essential faith that openness improves national welfare.

Heterodox economists view many tenets of the mainstream approach with skepticism (at least). Perhaps most generally, heterodox economists have considerably less faith than their mainstream counterparts in the ability of markets to solve important economic problems fairly and efficiently. They reject the assumption that labor markets clear; they believe that economic growth is often demand constrained; and they believe that economic and political power are critical in shaping political-economic outcomes. The meanings of mainstream and heterodox economics are spelled out, to a considerable degree, in the sections II and III.

Marxists and Dependency Theorists clearly qualify as heterodox thinkers. But their critiques of free trade, markets, unregulated capital flows and capitalism are broader and more fundamental than those of many other economists I include in this category. Marxists and Dependency theorists typically call for quite fundamental changes in the world economy, and many of them would find proposals by "heterodox" economists inadequate, because they do not address the essential contradictions of global capitalism. Other heterodox economists (Blecker (1996), Bluestone and Harrison (1982), Faux and Lee (1992), Gordon (1988), Koechlin and Larudee (1992), Skott and Larudee (1994), and Stanford (1993, 1996), for example) have argued for interventions in the domestic and international economies that do not necessarily threaten the essential nature of the capitalist system -- although many of them are clearly interested in changes of this sort as well.

The line between "mainstream" and "heterodox" economic theory is thus quite arbitrary. Indeed, many Marxists (and perhaps Marx himself) would likely count many of the heterodox economists listed above as "bourgeois economists." And there are, of course, important differences between dependency theory and Marxism.

This chapter clearly does not provide a detailed review of perspectives on openness. It provides, rather, a useful analytical contrast between those who hold a basic faith in markets and free trade, and those who view these institutions with serious concern and skepticism.

3. For example, this is true of every study presented in US ITC (1992).

4. See James Stanford (1993) for an excellent critique of general equilibrium models of trade.

5. While the HOS model is quite clear that free trade may hurt workers (or capital owners) in the aggregate, aggregate income always grows with free trade. By assumption, free trade does not result in a larger trade deficit, a tighter aggregate demand constraint or net job loss.

6. Some trade models, particularly those that assume increasing returns to scale, dynamic gains from trade, and/or product differentiation, suggest that trade liberalization may increase wages even in a country with a high ratio of capital to labor.

7. See US ITC (1992) for several examples.

8. See note 2 for a brief discussion of the meaning of "heterodox" economics in the context of this essay.

9. See Blecker (1996), Faux and Lee (1992), Koechlin and Larudee (1992), Skott and Larudee (1994) and Stanford (1996), for example.

10. With few exceptions, models of NAFTA's effects assumed full employment. And so the question of whether NAFTA would result in net job loss was "resolved" by assumption. See, for example, the studies published in US ITC (1992) and those reviewed in Lustig, Bosworth and Lawrence, eds. (1992).

11. Again, the NAFTA debate is illustrative. The most common case against NAFTA focused on the likelihood this agreement would motivate a relocation of investment from the US to Mexico, destroying jobs and eroding wages in the US. See Koechlin and Larudee (1992) and Faux and Lee (1992).

12. See Koechlin and Larudee (1992) for a discussion of this issue.

13. Mehrene Larudee (1993) argues, for example, that openness has hurt many US workers in recent decades but that, on balance, openness benefitted US workers in the twenty-five or so years following World War II.

14. Sheldon Friedman (1992), for example, argued that NAFTA would have precisely these effects on US workers.

15. See Crotty (1993) and Friedman (1992).

16. See, for example, Reich (1991) and Bluestone and Harrison (1982).

17. Capital expenditures are purchases of plant, equipment and structures by affiliates of US parents. Capital expenditures are arguably a better measure of investment than is DFI, but capital expenditure data are not available for many countries.

18. See Koechlin and Larudee (1992) and Buckley and Artisien (1987) for discussions of this issue.

19. The paper presents a number of specifications for each of the seven countries and estimates pooling data from the seven countries.

20. There is a vast literature which attempts to measure the integration of domestic financial markets in a similar way. See Obstfeld (1993) for a summary and discussion of this literature.

21. Slaughter's study is limited in a number of ways. Most importantly, it only considers outsourcing from parents to foreign affiliates.

22. See Koechlin (1992b) and sources cited therein.

23. See Stanford (1996) and Campbell (1991) for discussions of the effects of free trade with the US on Canadian workers.

24. Data on outsourcing by US firms to foreign firms (other than affiliates) is not available. But this is clearly an important area for future research.

25. This discussion of trade is clearly far from comprehensive. It is merely meant to suggest that my argument about capital mobility -- the main thrust of this paper -- is not contradicted by the evidence on trade.

26. Wood (1994) and Sachs and Shatz (1994) argue that the effects of trade on Northern labor markets have been notable. Larudee (1995) argues that trade liberalization is likely to increase income inequality in poor countries. Krugman (1994); Slaughter (1995) and Lawrence and Slaughter (1993) conclude that the effects of trade on wages and employment in the US have been small. See Belman and Lee (1995) for an excellent review of this literature.

27. While financial capital is clearly more mobile than productive capital, the evidence suggests that it is far from perfectly mobile. See Obstfeld (1994); Tesar and Werner (1992) and Epstein and Gintis (1989).

References

Belman, Dale and Lee,Thea M. "International Trade and the Performance of US Labor Markets," in Robert Blecker (ed) *US Trade Policy and Global Growth*, Armonk, NY: M.E. Sharpe, 1996.

Bluestone, Barry and Harrison, Bennett. *The Deindustrialization of America*, New York: Basic Books, 1982.

Buckley, Peter J. and Artisien, Patrick."Policy Issues of Intra- EC Direct Investment," *Journal of Common Market Studies*, 1987. 26 (2).

Campbell, Bruce. "Canada Under Siege: Three Years into the Free Trade Era," Ottawa: Centre for Policy Alternatives, 1991.

Crotty, James. "The Rise and Fall of the Keynesian Revolution in the Age of the Global Market Place," in Epstein, Graham, Nembhard (eds) *Creating a New World Economy*, Philadelphia: Temple University Press,1993.

Epstein, Gerald A. "Profit Rate Equalization and Foreign Direct Investment: A Study of Integration, Instability and Enforcement," in Epstein and Gintis (eds), *Macroeconomics After the Conservative Era.* Cambridge: Cambridge University Press, 1995.

Faux, Jeff and Lee, Thea. "The Effect of George Bush's NAFTA on American Workers: Ladder Up or Ladder Down?," Washington, D.C.: Economic Policy Institute, 1992.

Frobel, F.; Heinrichs, J. and Kreye, O. *The New International Division of Labor.* Cambridge: Cambridge University Press, 1980.

Glyn, Andrew.. "Internal and External Constraints on Egalitarian Policies in Europe," presented at Economic Policy Institute conference on "Globalization and Progressive Economic Policy," Washington, D.C., June 1996.

Hufbauer, Gary C. and Schott, Jeffrey J. *North American Free Trade: Issues and Recommendations*, Washington D.C.: Institute for International Economics 1992.

_____. *NAFTA: An Assessment*, Washington D.C.: Institute for International Economics, 1993.

Hymer, Stephen. "The Multinational Corporation and the Law of Uneven Development," in Radice (ed), *International Firms and Modern Imperialism.* Middlesex, England: Penguin, 1975.

Goodstein, Eban. "Malthus Redux?: Globalization and the Environment," presented at

Economic Policy Institute conference on "Globalization and Progressive Economic Policy," Washington, D.C., June 1996.

Gordon, David M. "The Global Economy: New Edifice or Crumbling Foundations," *New Left Review*, March/April 1988.

Kindleberger, Charles P. *American Business Abroad: Six Lectures on Direct Investment*, Yale University Press, New Haven 1969.

Koechlin, Timothy. "Accumulation and the Nation State," forthcoming in *Economic Geography* 1996.

_____."The Globalization of Investment."*Contemporary Economic Policy*, January 1995, pp. 92-100.

_____. "The Responsiveness of Investment to Foreign Economic Conditions," *Journal of Post Keynesian Economics*, 1992a., vol. 15, no. 1, pp.63-83.

_____. "The Determinants of the Location of US Direct Foreign Investment," *International Review of Applied Economics*, 1992b, vol. 6, no. 2, pp.203-216.

_____ **and Larudee, Mehrene.** "The High Cost of NAFTA," Challenge, October/November 1992, pp. 19-26.

Krugman, Paul R. "Growing World Trade: Causes and Consequences," *Brookings Papers on Economic Activity*, 1:1995.

_____. "Competitiveness: A Dangerous Obsession," *Foreign Affairs*, 1994, vol. 73, no. 2, pp. 28-44.

_____. "Is Free Trade Passe?," *Journal of Economic Perspectives*, 1987, vol. 1, no. 2, pp. 131-143.

Larudee, Mehrene. "Integration and Income Distribution Under the North American Free Trade Agreement (NAFTA)," presented at Economic Policy Institute conference on "Globalization and Progressive Economic Policy," Washington, D.C., June 1996.

_____. "Free Trade: Who Wins? Who Loses?," in Epstein, Graham, Nembhard (eds) *Creating a New World Economy,* Philadelphia: Temple University Press,1993.

Lawrence, Robert Z. and Slaughter, Matthew. "International Trade and American Wages in the 1980s: Giant Sucking Sound or Small Hiccup?," *Brookings Papers on Economic Activity: Microeconomics*, 1993, No. 2, pp. 161-210.

Lustig, Nora; Bosworth Barry and Lawrence Robert Z. (eds.), *North American Free*

Trade: Assessing the Impact, Washington, D.C.: Brookings Institution, 1992.

Obstfeld, Maurice. "International Capital Mobility in the 1990s," NBER working paper # 4534, 1993..

Pieper, Ute and Taylor, Lance. "The Revival of the Liberal Creed: The IMF, World Bank and Inequality in a Globalized Economy," presented at Economic Policy Institute conference on "Globalization and Progressive Economic Policy," Washington, D.C., June 1996.

Reich, Robert B.. *The Work of Nations.* New York: Alfred A. Knopf, 1991.

Sachs, Jeffrey D. and Shatz, Howard J. "Trade and Jobs in U.S. Manufacturing," *Brookings Papers on Economic Activity*, 1994, 1, pp.1-84.

Skott, Peter and Larudee, Mehrene. "Uneven Development and the Liberalization of Trade and Capital Flows: the Case of Mexico," University of Aarhus, Economics Institute, 1994-23, Aarhus, Denmark, 1994.

Slaughter, Matthew J. "Multinational Corporations, Outsourcing, and American Wage Divergence," NBER working paper #5253, 1995.

Stanford, James. "Continental Economic Integration: Modeling the Impact on Labor," *Annals of the American Academy of Political and Social Science*, March 1993.

_____. "Openness and Equity: Regulating Labor Market Outcomes in a Globalized Economy," presented at Economic Policy Institute conference on "Globalization and Progressive Economic Policy," Washington, D.C., June. 1996.

Tesar, Linda L. and Werner, Ingrid M. "Home Bias and the Globalization of Securities Markets," NBER working paper no. 4218, Cambridge, MA, 1992.

UNCTAD (United Nations Conference on Trade and Development). *World Investment Report 1995*, New York: United Nations.1995.

US ITC (International Trade Commission). *Economy-Wide Modeling of a FTA with Mexico and a NAFTA with Canada and Mexico.* US ITC Publication no. 2508. Washington: D.C.: US International Trade Commission, 1992.

Wood, Adrian. *North-South Trade, Employment and Inequality*, Clarendon Press: Oxford, 1994.

5

THE "GLOBALIZATION" OF TRADE:
What's Changed and Why?
Beth V. Yarbrough
Robert M. Yarbrough

Amherst College, USA

"Globalization" is widely cited as the dominant international economic trend of the post-Second World War era. However, perceptions of the extent and importance of globalization depend on how we define and attempt to measure it. The sheer magnitude of trade has grown; but probably more important are changes in the kinds of trade and in patterns of participation. These changes, in turn, have been facilitated by advances in communication and transportation technologies and by changes in governments' policies toward international trade.

Most observers of the world economy, if asked to name the most important trend since the Second World War, probably would cite a growing internationalization of economic activity, or "globalization." Evidence of the perceived importance of this trend can be seen in expanded news coverage of international economic events, more tendency to attribute domestic economic developments to international causes, and frequent claims that the fundamental rules of economic policy making have changed as a result of an increasingly dense network of international economic interactions.

In this chapter, we focus on possible meanings of *globalization* and briefly examine some basic empirical data to determine which meanings best capture important aspects of actual changes in the world economy related to international trade. The exercise reveals, among other things, that the way we measure trade influences our perception of the globalization phenomenon and its apparent magnitude. We then turn our attention to the relative roles of policy-induced and non-policy-induced factors in the process of globalization.

Globalization Indicators

In popular discussion, the term *globalization* often seems to symbolize a vague perception, by either private citizens or policy makers, of increased international economic interdependence or increased vulnerability to economic events occurring abroad. But what exactly has changed; or, in what senses has economic activity become more "global"?

More Trade?

Perhaps the most obvious margin on which we might measure globalization is the sheer magnitude of international trade. Total world exports grew by a factor of seventeen in the quarter-century between 1968 and 1992.[1] Figure 1 illustrates this trend. As a benchmark for comparison, U.S. gross domestic product increased over the same period by only a factor of six, approximately half real and half due to price increases.[2]

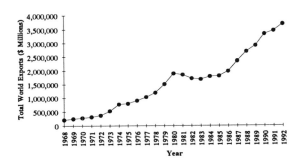

Figure 1: Total World Exports, 1968-1992 ($ Millions).
Source: International Monetary Fund.

A longer time horizon provides an alternative and somewhat different perspective on recent trade growth. The period from 1913 through the Second World War consisted of more-or-less continual setbacks to open trade policy, most notably the U.S. Smoot-Hawley tariffs and other countries' beggar-thy-neighbor responses to the Great Depression. Therefore, a large part of the trade growth and liberalization after the Second World War can be seen simply as having erased the retrenchment and protectionism of the interwar period.[3] Only since the mid-1970s have trade-to-output ratios reached new post-1913 highs for the leading industrial countries. Thus, the longer perspective leads us to look beyond mere trade growth in our search for any historically unprecedented aspects of globalization.

More Countries Involved in Trade?

Another possible connotation of *globalization* is broader participation in international economic activity. Even if the overall level of international trade had remained constant as a share of output, we might nonetheless perceive a process of globalization if that trade came to be spread over a wider range of countries. In 1913, the four leading traders (the United Kingdom, Germany, the United States, and France) accounted for 45 percent of world trade.[4] By 1968, the same four countries still led, and their collective share of world exports had fallen to 38 percent, as illustrated in Figure 2. By 1992, Japan replaced the United Kingdom in the top four, whose collective share of total world exports stood at 36 percent. These figures suggest a modest decline in domination of world trade by the largest players, with the bulk of that decline occurring prior to 1968.

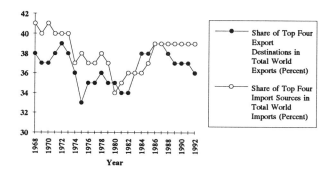

Figure 2: Share of Top Four in World Exports and Imports, 1968-1992 (Percent). *Source:* International Monetary Fund.

However, other measures, summarized in Figure 3, do reveal some broadening of participation in trade. In 1968, only 19 countries in the world absorbed as much as 1 percent of total world exports, and only 3 of the 19, or 16 percent, were developing economies (panel (a)). In the same year, just 17 countries shipped a share as large as 1 percent of total world exports, again only 3 of them (18 percent) developing countries (panel (b)). By 1992, among the 21 countries taking in as much as 1 percent of total world exports, 7 (33 percent) were developing economies. And 10 developing economies shipped at least 1 percent of total world exports, out of a total of 25 countries (40 percent). Therefore, developing countries' participation grew both absolutely and relative to world totals, and on both the import and export sides of trade.[5]

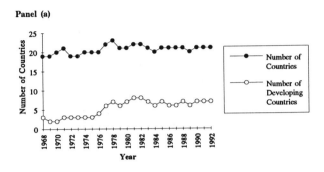

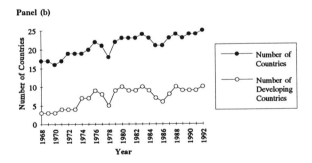

Figure 3: Number of Countries Absorbing 1% or More of Total World Exports (Panel (a)) and Shipping 1% or More of Total World Exports (Panel (b)), 1968-1992. *Source:* International Monetary Fund.

Changes in Who Trades with Whom?

One of the most often-cited changes in world trade patterns, at least in the United States, is increased industrial country imports from developing, especially low-wage, economies. Examination of trade in specific sectors of the economy, such as textiles, and of specific bilateral trading relationships, for example, that between the United States and China, does reveal significant changes even over a relatively short time horizon. However, at a more aggregated level, the trade pattern of industrial economies has remained remarkably stable over the last quarter-century.

Figure 4 panels (a) and (b) illustrate the shares of industrial-country exports and imports going to and coming from other industrial countries and going to and coming from developing countries.[6] Despite rapid trade growth overall, the patterns of both imports and exports remain virtually untouched in their *allocation* between industrial and developing trading partners.

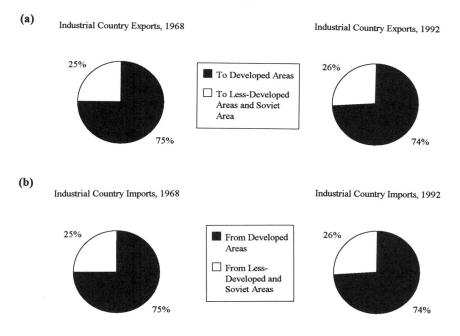

Figure 4: Destinations and Sources of Industrial Country Exports and Imports, 1968, 1992 (Percent). *Source:* International Monetary Fund.

The trade of developing economies shows significantly more change, illustrated in Figure 5. Developing economy exports increasing go to other developing countries; and their imports increasingly come from other developing economies. The change in export destination is especially pronounced, with a shift of 15 percent of developing country exports from industrial country destinations to developing country destinations between 1968 and 1992.

(a)

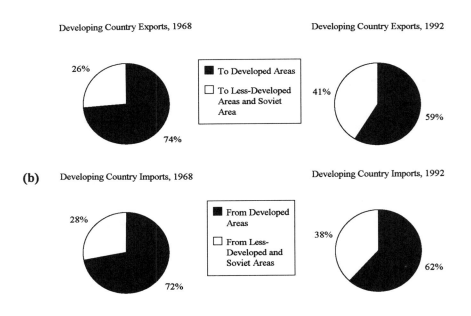

Developing Country Exports, 1968   Developing Country Exports, 1992

26%   74%   ■ To Developed Areas   □ To Less-Developed Areas and Soviet Area   41%   59%

(b)   Developing Country Imports, 1968   Developing Country Imports, 1992

28%   72%   ■ From Developed Areas   □ From Less-Developed and Soviet Areas   38%   62%

Figure 5: Destinations and Sources of Developing Country Exports and Imports (Percent). *Source:* International Monetary Fund.

Changes in the Type of Trade?

Another aspect of globalization consists of changes in the *types* of trade such as inter-industry, intra-industry, intra-firm trade, and trade in services.

Intra-Industry Trade. The traditional examples of international trade, dating back to the Classical economists, constituted inter-industry trade, such as the exchange of wine for cloth or food for clothing. This pattern fits much of historical trade, in which developed countries imported raw materials and exported manufactures, while developing countries' trade exhibited the opposite pattern. Increasingly, however, trade consists instead of intra-industry trade, in which both imports and exports occur within the same industry category. Intra-industry trade encompasses two basic types. The first type includes trade in similar but differentiated finished goods (for example, the exchange of Japanese Toyotas for German BMWs). The second type includes trade in components (for example, Mexican imports of automobile-engine components from the United States and re-export of finished engines to the United States).

Proper calculation of intra-industry trade indices, which indicate the share of total trade attributable to intra-industry trade, is a subject of some methodological controversy. However, most analysts agree that (1) the share of such trade has grown rapidly and (2) a much higher share of trade among developed countries represents intra-industry trade than among developing countries. For example, in 1978, samples of non-newly industrializing developing economies, newly industrializing countries, and industrial countries produced intra-industry trade shares averaging 14.5 percent, 41.9 percent, and 58.9 percent, respectively.[7] Table 1 reports the share of intra-industry trade for a sample of developed economies in 1980 and breaks the shares down by type of trading partner.

Table 1: Shares of Intra-Industry Trade in Total Trade, 1980 (Percent)

Country	*World*	*Trade with All Developing Countries*	*All Developed Countries*
Australia	35.8	29.2	22.7
Belgium	79.7	40.1	77.6
Canada	58.5	33.0	56.7
France	80.4	44.2	79.2
West Germany	65.4	34.6	74.1
Italy	65.4	44.3	59.8
Japan	28.8	17.6	33.6
Netherlands	74.2	45.5	70.3
Sweden	66.5	17.4	72.5
U.K.	79.1	44.2	77.5
United States	60.7	35.0	66.7

Source: Culem and Lundberg, 1986; reproduced in Grimwade, 1989, p. 110.

In what sense does intra-industry trade reflect globalization? Intra-industry trade in differentiated finished goods results from the spread of similar industries and production techniques, particularly in industries subject to economies of scale. Intra-industry trade in components, on the other hand, indicates increased cross-border production linkages, typically based on comparative advantage.

Intra-Firm Trade. An even more dramatic trend is the growth of intra-firm trade, or trade between parent firms and their affiliates abroad. Estimates such as those in Table 2 suggest that by the 1980s intra-firm trade had reached a level equal to a third of total trade for several industrial economies. Such intra-firm trade

Table 2: Intra-Firm Transactions as a Share of International Trade (Percent)

Country			*Share of intra-firm transactions in international trade*
United States:	Exports		
		1977	29.3
		1982	23.0
		1985	31.0
	Imports		
		1977	42.2
		1982	38.4
		1985	40.1
Japan:	Exports		
		1980	25.8
		1983	31.8
	Imports		
		1980	42.1
		1983	30.3
United Kingdom:	Exports		
		1981	30.0

Source: McKeown, 1991; data from United Nations, 1988, p. 92.

represents an important component of globalization because it captures a measurable dimension of the extension of corporate governance, a non-territorially defined institution, across international boundaries.[8]

Trade in Services. Until recently, in most discussions of international trade, services came up primarily as a set of easy examples of so-called "nontraded" items--including haircuts, health care, and retailing. Now, services comprise the fastest growing component of both international trade and foreign direct investment, accounting for roughly a quarter of world trade.[9] The services sector is also notable for the diversity of its components: banking, insurance, financial services, advertising, legal services, accounting, construction, transportation, and communication to mention just a few. Data entry, software design, and computing are new and fast-growing services rendered tradable by advances in communication and information technologies. Most analysts agree that balance-of-payments data, the primary sources of statistics on services trade, seriously understate the magnitude of trade in services; nonetheless, available indicators such as those in Table 3 show rapid growth, particularly for developing economies.

Table 3: World Trade in Services, 1980-1993

	1980	*1985*	*1990*	*1993*
Trade in commercial services ($ Billions)	358.0	379.6	790.9	933.7
OECD	283.3	298.5	648.2	752.0
Rest of the World	74.6	81.1	142.6	181.3
Share in total trade (Percent)	17.0	18.2	20.4	22.2
OECD	18.8	19.3	21.2	23.1
Rest of the World	12.7	15.3	17.5	19.1

Source: The World Bank, 1995a, p. 47.

Measurement Issues

We already have seen several cases where the precise indicators we choose to examine affects our perception of globalization: World trade has grown dramatically since the Second World War, but less so compared with pre-First World War figures. The share of world trade accounted for by the four biggest traders has not changed much since 1968; but over three times as many developing countries now ship as much as 1 percent of total world exports as was the case in 1968. But the way we measure international activity affects our perception of globalization in even more fundamental ways.

National Boundaries and Country Size.   International trade, by definition, consists of trade *across* national boundaries. Hence, the placement of national boundaries defines the extent and pattern of international trade; and changes in national boundaries alter the magnitude and pattern of trade in several ways. The first is simply definitional and takes the distribution of economic activity across geographic space as given. The 1990 unification of the former East and West Germanies reduced international trade because trade between the two, formerly international, became interregional trade on unification. The dissolution of the Soviet Union, in contrast, increased international trade as transactions among the Soviet republics, formerly interregional trade, became international trade with the Soviet breakup. This direct, definitional effect implies a positive relationship between the number of countries in the world and the extent of international trade, taking the spatial distribution of economic transactions as given.

Other effects of changing national borders on international trade occur once we allow the distribution of economic activity to be endogenous. For example, a second possible effect of changing national boundaries on international trade, suggested by a recent study of U.S.-Canada trade, is that national boundaries may discourage economic transactions even when formal border restrictions are low or nonexistent.[10] This effect may provide a partial offset to the definitional effect of boundary changes. If economic transactions do cluster within national boundaries, then a new national border (say, the division of the former Czechoslovakia into the Czech and Slovak Republics) may increase measured international trade in the short run due to the definitional effect; but eventually if the new border discourages transactions, trade may turn inward within the newly divided states, and measured international trade may decline back toward its original level.[11]

A third possible effect of boundary changes on measured international trade is policy induced. Even in today's relatively open and liberal trade environment, virtually all governments place more restrictions on international transactions than on domestic ones. Hence, more borders may translate into more restrictions and, therefore, into less trade. This third effect reinforces the second; that is, it mitigates the positive definitional relationship between the number of states and the magnitude of international trade.

Double-Counting Trade.   International trade is measured in a fundamentally different way than the common measures of economic output, gross national product (GNP) and gross domestic product (GDP).[12] Output measures attempt to avoid double-counting by including only newly produced *final* goods and services. For example, if aluminum is used in an auto-engine component, which is placed in an engine subassembly, which goes into a finished automobile, the GNP or GDP accountant would include only the value of the finished car. To do otherwise would count the value of the aluminum four times, the value of the engine component three times, and the value of the engine subassembly twice.

International trade accounting, however, follows different rules. Suppose Country A produces the aluminum, exports it to Country B which manufactures the engine component, after which Country B exports the component back to Country A, which completes the subassembly and exports it to Country B, which places the subassembly in the finished car and exports the car to Country A. The combined trade figures for the two countries will count the aluminum four times, the engine component three times, the engine subassembly twice, and the finished car once. Thus, growth of intra-industry and intra-firm trade in components and subcomponents can produce dramatic increases in measured international trade.[13]

Ceteris paribus, the more numerous the stages into which the production process is broken, the more times the value of upstream components enter international trade figures. And the more heavily involved a given country is in this geographically disintegrated intra-industry or intra-firm production, the larger will be its trade relative to its GNP or GDP, because the former includes multiple entries for the same value-added, while the latter do not.[14] Hong Kong and Singapore, for example, routinely report exports well in excess of their gross national products.

Sources of Globalization

The most often-cited reasons for recent globalization trends in international trade fall into two basic groups. The first emphasizes changes in technology and in product characteristics. The second emphasizes unilateral and multilateral changes in government policies toward international trade.

Technology

Effective systems of international communication and transportation, based on telegraphs, steamships, and railroads, united the major trading economies by the mid-nineteenth century. These systems played important roles in the evolution of worldwide markets for standardized commodities during that period, as well as in the development of continental markets in the United States. But, the systems were slow; and their lack of speed constrained the types of goods and information they could carry.

Steamships allowed Britain to import raw cotton and export cotton textiles to much of the rest of the world. Had Britain, however, attempted the equivalent of today's assembly of the Ford Escort from components produced in 15 countries and managed under just-in-time inventory techniques, steamship transport would have fatally constrained the system.[15] And the slowness of transportation limited the face-to-face contact among managers that modern business studies indicate is so important in enterprise performance. Similarly, trans-Atlantic telegraph cables kept British manufacturers informed about spot and futures commodity prices worldwide. But those cables would not have allowed British manufacturers to outsource their bookkeeping tasks to developing countries thousands of miles away. In other words, while mid-nineteenth century communication and transportation technologies clearly sufficed for the development of worldwide international trade-- especially inter-industry trade in standardized and nonperishable commodities--they just as clearly constrained the types of goods (and services) for which international trade was feasible.

Recent developments in transportation and communication technologies embody two important elements: increased speed and decreased cost. Jet-transport, electronic mail, faxes, and private satellite transmissions represent just a few new high-speed technologies. Average air-transport cost fell by over 80 percent between 1930 and 1990. The cost of a New York-to-London phone call is about one percent of its 1930 level. Ocean freight and port charges have fallen by about half since 1930.[16] And satellite utilization charges now equal approximately 10 percent of mid-1970s prices.

These improvements facilitate not just increased *quantities* of trade, but different *kinds* of trade with different partners. Assembling a Ford Escort from components produced in 15 different countries--a process requiring a substantial level of coordination--becomes not just technically feasible, but profitable. American Airlines can perform the data-entry operations to process its tickets and boarding passes in Barbados. Israel and Colombia can export fresh cut flowers to the United States. Programmers in Bangalore, India, can design computer software and transmit it back to Texas Instruments via satellite. Containerized 150-ton ocean transport ships can lower transport cost sufficiently to make Asian consumer electronics and automobiles competitive in U.S. and European markets.

Modern manufactured goods exhibit levels of sophistication and diversity that permit them to take advantage of the new transportation and communication potential. Earlier, inter-industry trade in standardized commodities consisted of goods whose production processes typically involved relatively few distinct stages; and technology limited firms' abilities to separate those stages geographically. Today's more complex manufactured goods--automobiles, computers, televisions--

embody more separable stages that can take fuller advantage of countries' diverse factor endowments and of economies of scale; and today's technologies facilitate geographically disintegrated production, even under the coordination of a single firm. Automobiles, for example, include windshield glass, plastic bumpers, and floor mats, as well as sophisticated electronic brake-monitoring and fuel-management systems. A single firm can use advanced transportation and communications technologies to coordinate production around the world, placing each production stage in its low-cost location.

Government Trade Policy

The dramatic decline of world trade during the interwar period highlights the important lesson that technology and potential gains from trade alone cannot suffice to maintain trade growth. Economic policy, both unilateral and multilateral, plays a vital role.[17] Since the end of the Second World War, governments have reduced barriers to international trade, especially tariffs, substantially. Table 4 reports the average levels of tariff reduction accomplished in the various GATT rounds.[18] During the early rounds, liberalization was concentrated in the developed industrialized economies; but more recently liberalization achieved under GATT auspices has spread with the organization's growing membership.

Table 4: GATT Tariff Reductions, 1934-1994

GATT Conference	*Average Cut in All Duties (Percent)*	*Remaining Duties as a Percent of 1930 Tariffs*	*Number of Participants*
Pre-GATT (1934-47)	33.2%	66.8%	23
First Round (1947)	21.1	52.7	23
Second Round (1949)	1.9	51.7	13
Third Round (1950-51)	3.0	50.1	38
Fourth Round (1955-56)	3.5	48.9	26
Dillon Round (1961-62)	2.4	47.7	26
Kennedy Round (1964-67)	36.0	30.5	62
Tokyo Round (1974-79)	29.6	21.2	99
Uruguay Round (1987-94)	38.0	13.1	125

Source: Lavergne, 1981; reproduced in Baldwin, 1984, p. 6; updated to include the Uruguay Round data from Schott, 1994.

Outside the GATT, recent liberalization has come in two major forms. First, smaller groups of GATT contracting parties, most notably members of the European Union and of the North American Free-Trade Agreement, have gone beyond their GATT obligations to lower barriers to intra-group trade.[19] These agreements include relaxation of foreign-investment rules in addition to reductions of tariff and nontariff barriers. Second, many developing economies and countries in transition have unilaterally lowered their trade barriers, ending decades of import substitution, trade diversion, and foreign-exchange controls. For example, during the late 1980s and early 1990s, developing countries enacted 58 out of the 72 unilateral liberalization policies reported to the GATT.[20]

Summary

Globalization is widely cited as the dominant international economic trend of the post-Second World War era. Our perceptions of the extent and importance of globalization depend on how we define and attempt to measure it. The sheer *magnitude* of trade has grown; but probably more important are changes in the *kinds* of trade and in the patterns of *participation*. These changes, in turn, have been facilitated by advances in communication and transportation technologies and by changes in governments' policies toward international trade.

Endnotes

1. Data for 1968 include 157 countries; data for 1992 include 161 countries.

2. Economic Report of the President, 1995.

3. See, for example, McKeown, 1991, and Krugman, 1995

4. Lake, 1988, p. 31.

5. For many developing countries, a substantial portion of their increased trade reflects intra-firm trade by foreign direct investors. However, such trade still can provide gains from trade, as well as technological and managerial know-how; therefore, it is important not to discount the role of such trade in the process of development.

6. The GATT's annual *International Trade and Statistics* publication provides a good source of additional source of information on trade patterns and trends. Country classifications used in Figures 4 and 5 follow usage by the International Monetary Fund. Industrial countries include the United States, Canada, Australia, Japan, New Zealand, Austria, Belgium-Luxembourg, Denmark, Finland,

France, Germany, Greece, Iceland, Ireland, Italy, Netherlands, Norway, Portugal, Spain, Sweden, Switzerland, and the United Kingdom. Between 1968 and 1992, the Fund shifted Turkey, Yugoslavia, and South Africa to the Developing Areas classification. Combining Developing Areas with Soviet Areas attempts to avoid problems associated with the reclassification of transitional economies, for which data are notoriously unreliable in both years.

7. Grimwade, p. 127.

8. Yarbrough and Yarbrough, 1992, Chapter Two.

9. The World Bank, 1995a, p. 43. Fieleke, 1995, presents an excellent summary of recent developments in trade in services, including its implications for developing countries.

10. McCallum, 1995.

11. Of course, economic activity can influence border placement, as well as *vice versa;* see Yarbrough and Yarbrough, 1994.

12. The distinction between GNP and GDP rests on whether the economy is defined based on territorial location or nationality of resource ownership.

13. We should recognize this "double counting" phenomenon in our evaluation of globalization trends. However, the trade captured in such double counting, whether based in comparative advantage or in economies of scale, still can provide gains from trade to the participating countries. Therefore, we should not underestimate its importance.

14. Note that *geographically* disintegrated production need not be *vertically* disintegrated in the sense of corporate ownership.

15. Dicken, 1986, p. 304.

16. The World Bank, 1995b, p. 51, and *The Economist,* 1991.

17. Krugman, 1995.

18. More inclusive measures of the level of trade protection are difficult to estimate because of the opaque and *ad hoc* nature of many non-tariff barriers, as well as their discriminatory application. On issues related to measuring tariff and non-tariff barriers, see Yarbrough and Yarbrough, 1997, Chapters Six and Seven. These measurement problems make empirical demonstration of the link between the volume of trade and the extent of protection difficult. McCallum, 1995, presents evidence that tariff cuts between the United States and Canada have been associated with substantial increases in bilateral trade, but the data omit non-tariff barriers.

19. Westhoff, Yarbrough, and Yarbrough, 1994.

20. The World Bank, 1995a, p. 1. In some cases, these unilateral policy changes were in part responses to external pressure from creditors and trading partners, especially during the debt-crisis decade (1982-1992); see Yarbrough and Yarbrough, 1997, Chapter Eleven.

References

Baldwin, Robert E. "U.S. Trade Policy Since World War II." In *The Structure and Evolution of Recent U.S. Trade Policy,* Robert E. Baldwin and Anne O. Krueger, eds. Chicago: University of Chicago Press, 1984.

Culem, C. and L. Lundberg. The Product Pattern of Intra-Industry Trade: Stability Among Countries and Over Time. Weltwirtschaftliches Archiv 1986; 122, pp.113-130

Dicken, Peter. *Global Shift.* London: Harper and Row, 1986.

Economic Report of the President. Washington, D.C.: U.S. Government Printing Office, 1995.

The Economist. July 20, 1991.

Fieleke, Norman S. The Soaring Trade in "Nontradables." Federal Reserve Bank of Boston New England Economic Review 1995, pp. 25-36.

General Agreement on Tariffs and Trade. *International Trade: Trends and Statistics 1994.* Geneva: GATT, 1994.

Grimwade, Nigel. *International Trade: New Patterns of Trade, Production and Investment.* London: Routledge, 1989.

International Monetary Fund. *Direction of Trade Statistics Yearbook.* Washington, D.C.: International Monetary Fund, various issues.

Krugman, Paul. Growing World Trade: Causes and Consequences. Brookings Papers on Economic Activity 1995;25, pp. 327-377

Lake, David A. *Power, Protection, and Free Trade.* Ithaca, NY: Cornell University Press, 1988.

Lavergne, Real Phillipe. The Political Economy of U.S. Tariffs. Ph.D. thesis, University of Toronto, 1981.

McCallum, John. National Borders Matter: Canada-U.S. Regional Trade Patterns. American Economic Review 1995;85, pp. 615-623

McKeown, Timothy J. A Liberal Trade Order? The Long-Run Pattern of Imports to the Advanced Capitalist States. International Studies Quarterly 1991;35, pp.151-172

Schott, Jeffrey J. *The Uruguay Round: An Assessment.* Washington, D.C.: Institute for International Economics, 1994.

United Nations Center on Transnational Corporations. *Transnational Corporations in World Development: Trends and Prospects.* New York: United Nations, 1988.

Westhoff, Frank H.; Yarbrough, Beth V. and Yarbrough, Robert M. Preferential Trade Agreements and the GATT: Can Bilateralism and Multilateralism Coexist? Kyklos 1994;47, pp.179-195

World Bank. *Global Economic Prospects and the Developing Countries.* Washington, D.C.: The World Bank, 1995a.

_____. *World Development Report: Workers in an Integrating World.* Oxford: Oxford University Press, 1995b.

Yarbrough, Beth V. and Yarbrough, Robert M. *Cooperation and Governance in International Trade.* Princeton: Princeton University Press, 1992.

_____. International Contracting and Territorial Control: The Boundary Question. *Journal of Institutional and Theoretical Economics* 1994;150, pp.239-264

_____. *The World Economy: Trade and Finance,* fourth edition. Fort Worth, TX: The Dryden Press, forthcoming 1997.

(εʋ)

F42 F02

6

LIMITS OF CONVERGENCE AND GLOBALIZATION[1]

Brigitte Unger

Vienna University of Economics and Business Administration, Austria

Historically, convergence has not been a smooth process. Though worldwide interdependence has increased, its outcome is neither homogenous nor foreseeable. Even in so called developed countries, with similar production facilities and access to technology, policy styles and economic policy outcomes vary. This chapter first gives an overview of the convergence debate in different disciplines, in order to show that institutional and policy aspects should not be ignored by economists. It then analyzes policy differences among countries of the European Union and why they persist. Market forces and competition work in favor of convergence, but institutions outside the market work against it. The latter are more important than the current debate admits. Channels of convergence such as imitation, competition, state competition and enforcement can be clogged due to institutional factors.

"In the long run, of course, it is hoped that the poorer Member States will become richer...as a result of a combination of continued efforts to promote cohesion and convergence.."
James Mc Kenna, EU-Commission, in 1993

Countries have different policy styles and policy outcomes. Per capita income and the development of the Welfare State differ substantially, even among so-called Developed Countries. Also unemployment and inflation rates, crime rates, average life expectancies, traffic death rates, statutory minimum wages, and literacy and education rates can vary significantly. There are many reasons for this rich diversity; geographic and demographic differences, culinary traditions, consumer preferences, culture, political ideas, social movements, voting systems, executive decision making structures, authority of the courts and extent of state regulation. In general, policies and policy outcomes are the result of successive combinations of ideas, interests, and institutions, whereby each combination pre-structures new combinations at a later point of this nation's history in a path dependent way. This is what makes each nation's specific history. Because much of policy substance, form, and outcome is linked to national cultures and institutions which are strongly rooted in history, they have been surprisingly persistent over time.

But will this diversity in policy goals, instruments, and outcomes decline or even vanish as history unfolds? Will there be an eventual convergence of policy styles and outcomes? One is tempted to think so, in an age of increasing economic, social, cultural, political, and legal interdependence. Technological innovations allow for much easier communication and travel across the globe, thus facilitating information exchanges and shared cultural experiences. Television connects worldwide audiences. Shared information and stimuli may provide for similar consumer tastes, and multinational companies will try to enhance this through world-wide advertising. More than one billion people from all over the world watch the Super Bowl game at one point in time. In between they are confronted with the same commercials, and a large percentage of them will munch Italian pizza during the game and flush it down with American coke. Is there a new species emerging? The "global man", identical and faceless, living in Sassen's (1991) "global city" ? Do we approach Fukuyama's (1992) *End of History* with identical patterns of production, behavior, taste and ideology across countries ?

In the following, I will first give a short overview of the convergence debate in sociology, economics, and political science. Then, I shall explore some econometric problems. Even a short glance at this discussion reveals that in none of the disciplines is convergence an uncontested theoretical construct. Sociologists have controversies about the end of ideology, economists have them about the end of income disparities and political scientists about the end of policies. Even so called precise sciences such as mathematics and econometrics struggle with the choice and operationalization of convergence measures.

The first part of this essay emphasizes that convergence is an interdisciplinary issue and has come and gone in historical waves of optimism and pessimism regarding its success. The second part of the paper emphasizes the channels through which convergence will occur. Limits to convergence and globalization will be identified as "clogged channels" of which I distinguish four; imitation, market competition, state competition and enforcement. While the first two channels are quite familiar to economists and can be placed in the economic convergence debate, state competition and enforcement problems are more often found under the heading of policy convergence. Yet, political factors have important impacts on economic convergence as a recent empirical study on policy convergence within the European Union for fourteen policy fields shows (Unger/Van Waarden 1995). The last sections on non-market conforming responses of political actors and on problems of enforcement provide an overview of some of the empirical results of this study. Main factors for convergence and divergence will be identified in the conclusion. If we include institutional and political factors into our analysis, we have to face new uncertainties concerning the outcome, because some of these factors work, at least partially, against convergence.

The Convergence Debate

Convergence has been defined in social sciences as "the tendency of societies to grow more alike, to develop similarities in structures, processes, and performances" (Kerr 1983: 3). The topic has recently gained in popularity, following the Maastricht Agreement among EU Member States that requires - for monetary union to occur - that several of their macroeconomic indicators should converge beforehand. This has no doubt stimulated the scholarly interest in convergence in the economic literature; at the same time that it has kept econometricians busy searching for ways to measure it.

However, the question of convergence of nations and their structures, policies and performances is an old one. It keeps reappearing, as if following some invisible cycle. The issue has been central to theory formation in most of the social sciences, in sociology, in economics, and in political science. As Boyer (1993) showed, the convergence debate seems to go in waves or swing like a pendulum: the strong belief in convergence in the Postwar period of the 1950s and 1960s was criticized and followed by a conviction in divergence in the 1970s and 1980s. In the 1990s, belief in harmonization and convergence seems to be back in vogue.

System Convergence - The End of Ideology?

The term "convergence" has been used often to refer to system convergence, the growing together of whole societies from initial points of extreme, if not polar, difference: the developed and developing, the industrialized and industrializing, the democratic and totalitarian, the capitalist and socialist. The classics of sociology, writing at a time when most European societies experienced common processes of industrialization, urbanization, secularization, state formation, and imperialism, all had implicit or explicit theories of convergence as part of their theories of modernization. Durkheim saw an increase in the societal division of labor and feared the replacement of organic by mechanical solidarity, resulting in a common situation of anomia. Marx predicted increasing tensions between the forces and relations of production, a gradual lowering in profit rates and eventually the end of capitalism.

In the Postwar period authors such as Tinbergen (1959) and Bell (1960) predicted the "end of ideology", as Fukuyama prophesies now the "end of history". The former two authors argued that the ideological and structural distinctions between communism and capitalism would gradually disappear. Countries in East and West would develop into more or less similar industrial societies. The global spread of technology, industrialization and economic growth would confront all countries with similar imperatives. The uniform imperatives of growth and technology would make ideological distinctions irrelevant and class differences would disappear. The convergence proponents strongly believed in technological determinism and a harmonious outcome from the diffusion of technology and growth.

However, such perspectives have been more popular in certain periods than in others. The 1960s were followed by the 1970s and 1980s with more attention focused on international differences and divergence. Kern and Schumann (1976) demonstrated empirically that technology did not have the unifying effect it has often been presumed to have. First of all, technological development tended to increase the level of required skills for higher level jobs, but to decrease them for lower level ones, resulting in a divergence in skill requirements, working conditions, and workers' consciousness. Secondly, the effects of technology differed by sector. Implicit here was the further argument that, since different societies have different sectoral portfolios, technology would affect them differently, thus leading to divergence, rather than convergence at the macro-level. Several other studies in the volume edited by Goldthorpe (1984) pertain to the political organization of classes and emphasized the differences between corporatist and pluralist systems, which complicated the simple dichotomy between capitalism and socialism that prevailed in the earlier convergence theories. According to their findings the specific and diverse institutional arrangements in capitalist societies mattered for differences in performance. For example, corporatist countries with well organized employers' associations and strong trade unions performed better than more market driven and "disorganized" Western Capitalist Societies.

Economic Convergence: The End of Income Disparities?

Convergence in economics refers to convergence of economic variables such as growth rates, interest rates, inflation or unemployment, indicators, which can also be seen as economic policy outcomes. There has been considerable disagreement as to the likelihood of convergence in the various theories. For every convergence theory there has been an opposing divergence theory.

Neoclassical growth theory expects convergence of living standards and productivity between poor and rich countries through the diffusion of similar technology. International Trade Theory stresses the convergence of factor prices (wages, interest rates) and good prices as a result of trade and competition The latest newcomer in the convergence debate is "Maastricht convergence". The Maastricht Treaty sets criteria for inflation rates, nominal interest rates, budget deficits, and public debts, to which Member States are supposed to converge in order for them to be allowed to join the planned European Monetary Union. If convergence should take place, it will be partly the result of the political enforcement of this Treaty commitment.

Neoclassical growth theory expects convergence through the channel of imitation. Poor countries will imitate the technology and know how of rich countries. Modern technology will diffuse worldwide. By taking advantage of Kuznets' "transnationally available stock of useful knowledge" and by replacing their entire capital stock with the latest high tech capital stock of developed countries, poor countries should eventually "catch-up".

Abramovitz (1986) showed that "falling behind and forging ahead" instead of catching up of income and growth will occur, if poor countries are unable to use the foreign technology due to "social inabilities". Poor countries will *not* catch up, if they cannot implement the technology of the rich countries on a one to one basis, e.g. because labor skills differ. Kuznets' "stock of knowledge" can then simply not be drawn upon by the poor. Thus, the convergence theory of growth rates found its divergence counterpart.

While orthodox growth theory sees convergence by means of imitation of technological progress, International Trade Theory expects convergence through competition and trade. The neoclassical factor price equalization theorem states that interest rates, profit rates, wages, prices, and income will converge due to the mobility of factors of production and the mobility of goods and services. Instantaneous, perfectly flexible reactions of market participants will guarantee arbitrage in all fields. Financial capital goes to the highest interest rate, i.e. to the poor countries, until interest rates are equal. Physical capital seeks the highest profit and thus results in a convergence of interest rates and profit rates. Labor goes to the highest wages and entrepreneurs to the lowest wages. Their claims meet at the international market clearing wage rate. If wages are below the equilibrium rate, labor would go abroad. If wages are above the equilibrium rate, capital would abandon the high-wage country. As a consequence, wages will converge due to market forces. If factors of production are somehow prohibited from smoothly flowing across borders, then the mobility of goods will bring about convergence. Consumers buy from the cheapest offer of goods. Prices of goods across countries should, therefore, converge. And since labor and technology are incorporated in goods, wages and profit rates will converge as a consequence of trade in goods.

A consequence of this overall mobility of factors and goods is that economic policies are constrained by exogenously, i.e. internationally, given prices, wages and interest rates. Policies are either impotent or forced to be the same across countries. They have to converge. The convergence hypothesis proclaims a smooth, automatic adjustment of economic outcomes and as a consequence also of economic policies.

As we have seen above, for every convergence hypothesis there is one of divergence. It usually stresses some imperfections and frictions. International trade theory of factor price equalization and income adjustment was criticized most prominently by Krugman (see e.g. Dehesa and Krugman 1992). He showed that convergence by means of trade depends on two crucial assumptions; the same efficiency in production among countries and constant returns to scale. Differences in efficiency may prevent physical capital from flowing from the rich to the poor countries. If capital flows to the rich, this would widen the gap of income differentials. Falling behind and forging ahead, instead of catching up, would be the outcome, due to differences in efficiency in production.

Economies of scale tend to promote agglomerations. Firms tend to cluster in order to be close to markets. Reduced barriers to trade make it also profitable for firms to concentrate production in a few locations to achieve economies of scale. It has been indicated that seen from an airplane, Europe at night looks like a "blue banana", with blue lights stretching from Milan to Copenhagen, rather than being evenly spread over Europe as in the shape of a grape (Dehesa and Krugman 1992). If so, regional disparities would become greater, rather than smaller, as trade theory would predict.

Financial capital does not behave well either. According to neoclassical theory, capital will go to the highest interest rates, provided that exchange rate risks are subtracted. Arbitrage will lead to a convergence of interest rates. Differences in interest rates only account for the risk. Due to diminishing returns, poor countries have higher returns than rich countries. Capital should flow from the rich to the poor. But capital also flows systematically from the poor to the rich countries. Financial capital follows expectations and primarily creates speculative waves instead of intertemporal smooth adjustment. Political risk and inefficient production in many poor countries make it unattractive for investors to place their capital there, even though interest rates are exorbitantly high and put poor countries in financial and economic crisis.

Labor mobility does not satisfy the assumption of international trade theory either. Convergence of wages is to be expected, only if labor mobility is high. But labor mobility can be very limited due to linguistic, cultural, and social barriers. Sassen (1995) casts doubt upon economists' assumption of a clear causal relationship between labor mobility and convergence of economic outcomes. If labor mobility is not exogenous but is itself dependent on capital mobility, if higher profits and not higher wages induce higher labor mobility, if migration policies increase migration instead of stopping it, a divergence of wages and incomes is to be expected.

Even if factors are immobile, the Stolper-Samuelson theorem claims that convergence should still be the outcome. Prices would converge as a consequence of trade (all sorts of transportation and other transaction costs would still allow for some differences in prices). Wages and incomes would also converge, since (immobile) capital and labor are incorporated in mobile goods. Immobile factors cross borders in their transformed version as commodities. However, critics would stress that trade does not take place by means of free and unlimited competition on markets. As Bellak (1995) shows, only one-third of worldwide trade is really free trade. The rest is managed trade and trade by the hierarchies of multinational firms. That is, non-market institutions determine a substantial portion of international trade.

Economic convergence theories usually refer to the real outcome of economic policy, to the convergence of real variables (physical measurable variables), such as real income distribution or growth of real GDP. Convergence of nominal variables was never an economic issue, since poverty, structural inequalities, or disparities in income were the long term economic concerns. Only recently, since the planned Monetary Union of Maastricht, did the convergence of nominal variables (inflation rates, nominal interest rates) become an issue. I will refer to these as "Maastricht-style convergence". The problem with this is that there is no theory, explaining why convergence of such variables should take place and through which mechanisms this should occur. As indicated, real convergence is mainly an issue in two fields of economics: (1) growth theory, and (2) international trade theory. In the latter the openness of the economy, barriers to trade, mobility of goods and factors explain convergence or divergence. In both theories convergence is the outcome of increased interdependence and market forces and not a prerequisite for integration to take place.

Maastricht-style convergence, which deliberately imposes a set of convergence criteria on countries wanting to join the currency club, addresses a third channel of convergence. Here convergence is not the result of imitation of technology or of market forces, but the result of political norms and collective enforcement. This form of convergence is of course not new, as throughout history states have invaded other states and imposed their culture, religion, or language on the conquered. In economics, however, this concept is new. For the first time, convergence of economic outcomes should be realized through political enforcement, rather than through imitation or market forces.

Maastricht-style convergence also has a much shorter time horizon (1997 or 1999) than real convergence. It, furthermore, does not have an explicit theory. The Maastricht criteria are quite arbitrary. The fiscal norms, for example, were set according to the status quo of the year in which they were decided, and turned out to be unfeasible in the years of crisis that followed. By 1994 no country fulfilled the Maastricht criteria anymore (see Buiter 1992, who heavily criticizes them).

The idea behind Maastricht-style convergence is that a monetary union should be a low-inflation union. Therefore, countries should be forced by means of nominal variable convergence to keep inflation low. The price a high inflation country has to pay in order to bring inflation down can be many years of recession, high unemployment and real income dispersion. Maastricht convergence can thus lead to divergence of real variables and to increased inequalities in welfare, since the price which countries have to pay for it, differs. The trade-off between different variables is a concern in the convergence debate. If nominal variables are forced to converge, real variables will have to bear the full burden of adjustment. This shows that the planned currency union is inherently unstable. Europe is no optimal currency area (Eichengreen 1991). Free riding of countries joining the currency club is obviously feared by those in favour of convergence criteria (Unger 1995). In other words, problems of collective action seem more important than traditional economic causes for the convergence of such economic policies and policy outcomes.

Policy Convergence: The End of Policies?

Whereas sociologists have studied the convergence of nation states, and economists the convergence of macroeconomic indicators, political scientists have focused on the policies with which authorities have tried to affect society and economy. These policy analysts have typically taken a single allegedly universal problem and then analyzed how different nations have reacted to it. Among the problems they have selected have been the demand for welfare, the fiscal crisis of the state, rising unemployment, the arms race, the new poverty, the increase in crime, or the decline of air and water standards. They have found that nations tend to react differently in their policy goals, instruments and styles. Dye (1991) compared policies of the fifty American states over time and found some evidence of convergence. Waltman and Studlar (1987) investigated whether the coming to power of neo-liberal governments produced a convergence of policies in the US and Britain. Döhler (1990) did the same for neo-conservative health policies in Britain and Germany, and Grande (1989) for French and German telecommunication policies. Vogel (1986) studied possible convergence in US and British environmental policies and Bennett (1988) did the same for data protection policies. The overall results have been somewhat inconclusive. The neo-liberal shift in policies during the early 1980s did not produce the degree of convergence, expected by the authors.

Policies do not change easily, since policy preferences are often rooted in systems of institutions. The more policy content, procedure or intended outcome affect the core of such institutions and the cultural values that underlie them, the stronger the resistance to change will be. For basic policy preferences, major shocks such as war, revolution, or severe economic depressions are usually required in order to induce change (Crozier 1964, Lehmbruch 1987).

Although not a sudden event, the persistent increase in economic and political internationalization could be the kind of shock that might elicit major policy change and possibly policy convergence. That it will have effects seems certain. This begs further questions: On what policies and policy choices will it have an effect? And how much of an effect?

More to the point, does this process of internationalization promote convergence or divergence in policy responses? And, if so, is it a deterministic and irreversible effect? Or does it leave room for choice and changes of mind with respect to change? Will nations that do not adapt their policies loose out in international competition and perform poorer? Is it a matter of survival of the fittest? Social Darwinism was one of the early approaches in sociology. It remains the dominant paradigm in economics, and it has recently reemerged among sociologists in the form of population ecology theory .

Interdependence does not necessarily require or produce similarity. On the contrary. Men and women are interdependent, as are employers and employees, precisely because they are dissimilar, i.e. capable of contributing differently to the production of the same product. Interdependence between nations may produce even greater differences, as nations specialize in a worldwide division of labor. However, interdependence may also enhance competition between nations in similar fields, and this competition may force them to act similarly or become more alike.

Some Problems of Measuring Convergence

According to the dictionaries the term 'convergence' means' to move towards each other or to a common point'. It originally stems from mathematics, where the idea of a 'limes' - a limit - to which indefinite series approach (converge) in infinity is very old. The concept of convergence is well defined and understood in mathematics and statistics: The difference between two (or more) series should become arbitrarily small (or converge on some constant a) as time elapses. For random series, such as most economic variables, this can be extended so that only the probability that the two series differ by a specified amount is required to become arbitrarily small (stochastic convergence).

However, even the discipline of econometrics, used to formalized models and precise definitions, has its problems when it comes to the operationalization of these intuitive criteria of convergence: "The principle of convergence arises in many contexts in the economics literature and each application seems to have evolved its own measure of convergence with little regard for existing measures" (see Hall/Robertson/Wickens (1992, p.100). There is, nowadays, a proliferation of measures of convergence in econometrics. A very simple and popular way is to calculate measures of dispersion (like the standard deviation or the coefficient of variation, i.e. the mean corrected standard deviation) for the series across countries. If the dispersion measure declines over time this is supposed to indicate convergence. More sophisticated methods are testing for cointegration of the series, i.e. one wants to make sure that the differences between the (non-stationary) series do not drift infinitely far apart (do not have infinite variances, cointegrate). In a further step one can ask whether their means tend to zero or an arbitrarily small number (see Grandner/Unger (1993) who apply this method to test for the convergence of unemployment and inflation rates). For a quite readable survey and for further techniques and measures see Hall/Robertson/Wickens (1992). For a more sophisticated but insightful survey see Bernard and Durlauf (1991).

The choice of convergence measures in practice is quite arbitrary. One problem that emerges is that while the dispersion measure indicates convergence, the cointegration test may indicate no convergence or even divergence. Convergence and divergence results are then arbitrary and only depend on the choice of model (this problem of econometrics is indeed not limited to convergence). Another problem, which is especially relevant in the current EU-Maastricht-convergence-discussion, is the arbitrary combination of variables. If convergence is measured by examining whether the sum of changes in inflation rates, interest rates and budget deficits of different countries becomes more similar, this pre-assumes a linear relationship between economic fundamentals. But, if the world is round, why should the economic world be linear? Even if each convergence indicator is calculated separately: how can we prove anything about convergence in general, if the decline of the dispersion measure in one variable (e.g. inflation) is causally related to a rise of the dispersion measure in another variable (e.g. nominal interest rate). Two variables might be dependent on each other differently in each country (e.g. monetary policy in order to reduce inflation has to raise interest rates a lot in order to restrict inflationary demand in one country, while in another a short talk among the social partners is sufficient to bring inflation down)? There is evidence for a trade- off between different kinds of convergence. Hall/Robertson/Wickens (1992) used a sophisticated time-varying parameter model to discover that, for EU countries, convergence in real exchange rates was associated with divergence in real interest rates between 1970 and 1991 (p.111).

Another problem is that the content of what convergence really means differs in different models. For example, a famous convergence study by Baumol (1986) analyzed whether there is a negative correlation between the initial per capita income of a country and its subsequent growth rates. He found empirical evidence for the catching up of poorer countries. But is this convergence as Baumol claims? Income inequalities need not vanish. If the world experienced a single technological change, we would observe a spill over from rich to poor countries and, hence, a catching up of the latter. We would also observe a negative correlation between income and growth. But this would not be sufficient to trigger a long-term growth development that would make income inequalities vanish.

Another statistical concept (see e.g. Streissler 1979, Bernard and Durlauf 1991) would speak of convergence only if this catching up leads to an eventual disappearance of income inequalities. Barro/Sala i Martin (1991, p.112) distinguish between these two forms of convergence by calling the first 'beta-convergence' (poor countries grow faster than rich ones) and the second 'sigma-convergence' (a decline over time in the cross-sectional dispersion of per capita income).

What we can conclude, so far, is that even in the 'precise sciences', convergence is an unclear concept. An agreed definition of it is still missing in econometrics and economics.

The 'Clogged Channels' of Economic and Policy Convergence

I shall analyze four main channels of divergence in greater detail to look for evidence of how they might become distorted or blocked. (1) What if imitation of technology is not always possible or wanted? (2) What if the assumptions of market competition fail, e.g. because factor mobility itself is a political variable? (3) What if political actors decide not to conform and try to avoid state competition? (4) What if collective actors decide to free ride?

Limited Imitation Possibilities

The belief in catching up through the diffusion of technical progress among countries can be traced to Veblen (1915), Gerschenkron (1952) and Kuznets (1966). Veblen claimed that Britain had to pay the penalty of low growth rates for its early industrialization and, hence, was overtaken by other countries. Gerschenkron (1952) drew attention to the 'advantage of backwardness', leaving space for catching up by poor countries. For Kuznets (1966, p.1), economic growth is a sustained increase in per capita or per worker product, most often accompanied by an increase in population and usually by sweeping structural changes. He discovered that modern economic growth is first and foremost characterized by growth of total factor productivity (efficiency). He came to the "inescapable conclusion..that the direct contribution of man-hours and capital accumulation would hardly account for more than a tenth of the rate of growth in per capita product.. The large remainder must be assigned to an increase in efficiency in the productive resources, or the effects of changing arrangements, or to the impact of technological change, or to all three" (Kuznets 1966, p.81). According to Kuznets, modern growth was based on the existence of a **'transnationally available stock of useful knowledge'.** This knowledge is "invariant to personal traits and talents and to institutional vagaries and hence..fully transmissible on a worldwide scale, in ways in which, say, handcraft techniques in traditional agriculture and industry were not, because they were based on personal knowledge of conditions specific to a given country..." (see Kuznets 1966, p.287 quoted in Terhal 1987, p.79f).

Nevertheless, Kuznets empirically found out that inequalities on a worldwide scale persisted or even widened. He attributed this to the fact that countries differ with respect to the date of full entry into the worldwide process of application of this knowledge. The main reasons for this 'divergence', he postulated, lay in the retardation of political and institutional adjustments, which have to occur before countries can 'take off' (see Kuznets 1966, p.468). His explanation for divergence,- i.e. the role of institutions and their policies - lay outside the field of neoclassical economics.

Many reasons are given nowadays for divergence of income and growth rates (see Helliwell/Chung 1990,p.2):

1.   the technologies of the richer countries may not be directly applicable to poorer countries (e.g. due to different relative factor prices and different levels of education),

2.   political and social systems of the poorer countries may not be willing to accept the degree of international interdependence (Abramovitz 1986 refers to it as "social capabilities" of poor countries),

3.   technologies are privately owned and not public goods (the rents on imported technology would then flow to the rich countries and raise their income instead the income of the poor),

4.   countries that have enjoyed economic progress in the past may lose their desire or ability to keep up with productivity improvements. A recent study by Windhoff-Heritier (1995) on environmental production standards gives empirical support for the argument that countries, once they implement a production technique are not willing to adjust it regularly. Therefore, the

leading and lagging of specific countries can occur consecutively over time.

As stated above, in the neoclassical growth model the rate of technological progress is assumed to be exogenous and identical in all economies. Lucas (1990) has expanded the neoclassical model by adjusting the rate of technological advance for effects resulting from the accumulation of human capital. According to this model, different levels of education, i.e. differences in the amount of human capital between countries, lead to differences in productive performance. Furthermore, human capital accumulation generates economies of scale. If one employee makes a technological innovation, other employees may benefit from it. As Buiter and Kletzer (1991) add, the presence of a non-traded (home-grown) human capital good which is an essential input for its own accumulation is sufficient for the existence of persistent international differentials in levels and growth rates of labor productivity, even if there is perfect capital mobility and even if technologies are identical across the world (p.43). Buiter and Kletzer show furthermore, that different policies (e.g. different levels of public spending on education) can increase growth rates. But even this expansion of the neoclassical model leaves out the decisive question, what leads to different policies and accumulation of human capital outside the sphere of economics. A somewhat more 'sociological' answer has been offered by Durlauf (1992), who incorporates the choice of neighborhood, and makes it responsible for human capital accumulation through education and cultural influences through things such as successful role models, in an intra-generational endogenous growth model. He shows that persistent income inequality and poverty can emerge from individual differences in the choice of neighborhood. This brings us precise technical results, but does not say very much about the content and conditions of these sociological choices.

Convergence of labor productivity levels or per capita income would thus occur if there is no impediment to the dissemination of technological knowledge, if there is no difference in country specific, non-traded, human capital accumulation and no barrier to the accumulation of capital. The hope that diffusion of technology will bring technical progress everywhere and will lead to the disappearance of income disparity and poverty in the long run depends on too many unrealistic assumptions. In the recent debate on the comparative advantage of the Japanese economy over the US economy, a new issue has been stressed. Imitation can be asymmetric due to the nature of the product. While Japanese firms are famous for their ability to imitate US technology of production, US firms have problems in imitating Japanese production advantages. The Japanese advantage consists mainly in better organizational know-how, which is much more difficult to copy than a production plant due to differences in culture and regulations (see Aoki 1988, Dore 1986).

Limited Mechanism of Competition

The reference model for economists is the perfectly competitive market. An indefinite number of anonymous suppliers and demanders trade goods and services at a market clearing price. A market economy consists of all kinds of sub-markets for labor, capital, goods, services and futures. If there is an oversupply in some market, the price will fall; if there is excess demand, the price will go up. As long as the state does not restrict any of the actors from doing what he or she likes to do and to bid and offer what he or she prefers to bid and offer, the price mechanism will work. Scarce resources will be allocated to their best and most efficient use. There are, of course, all kinds of market failures due to things as information asymmetries, externalities or natural monopolies which are treated as deviations from the standard model.

The neoclassical convergence theory strongly depends upon the functioning of the perfectly competitive market. Unfortunately, that model seems to be a very poor one for international trade. First, trade does not take place exclusively through markets. If only one third of trade goes through the market (see Bellak 1995) - and this market is far from being a perfectly competitive one! - and if two thirds of world trade is 'managed' trade or negotiated within firms, the market model would be manifestly inadequate. If international trade functions through hierarchies of firms and depends on political decisions, why should we expect convergence from competition on a perfect market? Convergence of prices and wages through competition and trade stems from the neoclassical design of a market economy which simply cannot be found at an international level, except for raw materials, coffee beans, sugar cane and wheat.

Moreover, many firms involved in international trade are not anonymous units too small to influence the market price. They are price setters, oligopolies, and hence strategic actors. Concentration instead of competition, hierarchy instead of the price mechanism are the principles of governance of multinational enterprises. They create their own capital and labor flows, which differ from the neoclassical market model.

Furthermore, the neoclassical convergence debate considers all factors as somehow equally mobile. But the penetration of borders has not generated an indefinitely smooth and quick flow of factor adjustments. Financial capital can cross borders with almost unlimited speed. The mere push of a button on a computer can transfer funds all over the globe, and this brings it closest to economists' perception of a perfect world. Physical capital is already less mobile, as it is more tied to sales markets, proximity to raw material markets, or the availability of qualified labor and transport facilities. Nevertheless, the number of multinational and transnational enterprises and the speed with which firms change their location has also increased over the time. Foreign direct investment (FDI) - an instrument by which multinational enterprises transfer whole packages of physical and financial capital - has increased dramatically since the 1980s. By the early 1990s, FDI has reached the importance of international trade. FDI outflows grew at an average annual rate of 24% between 1986 and 1990 (Bellak 1995, p.102). This is about four times the rate of world output growth (for further impressive numbers see Brigitte Levy in this volume). Yet, the mobility of physical capital is not indefinite and smooth. Firms agglomerate instead of spreading over space. Poor regions stay poor and in the periphery, while the core expands (see Dehesa and Krugman 1992).

A study by the Dutch Social Economic Council (SER-COB 1994) found that physical capital mobility was even low between official European border regions (Euregios) in Germany and the Netherlands, where national authorities cooperate across borders and try to stimulate similar patterns in the relations between private businesses. The survey showed that Dutch businessmen rarely look over the border for business (Van Houtum en Van Kerkhoff 1994, Corvers and Dankbaar 1994). Problems with language, legal regimes, differences in mentality and product preferences - coupled with the specialization of firms - all seem to limit mobility.

Labor mobility - the amount and speed with which workers move across national borders - has also increased, though to a still lesser degree. It is certainly much lower than capital mobility. Furthermore, labor mobility is not a homogenous flow across countries. It is institutionally, historically and culturally embedded. Whatever there is in terms of labor mobility follows specific and usually officially controlled patterns. Sassen (1995) shows that labor mobility takes place within specific segments of the labor market, is restricted to specific historical phases, typically occurs between a limited set of countries and thus affects some countries more than others, i.e. it creates divergence. Furthermore, migration streams between countries are often established by multinational corporations (MNCs). They create networks. People in the host country come to know the culture and opportunities of the MNCs country of origin and come to consider it as a potential migration country. Interestingly enough, immigrants often originate from countries which receive foreign aid, investment, and exports of consumer goods. Measures commonly thought to deter immigration seem to have precisely the opposite effect. On the one hand, labor mobility is socially produced by transnational enterprises and thus is not a migration influx suffered by the labor receiving country. On the other hand, labor mobility is also politically steered. Sassen's (1995) analysis of migration policies shows that the globalization process leads to converging anti-migration policies across nations and gives labor and capital an uneven chance to "cross the globe".

Labor mobility is very limited, except for some very specific, very high and very low skilled jobs. Even in the United States, with a more homogeneous working population than Europe that speaks basically the same language, labor mobility is not unlimited. Wage and unemployment rates still differ significantly and do not automatically trigger "compensating" flows of labor (Dye 1991). Unemployment rates by state varied in 1991 between 10.5 per cent in West Virginia and 2.7 per cent in Nebraska. In Europe, the language and cultural barriers to migration are much higher. Labor mobility in Europe is about one-third of the US. Unemployment rates in the European Union differ between 23.8 per cent for Spain and 6.0 per cent for Portugal (OECD 1993).

Pressures for internationalization are higher coming from capital than from labor due to these different factor mobilities, which are, in term, due to their intrinsic nature. Land cannot be transferred at all, while financial capital can be transferred almost effortlessly and at quasi zero cost. Labor is largely stuck with its cultural and linguistic endowment. The opening of territorial borders and the interdependence of economies give capital and labor an unequal chance to adjust.

The Non-market Conforming Responses of Political Actors

Even if production factors are not perfectly mobile, most countries are benefiting (and suffering) from the pressures of increased flows of capital, labor, and goods. Through these exchanges, they come more in contact with each other and have to compete for the same pool of production factors, goods, and consumers. They are under pressure to attract or keep capital, labor, and markets for their goods and services. Since a large share of international trade takes place within multinational companies, countries are also under pressure to compete for the location of such enterprises. Their competitive position in the world economy will depend in large part on their economic policies and policy outcomes. Do they have a secure currency, low inflation, a good infrastructure of transportation and communications, pleasant living conditions, low costs of living, high wages (to attract labor) or low wages (to attract capital), qualified labor, educational institutions, research and development facilities, attractive tax regimes, few regulations that bother industry, and whatever else goes in the making of the competitive position of nations? As international competition increases, so will the pressure to compete with other nation-states. Nations will have to adjust their economic policies and the chance is great that these policies will become more similar. Countries will try to offer similar infrastructures, tax regimes, inflation rates, wage levels and regulations on production and consumption. Insofar as convergence could take place, there are contrasting hypotheses as to the level at which this will happen. First there is the *thesis* that internationalization will produce a *"race to the bottom"*, i.e. a convergence at a low level of product regulation and consumer protection. A rival thesis is that it will promote a convergence toward a high level of regulation and protection, a *"race to the top"*.

The more well-known thesis of the race to the bottom implies that countries will try to surpass each other by offering lower wage levels, lower costs of social security, and less regulatory restrictions to business. Conservatives saw this as the great attraction of the Single European Market. Former British Prime-Minister Thatcher called it the "greatest deregulation operation in history". The financial speaker of the Social Democrats in the Austrian parliament, Ewald Nowotny, concurred: "Obviously, this is a race to the bottom. And obviously the one wins this race who is more mobile, better informed or also more ruthless. Hence, it is likely that this will be capital (notably financial capital) rather than labor, the large enterprise rather than the small, and actors with low social and ecological morals rather than responsible businessmen" (translated from Nowotny in *Der Standard*, November 1994).

There are however a number of qualifications to this theory of social dumping. The *first* relates to economic integration. Formal membership in the European Union does not immediately produce a uniform economic reality. That which exists *de jure*, say, in the Single European Act, does not immediately also exist *de facto*. The legal establishment of the "four freedoms" which allows capital, labor, goods and services to move freely within the Union, does not automatically create high factor and product mobility across borders.

A *second* qualification to the assumed 'race to the bottom' is that not all countries are equally affected by the pressures of internationalization. As indicated, labor mobility occurs typically between specific supplying and receiving countries.

Furthermore, the dependence of the various nation-states on foreign trade varies. The degree of openness of the economy to world markets varies between ten per cent of exports to GDP for the US, to about sixty percent for some small European countries such as the Netherlands. Hence, countries are not all affected to the same degree and this should influence the pressure for convergence.

Thirdly, wage levels, regulations and state expenditures are not as malleable as presumed. They serve specific purposes and interests, such as labor and environmental protection, which cannot be neglected for electoral reasons or due to the pressure of organized interest. What is more, they are often also in the interest of business itself. It is not always so clear what makes for an optimal competitive position in world markets. Often, there is a potential trade-off between different factors for improving competitiveness. Lower wages may attract foreign enterprises, however, the resultant lower qualification levels of personnel may keep them away. There is a similar trade-off between lower taxes and less infrastructural facilities, or between less environmental regulation and a worse image with consumers. As Mosley (1995) empirically shows, if all aspects that are favorable for business are taken into account, it is not clear which country is the most attractive for business' location.

Opposed to the race to the bottom thesis is the thesis of a " race to the top" via "Euro-welfarism". As more and more national regulations get invalidated, pressure has been mounting in the EU- Member States to replace national regulations with supranational ones. This has led to a veritable flood of directives from the European Commission. Political conflict has focused on the level of protection to be provided by this legislation. Should it be high or low? Countries which themselves have high levels of protection press for adoption of their norms by the EU. In this case, political integration - and political competition between Member States within this supranational unit - could fuel a race to the top, rather than to the bottom, i.e. to a convergence at a high level of protective regulation.

Both convergence theses could turn out to be wrong, if political actors decided not to compete with similar strategies but to differentiate themselves and to create niches. A specific bundle of location advantages could then attract specific firms and industries.

Some empirical results on European policy convergence can be found in Unger/Van Waarden (1995), where fourteen policy fields have been analyzed by various authors. Neither the social dumping nor the Euro-welfare thesis were confirmed. Bellak (1995) saw divergence of national **industrial policies** as a more likely outcome. Since Multinational enterprises do not have homogenous interests, governments may compete for the location of enterprises by means of specialization, by creating a unique environment for specific industries, necessitating different industrial policy measures. According to him, industrial policy will continue to differ, despite increases in physical capital mobility.

Kitzmantel and Moser (1995) argued that **tax policy** in EU Member States - a major economic instrument of redistribution - is substantially influenced by EU laws as well as by the high mobility of financial capital, which enhances tax competition between nations. Thus in most countries foreign operators are typically exempted from income taxation whilst domestic operators are not. Tax competition has been more important than joint action. Concerted measures have been mainly limited to harmonizing indirect taxes (VAT, excise duties), whereas direct taxation (company taxes, personal income taxes) has remained largely a subject of national initiatives. Notwithstanding some tendencies towards convergence, the authors do not expect a convergence to the bottom, to very low tax rates, since nations have financing needs that will prevent them from lowering taxes drastically. Furthermore, considerable discrepancies between national tax systems still exist, both with respect to tax rates and tax exemptions. Since the mobile factors cannot be taxed further due to international tax competition, the tax burden will be shifted more and more towards the immobile factor, in particular labor.

Mosley (1995) analyzed national **regimes of workers' protection** in Europe and argued that economic and political integration is unlikely to result in 'social dumping', but will not lead to an 'upward' convergence through high standards of social protection of a European authority either. While some EU countries have the competitive advantage of low labor costs (the periphery), others have the competitive advantage of higher welfare facilities (the core). Welfare state arrangements are not always a burden, but can create competitive advantages due to e.g. better training and health of workers. Regulations and welfare programmes differ among European countries, but "any hierarchy in the overall 'burden' on enterprises is difficult to discern". Nevertheless, center-core problems related to wage differentials could become important in certain sectors, such as labor intensive industries. Even though social dumping does not occur, social benefits are on the defensive in many EU-countries. Mosley attributes this "convergence towards the worse" to ideological trends and not to internationalization and European integration. Some convergence could emerge in the core countries, while divergence may appear in the core-periphery relation.

Engbersen (1995) investigated the concept of welfare states in his study of **poverty regimes** in Europe. He showed that poverty regimes in Britain, France, and the Netherlands differ, and so do their outcomes, the life chances of the European poor. The 'residual welfare state' in Britain produces material deprivation including lack of food and clothing, which would be unthinkable in the Dutch welfare state. In this well-developed welfare state, poverty means not so much financial deprivation as well as social isolation, structural exclusion, alienation of the poor from central societal institutions, and permanent dependence on the welfare state. The author expects and fears convergence towards a "residual welfare state". A continuation of the actual trend of lowering welfare benefits could bring about greater social inequality and social problems, such as anomie, in many European nations.

Keller (1995) analyzed **labor regulation policies.** He found some convergence to the bottom, towards minimal standards, but also differentiation at the firm, sectoral and national level. He agreed with Engbersen in that he neither expects a well-developed European welfare state. He argued that a European social policy - especially in the field of labor relations - is unlikely. A Europeanization of labor relations is not to be expected, given the divergent interests and different organizational structures of trade unions. Furthermore, the strengthening of the position of employers makes bargaining above the company level less attractive to them. Interest representation and participation at the company and factory level in transnational enterprises - though rare and difficult - is nevertheless easier to imagine than a centralized European system of collective bargaining.

Eichener (1995) studied **workplace health and safety standards** and neither perceives a convergence to the bottom. He argues that the fear of some countries that their high levels of protection would be undercut by social and ecological dumping is unjustified. Such expectations were based on political integration theories which analyzed European policy making primarily as intergovernmental bargaining, which would only lead to lowest common denominator agreements. European occupational health and safety regulation, however, provides a surprisingly high level of protection and develops even innovative approaches. This is because it is the outcome of interactions among complex configurations of actors, including not only national governments (as in intergovernmental bargaining theories) but also national interest groups and European actors, particularly the European Commission. The latter's institutional self-interest is an important factor explaining the innovativeness of health and safety regulation.

Héritier (1995) analyzed **clean air policies** in Europe. Air pollution is a policy problem which ideal-typically represents 'international interdependence'. Firstly, as atmospheric pollution transgresses national boundaries, it cannot effectively be dealt with within the territorial boundaries of one state. States which suffer from pollution (and from international treaties, designed to reduce the problem) will exert pressure on other states. Secondly, since emission regulation affects the competitive position of the regulated industries in an integrated market, harmonization is a prime concern especially of the high-level regulation countries. Therefore, environmental policy making has become increasingly a matter for European authorities, and for mutual influence between national and European agencies. As Mosley and Eichener, Héritier neither finds a race to the bottom. But whereas Eichener stresses the role of the European Commission in maintaining or creating a high level of protection, Héritier finds the cause in policy competition between Member States. Countries try to stay ahead of EU-regulations and regulatory intentions in their national policies. They try to assume a leadership role to save on costs of harmonizing national legislation with EU-legislation. But once they have installed new regulations they tend to stick to them and become "laggards" instead of "leaders". Upwards convergence takes thus place in a kind of catching up and forging ahead process. Nevertheless, policy differences persist, because of different geographic and geopolitical conditions which influence the concern with air pollution, of different political structures which give environmental groups and issues varying access to the political arena, of different administrative structures and traditions, which influence motives, concerns, and priorities of politicians and civil servants, and of different legal systems which prefer either voluntary self-regulation or detailed, mandatory regulations. These differences produce different perceptions and approaches to the problem of air pollution, which seem to be remarkably persistent.

Kelemen (1995) did not find a race to the bottom for **environmental policy** either, but was more pessimistic about a race to the top, since EU-countries with low environmental standards get delays for adjustments. He took as his point of departure the potential conflicts between European competition and environmental policy. This gives the European Court of Justice leeway in deciding which should prevail over which. Kelemen showed that Decisions of the Court and the Commission have tended to advance environmental protection but that the Council, where intergovernmental bargaining between high and low standard countries takes place, tends to retard the development of EU environmental policy. The Treaties agreed upon by the Member States can hence be read as steps backward, which should correct for steps forward, made by the Court.

As soon as we take institutional differences among countries into account, the likelihood of convergence declines. There is, of course, also an ongoing debate, whether institutions will converge in the process of internationalization and globalization. Given first empirical results of a volume forthcoming by Unger/Van Waarden on institutional Convergence, this does not seem very likely either.

Problems of Enforcement (Maastricht Problems)

As already mentioned, the idea of enforcing economic adjustment by fixing targets for some monetary indicators, is quite new in economics. This raises the question of which problems of enforcement could occur. On the one hand, **problems of collective action** might oppose the original idea of convergence. As Unger (1995) showed for **fiscal policy**, even if countries fulfilled all Maastricht criteria by 1997 or 1999 and were allowed to enter the currency union, it will be very difficult to exclude free riders afterwards. Whether fiscal policies will converge or not will depend mainly on whether financial markets believe that the European Union will not bail out bad debtors. The solemn declaration of the "no bail out clause" in the Maastricht Treaty itself is insufficient to solve the collective action problem.

Even if all countries planned to fulfill all EU norms and laws, the national outcome may still differ because of differences in policy implementation. To translate laws into different languages and law systems can already be a problem. Van Waarden (1995) argued that countries differ in their dominant styles of **policy implementation** and described the typical styles of the US, Britain, France, Germany, and the Netherlands. While British top civil servant perceive themselves as civilized gentleman, serving society, the French perceive themselves as elite, serving the interest of *la grande nation*. The British civil servants have a relatively high status, allowing for informality and discretionary authority, while the French civil servants distrust particularism. The Germans have legal training and concentrate on legalistic interpretations of law. The `mediating' role between business and the state that they consider their task would be viewed as `corruption' and `capturing' by US civil servants. Van Waarden argued that these differences are not incidental nor accidental, but structural, in that they are strongly rooted in national state institutions, such as legal systems and structures and traditions of the public administration. This makes these policy styles rather resistant to change. Even the pressures of internationalization will be resisted, which is not to say that change could not take place of course. However, as long as implementation styles are different between Member States, this will also affect the degree of real integration. The differences in national styles imply that European policy may be implemented differently - and unequally - in different countries - as long as EU-policies are implemented by national state agencies.

Conclusion

Forces towards convergence and towards divergence exist and interact within the same time-frame. Sometimes the one is stronger, sometimes the other. Phases of convergence are followed by periods of divergence. Peace follows war; the Post-Fordist period of specialization and selective tastes follows the Fordist period of mass production and homogenous tastes. Convergence wins over divergence and vice versa with the pendular swings of history.

Economic policies which depend on the most mobile factors, i.e. financial and physical capital, lose room for maneuver due to internationalization. A typical example is the inability of monetary policy to set interest rates autonomously. Economic policies which depend on the least mobile factor, i.e. labor, gain in importance. A typical example is wage policy which has still room for maneuver left. These asymmetries of factor mobility and institutional differences make for persistence of differences in outcomes.

The Unger/Van Waarden (1995) comparison of fourteen policy fields within the European Union showed that financial market liberalization, multinational firms' threats of relocation, the spread of political ideologies, and EU-harmonization laws are the main factors of internationalization affecting national economic policies in this part of the world. Of these, state competition for the location of firms seems to be more important for convergence than has been the enforcement of EU-harmonization laws. And imitation of political ideology seems more important than market forces. As has been shown above, internationalization or globalization does not necessarily imply that market forces become more important. Globalization may also mean that hierarchies (such as multinationals), or niches or conglomerates will gain in importance. And these factors work partly against convergence. Even for Western Capitalist Societies, we cannot conclude that poor countries will ever cease to be poor in relative terms. Within the EU, we have seen that some poor countries are catching up, such as Portugal, while others do not, such as Greece. Let us hope with McKenna from the EU Commission that in the long run poorer countries will become richer, but let us not pretend that they necessarily will.

Endnotes

1 . Parts of this paper draw heavily on the Introduction of Unger/Van Waarden (1995). I would like to thank Frans van Waarden for his permission of using our joint paper and for having made this interdisciplinary work possible. I would also like to thank Philippe C. Schmitter for helpful comments and for important style corrections. Thanks to an anonymous referee who gave stimulating advice for the reorganization of the paper.

References

Abramovitz, Moses A. "Catching up, forging ahead, and falling behind." *Journal of Economic History,* June 1986, vol. XLVI, no. 2.

Alber, Jens. *Vom Armenhaus zum Wohlfahrtsstaat. Analysen zur Entwicklung der Sozialversicherung in Westeuropa,* Frankfurt am Main, Campus, 1982.

Anderson, Kym, and Blackhurst, Richard (eds). *Regional Integration and the Global Trading System,* New York: Harvester Wheatsheaf, 1993.

Aoki, Masahiko. *Information, Incentives and Bargaining in the Japanese Economy,* Cambridge: Cambridge University Press, 1988.

Barro, Robert J. and Xavier, Sala I Martin.. "Convergence across States and Regions." *Brookings Papers on Economic Activity,* Washington DC, 1991; 1, pp. 107-82.

Baumol, W. J. "Productivity Growth, Convergence and Welfare: What the Long Run Data Show." *American Economic Review,* December 1986; 76: pp. 1072-85.

Bell, Daniel . *The End of Ideology,* New York: Free Press, 1960.

Bellak, Christian. "International Trade, multinational enterprises, and industrial policy choice," in B. Unger and F. Van Waarden (eds), *Convergence or Diversity, Internationalization and Economic Policy Response* , Aldershot: Avebury, 1995.

Bennett, Colin J. "Review article: what is policy convergence and what causes it?." *British Journal of Political Science,* 1991, vol. 21.

Bernard Andrew B. and Durlauf, Steven N.. 'Convergence of International Output Movements' NBER (Cambridge, MA) Working Paper No. 3717, May 1991.

Boyer, Robert. 'The Convergence Hypothesis Revisited: Globalization but Still the Century of Nations?' CEPREMAP No. 9403, Paris, August 1993.

Buiter, Willem. "Should we worry about the fiscal numerology of Maastricht?" CEPR Discussion Paper No. 668 , Center for European Policy Research, London, June 1992.

_____ **and Kletzer, Kenneth M.**. "Persistent Differences in National Productivity Growth Rates with Common Technology and Free Capital Mobility: The Roles of Private Thrift, Public Debt, Capital Taxation and Policy Towards Human Capital Formation" NBER (Cambridge, MA) Working Paper No. 3637, February 1991.

Corvers, F. and Dankbaar, B.. "Bedrijven in Euregio Maas-Rijn kijken amper over de grens." *Geografie*, 1994, no. 3.

Crozier, Michel. *The Bureaucratic Phenomenon*, Chicago: University of Chicago Press, 1964.

Dehesa, Guillermo de la and Krugman, Paul. "EMU and the regions, Group of Thirty", *Occasional Papers*, Washington DC, 1992, No. 39.

Döhler, Marian. `Gesundheitspolitik nach der 'Wende'. Policy-Netzwerke und ordnungspolitischer Strategiewechsel in Großbritannien, den USA und der Bundesrepublik Deutschland*, Berlin: Sigma Bohn, 1990.

Dore, Ronald. "Goodwill and the spirit of market capitalism." *The British Journal of Sociology*, 1983, vol. 34.

_____. *Flexible Rigidities. Industrial Policy and Structural Adjustment in the Japanese Economy, 1970 - 1980*, London: Athlene Press, 1986.

Dye, Thomas R. *Politics in States and Communities*, Englewood Cliffs, New Jersey: Prentice Hall, 1991.

Eichener, Volker. "European health and safety regulations: No 'race to the bottom', " in B. Unger and F. Van Waarden (eds), *Convergence or Diversity? Internationalization and Economic Policy Response*, Aldershot: Avebury, 1995.

Eichengreen, Barry. "Is Europe an optimum currency area?" NBER (Cambridge,MA) Working Paper No. 3579, January 1991.

Engbersen, Godfried, "Poverty regimes and life chances: The road to anomia?," in B. Unger and F. Van Waarden, *Convergence or Diversity? Internationalization and Economic Policy Response*, Aldershot: Avebury, 1995.

Fukuyama, Francis. *The End of History and the Last Man*, New York, Free Press, 1992.

Gerschenkron, Alexander. "Economic Backwardness in Historical Perspective," in Bert F. Hoselitz, (ed) *The Progress of Underdeveloped Areas,* Chicago: Chicago University Press, 1952.

Goldthorpe, John H. "The end of convergence: Corporatist and dualist tendencies in modern western societies," in John H. Goldthorpe (ed), *Order and Conflict in Contemporary Capitalism*, Oxford: Oxford University Press, 1984.

Grande, Edgar. *Vom Monopol zum Wettbewerb? Die neokonservative Reform der Telekommunikation in Großbritannien und der Bundesrepublik Deutschland - eine vergleichende Analyse ökonomisch-politischer Konfiguration,* Wiesbaden: Deutscher Universitäts Verlag, 1989.

Grandner Thomas and Unger, Brigitte. 'The role of governance institutions for the change of economic politics'. Paper prepared for the Conference of the Society for Socioeconomics (SASE) New York, March 26-28, 1993.

Hall, S.G.; Robertson, D. and Wickens, M.R.. "Measuring convergence of the EC Economies." *The Manchester School*, supplement, June 1992, vol. LX.

Helliwell, John F. and Chung, Alan. 'Macroeconomic Convergence: International Transmission of Growth and Technical Progress' NBER (Cambridge, MA) Working Paper No. 3264, February 1990.

Hollingsworth, J. Rogers; Schmitter, Philippe C. and Streeck, Wolfgang (eds). *Governing Capitalist Economies. Performance and Control of Economic Sectors*, Oxford: Oxford University Press, 1994.

Immergut, Ellen. *Health Politics, Interests and Institutions in Western Europe*, Cambridge, Mass: Cambridge University Press, 1992.

Inkeles, Alex. "Convergence and divergence in industrial societies," in Mustafa O. Attir, Burkart Holzner, and Zdenek Suda (eds), *Directions of Change: Modernization Theory. Research and Reality*, Boulder, Colo: Westview Press, 1981.

Kelemen, Daniel R. "Environmental policy in the European Union: The struggle between Court, Commission and Council," in B. Unger and F. Van Waarden (eds), *Convergence or Diversity? Internationalization and Economic Policy Response*, Aldershot: Avebury, 1995.

Keller, Berndt. "European integration, workers' participation and collective bargaining: A Euro-pessimistic view," in B. Unger and F. Van Waarden (eds), *Convergence or Diversity? Internationalization and Economic Policy Response*, Aldershot: Avebury, 1995.

Kern, Horst and Schumann, Michael. *Industriearbeit und Arbeiterbewustsein,* Frankfurt am Main: Europaeische Verlagsanstalt, 1976.

Kerr, Clark. *The Future of Industrial Societies: Convergence or Continuing Diversity?*, Cambridge, Mass.: Harvard University Press, 1983.

Kitzmantel Edith and Moser, Erhard. "State competition with tax policy," in B. Unger and F. Van Waarden (eds), *Convergence or Diversity? Internationalization and Economic Policy Response*, Aldershot: Avebury, 1995.

Kuznets, S. "Economic Growth and Income Inequality." *American Economic Review*,1955, Vol. 45, no 1.

Lehmbruch, Gerhard. "Administrative Interessenvermittlung," in Adrienne Windhoff-Héritier (ed.), *Verwaltung und ihre Umwelt. Festschrift für Thomas Ellwein*, Opladen, 1987.

Lucas, Robert. "Why doesn't capital flow from rich to poor countries?." *American Economic Review*, Papers and Proceedings, 1990, Vol. 80, no. 2.

Mosley, Hugh. "The 'social dumping' threat of European integration: A critique," in B. Unger and F. Van Waarden (eds), *Convergence or Diversity? Internationalization and Economic Policy Response*, Aldershot: Avebury, 1995.

OECD, *Economic Outlook*, Paris: OECD, December 1993.

Sassen, Saskia. *The Global City: New York London Tokyo,* Princeton: Princeton University Press, 1991.

_____. "Labour mobility and migration policy: Lessons from Japan and the US," in B. Unger and F. Van Waarden (eds), *Convergence or Diversity? Internationalization and Economic Policy Response*,Aldershot: Avebury, 1995.

SER-COB. *Nieuwe kansen voor bedrijven in de grensregio's*, Staatsuitgeverij: The Hague, 1994.

Streissler, Erich. "Growth Models as Diffusion Processes: II. Empirical Implications." *Kyklos*, 32, 1979, 3: pp. 571-86.

Terhal, Petrus H. J. J. *World Inequality and Evolutionary Convergence, A Confrontation of the Convergence Theory of Pierre Teilhard de Chardin with Dualistic Integration*, PhD thesis, Erasmus University, Rotterdam, 1987.

Tinbergen, Jan. *The Theory of the Optimum Regime*, Amsterdam, North Holland, 1959.

_____. "Do communist free economies show a converging pattern?." *Soviet Studies*, 1961, vol. XII, no. 4.

Unger, Brigitte. "European integration and fiscal policy options," in B. Unger and F. Van Waarden (eds), *Convergence or Diversity? Internationalization and Economic Policy Response*, Aldershot: Avebury, 1995.

_____ and Van Waarden, Frans, (eds). *Convergence or Diversity? Internationalization and Economic Policy Response*, Aldershot: Avebury, 1995.

_____. "Introduction: An interdisciplinary approach to convergence," in B. Unger and F. Van Waarden (eds), *Convergence or Diversity? Internationalization and Economic Policy Response*, Aldershot: Avebury, 1995.

Van Waarden, Frans. "Persistence of national policy styles: A study of their institutional foundations," in B. Unger and F. Van Waarden (eds), *Convergence or Diversity? Internationalization and Economic Policy Response*, Aldershot: Avebury, 1995.

Veblen, Thorsten. *Imperial Germany and the Industrial Revolultion,* New York: Macmillan, 1915.

Vogel, David. *National Styles of Regulation. Environmental Policy in Great Britain and the United States,* Ithaca and London: Cornell University Press, 1986.

Waltman, Jerold L. and Studlar, Donley T. (eds). *Political Economy: Public Policies in the United States and Britain,* Jackson, Miss.: University Press of Mississippi, 1987.

Windhoff-Heritier, Adrienne. " 'Leaders' and 'Laggards' in European clean air policy," in B. Unger and F. Van Waarden (eds), *Convergence or Diversity? Internationalization and Economic Policy Response*,Aldershot: Avebury, 1995.

(global)   F16   129 - 46
519 531
532

7

DOES TRADE WITH THE SOUTH DISADVANTAGE UNSKILLED WORKERS IN THE NORTH?

S. Mansoob Murshed

University of Bradford, England

A theoretical macroeconomic model of North-South interaction is constructed to examine the impact of inter-regional trade on unskilled wages in the North. The model allows for process innovation in the form of R&D activities; both skilled and unskilled labour inputs enter into Northern production; real wages could be fixed by institutional considerations; and trade policy initiated by both regions is analyzed. It is not trade with the South, per se, which hurts unskilled labor in the North, but the nature of labor market imperfections and the process of technical change.

This chapter will present a macroeconomic model of North-South interaction to examine the effect of trade between the two regions on the welfare of unskilled workers in the North. The chapter is organized as follows. The next section provides a brief sketch of the background to the issues being considered and the literature on the subject. We then consider a detailed outline of the model that we employ. The section following that contains the analysis involved in varying parameters. We conclude by way of a summary with some policy implications.

Background and Motivation

The changing pattern of the international division of labor is one of the most topical economic issues of our times. In particular, the shift of competitive advantage in labor intensive manufacturing production from the richer OECD countries (North) to the poorer developing countries (South) has attracted a good deal of attention from commentators in developed countries.   These commentators include politicians, such as the American Presidential candidate Ross Perot and the former President of the European Commission Jacques Delors; journalists; trade unionists; and even church groups.   The reason for this concern is the recent decline in employment in the North's *traditional* manufacturing sector.   This has been accompanied by either or both rising unemployment or a fall in the wages of the unskilled group of the North's manufacturing labor force, the blue collar worker. This phenomenon of declining employment/wages of the less privileged group in the North's labor force is said to have sparked off major social unrest, as well as promoting increased inequality in income, wealth and opportunity.   More often than not, protection from the invidious sources of the competition driving these processes is sought for.   The culprit is usually identified to be the relatively poorer countries in the developing world or South; where it is stressed that low wages and generally exploitable conditions have led to the wholesale movement of certain manufacturing activities.

Perhaps so.   It is certainly true that total employment in manufacturing has declined in the North, whereas it has risen in the South.   As Lawrence and Slaughter (1993) indicate there has been a secular tendency for a decline in manufacturing employment, as a share of total employment, in the USA.   The same is true for most of the other industrialized OECD nations.   Accompanying this tendency there was a decline in *average* real wages in the USA during the 1980s (but not in other OECD countries).   Measured in terms of 1982 consumer prices, average real hourly earnings in the USA in 1992 were 13.1% below their 1973 level (Lawrence and Slaughter, 1993).   This decline in real wages took place in the 1980s.   Moreover, the burden of falling real earnings fell disproportionately on the unskilled segment of the labor force, increasing the earnings gap between skilled and unskilled in manufacturing.   This rise in income inequality between the skilled (who are often defined as non-production workers in empirical studies such as Lawrence and Slaughter, 1993) and unskilled (who are categorized as blue collar production workers), is in contrast to the 1945-79 period when the skilled-unskilled wage differential narrowed in the USA.   Many erstwhile production workers were forced into lower paying, low productivity, service sector jobs.   In the Western European segment of the North, real wages of all workers have not declined, due, perhaps, to the more generous compensation to the unemployed (including the long-term unemployed). But that part of the North has also witnessed a decline in traditional manufacturing employment.   The disadvantaged group (either in terms of employment or real earnings) are the unskilled part of the workforce in the entire North.

Meanwhile, employment in manufacturing has grown in the South; especially in East Asia and in those activities where the North has lost competitiveness. These regions of the South have sharply increased their share of manufactured exports to the North. This has led to the inevitable conclusion that North-South trade is inimical to the interests of unskilled production workers in the North, in terms of jobs and living standards. But equally there must be other factors, *internal* to the North, which contribute to this process of loss of competitiveness. These include technological change and innovation of new products in the North, as well as the nature of labor markets in the North. The purpose of this chapter is to present a macroeconomic model of North-South interaction with a role for process innovation (R&D) and a skilled/ unskilled labor dichotomy in the North.

Broadly speaking, there are five strands of literature relevant to North-South interaction which could lead to industrial relocation to the South, as well as disadvantaging unskilled labor in the North. The *first* can be described as the technical diffusion process. The paradigms here rely on an imperfectly competitive market structure (monopolistic competition) leading to the production of an increased variety of goods, see Dixit and Stiglitz (1977) on this. Krugman (1979) extends this idea to the North-South sphere. In his model the North innovates new products which the South eventually imitates. The number of the older goods produced in the South depends on the real wage differential between the two regions. Grossman and Helpman (1991) endogenize the process of innovation in the North and imitation in the South. Dollar (1986) constructs a North-South model with technical diffusion and two factors of production, where capital is internationally mobile. An increase in the South's labor supply and/or technical diffusion from the North eventually leads to a rise in its equilibrium capital stock, productive capacity and real wages in the South increase in comparison to the North. Related to this literature are the ideas of the endogenous growth theory, with its emphasis on human capital (skills) formation as being crucial to growth, see Romer (1990) for example. If the South manages to accumulate an impressively high stock of human capital, and this feature is combined with low relative wage costs, it gives that region added competitive advantage.

The *second* approach concerns itself with labor market imperfections in the North, see Layard *et al* (1991). Real wage rigidity could cause unskilled wages in the North to become too high. This may lead to the relocation of unskilled labor intensive manufactures to the South. Furthermore, it may induce labor saving technical progress in the North. The social security system has a role to play in this. In the Western European segment of the North there is a strong tendency for the unemployment benefit system to preserve the living standards of the unwaged. A decline in unskilled labor demand leads to quantity rationing, increased unemployment. By contrast, in the USA the same decline in demand can lead to a fall in real wages or employment in less remunerative jobs in the service sector, due to the less extensive benefit structure there for the long term unemployed.

The *third* strand can be described as the managed trade or the anti-free trade approach of many a policy maker. These arguments are most succinctly stated in Bhagwati (1994). Free trade with the South should be eschewed as it pauperizes unskilled labor in the North, as well as being detrimental to human rights and the environment. Indeed, much of the South's exports to the North is already heavily subject to protectionist measures in the North (see Page, 1994). Also, Krugman (1994) cites the calls made in certain quarters for *all* trade to be regulated along the lines of the Multi-Fibre Agreement, which assigns strict quotas to the textile and apparel exports of developing countries in industrialized countries.

The *fourth* type of paradigm can be characterized as the inverse "unequal exchange" approach, see Wood (1994) for a statement of these arguments. Unlike in the bulk of the traditional North-South literature, where the unequal exchange emanates from the North, the argument contained in Wood (1994) stresses that the very increase in trade itself, between the two regions, is disadvantageous to the unskilled in the North. The mechanism invoked is the Heckscher-Ohlin-Samuelson paradigm of international trade and the related Stolper-Samuelson theorem about relative factor payments. The North is relatively more abundantly endowed with skilled labor compared to the South. An increase in trade with the South will therefore raise that region's exports of unskilled labor intensive manufactured products. Employment in the unskilled manufacturing sector in the North will decline. Given the presence of specific factors and inter-sectoral labor immobility (unskilled labor), unemployment ensues in the North. He also argues that the disadvantaging aspects of trade with the South will bear most heavily on the most unskilled segment of any contracting industry in the North. With regard to falling relative wages of unskilled manufacturing workers in the North, this can only occur if and only if the relative *price* of unskilled labor intensive goods decline, by the Stolper-Samuelson theorem.

The empirical evidence on the contribution of the Stolper-Samuelson process towards the lowering of the unskilled manufacturing relative wage in the USA is the subject of some controversy. Lawrence and Slaughter (1993) show that the relative price of unskilled labor intensive manufactured goods actually rose in the 1980s, compared to skill intensive manufactures such as computers, whose prices fell reflecting technical progress in those industries. This is disputed by Sachs and Shatz (1994), who use different data sets to demonstrate their opposite point of view. As far as the competing hypothesis is concerned, the empirical contribution of labor augmenting technical progress towards lowering the relative real wage of the unskilled in the USA (defined as non-agricultural production workers); Lawrence and Slaughter (1993) find considerable empirical evidence to support this process. In fact, they find that technical change in manufacturing was *biased* towards skilled labor (non-production workers) and more concentrated in activities using more skilled labor (computers, for example). Thus, according to them, the relative decline in the real compensation of unskilled manufacturing labor in the USA is explained mainly by biased technical progress raising the productivity of the skilled. Trade with the South cannot explain the fall in unskilled labor's relative wages, as the prices of manufactures intensively utilizing this factor actually increased. Thus, if anything, by the Stolper-Samuelson theorem, the relative wages of the unskilled should have risen.

Productivity and wages in the service sector might help explain the puzzle of the falling relative wage of the unskilled in the USA. As Leamer (1995) points out, declining employment in manufacturing need not cause a fall in average real wages, if the workers released from manufacturing can be reabsorbed in a high paying/ highly productive service sector. In the USA and the UK the recent expansion in the service sector has mainly been in low paid occupations. This points to a low productivity increase, in contrast to the experience of nations such as Germany, France and Japan. Since the employment share of services and non-traded goods has increased, implying that displaced unskilled workers and new unskilled entrants to the labor market work in low productivity/low wage service sector jobs, this partially explains the skilled (non-production)- unskilled (production) wage gap in manufacturing, at least in the USA.

Another contributory process at work might be the impact of greater globalization, and increased trade, on the level of worker unionization and the willingness of firms to recruit from a pool of unionized labor. Adamson and Partridge (1997, this book) empirically demonstrate the indirect impact of trade on wages via the unionization mechanism in the USA. Increased international exposure might reduce the probability of firms hiring unionized workers, lowering union rents extracted by production workers.

Increased long-term capital flows from North to South in the form of foreign direct investment can also raise the relative size of the South's capital stock, especially that part devoted to manufacturing unskilled labor intensive products.

This process, when combined with the South's lower wage structure, can further disadvantage the unskilled in the North. This point was emphasized in Sachs and Shatz (1994). Given that the 1980s saw substantive negative net transfers to the South, in the form of the South's debt servicing to the Northern financial sector; and the fact that foreign direct investment from North to South has only recommenced substantially very recently, we may be skeptical of the actual empirical weight of this process.

As such the trade based argument, favored by Wood (1994) as well as Sachs and Shatz (1994) as an explanation for declining real wages and employment of the unskilled in the USA, is subject to the same critique as was Emannuel's (1972) notion of the opposite type of unequal exchange. That is to say, North-South trade is more a symptom than the cause of disadvantaging tendencies. This argument is also stated by Deardorff in his comments on Sachs and Shatz (1994, page 71), where he argues that international trade cannot be viewed as an independent *exogenous* process; but rather that trade *reflects* the effects of other processes in motion such as technical change. Clearly, greater globalization results from changes, which include *inter alia* phenomenon such as a higher degree of openness and trade liberalization.

Finally, a *fifth* strand is related to the macroeconomic policies pursued with varying rigor in all the countries of the North in the 1980s. Contractionary monetary policy (all major OECD nations), expansionary fiscal policy (the budget deficits in the USA) and the effects of natural resource based revenues (UK's North Sea oil revenues) can all contribute to exchange rate over-valuation. If this feature is persistent, as in the case of the dollar and sterling in the 1980s, it might go a long way towards contributing to de-industrialization. Some of these industries could relocate in the South.

The innovation in the model in this chapter is that it marries at least the first three of the different strands mentioned above into one single model. The first strand is present as our model allows for process innovation, along the lines suggested in Shell (1966). The North is the technological leader, and part of its R&D spills over to the South as common knowledge. We accommodate the second, as we not only have both skilled and unskilled labor inputs in Northern production, but also let real wages be fixed by institutional considerations, allowing for both quantity as well as wage adjustments in the Northern labor market. Our model explicitly analyzes trade policy initiated by the North to restrict competition from goods produced in the South, as well as export promoting subsidies in the South aimed at boosting its market share in the North. The model is in the macro-structuralist genre, see for example Taylor (1983) and Murshed (1992).

The Model

Both North and South produce a composite good which is traded between the regions. R&D expenditures augment aggregate supply in both regions. Equilibrium in the goods market, for both the regions (two composite commodities), implies the equality of aggregate demand (expenditure) with aggregate supply (income). In both regions excess demand (supply) causes output to increase (decrease). We could, however, make excess demand respond positively to the terms of trade (prices) without altering our results.

$$Q_N(R^N) = D_N(Y_N^D) + R^G + X_N (Y_S^D ; P_S) - P_S X_S (Y_N^D ; P_S) \tag{1}$$

Let us begin by outlining equilibrium in the Northern goods market: The right hand side denotes aggregate demand and the left hand side aggregate supply. Q_N is output in the North which is an increasing function of R&D (R^N) relevant to the North described in greater detail below; Y_N^D is disposable income in the North; D_N is total absorption, inclusive of imports; R^G indicates public expenditure on R&D in the North, which also benefits the South; X_N are exports of the North; X_S are the imports of the North; P_N, the Northern price is set equal to unity, P_S is thus the North-South terms of trade. Note that the absorption, import and export functions can be derived from the utility functions of representative consumers in the North and South. Disposable income is defined by:

$$Y_N^D = [1 - \tau_r] Q_N (R^N) \tag{2}$$

where, τ_r is a tax imposed on output to finance the public component of R&D, R^G.

The manner in which R&D is incorporated in the model is that: (i) in the North it lowers the input requirement of unskilled labor in production, corresponding to biased technical progress in favor of the skilled; and (ii) in the South it augments output supply. These two processes are similar in an aggregate macroeconomic sense, as will become apparent presently.

The total supply of R&D contains a public goods part in both the North and the South, and a private component in the North. Total R&D activities in both regions is thus:

$$R = R^G + R^P \tag{3}$$

where R^G is publicly financed R&D and is a public good financed through taxation. Each region's R&D results in expenditure in that particular region. In the North the public goods component of R&D expenditure adds to a fund of non-excludable general knowledge as in Romer (1990) and Grossman-Helpman (1991). This is in line with an idea going back to Shell (1966), also used by Lahiri and Mehran (1991) in a North-South model. Basically the idea is that a part of inventive activity and innovation is a public good, financed by taxation.

Northern public R&D spills over to the South as common general knowledge, but the South's R&D does not benefit the North. This is a fundamental asymmetry in the model. This is justified by the North's technological superiority and leadership over the South. The South merely follows and imitates the North, as in Krugman (1979) and Dollar (1986). The nature of Southern R&D can be described as a public investment process in human capital, which allows the South to imitate the North. This activity is publicly financed and leads to an increase in output supply in the model. In summary, therefore, total public R&D in both regions is:

$$R_N^G = \tau_r Q_N$$
$$R_S^G = \tau_s Q_S \tag{4}$$

τ_s is the tax imposed on the output of the South, Q_S, to finance the South's public R&D.

Private R&D activities are conducted exclusively in the North:

$$R^P = R^P(\theta) \tag{5}$$

Private R&D is similar to the firm specific "blueprint" idea contained in Romer (1990). Private R&D in the North is part of the Q_N production process. Note that private R&D in the North does not directly benefit the South, an assumption that we can easily alter. An increase in θ increases the productivity of existing private

R&D, R^P, in the North. This increase could represent a response to the real wages of the unskilled being too high (real wage resistance); and/or a result of exogenous technical progress. We choose not to endogenize the technical progress element of R&D as we regard this process to be exogenous for the aggregate macroeconomy.

Thus, the R&D relevant to the North which raises Northern output is:

$$R^N = R^P(\theta) + \tau_r Q_N$$
$$or \quad Q_N = (\tau_r; R^P(\theta)) \tag{6}$$

For the South, the amount of R&D which raises its output is:

$$R^S = [\tau_r Q_N + \tau_s Q_S]$$
$$or \quad Q_S = (\tau_r ; \tau_s) \tag{7}$$

Thus, the South benefits not only from the R&D it pays for itself, but also from Northern public R&D.

Note that R&D expenditures contain an endogenous element and an exogenous component. The endogeneity is because R&D rises as output rises. Also in the North private R&D may be increased if the real wages of the unskilled are too high. The exogeneity emanates from the choice of tax rates to finance public R&D, and the exogenous productivity of private R&D in the North.

Let us outline the supply relationship for Q_N. We fix the capital stock and postulate the input of two types of labor, skilled and unskilled in the Northern production process. Skilled labor in Q_N production is employed in private R&D, the process of producing, improving and implementing the blueprint type of R&D. Employing a mark up process which is consistent with profit maximization under imperfect competition:

$$P_N = [1 + \pi][a_u(R^N)W_u + a_r W_r]$$
$$where \quad a_u = L_u/Q_N \; ; \; a_r = L_r^P/Q_N \tag{8}$$

here a_u and a_r are the labor (L)-output ratios involved in the input of ordinary (unskilled) labor and skilled (private R&D) labor in Q_N production; W indicates the wage rates of the two types of labor; π is the desired profit rate of firms engaged in production.

Two points are noteworthy here. The first is that an increase in R&D lowers the demand for unskilled labor's input in the production process. Secondly, wage rates could be subject to labor market imperfections as discussed in Layard et al (1991). For example, a fall in demand for unskilled labor can lead to the increased unemployment of the unskilled at going wage rates as is more prevalent in Western Europe, or in the fall in unskilled wages as is common in the USA; or both a fall in wages and employment. At different times either or both of these processes may be applicable. Noting that $P_N = 1$, we can re-write (8) as:

$$Q_N = [1 + \pi][L_u(R^N)W_u + L_r^P W_r] \tag{9}$$

From (9) it is apparent that if the share of the skilled in national income ($L_r^P W_r$) rises, it has to be at the expense of the unskilled ($L_u W_u$) given fixed profit rates. This means a decline in either the wages or the employment of the unskilled, or both.

Turning finally to the economy of the South, equilibrium in the goods market can be described as:

$$P_s Q_s(\tau_r ; \tau_s) = P_s D_s(Y_s^D) + \tau_s P_s Q_s + P_s X_s(.) - X_I \tag{10}$$

the South's output Q_s increases with public R&D in both North and South. Disposable income in the South is written as:

$$Y_s^D = [1 - \tau_s]P_s Q_s(R^S) \tag{11}$$

where as noted a fraction of income, τ_s, is taxed to finance, say, human capital formation which enables skills to be accumulated and more output to be produced. Notice that we do not explicitly specify an equation for production in the South. For the sake of simplicity we say that the employment of one type of homogenous labor rises in the South as output increases. This is in line with Wood's (1994) notion that (manufacturing) output in the South utilizes mainly basically skilled labor.

Variations in Parameters

A Rise in the Productivity of the North's Private R&D

An increase in the productivity of the North's R&D arises because of technical progress and/or real wages of the unskilled being too high.   The effect on *equilibrium* output in the North is not clear cut. This is because, although output supply rises due to an increase in R&D productivity, demand rises less than proportionately. Also, a part of the rise in output is subject to a proportionate tax to finance public R&D.

The South's output is totally unaffected by the rise in the productivity of the North's private R&D. This is because we did not make the South's output an increasing function of private R&D in the North. If we had done so, the output of the South may have risen.

The above results can be depicted diagrammatically in Q_N and Q_S space (figure 1). The NN schedule depicts equilibrium in the Northern goods market; the SS does the same for the South. They are both upward sloping because a rise in output in one region increases the demand for the output in the other. In figure 1, the rise in the Northern tax rate shifts the NN rightwards and the SS downwards from the initial equilibrium at point A. The new equilibrium is at point B.

As far as the employment of unskilled labor in the North is concerned, this can be deduced by totally differentiating (9) with respect to θ:

$$\frac{dL_u}{d\theta} = \frac{dQ_N}{d\theta} = (1+\pi)[L_u \frac{dW_u}{d\theta} + W_u \ L_{uI} \frac{dR^N}{d\theta} + W_r \frac{dL_R^P}{d\theta} + L_R^P \frac{dW_r}{d\theta}] \tag{12}$$

There is an unambiguous decline in the employment and/or wages of unskilled labor in the North. Input of skilled labor and/or their wages will increase.

An Increase in the Southern Tax Rate (Rise in Public R&D)

This would be a consequence of a move by the South to raise its R&D activities or human capital formation financed by taxation. As far as output in the North is concerned, there will be no effect. This is because public R&D in the South does not spill over to benefit output supply in the North.

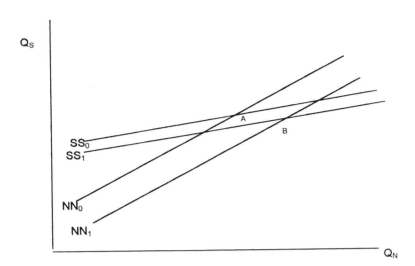

Figure 1: Rise in the productivity of private R&D

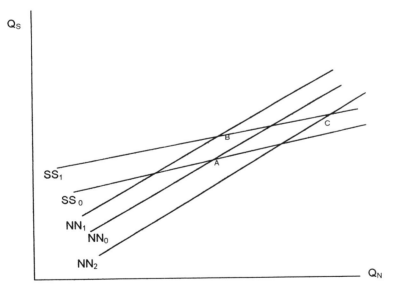

Figure 2: Increases in tax rates

A necessary condition for an expansion in the South's output after a rise in publicly financed R&D is a high supply elasticity of output with respect to an increase in R&D. This will ensure that the rise in output and the increase in demand is substantial. Formally we require:

$$\gamma_s = \tau_s Q_{S2} / Q_S$$

In figure 2 the SS schedule moves upwards, and the NN leftwards with the new equilibrium at point B.

An Increase in the Northern Tax Rate (Rise in Public R&D)

A similar rise in public R&D in the North results in ambiguous output effects. Again, however, a high value of output supply elasticity with respect to public R&D is necessary for a rise in equilibrium Northern output. Formally we require a high value of the following:

$$\gamma_n = \tau_r Q_{N1} / Q_N$$

Unlike in the case of a rise in public R&D in the South, which did not benefit the North; the rise in Northern publicly financed R&D does spill over and has a positive impact on Southern output. The necessary condition for a rise in the South's output are similar to that for a rise in the North's output. In figure 2, from point A, the new equilibrium is depicted at point C, showing a rise in output in both regions.

As far as employment of unskilled labor in the North is concerned:

$$\frac{dL_u}{d\tau_r} = \frac{dQ_N}{d\tau_r} = (1+\pi)[L_u \frac{dW_u}{d\tau_r} + W_u L_{u1} \frac{dR^N}{d\tau_r} + W_r \frac{dL_R^P}{d\tau_r} + L_R^P \tag{13}$$

The effect on unskilled labor is negative, the impact on skilled labor in Northern production will be positive.

An Export Subsidy by the South

An export subsidy by the South on its own goods, lowers the price of its exports to the North to $P_S(1-s)$. Our idea here is to encapsulate the variety of export promotion strategies adopted by successful exporting nations in the South. The object of the subsidy is to ensure expenditure switching away from Northern towards Southern goods in the North. This subsidy is financed by a tax on domestic disposable income $= sP_SQ_S$. Thus disposable income in the South is further curtailed. We need to rewrite the equilibrium conditions for the North and South:

$$Q_N(R^P(\theta);\tau_r) = D_N(Y_N^D) + \tau_r Q_N(.) + X_N(Y_S^D;P_S) - P_SX_S(Y_N^D; P_S(1-s)) \qquad (14)$$

where disposable income in the South becomes:

$$Y_S^D = P_SQ_S - \tau_s P_SQ_S - sP_SX_S \qquad (15)$$

Similarly for the South, (10) becomes

$$P_SQ_S(\tau_r; \tau_s) = P_SD_S(Y_S^D) + \tau_s P_SQ_S + P_SX_S(Y_N^D;P_S(1-s)) - X_N(.) \qquad (16)$$

Northern output declines as the South increases its export share in the North. The employment of the unskilled will also decline. The South's output will rise only if the price elasticity of its exports is greater than unity (elastic). This is the condition for the export subsidy to work and ensure a sufficient rise in export demand to boost output.

In figure 3, the initial equilibrium at point A; and the new equilibrium is at point B showing a rise in output in the South and a decline in Northern output.

An Import Tariff Imposed by the North on the South's Goods:

Commercial policy is engaged in by the North to protect its import competing sectors from competition in the South. The *ad-valorem* tariff, m, imposed by the North raises the price of the South's good in the North, the revenue from the tariff is redistributed back (in a lump sum manner) to the public in the North. The Northern goods market equation becomes:

$$Q_N(R^P(\theta); \ \tau_r) = D_N(Y_N^D) + \tau_{rQ_N}(.) + X_N(Y_S^D; P_S) - P_S X_S(Y_N^D; \ P_S(1+m)(1+m) \quad (17)$$

Disposable income in the North becomes:

$$Y_N^D = Q_N - \tau_r Q_N + mP_S X_S \quad (18) \tag{18}$$

Thus the North's disposable income rises with the tariff. The South's equilibrium relation is:

$$P_S Q_S(\tau_r \ ; \tau_s \ ) = P_S D_S(Y_S^D) + \tau_s P_S Q_S + P_S X_S(Y_N^D; \ P_S(1+ \ m)) - X_N(.) \quad (19)$$

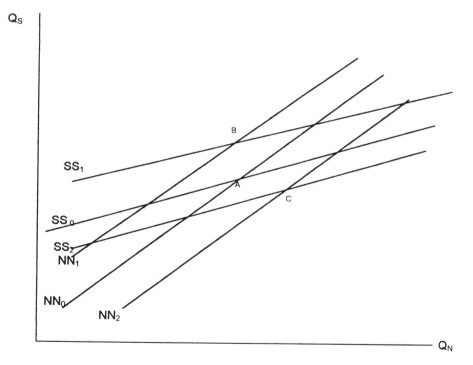

Figure 3: Commercial policy

The necessary condition for a rise in the North's output is the same as the condition for a rise in the South's output when an export subsidy was instituted by the South: the South's exports must be price elastic. The object of the tariff is to switch expenditure from Southern to Northern goods. A high price elasticity guarantees its success. If Northern output rises, employment of the unskilled is likely to increase, other things being equal. Southern output declines as a result of Northern commercial policy. In figure 3 the outcome of a Northern tariff is shown at point C with Northern output rising and the South's output declining.

Commercial policy initiated by either the North (import tariff) or the South (export subsidy) is similar to a zero sum policy move.

Summary and Policy Implications

To conclude briefly our model demonstrates that technical change (R&D involving process innovation) in the North can disadvantage unskilled labor in that region. In some circumstances the benefits of Northern R&D spill over to the South. It is not trade with the South, *per se*, which hurts the unskilled labor in the North. Rather it is the innovative nature of capitalism and labor market characteristics that are responsible. International trade is, ultimately, a reflection of the processes in motion in the global economy, and not a cause of events. Furthermore, it is implausible to suggest that the North with its dominant economic and political power is in any overall sense disadvantaged by interaction with the South.

Successful export promotion by the South does displace Northern labor. But this is often engaged in at the behest of Northern governments and international agencies, who in the past actively encouraged market penetration by selected countries in the South, motivated by strategic considerations during the cold war. Protectionism in the North directed towards the goods of the South does appear to promote the interests of Northern unskilled workers in the short run. It should be noted that such protectionist measures are *already* well in place in the North (Bhagwati, 1994). But this sort of protectionism flies in the face of the received capitalist wisdom of the last three centuries, which accepts that comparative or competitive advantage moves on, and is ultimately self-defeating. Also, some of the developing countries of the present are important markets of the future.

The vast social problems engendered by the mass unemployment/low wages of the unskilled in the North does merit more than passing attention. The answers lie in labor markets. The solutions could be: (i) Promoting the acquisitions of skills in Northern labor markets. This is indicated by the effects of increased taxation in the North to finance more public R&D in our model. (ii) Encouraging flexibility of wages in West European labor markets. (iii) Providing more income support to the long term unemployed, particularly in the USA. (iv) Providing more publicly supported employment for the long-term unemployed, especially in Europe. In the final analysis, the political will and a collective social decision to meet the considerable *costs* of these measures has to be present. The alternative is a growing social acceptance of increased inequality and deprivation amongst a segment of the population, akin to the situation prevalent a century ago.

References

Adamson D. and Partridge, M. D.. "The Influence of International Trade on Union Firm Hiring and Worker Union Choice," in Satya Dev Gupta, ed. *Political Economy of Globalization*, Norwell, Mass: Kluwer Academic Publishers, 1997.

Bhagwati, J. "Free Trade: Old and New Challenges." *Economic Journal,* 1994; 104: pp. 231-46.

Dollar, D. "Technological Innovation, Capital Mobility, and the Product Cycle in North-South Trade", *American Economic Review* ,1986, 76, pp. 177-90.

Dixit, A. and Stiglitz, J. E. "Monopolistic Competition and Optimum Product Diversity." *American Economic Review,* 1977, 67, pp. 297-308.

Dornbusch, R. *Dollars, Debts and Deficits*, Cambridge: MIT Press, 1986.

Emmanuel, A. *Unequal Exchange: A Study of the Imperialism of Trade*, New York: Monthly Review Press, 1972.

Grossman, G. M. and Helpman, E. "Endogenous Product Cycles." *Economic Journal,* 1991, 101, pp. 1214-29.

Krugman, P. "A Model of Innovation, Technology Transfer, and the World Distribution of Income." *Journal of Political Economy*, 1979, 87, pp. 253-66.

Krugman, P. "Does Third World Growth Hurt First World Prosperity?" *Harvard Business Review*, 1994, July-August, pp. 113-21.

Lahiri, S. and Mehran, H. A. "Terms of Trade, Endogenous Technological Progress and Equilibrium Growth in a North-South Model", University of Essex Discussion Paper, 1991.

Lawrence, R. Z. and Slaughter, M. J. "International Trade and American Wages in the 1980s: Giant Sucking Sound or Small Hiccup?', *Brookings Papers in Economic Activity*, 1993, Microeconomics (2), pp. 161-226.

Layard, R.; Jackman, R. and Nickell, S. *Unemployment: Macroeconomic Performance and the Labor Market*, Oxford: Oxford University Press, 1991.

Leamer E. A. "The Heckscher-Ohlin Model in Theory and Practice." *Princeton Studies in International Finance*, 1994, vol. 77

Murshed, S. M. *Analytical Models of North-South Interaction*, London: Academic Press, 1992.
Page, S. *How Developing Countries Trade: The Institutional Constraints*, London: Routledge, 1994

Romer, P. "Endogenous Technical Change." *Journal of Political Economy*, 1990, 98, pp. S71-102.

Sachs, J. and H. J. Shatz. "Trade and Jobs in U S Manufacturing." *Brookings Papers in Economic Activity*, 1994, 1, pp. 1-84.

Shell, K. "Towards a Theory of Inventive Activity and Capital Accumulation." *American Economic Review*, 1966, 56, pp. 62-68.

Taylor, L. *Structuralist Macroeconomics*, New York: Basic Books, 1983.

Wood, A. *North-South Trade, Employment and Inequality: Changing Fortunes in a Skill Driven World*, Oxford: Clarendon Press, 1994.

8

THE INFLUENCE OF INTERNATIONAL TRADE ON UNION FIRM HIRING AND WORKER UNION CHOICE

Dwight W. Adamson

South Dakota State University, USA

Mark D. Partridge

St. Cloud State University, USA

Recently, income inequality in advanced countries has increased. Empirical evidence suggests that declining labor movements is one cause. Union opposition to free trade policies suggests that trade damages the union movement, which indirectly increases income inequality. Greater trade shares may hinder unions by reducing the likelihood that workers enter the union sector. A bivariate partial observability probit model is used to predict union choice. The model estimates the probability of workers wanting to belong to a union and the probability of union firms hiring these workers. The results suggest that trade has had some adverse effects on union choice.

The U.S. labor market has undergone dramatic transformations since the late 1960s (Bound and Johnson 1992; Freeman and Katz 1994). First, after 1973, growth in real wages for most Americans dramatically slowed and outright declined for many low-skilled workers. Second, income inequality began to increase sometime in the 1970s and accelerated in the 1980s, reflecting the greater returns to education and skill over this time period (Bound and Johnson 1992). Third, the U.S. labor movement suffered a precipitous decline in the share of the labor force that it represented. The declining labor movement has been offered as one reason for increased income inequality (Freeman 1993; Freeman and Katz 1994). That is, blue collar and less-skilled worker wages tend to be greater if they are unionized.

Moreover, unions can indirectly increase nonunion blue collar wages through a union threat effect, where nonunion employers essentially "bribe" their work force with higher compensation to deter union organizing.

Since these labor market transformations have occurred concurrently with rapid increases in foreign trade, one possible explanation for these labor market changes is that greater trade has altered basic labor market institutions such as unions. For example, union opposition to the North American Free Trade Agreement (NAFTA) and to GATT exemplifies the staunch resistance to free trade in general by U.S. union leaders. However, research has indicated that trade has relatively little influence on average U.S. wages (e.g., Partridge 1993; Freeman and Katz 1991). Notwithstanding, union opposition may have arisen because trade influences the likelihood that individuals belong to unions. That is, greater trade either reduces the likelihood individuals are willing to work in the organized sector or it reduces the likelihood that unionized employers will expand their work force. By separating workers' demand for unionization from unionized firms' hiring decisions, the effects of trade on union strength, and ultimately on income inequality, can be better understood. Therefore, this chapter focuses on trade's impact on U.S. labor union strength and the implications for economic restructuring and equity.

International Trade and Labor Market Earnings

There is a theoretical basis to believe that trade is a major cause in the decline in U.S. wage growth and in greater income inequality.[1] First, international convergence of European and Japanese industries since World War II, along with more recent convergence of middle income nations such as Korea, have weakened many U.S. industries (e.g., Johnson and Stafford 1993). Specifically, Johnson and Stafford suggested greater trade may have reduced wages in U.S. industries where the "U.S. level" of technology was attained in other countries. Likewise, Borjas and Ramey (1994) contend that trade's influence on durable good manufacturing plays a prominent role in the U.S. labor market. Generally, the arguments of Johnson and Stafford and Borjas and Ramey suggest that greater foreign competition has reduced the availability of quasi-rents for the affected American industries. This reduction in quasi-rents could reduce U.S. union wages when unions are extracting industry rents. Less-skilled blue collar workers also tend to predominate in industries where the technology is more readily available throughout the world (e.g., durable good manufacturing). Hence, less-skilled workers' wages may have been especially hurt by international convergence and the resulting increase in foreign competition. A second reason to expect that international trade may affect the labor market and increase U.S. income inequality is the Heckscher-Ohlin-Samuelson (HOS) trade model. The HOS model implies that greater trade will increase the returns of a nation's abundant factor relative to the less abundant factor. Thus, the HOS model suggests that U.S. skilled labor will fare relatively better than unskilled labor.

Empirical studies, nonetheless, have found mixed results regarding the influence of trade on earnings. Several studies have examined the response of average industry wages to changes in industry import and export shares. The typical finding is that changes in trade shares have only a modest impact on wages (e.g., Freeman and Katz 1991). Using individual or union contract data, Macpherson and Stewart (1990), Partridge (1993; forthcoming), and Blumenfeld and Partridge (1996) found that trade has had little influence on average earnings but that the actual effect depends on the industry's level of unionization.

Using a labor supply and demand framework, other studies have examined the impact of foreign trade on wages. These studies typically assess the net number of low-skilled and high-skilled jobs created by changes in imports and exports. A representative study is by Borjas et al. (1992), which found only modest trade impacts on wages and income inequality. Wood (1994) also uses a factor-content-of-trade calculation and found that trade between developed and developing nations has lowered the wages of less-skilled workers in advanced countries by a greater amount than what has been previously suspected. Specifically, Wood argues that workers in a particular industry that are displaced by developing country imports are more likely to be less skilled than the typical worker in the industry. However, others are skeptical that developing-country imports have played an important role in the U.S. labor market. This follows because the U.S. share of GDP that is accounted by imports from low-wage countries (besides oil) is less than 3% and has not dramatically increased in the last 30 years (Burtless 1995).

Other studies have examined how changes in import and export prices have influenced the U.S. labor market. Lawrence and Slaughter (1993) argued that relative price changes have *favored* low-skill-intensive industries versus high-skill-intensive industries. They suggest that this implies that trade has played little role in recent U.S. labor market trends. Conversely, Sachs and Shatz (1994) argued that relative price changes have instead favored high-skill-intensive industries, suggesting trade has played an important role in recent labor market trends--but they acknowledge that other factors are also at work.

Overall, one of the most effective ways for less-skilled workers and blue collar workers to earn better wages has been through collective bargaining. In 1983, among full-time wage and salary earners, the median usual wage for union members was 34.7% above nonunion workers (U.S. Department of Labor). This gap rose to 37.0% by 1994. Thus, to the extent that international trade indirectly affects the labor market by reducing unionization, it reduces wages for many less-skilled workers. In fact, the superficial evidence is consistent with greater foreign trade reducing unionization. The annual 1960-1994 correlation between the percent of the nonagricultural labor force that belongs to a union with the manufacturing trade share (imports plus exports divided by shipments) equaled -.93, where similar correlations follow for import and export shares.[2] Thus, the evidence is consistent with greater trade being one cause of the decline of the labor movement. However, correlation does not mean causation. For example, other industrial nations which are exposed to significantly greater foreign trade shares than the United States (e.g., Canada, Germany) have not experienced major declines in unionization (Freeman 1988). Therefore, trade may not be a major cause of the decline in U.S. unions.

Given that trade has been increasing while unionization has been decreasing, the influence of foreign trade and unionization on wages should be further investigated. Data from the NBER Immigration, Trade, and Labor Markets Data Files (Abowd 1991) along with data derived from other sources will be used. The data set contains complete data on 428 four-digit manufacturing industries (22 relatively small industries had incomplete data and were omitted).

Because the most rapid trade growth occurred between 1960 and 1985--especially for imports, a closer examination of that period should provide insights into the effects of trade. Panel 1 of Table 1 contains descriptive statistics for some important manufacturing variables for 1960 and 1985. Note that the typical manufacturing industry became exposed to significantly more trade and that exports grew much less than imports over the period. In fact, the typical U.S. import share grew about 400%.

Industry composition also changed during the period. Following Lawrence (1984), Partridge (1993), and Blumenfeld and Partridge (1996), manufacturing is divided into four sectors to illustrate these changes. The first sector is high-tech (HT), characterized by high degrees of both human capital and R&D, and by short product cycles (e.g., chemicals, aerospace, computers, some industrial machinery). The next two sectors are characterized by a common technology that is readily available throughout the world. The first is the labor-intensive common technology sector (CTL) (e.g., apparel, footwear) and the second is the capital-intensive common technology sector (CTK) (e.g., steel, autos). The final sector is the natural resource-intensive sector (NR), which is characterized by the intensive use of natural resources in the manufacturing process (e.g., food processing, lumber, refined oil).

Table 1 shows that the U.S. HT share of manufacturing employment increased from about 27% to 34% over the period, while the other three sectors declined. The relative gain of the HT sector is consistent with Johnson and Stafford's (1993) international convergence hypothesis.[3] Also, to the extent that the CTL and CTK industries comprise the medium technology industries referred to by Johnson and Stafford, changes in relative earnings support their hypothesis. Specifically, average real earnings for HT nonproduction workers increased by 15.8% between 1960 and 1985, while they increased by only 8.9% and 11.6% in the CTL and CTK industries. A similar pattern followed for production earnings.

To examine trade's impact on earnings, the following model of the 1960 to 1985 change in manufacturing earnings at the four-digit industry level is specified:

$$\Delta \log \text{Earning}_i = \alpha + \beta_1 \Delta \text{Export Share} + \beta_2 \Delta \text{Import Share} +$$
$$\beta_3 \Delta \text{Export*Unionization} + \beta_4 \Delta \text{Import*Unionization} + \beta_5 \text{HT} + \qquad (1)$$
$$\beta_6 \text{CTL} + \beta_7 \text{CTK} + \beta_8 \Delta \text{Unionization} + \beta_9 1974 \text{ Unionization} + \Gamma Z + e_i.$$

where i denotes industry and e is an error term.[4] Equation (1) is estimated separately for production and nonproduction workers to capture different patterns that exist between relatively less-skilled production workers and more-skilled nonproduction workers.

Import share, export share, and in some specifications, their interaction with unionization are included as independent variables to account for the changes in trade intensity. The import and export share coefficients are respectively expected to be negative and positive. Based on the findings of previous studies (e.g., Macpherson and Stewart 1990; Partridge 1993), the import share-unionization and the export share-unionization coefficients are expected to be positive and negative (i.e., the direct influence of trade share on wages is mitigated in more unionized industries). Dummies for the HT, CTL, and CTK sectors are included to account for differences by sector, where the NR sector is the omitted

Table 1. Variable Definitions and Means (PANEL 1[a])

VARIABLE	DEFINITION	1960 MEANS	1985 MEANS
Avg. Non Prod. Earnings	Average nonproduction worker annual earnings deflated by the Consumer Price Index (1982-1984=100).	24048.0 (4230.5)	27543.0 (5004.4)
Avg. Prod. Earnings	Average production worker annual earnings deflated by the Consumer Price Index.	15734.0 (3973.3)	18401.0 (5662.7)
Export Share	Exports divided by domestic output multiplied by 100.	4.28 (5.93)	8.50 (11.1)
Import Share	Imports divided by domestic output plus imports multiplied by 100: Import Share=(Imports/(Output+Imports))*100.	2.30 (4.62)	10.98 (11.39)
High-Tech	A dummy variable for a high-tech manufacturing industry.[b]	0.267 (0.44)	0.337 (0.47)
Labor-Inten. Common-Tech	A dummy variable for a labor-intensive common-tech manufacturing industry.	0.184 (0.39)	0.159 (0.37)
Capital-Inten. Common-Tech	A dummy variable for a capital-intensive common-tech manufacturing industry.	0.324 (0.469)	0.320 (0.47)
Natural Res.	A dummy variable for a natural resource-intensive manufacturing industry.	0.226 (0.42)	0.184 (0.39)
Percent Union	The percent of the labor force that is unionized.[c]	38.68 (15.10)	27.62 (13.64)
1974 %Union	Union density in 1974.	36.9 (14.3)	36.9 (14.3)

Table 1. 1960-1985 Change in Annual Earnings Regression Results (PANEL 2ᵃ)

VARIABLE	PRODUCTION WORKERS			NONPRODUCTION WORKERS		
	(1)	(2)	(3)	(4)	(5)	(6)
ΔExport Share	0.002 (2.51)	0.004 (2.04)	0.003 (1.74)	0.0008 (1.43)	0.004 (3.02)	0.005 (3.25)
ΔImport Share	-0.002 (1.90)	-0.004 (1.96)	-0.003 (1.57)	-0.0003 (0.31)	-0.002 (0.70)	-0.0008 (0.36)
Δ(Export x Unionization)		-5.5E-5 (1.13)	-5.2E-5 (1.10)		-0.0001 (2.78)	-0.0001 (3.14)
Δ(Import x Unionization)		8.0E-5 (1.28)	6.9E-5 (1.09)		3.9E-5 (0.46)	2.7E-5 (0.32)
High-Tech			-0.023 (0.63)			-0.014 (0.31)
Labor-Intensive Common-Tech			-0.080 (2.89)			-0.081 (1.71)
Capital-Intensive Common-Tech			-0.073 (2.32)			-0.014 (0.33)
Δ %Union	0.002 (1.38)	0.001 (1.00)	0.002 (1.37)	0.004 (3.77)	0.005 (3.83)	0.005 (4.15)
1974 %Union	0.003 (5.49)	0.003 (3.89)	0.003 (3.38)	-0.0001 (0.11)	1.4E-5 (0.01)	0.0004 (0.28)

Table 1. 1960-1985 Change in Annual Earnings Regression Results (Panel 2), *Continued:*

VARIABLE	PRODUCTION WORKERS			NONPRODUCTION WORKERS		
	(1)	(2)	(3)	(4)	(5)	(6)
R^2	0.34	0.35	0.37	0.21	0.23	0.24
F-Exports[e]	na	3.94 (p=.020)	2.11 (p=.123)	na	4.57 (p=.011)	5.37 (p=.005)
F-Imports[f]	na	2.46 (p=.086)	1.52 (p=.220)	na	0.35 (p=.704)	0.06 (p=.938)
F-HT,CTL,CTK[g]	na	na	4.92 (p=.002)	na	na	1.68 (p=.170)

Notes for Table 1:

a. Each observation is weighted by total industry employment. Standard deviations are in parentheses.

b. The sources for the HT, CTL, CTK, and natural resource classification are Lawrence (1984) and Partridge (1993).

c. Data limits the earliest union density to 1974 (Abowd, 1991). The 1985 union density is from Curme et al. (1990).

d. Each observation is weighted by production or nonproduction industry of employment. The absolute values of the White heteroskedastic-consistent t-statistics are in parentheses. The sample size is 428 four-digit SIC manufacturing industries.

e. The F-statistic (and p-value) for the joint significance of the export share and the export share*unionization coefficient.

f. The F-statistic (and p-value) for the joint significance of the import share and the import share*unionization coefficient.

g. The F-statistic (and p-value) for the joint significance of the high-tech and the two common-tech coefficients.

category. Thus, the HT, CTL, and CTK coefficients are measured relative to the NR sector. From the above discussion, the HT coefficient is expected to be greater than the CTL and CTK coefficients.

Two different unionization measures are also specified. First, the 1960 to 1985 change in unionization is included. Earnings are expected to be positively related to changes in industry unionization rates due to union monopoly effects for union wages and union threat effects on nonunion wages. In addition, beyond changes in unionization, unions also may have a greater ability to increase wages, or resist downward wage adjustments, in industries where the *level* of unionization is higher. Thus, the 1974 percent unionization is included in the model, where 1974 is approximately the midpoint of the period. Finally, the Z vector controls for other factors.[5]

Panel 2 of Table 1 presents the regression results of interest. The Z vector results are available on request from the authors. To show the sensitivity of the results, different production worker specifications are shown in columns (1)-(3) and analogous nonproduction worker specifications are in columns (4)-(6). Columns (3) and (6) reflect the most complete specifications.

Using columns (3) and (6), HT production wages are greater than in the two common technology sectors, but for nonproduction workers, the CTK and HT coefficients are equal. The bottom of Panel 2 shows three joint F-tests on the statistical significance of the two export variables, the two import variables, and the three sectoral dummies. Regarding sectoral effects, the F-test indicates that they are jointly statistically significant at the 5% level for production workers but not for nonproduction workers. The two import share variables, however, are not jointly significant for production and nonproduction workers. The two export variables are jointly significant at the 5% level with the exception of the production worker model in column (3).

Overall, the direct impact of imports on earnings is not statistically significant, but there is stronger evidence that exports statistically influence earnings. Using the estimates in columns (3) and (6), a one standard deviation increase in the 1960-85 change in the export share (3.88%) increases production and nonproduction earnings by about 1.2% and 1.75% when measured at a *zero* level of unionization. However, when measured at the mean 1974 level of unionization, a one standard deviation greater shift in the export share changes production and nonproduction worker earnings by only 0.5% and 0%. Thus, even in the case of exports, the typical worker is not strongly affected by its direct impact, but this is not necessarily the case at extreme union densities.

Although the statistical significance varies for production and nonproduction workers, changes in unionization and the 1974 level of unionization are positively related to earnings. Using the estimates in columns (3) and (6), an additional one standard deviation *decrease* in unionization between 1960 and 1985 (%Δunionization) would reduce average annual earnings by about 1.2% and 3.3% for production and nonproduction workers. Production and nonproduction earnings were 4.1% and 0.5% lower in industries with a one standard deviation lower 1974 union density. The strong effect that the change in industry union density has on nonproduction earnings indicates that the effects of industry unionization can spill over to relatively nonunionized groups. The strong influence that unionization has on earnings also suggests an indirect avenue for foreign trade to influence earnings. Specifically, if trade reduces unionization, it can have large indirect effects on earnings. Moreover, if trade reduces production worker unionization rates, trade can increase income inequality. Thus, the following sections will analyze how trade affects the willingness of union firms to hire workers and the willingness of workers to join a union.

International Trade and Union Membership

Even assuming that trade affects union trends, it is not easy to determine the precise avenues for trade to affect unionization. Specifically, trade may have a different influence on U.S. workers' demand for unions and U.S. unionized firms' hiring decisions. Conversely, Martinello and Meng (1992) and Belman (1988) considered whether import shares influence the likelihood a worker belongs to a union by employing simple probit specifications.[6] However, simple probit does not distinguish between the choice that individual workers make regarding whether to enter the queue for union jobs from the union firm's selection of workers from the queue. Thus, this analysis should advance our understanding of the precise mechanism that trade influences union strength by using a partial observability probit model. Also, unlike previous studies (except Partridge 1994), this analysis also considers whether exports affect union status and how the relative comparative advantage of a sector affects the union choice decision.[7]

Changes in trade shares can influence union status in three ways. First, trade directly affects domestic product market power. Second, because trade is a signal of the future viability of the industry and future employment possibilities, trade can influence *strategic behavior* by unions and management. Third, greater trade can trigger risk averse behavior by unions and management. These three hypotheses are summarized in Table 2. Closely related to these points is that an individual's union status can be affected by technological characteristics that determine the relative comparative advantage of a given sector of employment, which is addressed below.

The basis for most union choice studies is that workers decide to join a union when the benefits of unionism outweigh the costs. Net benefits of unionism are influenced by many factors, including the workers' demand for unionization, the supply of unionization, and employer hiring decisions. Union choice is positively related to the union-nonunion wage gap, $(W^U-W^N)/W^N$, and other factors including industry, trade, labor market, and individual characteristics (Hirsch and Berger 1984).[8] Equation (2) represents the union choice decision:

$$U = G((W^U-W^N)/W^N, Z, L, I), \quad G_{(W^U-W^N)/W^N} >0, \tag{2}$$

where U is a union choice indicator variable, and Z, L, and I represent industry characteristics, labor market characteristics, and individual attributes.

The model in (2) does not fully illustrate the sequential decision undertaken by workers and their employers. Workers decide whether to belong to a union and join the union queue; second, union employers decide which workers to hire from the union queue or whether to hire workers at all. This sequential model has been previously considered by Abowd and Farber (1982) and DeFreitas (1993). However, both studies considered individual attributes and not industry characteristics (trade shares, etc.) which are the subject of this analysis. A worker's decision to join the union queue is represented by:

$$Q=X_1\beta_1 + e_1, \tag{3}$$

where Q is a union queue indicator variable, X_1 is a vector of individual and industry characteristics, and e_1 is an error term.. The firm's decision to hire from the queue is shown in (4):

$$HFQ=X_2\beta_2 + e_2, \tag{4}$$

where HFQ is an indicator variable, X_2 is a vector of relevant individual and industry characteristics, and e_2 is an error term. A worker is only hired for a union job if both Q and HFQ equal 1 (i.e., both conditions are true).

Table 2. Summary of Union Status Models
(PANEL A: Reduced Form Univariate Probit)

Model	Imports' impact on union status	Exports' impact on union status	Trades' Total Impact on union status	Net Exports' impact on union status
Product Market/Rent Sharing: Predicts that imports (exports) are positively (negatively) related to labor demand elasticity and negatively (positively) related to profits. Thus, imports (exports) are negatively (positively) related to the union wage gap.	(-)	(+)	?	(+)
Strategic Behavior (End Game): Predicts that unions tradeoff current wages with the probability of future employment. Greater imports (exports) increase (reduce) the union wage gap.	(+)	(-)	?	(-)
Risk Aversion/Uncertainty: Predicts that greater trade increases the uncertainty of union members (and management's uncertainty).	(-)	(-)	(-)	?

Table 2 (PANEL B: Bivariate-Partial-Observability Probit, Probability of Joining the Union Que)

Model	Imports	Exports	Total Trade	Net Exports
Product Market/Rent Sharing: See above.	(-)	(+)	?	(+)
Strategic Behavior (End Game): See above.	(+)	(-)	?	(-)
Risk Aversion/Uncertainty: See above.	(-)	(-)	(-)	?

Table 2 (PANEL C: Bivariate-Partial Observability Probit, Probability of Being Hired from the Union Que)

Model	Imports	Exports	Total Trade	Net Exports
Product Market/Rent Sharing: Predicts that greater imports (exports) reduce (increase) profits and (likely) union wages. This reduces (increases) the quality of the applicant pool, *ceteris paribus*, which increases (reduces) firm resistance to hiring union workers.	(-)	(+)	?	(+)
Strategic Behavior (End Game): Predicts that greater imports in a declining industry result in greater wages. This increases firm resistance to hiring more union workers. Greater exports in an expanding industry result in lower wages. This reduces firm resistance to hiring union workers.	(-)	(+)	?	(+)
Risk Aversion/Uncertainty: Predicts that greater trade increases uncertainty about the future prospects of the industry. Risk averse behavior by management increases firm resistance to hiring union workers.	(-)	(-)	(-)	?

Trade Share Influence

An individual's union status using simple reduced form *probit models* has been examined before (e.g., Hirsch and Berger 1984; Belman 1988). Most of these studies emphasize the role of the domestic industry's *product market power* in determining individual union status. For example, the product market power of a domestic industry may be positively related to its four-firm concentration ratio (CR4) and exports but negatively related to its imports. Greater product market power implies a smaller labor demand elasticity and greater profits. Assuming that unions extract "excess profits" (Abowd 1989) or that unions act as a monopoly supplier of labor (McDonald and Solow 1981), greater product market power implies a larger union-nonunion wage gap and a greater worker *demand* for union coverage. Thus, the *product market* analysis suggests that imports (exports) are negatively (positively) related to the demand for unionization. That is, a worker's likelihood of belonging to a union in a reduced form probit model or a worker's probability of joining the union queue in the partial observability probit model is negatively (positively) related to the industry's import (export) share. Greater wages as a result of product market power should also increase the quality of the applicant pool (e.g., from efficiency wage theory). Thus, exports should be positively related to union firms hiring from the union queue with the opposite applying for imports.

The product market model, however, ignores potential long-run union *strategic* responses to changes in trade. For example, increased imports can signal a greater likelihood that the firm will fail, while increased exports signal the opposite.[9] Clearly, one dimension of long-run union-management cooperation is the tradeoff between short-term wages and the likelihood of long-term employment. Farber and Saks (1980) show that employment security plays an important role in individual decisions to vote for union certification; thus, employment security likely plays a role in union bargaining strategy. Similarly, Lawrence and Lawrence (1985) examine the influence of foreign competition on union behavior through an end game, which is essentially a tradeoff between current wages and the probability of long-term employment.

Lawrence and Lawrence suggest that slow demand growth reduces the opportunity for an industry to invest in new plant and equipment.[10] Unions can extract *higher* wages because a slowly growing firm has more difficulty substituting capital for labor (i.e., smaller elasticities of factor substitution σ_{KL} and/or labor demand). Yet, the tradeoff for higher current wages is ultimately a reduction in long-term employment. Because greater imports are negatively related to the firm's (or industry's) demand growth and positively related to its failure rate, greater imports can induce a less cooperative union-management atmosphere. The implication is that greater imports could actually increase the union-nonunion wage gap. Conversely, robust product demand growth encourages the industry to expand its capacity. The union fears that if its wages are too "high," the firm will adopt a capital-intensive technology which could result in lower long-run union employment. Hence, greater exports, by inducing increased demand growth and union-management cooperation, can actually reduce the union-nonunion wage gap.

The strategic behavior hypothesis suggests a positive (negative) relationship between the union wage gap and imports (exports) and implies that greater imports (exports) are associated with a greater (reduced) demand for unionization.[11] Thus, strategic behavior suggests that the likelihood of belonging to a union or joining the union queue is positively (negatively) related to imports (exports). Moreover, because greater import competition increases union wages and induces an uncooperative union-management atmosphere, greater import shares reduce the likelihood that unionized firms will hire from the union queue, while greater export shares imply the opposite.

In addition to product market power and strategic behavior, union membership may be influenced by the increased *uncertainty* associated with foreign trade. Industries with a high export or import share are exposed to changes in tariffs, exchange rate risk, and other risks due to changes in the terms of international competitiveness (Dornbusch 1987). Moreover, foreign product markets and cost structures may not be completely understood by domestic firms. Since domestic production in high trade share industries is at a higher risk of displacement by foreign producers, these industries may suffer from greater variability in output and profitability.

Collective bargaining has characteristics that may add to the uncertainty of trade. Union contracts are typically set for three years and may inhibit labor market flexibility in reacting to foreign trends. Also, if unions extract higher wages, unionized firms will have a labor cost disadvantage and will be less competitive. Consequently, as risk aversion increases, firms exposed to greater foreign competition will be less likely to hire from the union queue. Workers may also be willing to trade off greater job security for lower wages and forego the benefits of unionization. Greater foreign competition in the union sector increases the risk of union busting tactics, lay-offs, or wage concessions. Thus, as workers' risk aversion increases, they will be less likely to enter the union queue. Overall, the uncertainty effect may have a stronger influence on firms than on employees because it affects firm behavior most directly.

The three competing hypotheses regarding trade's influence on union status: (1) product market, (2) strategic behavior, and (3) risk aversion/uncertainty are summarized in Table 2. Note that product market effects offset strategic behavior effects on the demand for unionization. That is, product market analysis suggests that greater *imports* (*exports*) *reduce* (*increase*) the likelihood of a worker joining the union queue, while strategic behavior implies the converse. The uncertainty hypothesis implies that greater trade has a negative impact on the probability of both joining the union queue and being hired from the union queue. Overall, it is an empirical question as to which effect dominates and it is possible that trade has very little influence on unionism because the three effects offset.

Sectoral Effects

The discussion above focused directly on how import and export shares alter union behavior. Aside from a sector's import and export shares, there are other technological characteristics inherent within a sector which determine its level of international competitiveness. For example, standard HOS trade theory emphasizes the role of factor intensities such as physical capital or human capital in determining trade flows. In fact, traditional trade models do not point to trade shares, *per se*, as a measure of how trade influences a sector.

To further investigate these matters, the four-way HT, CTL, CTK, NR division will be used again, where it is likely that each sector has its own *separate* impact on union status. Standard HOS trade theory suggests that the more skilled HT unionized labor force should fare relatively better than CTL and CTK union workers in response to trade. The product market analysis from above reinforces HOS trade theory. That is, the positive relationship between product demand and labor demand elasticities suggests that HT unions have a superior wage-employment relationship to exploit, while CTL and CTK unions have an inferior wage-employment relationship. The implication is that the demand for unionization should be *greater* (*smaller*) in the HT (CTL, CTK) sector(s) *on average*.[12] The superior union wage and long-run employment tradeoff in the HT sector also suggest that the quality of the applicant pool will be superior in the HT sector. Thus, unionized HT firms should be more willing to hire workers than unionized firms in the CTL and CTK sectors.

Empirical Methodology and Results

Following DeFreitas (1993), the sequential union model suggests that a worker will be unionized only if equations (3) and (4) are true (i.e., Q=1 and HFQ=1). A worker first decides whether to join the queue and second, the worker is hired from the queue. Unfortunately, we do not observe whether a worker has joined the queue or whether a firm has refused to hire a worker if they were in the queue. Instead, we observe the product of Q and HFQ. To account for this problem, a partial observability probit model is used by assuming that the errors in equations (3) and (4) are normally distributed. The estimates of β_1 and β_2 are derived from maximizing the following likelihood function:

$$L=\prod_{U=1}\{F(X_1\beta_1)F(X_2\beta_2)\}\cdot\prod_{U=0}\{1-F(X_1\beta_1)F(X_2\beta_2)\}. \tag{5}$$

To identify β_1 and β_2, the variables in X_1 cannot be identical to the variables in X_2. Therefore, the longitudinal nature of our data set is used to identify the model. Specifically, the worker's decision to join the union queue is based on 1978 data and the firm's decision to hire from the queue is based on 1980 data, meaning that the dependent variable is the worker's union membership status in 1980.[13]

A reduced form probit is also estimated to measure the likelihood an individual belongs to a union. Like DeFreitas (1993), the reduced form estimates will be compared to partial observability probit estimates. The specification for individual i is:

$$P(U=1) = P(Y\Gamma + \epsilon_i) > 0, \qquad \epsilon_i \sim i.i.d. \ N(0,1). \tag{6}$$

The dependent variable is the worker's 1980 union status (i.e., *union: U=1*). Vector **Y** contains variables that control for the net benefits of union membership including variables that influence the union wage gap, and ϵ_i is the error term.

Equation (6) is a reduced form of equation (2), which allows us to estimate the *total impact* of trade on union choice. Analogously, we estimate a reduced form representation of equation (5). Thus, the empirical specifications will measure the direct impact of the trade variables (e.g., on employment and on elasticities) *plus* their indirect influence through the union wage gap.

Data

Given the complex interaction between firm and individual worker characteristics in determining union status, micro-data is necessary for this analysis. Thus, data from the National Longitudinal Survey of Young Men from 1978-1980 is combined with three-digit industry data for the empirical analysis, resulting in a sample of 734 workers. The advantage of this time period is that the U.S. trade balance was approximately zero and the wild currency fluctuations of the 1980s had not affected manufacturing, which implies that we are considering a period that was approximately in equilibrium. This period is also before the dramatic declines in unionization and the major changes in management attitudes towards unions during the 1980s and 1990s. Hence, these other effects are not confounded with trade's influence.

The trade variables consist of the import share (M=imports /(imports +output)) and the export share (X=exports/output). The trade variables are from U.S. Department of Commerce data. As discussed above, there are three conflicting hypotheses regarding the signs of the trade share coefficients. For a sensitivity analysis, we will also specify an alternative model that uses a total trade share variable (export share + import share) and a net industry trade share variable (export share - import share) in place of the import and export share variables. The uncertainty hypothesis suggests that the more open an industry is to foreign competition, whether due to exports or imports, the less likely are workers or firms to be unionized. Conversely, neither the product market or the strategic behavior hypotheses are directly related to the industry's *total* trade share. Thus, in all of the models, a negative total trade share coefficient would support the uncertainty hypothesis.

With regard to the net trade balance of an industry, the product market hypothesis suggests a positive relationship between net trade balance and individual union status in both the nonqueue probit model and the partial observability model for workers deciding to enter the union queue, while strategic behavior suggests the opposite (see Table 2). The product market and strategic behavior hypotheses both imply that the net trade balance should be positively related to firms hiring from the union queue. However, the effect of the uncertainty hypothesis on the net trade balance is less clear. Assuming that the relative effects of import and export shares on union choice are equal, the uncertainty hypothesis suggests that net exports would have no effect on union choice since the negative uncertainty effect of imports and exports would offset. Consequently, the sign of the net trade balance variable may help in sorting out the relative effects of the product market and strategic behavior hypotheses.

To assess how sectoral comparative advantage influences union choice, NR, CTL, and CTK dummies are included where HT is the omitted category. Therefore, the sectoral dummy coefficients are measured relative to the HT sector, and the CTL, CTK, and NR t-statistics measure whether these sectors have statistically different effects than the HT sector. *A priori*, we expect workers in the CTL, CTK, and NR sectors have a lower probability of union choice since HT firms typically have expanding markets, are more profitable, and may be less resistant to unionization.

Several industry variables are included in **Y** to measure industry effects on the net benefits of union membership (e.g., the supply and demand for unionism) as well as variables to control for regional labor market differences and attitudes towards unions. Individual specific characteristics are also in **Y** to control for the demand for unionism and the probability of being hired by a union employer.[14] Previous studies use similar individual and industry controls (e.g., Martinello and Meng 1992; DeFreitas 1993) and we will only emphasize the variables unique to our analysis.

Empirical Results

In Panel 1 of Table 3, column (1) shows the descriptive statistics for the relevant variables. Column (2) reports the trade and technology parameter results for the nonqueue or traditional univariate probit model. The sequential bivariate queuing model results follow in the next two columns. Column (3) reports the results for entering the queue and column (4) shows the results for being hired from the queue. Note that the bottom of Panel 1 also reports the model specification where total trade share and the net export share are used in place of the import and export share.[15] The union queue model suggests that separate worker and firm considerations are important in determining union choice. This point is shown by the union queue model being a statistically significant improvement over the simple reduced form probit model.[16]

The results, however, are complicated by the integration of individual micro-data with aggregate industry data. Since the data have been "stretched" by combining the NLS micro-data set with industry data, the parameter coefficients and the t-statistics should be interpreted cautiously.[17] To enhance the interpretation of the estimated results, a likelihood ratio test is utilized to evaluate the *joint* restriction that the trade share and technological-based sectoral variables have no effect on union choice. The likelihood ratio test results for all three models are reported at the bottom of Panel 1 in Table 3. Generally, these *joint* significance tests indicate that the trade share variables and the sectoral dummies are *jointly significant* in all three probit models and influence union status as a group.

Panel 2 of Table 3 illustrates the change in the probability of union choice after a one standard deviation change from the mean export share and the mean import share, as well as for the alternative specification of total trade and net export share. Panel 3 of Table 3 shows the change in the probability of union choice in the CTL, CTK, and NR sectors relative to the HT sector.

International Trade. For the nonqueue model, Panel 2 of Table 3 shows that the probability of union coverage declines by 8.0% with a one standard deviation increase in the import share. The large export share effect reflects the highly significant parameter in column 2 of Panel 1, while the negligible import share effect on the probability of union choice in Panel 2 is not surprising since the parameter estimate is small and insignificant. Similarly, when the alternative trade share variables are used in the specification, a one standard deviation change in the total trade share and the net export share reduces the union choice probability by 5.7% and 5.9%. The results reflect the significant trade estimate and the nearly significant net export estimate in Panel 1 of Table 3. From Panel A of Table 3, the negative export effect implies that either the uncertainty or strategic behavior effect dominates any product market effects. However, the results suggest that imports have little if any effect on union choice in the univariate probit model, perhaps because the theoretical effects in Table 2 offset. Similarly, the negative net export effect is also consistent with strategic behavior.[18] The total trade share result, conversely, suggests that as the volume of total trade increases, firms' risk aversion to unions also increases, indicating that the uncertainty effect plays an important role. Overall, the total trade share result indicates that greater openness in the U.S. economy is reducing unionism and, in turn, increasing income inequality.

To sort out how individual workers or firms alter their behavior in response to changes in the international environment, we turn to the bivariate union queue model's results. Panel 2 of Table 3 suggests that entering the union queue has a small negative relationship to exports and a slight positive relationship to imports. However, in Panel 1, neither parameter estimate is significant. The entering the queue model indicates that trade may not have any impact on a worker's entry decision. This finding is further supported by the result in Panel 2 of Table 3,

Table 3. PANEL 1: Impact of Trade and Technology on the Probability of Union Choice

	(1) Means (Standard Dev)		(2) Nonqueue Probit Model	(3) Enter Union Queue Probit Model	(4) Hired From Queue Probit Model
Explanatory Variables:[b]	1978	1980	1980	1978	1980
Natural Resource (=1 if Technology Class)	0.24 (0.43)	0.30 (0.43)	-.1740 (0.69)	-.4171 (0.72)	-.6576 (1.41)
Common-Tech Labor (=1 if Technology Class)	0.19 (0.37)	0.19 (0.37)	-.2179 (0.73)	-1.071 (1.50)	-.4410 (0.81)
Common-Tech Capital (=1 if Technology Class)	0.27 (0.44)	0.27 (0.44)	-.7933 (2.84)‡	-1.264 (1.99)†	-1.087 (2.07)†
High-Tech (=1 if Technology Class)	0.30 (0.43)	0.24 (0.40)			
Import Share	0.08(0.06)	0.09 (0.07)	0.1978 (0.17)	1.476 (0.60)	-.4301 (0.21)
Export Share	0.08 (0.06)	0.09 (0.07)	-2.843 (1.98)†	-1.474 (0.40)	-5.290 (2.08)†
Total Trade Share	0.18 (.011)	0.18 (0.11)	-1.323 (1.66)§	0.0006 (0.00)	-2.859 (1.97)†
Net Export Share	0.01 (0.10)	0.01 (0.10)	-1.521 (1.48)	-1.485 (0.63)	-2.429 (1.36)
Dependent Variable:					
Union in 1980		0.41 (0.49)			
Number of Observations	734	734			
Log-Likelihood Statistic			-346.7	-308.8	-308.8
Likelihood Ratio Tests:					
1. Exports=Imports = 0			$\alpha=.1281\ (\chi^2_{(2)}=4.11)$	$\alpha=.0048\ (\chi^2_{(4)}=15.0)$	$\alpha=.0048\ (\chi^2_{(4)}=15.0)$
2. Net Exports=Trade = 0			$\alpha=.1281\ (\chi^2_{(2)}=4.11)$	$\alpha=.0048\ (\chi^2_{(4)}=15.0)$	$\alpha=.0048\ (\chi^2_{(4)}=15.0)$
3. HT=CTK=CTL = 0			$\alpha=.0046\ (\chi^2_{(3)}=13.04)$	$\alpha=.0001\ (\chi^2_{(3)}=35.2)$	$\alpha=.0001\ (\chi^2_{(3)}=35.2)$

Table 3. PANEL 2: Impact of a 1 Std. Dev. Change in the Trade Variables on the Probability of Being Union

	Exports	Imports	Trade	Net Exports
	Mean = 9.3%	Mean = 8.3%	Mean = 17.5%	Mean = 1.0%
	1 std. dev. = 7.3%	1 std. dev. = 7.7%	1 std. dev. = 11.1%	1 std. dev = 10.1%
Nonqueue Probit Model:[c]	-8.0%	0.6%	-5.7%	-5.9%
Entering Union Queue Model:[d]	-1.3%	1.4%	0%	-1.2%
Hired From Union Queue Model:[d]	-10.8%	-0.9%	-11.2%	-8.6%

Table 3. PANEL 3: Impact of the NR, CTL, and CTK Sectors Compared to the HT Sector

	NR	CTL	CTK
Nonqueue Probit Model:	-6.7%	-8.4%	-30.5%
Entering Union Queue Model:	-5.2%	-13.3%	-15.7%
Hired From Union Queue Model:	-18.3%	-12.3%	-30.3%

Notes for Table 3.

a. Standard Deviation and the absolute values of the t-statistics are in parentheses.

b. Only estimates for the technology, import, export, total trade, and net export share variables are reported.

c. Estimates are based on the coefficients in panel 1. The estimated impact of a one standard deviation change in the export (or import) share is measured by using the derivative of exports (imports). The probability estimates for the trade and net export variables are calculated in a similar manner. The normal probability density function is evaluated at the 1980 sample mean union density of 0.394 (using data from Kokkelenberg and Sockell, 1985). The pattern would be similar if the normal probability density function was instead evaluated at the mean for all of the variables.

d. Entering union queue and hired from queue estimates are calculated using Abowd and Farber's (1982) procedure.

e. Estimates each sector's probability of being union relative to the HT sector (the omitted category).

[‡]Significant at a 99% level. [†]Significant at a 95% level. [§]Significant at a 90% level.

where total trade share has no influence on the probability of entering the union queue, reflecting the insignificant estimate for the trade variable.

Panel 2 of Table 3 shows that the probability of being hired from the union queue has a substantial negative association with the export share (10.8% decline after a one standard deviation increase), reflecting the significant export share parameter estimate in Table 3. This result is consistent with the uncertainty argument, hypothesized in Panel C of Table 2, that unions increase the risk of export competition. This suggests that firms resist unionization as their exports increase because management apparently views collective bargaining contracts as too costly (i.e., greater wages) or too confining for rapid response to maintain export competitiveness. This may be especially the case when the terms of trade are rapidly changing, causing employers to substitute low-wage nonunion workers for high-cost union members. The probability of being hired from the union queue has a slight negative relationship to the import share, which is consistent with all three of the arguments in Panel C of Table 2. However, the import share parameter estimate in Table 3 is small and insignificant, suggesting that imports play little role in determining the union firms' hiring response (as in the entry to the queue model).

Total trade share, in the alternative trade variable specification, has the strongest negative effect on the probability of union choice--11.2% decline per standard deviation increase in total trade volume. Since total trade share also theoretically explains union risk aversion, this result reinforces the export-uncertainty findings. These results imply that union contracts impose restrictions on a firm's ability to quickly respond to increased international competition, which would increase resistance to hiring union workers. Net trade share also has a negative impact on the probability of union choice, but the result is statistically insignificant. Nonetheless, the negative coefficient could be further evidence of an export uncertainty effect, where exports have a stronger effect on union choice than imports (see endnote 18).

The union queue model is consistent with union claims that trade has been a significant factor in the decline in union membership. As in the nonqueue model, the results suggest that exports rather than imports have the largest impact on union employment. The union queue results also show that trade's influence on union employment affects firm choice differently than worker choice, which cannot be identified with an ordinary probit model. The difference in the models is exemplified by the apparent lack of a trade effect on workers' decisions to enter the union queue while employers' aversion to hiring union workers is primarily caused by exports (since imports appear to have no effect on employer hiring).

The results further suggest that rather than export expansion offsetting the negative effects of import competition, exports have even further hindered the union movement and added to the increasing wage disparity of low-skilled, less-educated workers. Consequently, it is understandable that union leaders feel threatened and oppose free trade measures such as NAFTA or GATT. They see no benefit for unions even if the free trade legislation provides the expected increase in exports. These results, however, may be unique to the United States because in other industrial nations, where trade accounts for a much greater proportion of GDP, labor movements have typically fared better.

The HT, CTL, and CTK Impact. The CTK sectoral variable is significant in all of three models in Table 3, while the CTL and NR variables are generally insignificant.[19] Also, the sectoral dummies are jointly significant; consequently, worker union choice appears to vary by sector of employment. After controlling for industry and worker characteristics, Panel 3 of Table 3 shows the difference in the nonqueue union choice probability for each sector *relative* to the HT sector. Compared to HT workers, NR, CTK, and CTL employees are less likely to be in a union, *ceteris paribus*. These results are consistent with *a priori* expectations and show that CTK sector employees have the lowest likelihood of joining a union (the probability of union choice is 30.5% lower), which was expected since U.S. CTK firms face intense foreign competition. Overall, the sectoral differences in international comparative advantage appear to be at least as important as the impact of trade shares in determining union status.

The results for the union queuing model parallel the standard probit estimates. Panel 3 suggests that HT workers are relatively more likely to join the union queue than workers in the common-technology sector industries. The finding that CTK and CTL workers are less likely to enter the union queue probably reflects the perceived susceptibility of these sectors to greater domestic and foreign competition. Panel 3 also implies that HT workers have the greatest probability of being hired from the union queue while CTK workers clearly have the lowest probability of being hired from the union queue, which is likely linked to intense foreign competition.

Panel 3 also shows that sectoral differences in union choice are influenced by the difference in the firm's willingness to hire from the queue as well as a worker's willingness to join the union queue (again, this cannot be identified in the ordinary probit model). Overall, the sectoral dummy coefficients suggest that the technological factors that determine both sectoral comparative advantage and the relative degree of foreign technological convergence have an impact on union membership that is separate from the influence of the sector's trade share (because trade shares are separately controlled for). Moreover, future foreign competition will likely force further industrial restructuring that should favor the HT sector at the expense of the CTL and CTK sectors.

The sectoral results are consistent with Johnson and Stafford's (1993) claim that U.S. medium technology industries are under competitive pressures from foreign economic convergence. The resulting loss of quasi-rents in these industries hurt CTK and CTL union workers and reduce their union membership.[20] This suggests that low-skilled, less-educated workers' relative incomes are adversely affected in two ways. First, foreign competition and economic convergence lower wages in the common-technology sectors, which has been the domain of less-skilled workers. Second, foreign competition weakens the union sector, which means that a large number of less-skilled workers lose their union wage differential, causing their relative incomes to decline. Foreign economic convergence in the common-technology industries can help explain why other industrial nations' labor movements have not fared as poorly as in the United States. Presumably, the other industrial nations' economic convergence after World War II was concentrated in their common-technology industries. Because international convergence favorably influenced their common-technology sector, it did not pull down their union movement as in the United States. However, now that this convergence has run its course, other industrial nations' unions may increasingly feel the pressures that have been felt in the United States.

Conclusion

This study examined how international factors have affected individual union choice along with the resulting implications for U.S. income distribution. First, we found that changes in trade shares since 1960 were negatively correlated with the level of unionization, implying that changes in trade shares indirectly affect the labor market by reducing unionization. We then presented a model that distinguishes between the effects of trade shares and the factors which influence international competitiveness in the determination of union choice. The probit results, in general, suggest that exports have a greater negative influence on union choice than imports. Of the theoretical impacts, the most consistent explanation is that greater trade shares result in more uncertainty about union employment, which reduces the probability of union hiring by employers. However, neither exports or imports appear to affect the likelihood that employees join the union queue.

The typical HT worker appears more likely to belong to a union than the typical CTK or CTL industry worker. The differing sectoral effects in union status were found to be consistent with HOS trade theory and they are at least as important as the effect of trade shares. Overall, the results suggest that trade may have damaged unionism, but greater trade is not a death knell for the labor movement. If unions can adjust to industrial restructuring by increasing their organizational efforts in the expanding HT sector, unions may well offset the losses to the decline of the CTK and CTL sectors.

Endnotes

1. Lawrence and Slaughter (1993), Sachs and Shatz (1994), and Burtless (1995) summarize the literature on how foreign trade affects U.S. wages.

2. Imports, exports, and manufacturing shipments are from U.S. Department of Commerce data. Unionization are from the *Statistical Abstract of the U.S.*, R. Ehrenberg and R. Smith, *Modern Labor Economics*, New York: Harper Collins, 1994, and various January issues of *Employment and Earnings*.

3. For further perspective, the HT sector was the only sector with a net trade surplus (export share minus import share) in 1985. Specifically the HT, CTL, CTK, and the natural resource-intensive 1985 net trade balances were 5%, -15%, -4%, and -4%.

4. We follow the traditional approach of most studies of trade's impact on the labor market in that we use trade quantities rather than import and export prices. This is due to the limited availability of foreign price data, measurement errors in international price data, and price endogeneity. Given the empirical difficulties of price data, industrial organization and labor economists generally prefer market share data. International economists, conversely, tend to prefer import and export prices and typically assume perfect substitutability between products. However, if goods are not perfect substitutes, then market share matters. Imperfect substitutability generally characterizes most manufactured goods (Dornbusch 1987). Labor studies that have used foreign price data rather than quantities have found very similar results (e.g., see Freeman 1995 and Revanga 1992 for more details).

5. There are three types of control variables in vector Z. First, firm effects are controlled for by the 1960-85 change in capital/labor ratio and the change in the natural log of the average establishment size. Second, other industry effects are accounted for by dummies for industries that produce equipment, durable goods, nondurable goods, and intermediate goods, where the auto industry is the omitted category. Also, a separate steel industry dummy is included in the model. Third, human capital and related effects are controlled for by the initial 1960 one-digit production and nonproduction worker occupation shares along with the 1960-85 changes in these occupational shares. The source for the auto, equipment, durable, non durable, and intermediate classification is Lawrence (1984). The occupation shares are derived from the 1960 *Census of Population* and the 1986 *Current Population Survey*.

6. Belman emphasized the influence of product market concentration on the union wage gap where he only controlled for the import share. Martinello and Meng only considered Canadian data, making it unclear how their results generalize to the United States.

7. The exact opposite issue is whether unionization, in turn, influences export and import shares. However, Karier (1991) finds no evidence that union wages or coverage affects trade share levels.

8. Assuming workers have freedom over job choice, a union choice model is useful because unionization is one factor which workers consider in accepting a job (Hirsch and Berger 1984).

9. Kahn (1993) examined the likelihood that labor and management cooperate in repeated games. Kahn found that union-firm cooperation is negatively related to an industry's or firm's bankruptcy or failure rate, where a greater failure rate reduces the expected gains for the union from long-run cooperation.

10. Lawrence and Lawrence suggest that the steel and auto industries of the late 1970s and early 1980s are good examples of end game behavior by unions.

11. Note that the product market and strategic behavior models imply offsetting impacts on *union wages*. Partridge (1993) and Macpherson and Stewart (1990) present results similar to this pattern.

12. The HT/CTL-CTK union choice relationship should hold *after* controlling for the individual characteristics of the labor force, especially education.

13. Abowd and Farber (1982) and DeFreitas (1993) identified their models by omitting union and nonunion tenure from the firm's hiring equation, where they did not use longitudinal data.

14. Industry variables in the probit models include an international trade adjusted industry concentration ratio (CR4), the three-year percentage change in real industry output, and dummies for the steel, durable goods and nondurable goods industries. Regional labor market variables include the local unemployment rate and dummies for residents in the South and metropolitan areas. Individual characteristic variables include years of completed education, potential work experience and its square, months of tenure and its square, dummy variables for part-time employment, marriage, health problems in the last year that have affected work, and occupation. The entire specification of the traditional univariate and bivariate union queuing probit models is available from the authors in an unpublished appendix.

15. The parameter estimates for the control variables in the total trade share and net export share model specification are virtually identical to the coefficients in the export and import share specification. Again, the complete model results are available from the authors.

16. The standard probit model places 29 restrictions on the union queue model. As shown in Table 2, the negative of the log likelihood ratio for the standard probit is 346.7, and for the union queue model it is 308.8. This gives a likelihood ratio statistic of 75.8 with 29 degrees of freedom, which suggests that the restrictions are significant at the 0.001% level.

17. There are two offsetting effects when using aggregate industry level data in a micro data set. First, Greenberg *et al* (1989) argue that data stretching of this type leads to an errors-in-variables problem which leads to parameter estimates that are biased toward zero. That is, the results should be viewed

as a lower bound estimate. Second, Moulton (1990) shows that if the random disturbances within variable groups are correlated, then the standard errors are downward biased and the t-statistics are inflated.

18. If exports have a stronger effect on union choice than imports, as suggested in Table 3, the net export result could reflect union risk aversion precipitated by a dominating export share influence.

19. The CTL variable is nearly significant in the entry into the queue model (p-value=.1342).

20. These results are also consistent with standard HOS trade theory where higher skilled HT union workers should fare better than less skilled CTK and CTL union workers. Thus, only examining the effects of trade shares may have led to the incorrect conclusion that HOS theory has little impact.

References

Abowd, John. "The Effect of Wage Bargains on the Market Value of the Firm," *American Economic Review*, September 1989, vol. 79, pp. 774-809.

_____. "The NBER Immigration, Trade and Labor Markets Data Files." in J. Abowd and R. Freeman eds., *Immigration, Trade, and the Labor Market*, Chicago: University of Chicago Press, 1991, pp. 407-421.

_____, and Farber, H. "Job Queues and the Union Status of Workers," *Industrial and Labor Relations Review*, April 1982, vol. 35, pp. 354-376.

Belman, Dale. "Concentration, Unionism, and Labor Earnings: A Sample Selection Approach," *Review of Economics and Statistics*, August 1988, vol. 70, pp. 391-397.

Blumenfeld, Stephen and Partridge, Mark D. "The Long-Run and Short-Run Effects of Global Competition on U.S. Union Wages," *Journal of Labor Research*, Winter 1996, vol. 17, pp. 149-171.

Borjas, George J.; Richard, Freeman and Lawrence, Katz. "On the Labor Market Effects of Immigration and Trade," in G. Borjas ed., *Immigration and the Work Force*, Chicago: University of Chicago Press, 1992, pp. 213-244.

_____, and Ramey, Valerie A. "Time-Series Evidence on the Sources and Trends in Wage Inequality," *American Economic Review*, May 1994, vol. 84, pp. 10-16.

Bound, John and Johnson, George. "Changes in the Structure of Wages in the 1980s: An Evaluation of Alternative Explanations," *American Economic Review*, June 1992, vol. 82, pp. 371-392.

Burtless, Gary. "International Trade and the Rise in Earnings Inequality," *Journal of Economic Literature*, June 1995, vol. 33, pp. 800-816.

Curme, Michael A.; Hirsch, Barry T. and Macpherson, David A. "Union Membership and Contract Coverage in the United States, 1983-1988," *Industrial and Labor Relations Review*, October 1990, vol. 44, pp. 5-33.

DeFreitas, Gregory. "Unionization Among Racial and Ethnic Minorities," *Industrial and Labor Relations Review*, January 1993, vol. 46, pp. 284-301.

Dornbusch, Rudiger. "Exchange Rates and Prices," *American Economic Review*, March 1987, vol. 77, pp. 93-106.

Farber, Henry S. and Saks, Daniel H. "Why Workers Want Unions: The Role of Relative Wages and Job Characteristics," *Journal of Political Economy*, April 1980, vol. 88, pp. 349-369.

Freeman, R. B. "Contraction and Expansion: The Divergence of Private Sector and Public Sector Unionism in the United States," *Journal of Economic Perspectives*, Spring 1988, vol. 2, pp. 63-88.

_____. "How Much has De-Unionization Contributed to the Rise in Male Earnings Inequality," in S. Danziger and P. Gottschalk eds., *Uneven Tides, Rising Inequality in America*, New York: Russell Sage Foundation, 1993, pp. 133-163.

_____. "Are Your Wages Set in Beijing?," *Journal of Economic Perspectives*, Summer 1995, vol. 3, pp. 15-32.

_____ **and Katz, L.** "Industrial Wage and Employment Determination in an Open Economy," in J. Abowd and R. Freeman, *Immigration, Trade, and the Labor Market*, Chicago: University of Chicago Press, 1991, pp. 235-260.

_____. "Rising Wage Inequality: The United States Vs. Other Advanced Countries," in Freeman R. Ed., *Working Under Different Rules*, New York: Russell Sage Foundation, 1994, pp. 29-62.

Greenberg, E.; Pollard, W. and Alpert, W. "Statistical Properties of Data Stretching," *Journal of Applied Econometrics*, October-December 1989, vol. 4, pp. 383-391.

Hirsch, Barry T. and Berger M. C. "Union Membership Determination and Industry Characteristics," *Southern Economic Journal*, January 1984, vol. 50, pp. 665-679.

Johnson, George E. and Stafford, Frank P. "International Competition and Real Wages," *American Economic Review*, May 1993, vol. 83, pp. 127-130.

Kahn, Lawrence M. "Unions and Cooperative Behavior: The Effect of Discounting," *Journal of Labor Economics*, October 1993, vol. 11, pp. 680-703.

Karier, Thomas. "Unions and the U.S. Comparative Advantage," *Industrial Relations*, January 1991, vol. 30, pp. 1-19.

Kokkelenberg, E. and Sockell, D. "Union Membership in the United States, 1973-1981," *Industrial and Labor Relations Review*, July 1985, vol. 38, pp. 497-543.

Lawrence, C. and Lawrence, R. Z. "Manufacturing Wage Dispersion: An End Game Interpretation," *Brookings Papers on Economic Activity*, 1985, pp. 47-106.

Lawrence, Robert Z. *Can America Compete?* Washington, D.C.: Brookings Institution, 1984.

_____ **and Slaughter, Mathew J.** "International Trade and American Wages in the 1980s: Giant Sucking Sound or Small Hiccup?," *Brookings Papers on Economic Activity*, Microeconomics (2), 1993, pp. 161-226.

Macpherson, D. A. and Stewart, J. B. "The Effects of International Trade on Union and Nonunion Wages," *Industrial and Labor Relations Review*, April 1990, vol. 43,pp. 434-446.

Martinello, F. and Meng, R. "Effects of Labor Legislation and Industry Characteristics on Union Coverage in Canada," *Industrial and Labor Relation Review*, October 1992, vol. 46, pp. 176-190.

McDonald, I. M. and Solow, R. M. "Wage Bargaining and Employment," *American Economic Review*, December 1981, vol. 71, pp. 896-908.

Moulton, Brent R. "An Illustration of a Pitfall in Estimating the Effects of Aggregate Variables on Micro Units," *Review of Economics and Statistics*, March 1990, vol. 72, pp. 334-338.

Partridge, Mark D. "Technology, International Competitiveness, and Union Behavior," *Journal of Labor Research*, Spring 1993, vol. 14, pp. 131-149.

_____. "The Effect of International Trade on Worker Union Choice," *Journal of Economics*, Spring 1994, vol. 20, pp. 63-71.

_____. "International Trade and the U.S. Wage Structure," *Journal of Economics and Finance*, forthcoming.

Revanga, Ana. "Exporting Jobs? The Impact of Import Competition on Employment and Wages in U.S. Manufacturing," *Quarterly Journal of Economics*, February 1992, vol. 107, pp. 255-282.

Sachs, Jeffrey D. and Shatz, Howard J. "Trade and Jobs in U.S. Manufacturing," *Brookings Papers on Economic Activity*, 1994, vol. 1, pp. 1-84.

U.S. Bureau of the Census. *Annual Survey of Manufactures*, Washington, D.C.: Government Printing Office, various years.a.

_____. *Census of Manufacturing*, Washington, D.C.: Government Printing Office, various years.b.

U.S. Department of Commerce. *U.S. Commodity Exports and Imports as Related to Output*, Washington, D.C.: Government Printing Office, various years.

U.S. Department of Labor. *Employment and Earnings*, Government Printing Office. various issues.

Wood, Adrian. *North-South trade, employment and inequality: Changing fortunes in a skill-driven world*. Oxford: Clarendon Press, 1994.

9

URUGUAY ROUND REFORMS AND THE DEVELOPING WORLD

Francis Adams
Old Dominion University, USA

The Uruguay Round of the General Agreement on Tariffs and Trade represents a significant advance in multilateral trade negotiations. The Final Accord expands market access, extends foreign investment rights, and liberalizes trade in services. This paper considers the implications of Uruguay Round reforms for developing nations. Although the Accord offers some short-term advantages for these nations, it jeopardizes their long-term prospects for development. Overall, the Accord represents a further step toward the consolidation of economic power in the North and the subordination of national interests to the logic of global markets.

The Uruguay Round of the General Agreement on Tariffs and Trade (GATT) was brought to a close in April 1994. Promoters immediately labeled the new Accord the most significant advance in multilateral trade negotiations since the GATT was founded in 1947. The 123 member nations agreed to reduce tariffs, eliminate non-tariff barriers, introduce new rules governing foreign investment, and incorporate service industries into the multilateral framework. Moreover, a new institution, the World Trade Organization (WTO), was established to oversee implementation of the Accord and to settle disputes among member nations.

The Uruguay Round Agreement (URA) clearly reflects the original objectives of the GATT. Under this free trade regime, member nations are expected to reduce tariffs and dismantle non-tariff barriers. Signatories must also respect the "Most Favored Nation" (MFN) principle wherein any trade privilege granted to one nation must be extended to all other nations.

Liberal economists contend that maintenance of this free trade regime is especially important for the developing nations of Latin America, Africa, and Asia. Because these nations have little bargaining power in the global political-economy, access to foreign markets would be minimal without the GATT framework.[1] Expansion of each nation's export sector is then expected to stimulate other sectors of the economy, laying the foundation for national development and long-term participation in global markets.

This paper considers the implications of the Uruguay Round Accord for developing nations. Of course, one should proceed cautiously when referring to the "developing world." There are important social, economic, and political differences among the nations of Latin America, Africa, and Asia. The effects of the Uruguay Round reforms will obviously vary from one nation to the next. At the same time, we still live in a world divided between the relatively prosperous nations of the North and the relatively impoverished nations of the South. In many respects, the distributional effects of the Uruguay Round reforms will mirror this North-South division.

Uruguay Round Reforms

The Uruguay Round Accord reflects a belief in the basic principles of economic liberalism. The text states that all participating governments ". . . recognize the contribution that liberal trading policies can make to the healthy growth and development of their own economies and of the world economy as a whole."[2] This section reviews the central provisions of the Accord, including measures to reduce tariffs, eliminate non-tariff barriers, promote foreign investment rights, and bring service industries into the GATT disciplines.[3]

Tariffs

A central objective of the Uruguay Round negotiations was to reduce tariff rates among member countries. Here considerable progress was achieved. The signatory nations agreed to reduce average tariff rates by about one-third on most manufactured goods, with minimum reductions required in each tariff line.[4] They also agree to multilateral harmonization of tariffs for a wide variety of products.

Moreover, significant tariff reductions were achieved in sectors which had previously been outside of the GATT disciplines. For example, the Accord brought agriculture into the multilateral negotiations for the first time. Northern nations have a long history of zealously protecting their agricultural sectors.[5] This has been especially true in Western Europe where governments traditionally placed relatively high variable duties on agricultural imports. In addition, most Western European nations and Japan have massively subsidized their agricultural sectors.[6]

Under the Uruguay Round Accord industrialized nations agreed to reduce their agricultural tariffs by about 36 percent over a six-year period. These nations also agreed to reduce the value of their agricultural subsidies to a level 36 percent below the 1986–90 base period level and to reduce the quantity of subsidized exports by 21 percent below the same base period.

The Uruguay Round Agreement also brought textiles and clothing into the multilateral negotiations. Since 1974 textile and clothing exports from developing nations have been limited by quota under the Multilateral Fiber Accord (MFA).[7] Negotiated as a "temporary derogation" to normal GATT disciplines, the MFA has allowed industrialized nations to protect their domestic textile industries.[8] The MFA has been extended four times, most recently in July 1991.

Under the Uruguay Round Agreement, the MFA will be phased out over a ten year period and quotas will be replaced by less restrictive tariffs. Moreover, many countries have agreed to tariff bindings, such that no tariff can be increased beyond a certain level without compensation. A Textiles Monitoring Body was established to oversee implementation of these commitments and to settle disputes among member nations.[9]

Non-Tariff Barriers

Non-tariff barriers were also a central concern during Uruguay Round negotiations. While tariff rates have steadily declined throughout the postwar period, nations have frequently employed non-tariff barriers to protect domestic markets (see Rode, 1990, p. 103). In many respects, non-tariff barriers have emerged as the single greatest threat to the free trade regime.

The Uruguay Round Accord calls for the reduction or elimination of a wide variety of non-tariff barriers. Quotas and import licensing schemes, for example, are to be replaced by tariffs for a number of products. New anti-dumping rules were also introduced. There are now more detailed rules for determining whether a product is dumped and for the implementation and duration of antidumping measures. The Agreement also calls for phasing out safeguards, such as voluntary export restraints (VERs) or orderly marketing arrangements.[10]

Comprehensive rules were also put in place with respect to product standards, such as health, safety, environmental regulations. Such standards cannot be employed without adequate scientific justification and must be both transparent and nondiscriminatory.[11] Similarly, new rules governing balance of payments related trade restrictions were introduced. The text provides that when a country is experiencing serious balance of payments problems, it will impose the least trade-distortive measures (import surcharges instead of quantitative restrictions) for the shortest period of time possible.[12] The Agreement also calls for harmonization of "rules of origin" among the GATT contracting parties including provisions for establishing transparency, notification, consultation, and dispute settlement procedures for origin decisions.[13] Lastly, the Agreement calls for the non-discriminatory access of foreign firms to the goods procurement contracts of signatory governments.

Foreign Investment Rights

Inclusion of foreign investment rights in the Uruguay Round negotiations represented a significant departure from previous rounds of the GATT. Again, justification for the inclusion of these rights follows liberal precepts, with the Final Text explicitly linking the expansion of foreign investment with global economic growth.

The Agreement on Trade Related Investment Measures (TRIMs) removes some of the most common restrictions on foreign investment.[14] For example, the TRIMs text calls for phasing out local content requirements (where some of the materials used to produce a good must be purchased from local sources), trade balancing requirements (which require investors to export an amount equivalent to some proportion of imports), foreign exchange balancing requirements (which link the volume of imports to the level of foreign exchange inflows), product mandating requirements (which require investors to produce specific products), and export performance requirements (which require investors to export a minimum percentage of their production) (Articles 1–9). The text also establishes a Committee on TRIMs to monitor implementation of these commitments.

Service Industries

The Uruguay Round negotiations also brought service industries into the multilateral trade regime. Service industries are defined as those economic activities whose outputs are other than tangible goods. This includes such industries as banking, insurance, securities, legal services, transportation, communication, data processing, retail and wholesale trade, advertising, accounting, construction, design, engineering, management consulting, real estate, education, health care, entertainment, and tourism. Service industries presently account for about $810 billion in global trade per year or roughly 19 percent of total trade (Broadman, 1994, p. 283).

Under the General Agreement on Trade in Services (GATS), member nations subscribed to new rules in more than 150 service industries. The Agreement prohibits measures which limit foreign service suppliers (Article XVI). It also calls for removing limitations on the number of service suppliers, the total value of service transactions, the total number of service operations, or the total number of natural persons that may be employed in a particular service sector (Article XVI). Again these rules are designed to assure foreign service providers the same advantages as their domestic competitors. As stated in the text,

. . . each Member shall accord immediately and unconditionally to services and service suppliers of any other Member treatment no less favorable than that it accords to like services and service suppliers of any other country. (Article II.1)

A Council for Trade in Services was established to oversee implementation of these rules (Article XXIV).

It is important to note that the GATS Accord is fairly minimal. Each government was simply asked to submit a voluntary schedule of commitments for market access in various service sectors. After a period of three years, countries can withdraw or modify commitments made in their schedules (Article XXI). However, the Agreement does establish the basis for progressive liberalization in services through successive rounds of multilateral negotiations.[15]

Developing Countries

Does the Uruguay Round Agreement further the interests of the world's developing nations? Again, there is no simple answer to this question. Given the heterogeneity of the developing world, the specific impact of these reforms will vary cross-nationally. The degree to which an individual nation gains or looses from the Accord will depend on a multitude of factors, including its overall level of development, the size of its economy, and the specific products which it exports.

At the same time, some general observations concerning the likely implications of the Uruguay Round Accord for developing nations can be advanced. First, it is important to note that the text continually refers to the special needs of developing countries, particularly those countries which are considered "least developed."[16] As stated in the text,

. . . there is need for positive efforts designed to ensure that developing countries, and especially the least developed among them, secure a share in the growth in international trade commensurate with the needs of their economic development.[17]

As such, developing countries are not required to open their markets to the same extent as industrial nations and have a longer period to complete the reforms. Least developed countries are only required,

. . . to undertake commitments and concessions to the extent consistent with their individual development, financial and trade needs, and their administrative and institutional capabilities.[18]

Clearly, recognition of the special needs of developing countries is important. The reforms which these nations must implement are, for the most part, less onerous than those required of industrialized nations. However, close analysis of the Accord reveals various ways in which these reforms undermine the long-term development prospects of Southern nations. Most notably, the Accord limits market access for developing nations, erodes the Generalized System of Preferences (GSP), and jeopardizes domestic manufacturing and service industries.

Market Access

Leaders in the developing world have traditionally complained that the GATT framework favors the industrialized nations. In previous GATT agreements, tariffs and non-tariff barriers were lowered for manufactured and capital-intensive goods while they remained high in those areas most important for developing nations.[19] As such, developing nations were expected to open their markets in precisely those sectors in which they were least competitive, while their own export products were excluded from foreign markets.

In some respects, the Uruguay Round Accord replicates this unequal arrangement. While the United States and the European Community agreed to cut their tariffs with each other in half, their average tariffs on goods from the rest of the world will decline by less than one third. Moreover, the tariff reductions of Northern nations are even lower on products of high export importance to developing nations.[20] As such, trade weighted post Uruguay Round tariffs facing developing country exports will be higher than those facing developed country exports in each others markets (Raghavan, 1994a, p. 15; 1994b).

Examination of the agricultural and textiles agreements also calls into question their presumed benefits for developing countries.[21] On the one hand, some of the language employed in the text is quite inclusive. For example, the text states that

. . . developed country Members would take fully into account the particular needs and conditions of developing country Members by providing for a greater improvement of opportunities and terms of access for agricultural products of particular interest to these Members, including the fullest liberalization of trade in tropical agricultural products.[22]

Specific provisions in the accord also seem to favor developing countries. Their tariff reductions are two-thirds those of the developed nations and can be stretched out over a longer period of time. Least-developed countries are not required to make any tariff reductions (Article 15.2). Moreover, as industrialized nations reduce export subsidies, developing countries should be able to compete more effectively in world food markets. Third world farmers have been at a distinct disadvantage in the past because their governments have not been able to provide comparable subsidies.[23]

However, the agricultural accord is also limited in a number of respects. Northern tariffs will remain high for many agricultural products from developing nations and will further increase as a result of tariffication. Moreover, in those sectors where developing countries achieve a significant degree of export competitiveness, they will be compelled to reduce their own tariffs and subsidies on a more accelerated basis. The Accord also restricts various agricultural policies which developing countries have employed in the past, such as minimum guaranteed prices, procurement prices, and price stabilization schemes (Raghavan, 1994b, p. 15).

The inclusion of textiles in the Uruguay Round Agreement has also been championed as an important victory for developing nations. These countries have long contended that their textiles are unfairly excluded from Northern markets.

However, it is important to note that the tariff reduction in textiles and clothing is only 15 percent in North American markets and 20 percent in Western European markets. Moreover, only those developing countries which decrease their own quotas on western fabric and clothing imports will be allowed increased access to Northern markets. Lastly, industrialized nations can still resort to safeguards when ". . . it is demonstrated that a particular product is being imported into its territory in such increased quantities as to cause serious damage, or actual threat thereof, to the domestic industry producing like and/or directly competitive products" (Article 6.2).

Preferential Treatment

The Uruguay Round Accord also erodes some of the key trading privileges which have been granted developing nations in the past. Under the Generalized System of Preferences, Northern nations have sometimes accorded more favorable tariff treatment to products imported from developing countries. Producers in developing countries thus enjoyed a price advantage over foreign products which continue to attract normal duties (OECD, 1983, p. 10). The GSP originated in 1965 when Part IV was added to the General Agreement making an explicit commitment to preferential access. In 1971 member nations approved a waiver to the "Most Favored Nation" principle of the General Agreement to allow preferences for third world exports for a period of ten years.[24] The 1979 "Enabling Clause" allowed for the extension of the GSP indefinitely.

The Uruguay Round Accord does call for the maintenance of such preferential treatment. The text states that "Members shall provide differential and more favorable treatment to developing country Members to this Agreement."[25] Again, the special needs of "least developed countries" are emphasized.

To the extent possible, the MFN concessions on tariffs and non-tariff measures agreed to in the Uruguay Round on products of export interest to the least-developed countries may be implemented autonomously, in advance and without staging. Consideration shall be given to further improve GSP and other schemes for products of particular export interest to least developed countries.[26]

At the same time, the Uruguay Round Accord does not go very far beyond these general appeals for preferential treatment. There are few specific provisions to assure such treatment. In fact, the Uruguay Round Agreement does not even mention the Enabling Clause. While the absence of specific provisions for preferential treatment is a marked difference from previous rounds of GATT negotiations, it does not necessarily indicate that such treatment is being reduced. However, as Michael Rom notes, it does suggest that such treatment is no longer an explicit right of developing countries (other than the least developed) and that such preferences are open to the discretion of developed countries (Rom, 1994, p. 8).

Clearly, the preferential price advantages accorded the exports of developing countries will be reduced, with GSP tariff margins expected to decline by 9 percent in the United States, about 15 percent in Japan, and by about 23 percent in the European Union (Raghavan, 1994c, p. 16). With GSP trade estimated at roughly ninety billion dollars per year, a reduction in these privileges constitutes a significant setback for developing nations.

The Agreement on Safeguards also grants industrialized nations the right to institute safeguard measures against third world products. Safeguards may be taken against a developing country if its share of imports of the product exceeds 3 percent, or developing countries collectively account for more than 9 percent of total imports of the product (Article 9). Similarly, a developing country is required to phase out export subsidies whenever its share of world trade in a particular sector reaches 3.25 percent during two consecutive years.[27]

In short, the Uruguay Round Accord erodes some of the key preferences which developing countries have achieved in previous rounds. At the same time, these nations are required to open their own markets to the products of industrial nations. As a result, small scale artisans with minimal access to capital, advanced technology, or marketing opportunities, will encounter increased competition from transnational firms. The expected influx of foreign products will undermine the market position of manufacturing enterprises in the South.

Once again, these nation will have to rely on a small number of primary product exports. Because trade relations take place in a highly monopolized world market, largely dominated by the industrialized states, primary products are often undervalued relative to manufactured goods. In fact, there has been a consistent decline in the terms of trade between primary and secondary products since the late 1960s. Participation in world markets thus prevents these nations from developing their own productive capabilities. They are left economically dependent on the manufactured goods, capital, and technology of the industrialized nations.

Foreign Investment and Services

Inclusion of foreign investment rights and trade in services in the multilateral trade negotiations also raises important concerns for developing nations. Again, the drafters of the Accord are careful to highlight the special needs of these nations. Both the TRIMs and GATS Agreements make special allowances for developing countries. They are expected to make fewer commitments, liberalizing fewer transactions at a slower pace.[28] Although the provisions on foreign investment rights and service industries are fairly minimal, these reforms do set the stage for progressive liberalization in the future. As Jeffrey Schott notes, the new GATT obligations ". . . would help lock in reforms in countries that already have reduced investment protectionism, encourage further liberalization, and protect against the erection of new barriers" (Schott, 1990, p. 31). For Pierre Sauve, inclusion of foreign investment rights constitutes ". . . an important watershed in international rule-making by subjecting investment related issues for the first time to the logic and disciplines of multilateral trade diplomacy" (Suave, 1994, p. 5).

Of course, liberal economists view the inclusion of foreign investment rights as a positive development for the South. The movement toward a multilateral regime for foreign investment is likely to increase North-South capital flows. Such investment, they argue, would bring an infusion of much needed capital and advanced technology to the South, modernizing the industrial base of these nations and increasing productive capacity.

However, foreign direct investment has often had the opposite effect on developing countries. Such investment typically creates small, capital intensive and labor displacing export enclaves, largely cut off from other sectors of the economy, which absorb local capital and pull resources toward primary rather than industrial production. Surplus generated domestically is then exported abroad rather than reinvested in the local economy. Once again, domestic production contracts as the human and material resources of these nations are used to benefit foreign economic interests.[29] As Emmanuel Awuku points out,

It is the aim of the North to put in place an international investment regime with rules and principles that will restrict and limit host-country policy and laws in relations to foreign investors and technology suppliers. (Awaku, 1994, p. 85)

The inclusion of service industries in the multilateral framework will also have a significant impact on the economies of developing countries. On the one hand, some developing nations have relatively competitive service industries.[30] This is especially true in those cases where labor costs are an important component of total costs (Snape, 1990, p. 6; Page, 1991, p. 43). Many service activities, such as tourism, maritime transport, data processing, and the distributional side of banking and financial services, are relatively labor-intensive (Heydon, 1990, p. 163). Developing nations could also benefit from the transfer of soft technology (management and technical skills) associated with the activities of foreign based service providers (Heydon, 1990, p. 161).

At the same time, the GATS Accord will certainly jeopardize the service sectors of many developing nations.[31] Access to markets in the North will necessitate reciprocal liberalization of Southern markets. The tremendous advantages which Northern firms presently enjoy over their Southern counterparts, most notably in financial services, can be expected to lead to the dismantling of a broad array of local service suppliers in the South. In fact, as Sheila Page notes, inclusion of services was one of the aims of the United States, mainly on the initiative of the major banks (Page, 1991, p. 40).

Domestic Equity

It is also important to consider the likely distributional effects of Uruguay Round reforms *within* the developing world. The question of domestic equity is frequently overlooked. Both promoters and critics of international trade tend to focus almost exclusively on the distribution of benefits between nations. Yet focusing exclusively on nation-states makes very little sense in societies characterized by strong class divisions. Considering the aggregate gains from trade, for example, overlooks the fact that some groups within these nations stand to gain considerably more than others.

Certain groups will clearly benefit from liberalized trade and investment regimes. Entrepreneurs in industry and agribusiness will benefit from access to foreign markets, while professionals and skilled laborers will find expanded employment opportunities with multinational firms, possibly with significantly better wages and benefits than they now enjoy.

However, the gradual reduction of tariffs and other barriers to trade and investment will not benefit the majority of working class and poor people. Rather, the flood of new imports can be expected to lead to the collapse of hundreds of family owned businesses, stores, restaurants, and repair shops. Moreover, small landowners will be displaced as production of cash crops for export replaces the production of staples to meet local needs and the best lands become concentrated in the hands of a small group of foreign and local exporters. As such, these reforms will simply exacerbate inequalities within developing nations, reinforcing the very conditions which generate such widespread poverty and destitution.

Conclusion: Transnational Capital

The Uruguay Round Agreement clearly represents an important development in the history of multilateral trade negotiations. The Accord calls for reducing both tariffs and non-tariff barriers, incorporates agriculture and textiles into the global free trade regime, introduces preliminary measures to extend foreign investment rights, and liberalizes trade in services.

This paper has examined the implications of this Accord for developing nations. Clearly, these reforms will benefit some groups in the developing world. Reduction in tariffs and non-tariff barriers will increase opportunities for third world exporters in Northern markets. Moreover, each section of the Accord includes special provisions for developing and least developed countries. Developing countries are almost always granted a longer period to implement the reforms and least developed countries are not required to make any commitments deemed inconsistent with their development needs.

However, it is important to recognize that these reforms will foreclose many of the policy options which developed countries employed in the past to protect their own infant industries and limit the export of capital. The Accord clearly threatens the economic position of most poor and working class people in the developing world. The market access agreements and inclusion of investment rights and service industries will place small and medium size local firms at a competitive disadvantage with transnational corporations. Moreover, because these reforms favor domestic elites over the rural and urban poor, they will preserve and intensify inequalities within these nations.

In short, the Uruguay Round Agreement reflects the rapidly changing nature of the global economy. Since the reproduction of capital now has a global logic, economic policy is structured to promote transnational rather than purely domestic accumulation. The distinction between a nation's domestic economy and the international economy has little significance when production is organized on a global basis and the cycle of accumulation is transnational. The Accord simply facilitates integration of national economies into the global economy. Rather than a vehicle for national development, the Uruguay Round Agreement represents a further step toward the subordination of national interests to the logic of global markets.

Endnotes

1. This perspective is reflected in Srinivasan (1982) and Hudec (1987).

2. Ministerial Decisions and Declarations, p. 387.

3. A comprehensive review of the Uruguay Round Agreement can be found in Schott (1994) and Steward (1993).

4. Tariff reductions are to be undertaken within six years by developed nations and within ten years by developing nations.

5. This history is chronicled by Avery (1993).

6. These protectionist policies are, of course, a function of the domestic politics of these nations. Agricultural groups constitute extremely powerful lobbies in the major European nations and represent a substantial part of the Liberal Democratic Party's constituency in Japan.

7. For a detailed history of the MFA see Erzan, Goto, and Holmes (1990).

8. In addition, both textiles and clothing are frequently subject to high tariffs in industrial countries. In the United States, for example, the average tariff rate is 17 percent, six times the average of other imports (Page, 1991, p. 27).

9. Both Bagchi (1994) and Blokker and Deelstra (1994), provide detailed analysis of the Uruguay Round reforms with respect to textiles and clothing.

10. Agreement on Safeguards, Articles 1–14. Safeguards are to be phased out within eight years after the date on which whey were first applied or five years after the Uruguay Round, whichever comes later.

11. Agreement on Technical Barriers to Trade, Articles 1–15.

12. Understanding on Balance of Payments Provisions of the General Agreement on Tariffs and Trade 1994.

13. Agreement on Rules of Origin, Articles 1–9.

14. It is important to note, however, that TRIMs are not precisely defined in the text but subject to future negotiations.

15. These negotiations are to begin not later than five years from the date of entry into force of the Agreement and are to be conducted periodically thereafter (Article XIX.1)

16. The United Nations list of least developed countries was used by Uruguay Round negotiators.

17. Agreement Establishing the World Trade Organization, p. 9

18. Agreement Establishing the World Trade Organization, Article XI.2.

19. Such as agricultural products, semi-processed commodities, and labor-intensive consumer goods.

20. See Raghavan (1994c, p. 17). This includes woolen, synthetic and cotton fabrics, footwear and leather products, certain ceramics and glassware, automotive vehicles, and consumer electronics.

21. This argument is more fully developed in Anderson and Tyers (1990).

22. Agreement on Agriculture, p. 43.

23. At the same time, the framers concede that subsidies may play an important role in the economic development programs of developing countries (Article 6.2). The text also recognizes that least-developed and net food-importing countries may encounter difficulties during the reform program. Therefore, a special Decision calls for the provision of food aid and basic foodstuffs to these countries.

24. For a history of the GSP see Whalley (1989) and Langhammer and Sapir (1987).

25. Agreement on Technical Barriers to Trade, Article 12.1

26. Decision on Measures in Favor of Least-Developed Countries, p. 385.

27. Agreement of Subsidies and Countervailing Measures, Article 27.6. Subsidies must be phased out over eight years for least developed countries and over two years for other developing countries.

28. Implementation of the agreed upon reforms is to be achieved within two years for developed countries, within five years for developing countries and within seven years for least-developed countries. The GATS Agreement also allows developing countries to attach requirements for access to technology, distributional channels, and information networks. However, since these special allowances are not legally binding, comprehensive implementation is not guaranteed.

29. This position is possibly best reflected in the writings of Chakravarthi Raghavan, who has emerged as one of the most outspoken critics of the Uruguay Round. See in particular his book *Recolonization: GATT, the Uruguay Round, and the Third World* (1990).

30. A cross-national analysis of service industries can be found in Messerlin and Sauvant (1990).

31. This perspective is further developed in Hindley (1988).

References

Anderson, Kym and Tyers, Rodney. "How Developing Countries Could Gain from Agricultural Trade Liberalization in the Uruguay Round," in Ian Goldin and Odin Knudsen, eds. *Agricultural Liberalization: Implications for the Developing Countries*, Paris: Organization for Economic Cooperation and Development, 1990.

Avery, William. *World Agriculture and the GATT*. Boulder: Lynne Rienner, 1993.

Awuku, Emmanuel Opoku. "How do the Results of the Uruguay Round Affect the North-South Trade," *Journal of World Trade* 1994, 28(2), pp. 75–93.

Bagchi, Sanjoy. "The Integration of the Textile Trade into GATT," *Journal of World Trade* 1994;28(6), pp. 31–42.

Blokker, Niels and Deelstra, Jan. "Towards a Termination of the Multi-Fibre Arrangement?" *Journal of World Trade* 1994, 28(5), pp. 97–118.

Broadman, Harry. "GATTS: The Uruguay Round Accord on International Trade and Investment in Services," *The World Economy* 1994, 17(3), pp. 281–92.

Erzan, Refig; Goto, Junichi and Holmes, Paula. "Effects of the Multi-Fibre Arrangement on Developing Countries' Trade: An Empirical Investigation." in Carl B. Hamilton, ed., *Textiles Trade and the Developing Countries*, Washington, D.C.: The World Bank, 1990.

Heydon, Kenneth. "Developing Country Perspectives." in Patrick A. Messerlin and Karl P. Sauvant, *The Uruguay Round: Services in the World Economy,*. Washington, D.C.: The World Bank, 1990.

Hindley, B. "Service Sector Protection: Considerations for Developing Countries," *World Bank Economic Review* 1988, 2(2).

Hudec, Robert. *Developing Countries in the GATT Legal System*. London: Trade Policy Research Centre, 1987.

Langhammer, Rolf and Sapir, Andre. *Economic Impact of Generalized Tariff Preferences*. London: Trade Policy Research Centre, 1987.

Messerlin, Patrick A. and Sauvant, Karl P. *The Uruguay Round: Services in the World Economy*. Washington, D.C.: The World Bank, 1990.

Organization for Economic Cooperation and Development (OECD). *The Generalized System of Preferences: Review of the First Decade*. Paris: OECD, 1983.

Page, Sheila. *GATT Uruguay Round: Effects on Developing Countries.* London: Overseas Development Institute, 1991.

Raghavan, Chakravarthi. "The WTO and the New Trade Order: Advantage for Whom?" *Third World Economics* 1994a, 101, pp. 11–20.

_____. "Detailed Analysis of Uruguay Round Results Sought," *Third World Economics* 1994b, 93/94, pp. 14–15.

_____. *Recolonization: GATT, the Uruguay Round, and the Third World.* Penang, Malaysia: Third World Network, 1990.

_____. "Third World Losers Either Way," *Third World Economics* 1994c, 90, pp. 15–17.

Rode, Reinhard. *GATT and Conflict Management: A Transatlantic Strategy for a Stronger Regime.* Boulder, Westview, 1990.

Rom, Michael. "Some Early Reflections on the Uruguay Round as Seen from the Viewpoint of a Developing Country," *Journal of World Trade* 1994, 28(6), pp. 5–30.

Sauve, Pierre. "A First Look at Investment in the Final Act of the Uruguay Round," *Journal of World Trade* 1994, 28(5), pp. 5–16.

Schott, Jeffrey. *The Uruguay Round: An Assessment.* Washington, D.C.: Institute for International Economics, 1994.

_____. *The Global Trade Negotiations: What Can Be Achieved?* Washington, D.C.: Institute for International Economics, 1990.

Snape, Richard H. "Principles in Trade in Services." in Patrick A Messerlin and Karl P. Sauvant, *The Uruguay Round: Services in the World Economy,.* Washington, D.C.: The World Bank, 1990.

Srinivasan, T. N. *Why Developing Countries Should Participate in the GATT System,* London: Trade Policy Research Centre, 1982.

Steward, Terrence. *The GATT Uruguay Round.* Boston: Kluwer, 1993.

Uruguay Round of Multilateral Trade Negotiations, Final Text. Office of the United States Trade Representative, Washington, D.C., 1994.

Whalley, John, ed. *The Uruguay Round and Beyond: Final Report from the Ford Foundation Supported Project on Developing Countries and the Global Trading System.* Ann Arbor: University of Michigan, 1989.

10

STRUCTURAL ADJUSTMENT AND CIVIL SOCIETY IN CONTEMPORARY AFRICA[1]

Sandra J. MacLean
Timothy M. Shaw
Dalhousie University, Canada

This chapter contributes to the debates surrounding the possible roles which various non-governmental organizations (NGOs) play in the democratisation and development of contemporary Africa. It argues that although more than a decade of externally dictated, neoliberal "reforms" have created "political space" for the actual, or at least potential (re)vitalisation of civil societies, dangers persist of regressions towards corporatism, authoritarianism and anarchy.

West Africa is becoming <u>the</u> symbol of worldwide demographic, environmental and societal stress, in which criminal anarchy emerges as the real "strategic" danger...West Africa provides an appropriate introduction to the issues, often extremely unpleasant to discuss, that will soon confront our civilization.

- Kaplan (1994: 46)

The trend is towards corporatism.
- Baskin (1993:2)

Structural adjustments and changes in both Africa and the global political economy which were apparent throughout the decade of the 1980s have become undeniable in the 1990s: the so-called "New" World (Dis)Order (Shaw, 1994). New social movements and contexts have stimulated prolonged debates about civil society's emerging central role in both the theories and practices of democratisation and development, as well as parallel debates on the dangers of regressions towards corporatism, authoritarianism and anarchy.

As a contribution to these debates, this paper focuses on the various non-governmental organisations (NGOs) which are central actors within newly- and re-established civil societies in Africa and elsewhere in the South. Despite the many contestations concerning the concept of civil society and the nuanced relations which exist among the various organisations of which it is composed, much of the recent literature posits an uncontradictory association with the institutions of liberal democracy. While acknowledging the relevance and necessity for democracy of constitutions, multipartyism and elections, the paper is concerned to go beyond such formal processes and institutions to underlying structures. Hence, it commences with an overview of Africa's political economy at the end of the twentieth century, seeking to situate the continent in the New International Divisions of Labour (NIDL) and of Power (NIDP) after more than a decade of externally dictated but internally digested adjustment "reforms". Then, informed by ongoing research of colleagues and by comparative typologies, it proceeds to an analysis of revitalised African civil societies. Finally, it concludes by identifying major challenges and opportunities confronting the continent as the next millennium approaches.

Africa's Political Economy/Culture in the 1990s

The political economy and political culture of Africa at the end of the twentieth century are quite different from those inherited by the new indigenous regimes at the end of the colonial era. Such changes are as much a function of the evolution of national and international economies and civil societies as of national policies or preferences; hence the relevance of international political economy (IPE) perspectives as opposed to rational choice. Indeed, the incidence and intensity of structural rather than state interventions have increased with the new conditionalities of the present "neo-liberal" period; ie since the start of the eighties. But the "lost decade" of structural adjustment programmes (SAPs) was but a formalisation and extension of pre- and post-independence dependency, the negative effects of which had been initially camouflaged by post-war growth and then -independence honeymoon. Unfortunately, SAPs coincided not only with the height and then demise of the Cold War but also with profound structural change, contraction and differentiation in the global economy.

Initially, in the first half of the 1980s, SAPs designed by the international financial institutions (IFIs) in Washington - the Bank and the Fund - were confined to "economic" policies and terms, but their range of conditionalities has grown in the last five years to include such "political" elements as democratic constitutions and elections, and more recently ecological and military factors such as increased environmental and decreased strategic expenditures. To be sure, SAP agreements are often honoured more in the breach than in implementation, with Western allies securing preferential treatment until the end of the Cold War: from slippages and changes in sequences to backsliding and abandonment. However, in an era of *neo-liberal hegemony*, some SAP terms get effected as aspects of contemporary policies; ie informal as well as formal negotiation and implementation. In short, the early stages of SAPs created the need for subsequent revisions and extensions.

The *negative impacts of SAPs* on lower classes and especially on "vulnerable" groups like women and children are now widely recognised. Much less acknowledged are their equally negative implications for middle and even upper classes. The declining quality and availability as well as escalating costs of basic welfare - education, health and infrastructure like electricity, housing and water - have hit the working class and un- and under-employed severely and incrementally since the early-1980s. But the *middle classes* have also been affected negatively, albeit somewhat belatedly but subsequently cumulatively as I) real incomes have declined precipitously, especially in terms of foreign exchange, and ii) costs of goods and services have escalated as inflation and user-fees have risen. Hence the frequency for the latter of the "exit" option involving activities ranging from migration to the creation of "instant" NGOs or consultancy think-tanks and moonlighting in several jobs simultaneously (see NGO typology below). This group's decline in prosperity has profound implications for redevelopment as well as for democracy; without a strong middle class, sustainable democracy is quite unlikely whatever the constitution. The proposition that SAPs would ultimately contribute to the emergence of thriving bourgeoisies throughout the continent amounts to a *fallacy of social composition* which parallels the economic fallacy that unlimited opportunity for diversification and expansion of exports exists even when most other Third World states are following similar SAP conditionalities[2].

In the initial *post-independence period*, most African regimes had sought to maximize their control over the hitherto colonial or settler state: interventions for indigenous power and property. These were relatively non-controversial given the prevailing social democratic environment in the global system: state capitalism or state socialism. And even declarations of peoples or communist systems were considered to be quite normal given the nature of some liberation struggles as well as of the bipolar system. In the absence of regular democratic elections, nationalist leaders were changed only by coups or by death. Thus, until the end of the 1970s, most African states were classic one-party or military regimes characterised by a high degree of centralisation and regulation, extending into the state-owned parastatal nexus.

Such *post-independence regimes* were neither developmental nor democratic. Wherever they could do so they placed severe limits on the role of civil society as well as on private capital. Such concentration of power was excused as a necessary reaction to previously exclusive colonial or settler orders in a Cold War era in which "half" the world enjoyed state communist government. Notions of democratic development or human rights were rejected as mere Western attempts to maintain economic influence and strategic balance.

Although at the level of the polity, the 1970s seemed to be a decade of continuity of African state control, at the level of the economy they constituted the beginning of a discontinuity. While some African countries, communities and classes grew along with most of the world economy in the 1960s, so reinforcing orthodox notions of international assistance and exchange as the means to growth if not development, the subsequent "shocks" of the 1970s wrought havoc even among the minority of "oil-producers" let alone among the majority of -importers. Exponential rises in the prices of both oil and money in the 1970s sowed the seeds of the next decade's debt "crisis" and made the continent vulnerable to hegemonic neo-liberal pressures.

The *conjuncture of the new decade of the 1980s* was marked by the appearance of two contradictory visions for post-nationalist Africa: the OAU"s "orthodox" pro-state *Lagos Plan of Action* and the IBRD's "radical" pro-market *Agenda for Action,* otherwise known as the (infamous?) "Berg Report". Despite initial resistance from both inside and outside the continent, the neo-liberal doctrines of both Bank and Fund became the new orthodoxy throughout Africa by the second half of the 1980s, in part because their conditionalities were effective. Given escalating debt obligations as well as forex shortages most regimes buckled under and began negotiations with Paris and/or London Clubs as well as with the IFIs in Washington.

In the process, the nature of the "development" discourse (Moore & Schmitz 1995) was transformed from acceptance of state intervention in the economy to a mix of deregulation, devaluation, privatisation, user-pay etc: a diminishing state (Nyang'oro & Shaw 1993). The distinction between state capitalism and state socialism was superseded by that between more or less "reform". And the space for non-state actors and activities expanded as it had done in the final days of colonialism when the nationalist movement successfully demanded a voice. Thus, by the start of the 1990s, African states were in general, however reluctantly at first, moving toward *liberalisation in both economics and politics,* whether these are compatible or not. In part this was in response to increasing Northern conditionalities or "interventions", which came to insist on democratic governance as well as open economies.

While orthodox Northern conditionalities have come to include democratic governance as an element in continuous aid/debt relief for reform negotiations, multi-party institutions and elections may not be enough to sustain "new" democracies into the next century. This is especially so as both global and continental economies are not exactly helpful given continued recessions and restructurings. To be sure, national conventions, constitutions and elections are crucial elements in any democratic system in the North as well as in the South. But these are only sustainable if continuously reinforced and supported by myriad non-state actors and activities; ie *"civil society".*

Civil Society in the Contemporary Continent

Civil society is usually conceived as the "...space of uncoerced human association and also the set of relational networks - formed for the sake of family, faith, interest and ideology - that fill this space" (Walzer 1991). In short, it is comprised of the various non-governmental organizations, human rights groups, cooperatives, unions, media, religious assemblages, professional associations, *et cetera* through which individuals collectively and voluntarily carry out their social enterprises. Such associations exist in dynamic tension with the state - hence, the contradictory treatments of civil society corresponding to various definitions and theories of state. *Liberals* tend to see state and civil society as distinct and oppositional - the former, possessing final coercive authority, mediates among competing interests in civil society, while the latter, in the collective and protected by the rule of law, limits the power of the state. By contrast, in the *Marxist* tradition, "(c)ivil society as such only develops with the bourgeoisie; the social organization evolving out of production and intercourse, which in all ages forms the basis of the state and the rest of the idealistic superstructure" (Marx & Engels 1976: 98). In short, the state is subordinate to civil society which is considered to be the realm of economic relations. *Gramscian* analysis provides yet a third version, accepting the Marxist idea of the primacy of a materialist base but placing civil society in the superstructure along with the state and including ideology with economics as primary forces (Carnoy 1984: 65-68).

The concept of *hegemony* which distinguishes the Gramscian notion of civil society from both liberal and Marxist versions is instructive in understanding post-independence state-societal relations in Africa. Whereas the term refers to the leadership by dominant classes by virtue of subordinate classes' submission - confirmed through consent rather than coercion - any hegemonic order which may have prevailed in countries in the early post-independence period was based on the unifying ideologies of nationalism and developmentalism which were unsustainable and short-lived. Although the characteristic African one-party and one-man state attempted in this period to monopolise political, economic and social life, it rarely achieved total, authoritarian control; weak economies do not allow for strong states. While hegemony in the Gramsican sense may have been nascent or fleeting in at least some of the post-independence societies, the combination of authoritarianism and weakness which ensued resembles a Gramscian "crisis of authority". Such a crisis results from the inability of the dominant class to retain its social consensus, following which control of civil society can be maintained only through coercion.

Nevertheless, while post-independence African states became increasingly adept at suppressing their civil societies, some features of the latter persisted, whether cooperatives, service clubs, trade unions, professional associations, religions or social organisations. And, in recent years, in response to states' comparative weakness, the range and diversity of forces in contemporary civil society has expanded once again. In particular, there has been a proliferation in *Non-Governmental Organisations* (NGOs) ranging from the small-scale indigenous associations which are the building blocks of effective local democracy to global NGOs which serve ideally in facilitating roles: another international "division of labour"? Over the last decade in particular various formations from grass-roots organisations and national structures to continental alliances represent a renaissance of civil society. In this reconstruction of societal relations, local and national, regional and global NGOs together with the media and religious institutions have a major part: pluralism as well as capitalism.

Although NGOs share a couple of essential features with each other and with other elements of civil society - they are non-state institutions beyond the family or household - they are otherwise characterised by *heterogeneity* rather than homogeneity. Such *diversity* is in part a function of changing demands and opportunities which have been presented by new divisions of labour and power as well as of longevity and evolution let alone competition within the NGO community itself. Therefore, just as African political economies have now to be recategorized in relation to their changing positions within the NIDL and NIDP, so NGOs in

Africa have to be retypologised as they are not all equal, neither in terms of functional attributes nor political character. Indeed, the increased heterogeneity of the rapidly expanding community of NGOs is such that it is impossible to generalise about NGOs' propensities for supporting or promoting democratic change or sustainable development. Moreover, critical analysis from "second wave" of scholarship on NGOs is skeptical about earlier positive claims regarding NGOs' inherent comparative advantage in micro development or a tendency to possess greater internal democracy (Hume and Edwards, 1996). It is beyond the scope of the overview presented in this chapter to attempt to disaggregate this community; however, many useful comparative analyses of specific NGOs or of NGOs within a particular country, region or area have begun to appear in the literature. One general, comparative attempt at such categorisation is offered by Korten (1990) who distinguishes among three "generations" of NGOs: 1) relief and welfare; 2) small-scale: self-reliant/local development; 3) sustainable: systems development. But this somewhat linear typology fails to treat changes in either external (global and/or international) contexts or internal (national and/or sub-national) structures, both of which can lead to complications, regressions and/or contestations.

Some distinctions found in other Southern regions may be relevant to Africa given the greater longevity and impact of NGOs in, say, parts of Asia and Latin America. Drawing on such comparative analyses, then (eg Heyzer *et al* 1995; Korten 1990; MacDonald 1996; Moore & Schmitz 1995; Wellard et al 1993), we can suggest the following set of overlapping *categories for African NGOs* which complement Korten's Asia-centric list of NGO generations:

1.   local versus national, international, regional and/or global;

2.   specific sector or multi-sectoral (eg agriculture, environment, education, gender, health, human rights, media, religion, etc);

3.   advocacy, communications, educational, welfare and/or production oriented;

4.   democratic or hierarchical in structure;

5.   primarily concerned with development issues and/or projects;

6.   part of broader NGO/civil society coalition or not;

7.   instant or long-established NGO;

8.   political orientation - conservative, mainstream, neutral and/or regressive; and

9.   antagonistic, cooperative or dependent relations with governments and/or transnational organisations.

In short, NGOs are distinguished not only by their normative commitments and functional operations, but also by the nature of their relations with other actors in both domestic and international environments. NGOs may exist in contradictory or complementary relationship with the state or, in Bratton's words, "engagement between state and society ... may be congruent as well as conflictual" (1989a: 418). The state-societal relationship may even degenerate to disengagement or anarchy, although, hopefully, not inevitably as Robert Kaplan's (1994) pessimistic and rather stereotypical perspective on Africa suggests.

But if the maintenance of a democratic social order implies some measure of engagement, by most definitions, NGOs (and civil society, generally) are distinct from the state. Indeed, *autonomy* is essential for the authority and integrity of such groups; popular or civic associations which fail to retain their independence are in reality only quasi- or semi-non-governmental.

However, creating and maintaining distance from partisan politics, government interventions and powerful companies is not easy. For example, elements in civil society which had been part of broad nationalist then democracy movements in the 1950s and 1980s, respectively, have had to distinguish themselves from political parties, especially those formally in power or in opposition. Such is the challenge for the civic movement in *South Africa*: the difficulty of playing a role of watchdog/conscience when closely allied with the transitional Government of National Unity (Lanegran, 1995).

Governments' attitudes toward NGOs extend from toleration and support to suspicion and hostility. In the latter instance, governments resort to various methods to coopt, control or repress (MacLean 1993a). Many of the actions tend to blur the legal and/or *de facto* distinction between state and societal institutions. Moreover, since external lending agencies now frequently fund NGOs directly, government officials in some countries have set up rival structures, awkwardly termed governmental-non-governmental organisations or GONGOs (Fowler 1992).

Given the proliferation of such quasi-NGOs (QUANGOs) under external pressures or incentives and in response to liberalised political economies/cultures, Bebbington & Farrington (1993: 202 & 216) suggest that a recent type of so-called NGO is "technocratic". These tend to result from the "economic displacement of middle class professionals from both public and private sectors"; any criticisms of government from them is "on the grounds of its inefficiency rather than its distributional and political biases". They go on to suggest in this context that "Technocratic is a generous term. They might also be called opportunistic NGOs...(even) 'yuppie NGOs'"(!)

The NGO world has become *big business*, especially since the start of the 1980s and SAPs: over US $5 billion annually, mainly through some 200+ Northern NGOs, but increasingly also via myriad Southern NGOs. Over 5% of Northern Official Development Assistance (ODA) is now distributed by NGOs, hence the controversies over an equitable and sustainable division of labour among them: from partnership to compact? (Kajese 1987) Many NGOs in both North and South now depend on ODA rather than private or members' donations. In turn, they are becoming more professional and bureaucratic, undergoing evaluations and upgradings themselves.

Such changes and realignments have fuelled debates concerning NGOs' legitimacy and accountability and generated questions on whether NGOs serve mainly as delivery agents for more powerful states and/or IFIs or whether they can maintain a democratising, developmentalist role in policy and/or political protest (Brown & Tandon, 1995; Covey, 1995; Hulme & Edwards, 1996). Even if NGOs are able to resist cooptation or external control, any active involvement in *policy debates* with state and interstate agencies is complicated. On the one hand, if they focus exclusively on "micro-level" projects then their efforts may be rendered pointless by macro-policy issues, such as SAPs. On the other hand, if they deal only with macro-policy issues, then local development may be disregarded particularly in the short-term (Bebbington & Farrington, 1993; Edwards, 1994). Clearly, some mix of macro- and micro-level roles, however elusive and problematic in practice, may be imperative in terms of the sustainability of both civil society and development.

Challenges for African Development in the Next Century

The NIDL and NIDP have together thrown up considerable challenges for the African continent as well as the rest of the world into the next century (Shaw 1994):

1.	*new states*, such as Eritrea and Somaliland in Africa:

2.	new factors ranging from the resurgent interest in democracy, concern for environmental issues such as biodiversity, ozone-depletion and global warming, the emergence of gender as a political issue and force, the increase in informal sector activity - including drug-trafficking and other crime, and the growing problem of social "emergencies" - such as viruses like AIDs and people migrations, to dramatic changes in production and labour practices, especially flexibilisation and feminisation.

3.   *new institutions* including the diversity of inter-governmental (eg G-7, -15 & -24), regional (eg AEC and SADC, etc), and transnational organisations (from MNCs, especially now from Asia, and trade unions to global religious arrangements and "ethnic" communities);

4.   *new relations*, especially globalization, regionalisation and hierarchisation, particularly differentiation between and within states, notably the rise of the Newly Industrializing Countries (NICs) and near-NICs and the roles of "middle powers" like China and India along with the relative decline of Fourth and Fifth Worlds; and

5.   *new responses or perspectives* from civil society including global commissions (eg Brandt, Brundtland, Carlsson & Ramphal) and "alternative global conferences" such as counter-conferences on the environment and women or at IFI annual meetings - ie global mobilisation by NGOs rather than by states - along with appropriate analytical or ideological formulations: popular participation, civil society, democratic development etc.

In addition to myriad development and foreign policy challenges perhaps especially for Africa, such changes also present some favourable contexts as well, albeit unintentionally[3]. Given the continuing global recession and restructuring, international and national aid agencies may not be able to maintain SAP terms much longer. Indeed, they have already proliferated conditionalities in part to disguise their inability to meet their terms of the apparent development "contract": less state intervention/oppression for more external assistance. Now regimes have to meet a range of political, ecological and strategic terms as well as economic. Meanwhile, economic contraction and aid fatigue in the North, along with diversion of attention and assistance to the East, mean that the South might be able to seize the current conjuncture to advance its *self-reliance.*

Not only has "post-socialist triumphalism" of the turn of the decade dissipated but neo-liberal confidence has also evaporated, symbolized by the Clinton White House's preoccupation with jobs rather than debt. In these circumstances, encouraged by the September 1992 Jakarta Non-Aligned conference that focused on the *Challenge to the South* (which should now include NAM's own internal democratisation?!) - the first post-Cold War (and -Yugoslavia meeting) - the South, including Africa, might still advance its national and collective self-reliance, thereby ultimately advancing global as well as Third World sustainable development. In short, even in spite of varying degrees of disarticulation between states and civil societies, the present conjuncture in the global political economy may provide opportunities of revi(s)ing old ideas and/or alliances which would lend support to development strategies based on 'popular participation' rather than on neoliberal economics.

Global change after the Cold War can no longer be the exclusive preserve of either states or interstate organisations. Both UN and IFI systems, continental and regional institutions, have been resistant to popular pressures, even although sustainable African cooperation and development cannot occur without direct popular participation. Thus, the current climate of democratic governance constitutes a unique conjuncture at which *civil society can demand attention* at inter- as well as trans-national arenas (Archibugi & Held, 1995; UNDP, 1994). To be sure, established agencies have not exactly brought international peace or development. And unless such global institutions are changed, they will continue to advocate inappropriate policies like SAPs.

Moreover, if NGOs do not insist on a direct role in international (and global?) (Nelson, 1995) as well as national decision-making they will run the risk of being coopted in such inappropriate projects on the terms of the UN, IFIs etc; ie parallel to the dangers of cooptation at national and local levels. This dilemma extends also to African continental and regional organizations, from the ECA & OAU to ECOWAS & SADC: how to facilitate and reinforce transnational connections among civil societies as essential elements in any sustainable pattern of integration? The challenge posed by the continental conference in Arusha on popular participation (OAU 1989) cannot be avoided by African (& other Southern, like NAM & G-77) inter-governmental organizations!

The *second* chance facing the South to effect democracy may also be its last. Just as novel multi-racial and -party constitutions and elections disappeared in the 1960s so the current *trend towards pluralism* may also evaporate. Given the largely negative consequences of SAPs, the environment for renewed democracy in many countries is hardly propitious. This is despite both 'neo-liberal rhetoric to the contrary' and the increased opportunities and various pressures for democratization from civil societies. Declining levels of living and basic needs satisfaction along with increasing inequalities and under/unemployment do not advance democratic practice. Exponential inflation along with the disappearance of the middle class undermine the prospects for sustainable development, whether brokered by NGOs or not.

If democracy proves to be unsustainable, in part because political and economic liberalizations are incompatible, then a return to authoritarianism or a retreat to anarchy are possible, particularly in the more marginal, Fourth or Fifth World states. Alternatively, especially in the more developed Third World political economies, some form of *corporatism* is likely: an exclusive understanding among capital, labour and the state which essentially excludes many of the other groups of civil society.

Corporatist arrangements have already been effected in some African states such as Zimbabwe (Nyang'oro & Shaw 1989) and others may be anticipated such as in a post-apartheid South Africa (Shaw 1994). As Baskin (1993: i) suggests: "There is a trend towards bargained corporatism in South Africa ... An institutionalized role for labour and capital in the formulation and regulation of economic policy is emerging". This conclusion is echoed from a more radical, materialist perspective by Johann Maree (1993: 24) who indicates that the combination of corporate concentration and high levels of un- and under-employment are likely to lead to both macro- and meso-level corporatism; ie from National Economic Forum to sectoral groups and summits:

There is a remarkably strong corporatist current flowing in South Africa. The major actors - labour, capital and the state - are so caught up in it that they are hardly aware of the fact that they have become part of the current.

Not all such possible scenarios - from democratization at global as well as local levels, through national corporatism and authoritarianism to anarchy - are incompatible; there may be a mixture or sequence of them depending on national and international contexts and pressures. While the cycle of state nationalization and liberalization may be repeated at the start of the next century, more likely is a further *divergence* of African political economies, in part as a consequence of adjustment reforms and external market opportunities or niches - authoritarianism or anarchy in the Fourth and Fifth Worlds and corporatism in the Third? Such differences would present problems throughout the continent for civil society in general and NGOs in particular as they would tend to become stronger in some states and weaker in others, so retarding prospects for regional and continental roles.

Whatever the specific character of internal social forces - ie the balance between civil society and the state - as already suggested, a range of relatively *"new" issues* confronts contemporary African political economies. These have typically been treated previously as "foreign policy" matters, open only to exclusive elite decision-making: the myth of "national security". However, in a post-bi-polar and -adjustment period, characterized by diminishing national borders and expanding transnational relations including "new" security threats, these increasingly become the concern of civil society as well, even if it lacks sufficient technical and financial resources to resolve them all at once. Elements in local or national civil society may, of course, seek to respond to many of these contemporary issues through regional or global levels of civil society, such as INGOs or international cooperative, media, religious or professional organizations. Complemented by pressure applied from such external sources, revitalized civil societies may yet force hitherto recalcitrant states into new, more democratic associations: from counter-hegemony to reestablished hegemony?

Conclusion: *What Prospects for Sustainable Democracy in the Twenty-first Century?*

SAP conditionalities and consequences have contradictory implications for African political economies/cultures. On the one hand, negatively, they have led to lower levels of basic human needs (BHN) satisfaction as well as to greater degrees of inequality. On the other hand, positively, they have legitimized political as well as economic liberalization, creating both demand and space for non-state actors and activities (Bratton 1990). However, the extent to which the latter promote sustainable democratic and developmentalist institutions and political cultures in particular countries varies depending upon unique sets of state, societal and external relations (Cox 1981). Moreover, the correlation between economic and political liberalization may be neither as direct nor non-contradictory as neo-liberal agencies' prescriptions would suggest.

Establishing appropriate civil society alliances surely constitutes the major *challenge confronting civil society, and especially the developmentalist NGOs within it, at the end of the twentieth century*: how to articulate and sustain local and global attention and resolution to critical issues? To be sure, it is quite unfair for the state system to deny its responsibility and capability, especially given the paucity of NGO resources. Yet while this challenge is rather unanticipated, the international context has never been more favorable: the new legitimacy and practice of democratic governance. If the 1980s in Africa was the pessimistic decade of SAPs, hopefully the 1990s and beyond can be the more optimistic one of the NGOs!

Such a possibility needs to be noticed and encouraged by analysts, whether academic or policy. Even now, the tenuous renaissance of pluralism in the continent tends to be overlooked by scholars and practitioners alike, particularly its civil society/NGOs if not so much its multi-party/elections aspects. Although they now symbolize the diminished stature and ambition of the hitherto dominant and dominating African state, the current dynamism of pluralism as well as capitalism herald the possibility of future democratic alliances between revitalized civil societies and reformed states. However, while the present conjuncture may offer opportunities to create such alliances, the possibility for less attractive scenarios is a troubling reality: corporatism, authoritarian and anarchy remain as potential and, in some countries, likely alternatives to democratic multipartyism and constitutionalism.

Endnotes

1. This is a revised version of a paper which will appear in the July, 1996 edition of the *Journal of Contemporary African Studies*.

2. For discussions on the *negative social effects of SAPs*, see, for example: Connelly et al. 1995; Dei, 1992; Hutchful, 1994; McLean, 1995; UNRISD, 1995. According to some analysts, such criticisms of SAPs miss the obvious - that structural adjustment became necessary because of the growing crisis in state management (cf. Van de Walle, 1994, p. 110). However, this so-called *counterfactual* argument which is based on a comparison of the situation with and without structural adjustment programmes disregards a second counterfactual which questions what the situation would be without a *different* structural adjustment, formulated on a social democratic rather than neo-liberal model. Or, as Richard Sandbrook (1995, p. 287) asserts, "(t)he alternative to adjustment is ... adjustment".

3. Certainly, Africa, as a continent, suffers more than any other region from the negative aspects of *new factors* such as AIDs and people migrations and at least as much from ecological strain, human rights violations and gender inequities. Moreover, with regard to *new relations*, and particularly *globalization*, Africa has become further marginalised within the increasingly *hierchical* global economy. At the same time, however, *new responses*, especially by civil societies, often supported by *new institutions* or new relations with existing institutions - eg. The UN and UN Conferences, offer unprecedented opportunities for positive change toward the integration of democratising initiatives from local, to national, regional, continental and global levels.

References

Adedeji, Adebeyo. "The African Challenges in the 1990s: new perspectives for development," *Indian Journal of Social Science,* 1990;3, pp.255-269

_____ and Shaw, Timothy, eds. *Economic Crisis in Africa*, Boulder: Lynne Rienner, 1985.

"Africa in the New World Order". *Review of African Political Economy* 1991, pp.50

African Leadership Forum. "Kampala Document from the Conference on Security, Stability, Development & Cooperation in Africa", May 1991.

All Africa Conference of Churches. "Emerging Power of Civil Society in Africa: report of workshop on approaches & skills in advocacy for development," September 1992, Nairobi.

Anyang' Nyong'o, Peter, ed. *Popular Struggles for Democracy in Africa.* London: Zed for UNU, 1987.

Archibugi, Daniele and Held, David. *Cosmopolitan Democracy: an agenda for a New World Order.* Cambridge: Polity Press, 1995.

Atkinson, Doreen, ed. Special Issue on the State & Civil Society.. *Theoria* 1992, 79, pp.1-104.

Barya, John-Jean B. The New Political Conditionalities of Aid: an independent view from Africa. *IDS Bulletin* 1993:24 (1), pp.16-23.

Baskin, Jeremy. Corporatism: some obstacles facing the South African labour movement, Research Report #30; Johannesburg: Centre for Policy Studies; April 1993.

Bebbington, Anthony & John Farrington. "Governments, NGOs & Agricultural Development," *Journal of Development Studies* 1993, 29 (2), pp. 199-219

Beckman, Bjorn." Whose Democracy? Bourgeois vs Popular Democracy," *Review of African Political Economy*, 1989; 45/46, pp. 84-97

Bratton, Michael. "Beyond the State: civil society and associational life in Africa," *World Politics* 1989a, 41 (3), pp. 407-30

_____. "The Politics of Government-NGO Relations in Africa," *World Development* 1989b, 17 (4), pp. 569-587

_____. " Non-Governmental Organizations in Africa: can they influence public policy?" *Development & Change*, 1990, 21 (1) , pp. 87-118.

_____ and van de Walle, Nicholas. "Popular Protest & Political Reform in Africa," *Comparative Politics*, 1992, 24 (4), pp. 419-442.

Brett, E.A. "Voluntary Agencies as Development Organizations: theorising the problem of efficiency and accountability," *Development and Change*, 1993, 24, pp. 269-303

Brodhead, Tim *et al. Bridges of Hope: Canadian voluntary agencies & the Third World.* Ottawa: North-South Institute, 1988.

Brown, L. David and Tandon, Rajesh.. "Institutional Development for Strengthening Civil Society," *Institutional Development: innovations in civil society*, 1994; 1 (1), pp. 3-17

Callaghy, Thoomas M. and Ravenhill, John, eds. *Hemmed In: responses to Africa's economic decline*, New York: Columbia University Press, 1993.

Campbell, Bonnie K. and Loxley, John, eds. *Structural Adjustment in Africa.* London: Macmillan, 1989.

Carnoy, Martin. *The State & Political Theory.* Princeton: Princeton University Press, 1984.

Carroll, Thomas F. *Intermediary NGOs: the supporting link in grassroots development .* Connecticut: Kumarian, 1992.

Chazan, Naomi. "Africa's Democratic Challenge: strengthening civil society & the state," *World Policy Journal*, 1992, 9 (2), pp. 279-307

Clark, John. *Democratizing Development: the role of voluntary organizations.* London: Earthscan, 1991.

Cleary, Seamus. *The Role of NGOs under Authoritarian Political Systems.* London: Macmillan, 1996.

Connelly, M. Patricia, *et al.*. Restructured Worlds / Restructured Debates: Globalization, Development and Gender, *Canadian Journal of Development Studies* (Special Issue) 1995, pp. 17-38.

Cornia, Giovanni Andrea, et al. *Adjustment with a Human Face: protecting the vulnerable & promoting growth.* Oxford: OUP for UNICEF, 1987.

_____. *Adjustment with a Human Face: ten country case studies.* Oxford: OUP for UNICEF, 1988.

_____; van der Hoeven, Rolph and Mkandawire, Thandika, eds. *Africa Recovery in the 1990s: from stagnation and adjustment to development.* London: Macmillan for UNICEF, 1992.

_____and Helleiner, Gerald K eds. *Adjustment & Development in Africa: is the current approach satisfactory?* London: Macmillan for UNICEF, 1994.

Covey, Jane G. "ccountability and Effectiveness in NGO Policy Alliances," Journal of International Development, 1995, 7 (6), pp. 857-67.

Cox, Robert W ."The Global Political Economy & Social Choice," in Daniel Drache & Meric S Gertler, eds, *The New Era of Global Competition: state power & market power,*. Montreal: McGill-Queen's, 1991.

Dei, George and Sefa, J.. "The Renewal of a Ghanian Rural Economy," *Canadian Journal of African Studies*, 1992, 26 (1), pp. 24-54.

"Democracy & Development". *Review of African Political Economy* , 1990, 49, pp. 3-110

Denham, Mark and Lombardi, Mark, eds. *Perspectives on Third World Sovereignty: problems without borders.* London: Macmillan, 1996.

Diamond, Larry et al. eds. *Democracy in Developing Countries.* Four volumes. Boulder: Lynne Rienner, 1988/9.

Drabek, Anne Gordon, ed. "Development Alternatives: the challenge for NGOs," *World Development*, 1987, 15 (Special issue), pp. 1-261

Economic Commission for Africa. *African Alternative Framework to Structural Adjustment Programmes for Socio-Economic Recovery and Transformation.* 1989 July, Addis Ababa.

_____. *African Charter for Popular Participation in Development & Transformation*, 1990 February, Addis Ababa.

Edwards, Michael. "NGOs in the Age of Information," *IDS Bulletin*, 1994; 25 (2), pp. 117-124

_____ and Hulme, David, eds. *Making a Difference: NGOs & Development in a Changing World.* London: Earthscan for SCF, 1992.

_____. "NGO Performance and Accountability in the Post-Cold War World," *Journal of International Development*, 1995, 7 (6), pp. 849-856

Ekins, Paul. *A New World Order: grassroots movements for global change.* London: Routledge, 1992.

Fatton, Robert. "Liberal Democracy in Africa," Political Science Quarterly, 1990, 105 (3), pp. 455-473

_____. "Africa in the Age of Democratization: the civil limitations of civil society," *African Studies Review*, 1995, 38 (2), pp. 67-99.

Fowler, Alan. "The Role of NGOs in Changing State-Society Relations: perspectives from Eastern & Southern Africa," *Development Policy Review,* 1991a, 9 (1), pp. 53-84.

_____. "Building Partnerships between Northern & Southern Development NGOs: issues for the 1990s," *Development in Practice,* 1991b, 1 (1), pp. 5-18

_____. "Democracy, Development and NGOs in Sub-Saharan Africa: where are we?". *Democracy and Development,* 1993, 7.

Friedman, Steven. "An Unlikely Utopia: state & civil society in South," Africa. *Politikon* 1991, 19 (1), pp. 5-19

_____. "Bonaparte at the Barricades: the colonization of civil society," *Theoria,* 1992, 79, pp. 83-95

Gibbon, Peter, ed. *Social Change & Economic Reform in Africa.* Uppsala: Scandinavian Institute of African Studies, 1993.

_____ et al. eds. Authoritarianism, Democracy & Adjustment: the politics of economic reform in Africa. Uppsala: SIAS, Seminar Proceedings #26, 1992.

Gordenkar, Leon and Weiss, Thomas eds. NGOs, the UN and Global Governance. *Third World Quarterly* (Special Issue) 1995;16(3), pp. 357-566.

Green, Andrew and Matthias, Ann. "NGOs - A Policy Panacea for the Next Millennium," *Journal of International Development,* 1995, 7 (3), pp. 565-573.

Healey, John and Robinson, Mark. *Democracy, Governance & Economic Policy: Sub-Saharan Africa in comparative perspective.* London: ODI, 1992.

Healey, John and Tordor, William eds. *Democracy, Development & Accountable Governance: votes & budgets in the South.* London: Macmillan, 1995.

Heyzer, Noeleen; Riker, James V. and Quizon, Antonio B. eds. *Government-NGO Relations in Asia: prospects and challenges for people-centred development.* London: Macmillan for APDC, 1995.

Hutchful, Eboe. "Smoke and Mirrors: The world Bank's social Dimensions of Adjustment Programmes", *Review of African Political Economy,* 1994; 62, pp. 569-84.

Hyden, Goran and Bratton, Michael, eds. *Governance & Politics in Africa* Boulder: Westview, 1992.

Hulme, David and Edwards, Michael eds. *NGOs, states and donors: too close for comfort?* London: Macmillan, 1996.

Kajese, Kingston. "An Agenda of Future Tasks for International & Indigenous NGOS: views from the South," *World Development* (Special issue), 1987, 15, pp. 79-85

Kaplan, Robert D. The Coming Anarchy. Atlantic Monthy, 1994, 273 (2), p. 44-75

Keane, John. *Democracy & Civil Society.* London: Verso, 1988.

Korten, David C. "Third Generation NGO Strategies: a key to people-based development," *World Development* (Special issue). 1987,15, pp. 145-159

_____. *Getting to the 21st century: voluntary action & the global agenda.* West Hartford: Kumarian, 1990.

Lanegran, Kimberly. "South Africa's Association Movement: ANC's Ally or Society's "Watchdog"? shifting social movement-political party relations," *African Studies Review,* 1995, 38 (2), pp. 101-126

Lehman, Howard P. *Indebted Development: strategic bargaining & economic adjustment in the Third World.* London: Macmillan, 1993.

Lewis, Peter M. "Political Transition & the Dilemma of Civil Society in Africa," *Journal of International Affairs,*1992, 46 (1), pp. 31-54

Lindberg, Staffan and Sverrisson, Arni, eds. *The Challenge of Globalization and Democratization.* London: Macmillan, 1996.

MacDonald, Laura. *Supporting Civil Society: the political role of NGOs in Central America.* London: Macmillan, 1996.

MacLean, Sandra J. "North-South NGO Relations & Sustainable Development in Africa: towards a study of Canadian & African partnerships," ASA Conference, December 1993a, Boston.

_____. "Possibilities & Problems in Building Partnerships between Canadian and African NGOs," CASID Conference, June, 1993b Ottawa.

_____. "The Effects of Structural Adjustment on civil Society in Zimbawe: Implications for Canadian Aid Policy," Paper presented at the Annual Meeting of the Canadian association for the Study of Internatiuonal Development, Montreal, June 1995.

_____. "'Managing' Development in Sub-Saharan Africa in the 1990s: states, markets & civil societies in alternative paradigms," in R. A. Siddiqui, ed., *Challenges to Democracy & Development: sub-Saharan Africa in the 1990s*, Westport: Greenwood, 1996.

Mamdani, Mahmood. "Africa: democratic theory & democratic struggles," *Dissent* , 1992,

Summer, pp. 312-318

Maree, Johann. "Trade Unions & Corporatism in South Africa," *Transformation,* 1993, 21, pp. 24-54

Martin, Matthew. *The Crumbling Facade of African Debt Negotiations: no winners.* London: Macmillan, 1991.

Marx, Karl and Engels, Frederick. *The German Ideology.* Moscow: Progress Publishers, 1976.

Moore, David and Schmitz, Gerald J. eds. *Debating Development Discourse: institutional & popular perspectives.* London: Macmillan, 1995.

Moore, Mick. "Introduction," *IDS Bulletin* 1993, 24 (1), pp. 1-6

_____, **ed.** Good Government?. *IDS Bulletin,* 1993, 24 (1), pp. 1-79

Mosley, Paul; Harrington, Jane and Toye, John. *Aid & Power: the World Bank & policy-based lending.* Two Volumes. *(1) Analysis & policy proposals; 2) Country case studies.* London: Routledge, 1991.

Nelson, Joan M. *et al. Fragile Coalitions: the politics of economic adjustment.* New Brunswick: Transaction, 1989.

_____, **ed.** *The Politics of Economic Adjustment in Developing Nations.* Princeton: Princeton University Press, 1990.

Nelson, Paul. *The World Bank & Non-Governmental Organizations: the limits of apolitical development.* London: Macmillan, 1995.

Nyang'oro, Julius E. *The State & Capitalist Development in Africa: declining political economies.* New York: Praeger, 1989.

_____. "The Receding Role of the State & the Emerging Role of NGOs in African Development" , Nairobi: AACC, 1993.

_____ **and Shaw, Timothy M., eds.** *Corporatism in Africa: comparative analysis & practise.* Boulder: Westview, 1989.

_____ **and Shaw, Timothy M., eds.** *Beyond Structural Adjustment in Africa: the political economy of sustainable and democratic development.* New York: Praeger, 1992.

Onimode, Bade. *A Future for Africa: beyond the politics of adjustment.* London: Earthscan, 1992.

Palmer, Ingrid. *Gender & Population in the Adjustment of African Economies: planning for change.* Geneva: ILO, 1991.

Please, Stanley. "Beyond Structural Adjustment in Africa," *Development Policy Review* 1992, 10(3), pp. 289-30.7

"Price of Economic Reform". *Review of African Political Economy* 1990, pp. 4.7

Ravenhill, John, ed. *Africa in Economic Crisis.* London: Macmillan, 1986.

_____. Adjustment with Growth: a fragile consensus. *Journal of Modern African Studies* 1988, 26 (2), pp. 179-210.

_____. "Reversing Africa's Economic Decline: no easy answers," *World Policy Journal* 1990a, 7 (4), pp. 703-732

Riley, Stephen. "Africa's Wind of Change," World Today," 1992, 48 (7), pp. 116-119

_____. "Debt, Democracy & the Environment in Africa," in Stephen Riley, ed. *The Politics of Global Debt* , London: Macmillan, 1993.

Robinson, Mark. "Political Conditionality: strategic implications for NGOs," in Olav Stokke, ed. *, Aid and Political Conditionality,* London: Frank Cass, 1995.

Rothchild, Donald and Chazan, Naomi eds. *The Precarious Balance: state and society in Africa.* Boulder: Westview, 1988.

Sandbrook, Richard. *The Politics of Africa's Economic Stagnation.* Cambridge: Cambridge University Press, 1985.

_____. "Liberal Democracy in Africa: a socialist-revisionist perspective," *Canadian Journal of African Studies*, 1988, 22, pp. 240-267

_____. "Taming the African Leviathan: political reform & economic recovery," *World Policy Journal,* 1990, 7(4), pp. 673-701

_____. *The Politics of Africa's Economic Recovery.* Cambridge: Cambridge University Press, 1993.

_____. "Bringing Politics Back In: the World Bank and Adjustment in Africa," *Canadian Journal of African Studies*, 1995, 29 (2), pp. 278-89.

_____ **and Mohamed Halfani, eds.** *Empowering People: building community, civil associations & legality in Africa.* Toronto: Centre for Urban & Community Studies, 1993.

Schmitz, Gerald J & David Gillies. *The Challenge of Democratic Development: sustaining democratization in developing societies*. Ottawa: North-South Institute, 1992.

Shaw, Timothy M. *Towards a Political Economy for Africa: the dialectics of dependence*. London: Macmillan, 1985.

_____. "Popular Participation in Non-Governmental Structures in Africa: implications for democratic development," *Africa Today*, 1990, 37 (3), pp. 5-22

_____. "Reformism, Revisionism & Radicalism in African Political Economy in the 1990s," *Journal of Modern African Studies*, 1991, 29 (2), pp. 191-212

_____. "Africa," in Mary Hawkesworth & Maurice Kogan, eds. *Encyclopeadia of Government & Politics*, London: Routledge, 1992. Volume II.

_____. *Reformism & Revisionism in Africa's Political Economy in the 1990s: beyond structural adjustment*. London: Macmillan, 1993.

_____. "The South in the 'New World (Dis)Order': towards a political economy of Third World foreign policy in the 1990s & Beyond any New World Order: the South in the 21st century," *Third World Quarterly*, 1994a, 15 (1), pp 17-30 & 139-146

_____. "South Africa: the corporatist/regionalist conjuncture," *Third World Quarterly* 1994b, 15 (2), pp. 243-255

Stein, Howard, ed. *Asian Industrialization & Africa: studies in policy alternatives to structural adjustment*. London: Macmillan, 1995.

Stewart, Frances. "Are Adjustment Policies in Africa Consistent with Long-run Development Needs?" Development Policy Review, 1991, 9, pp. 413-436

_____; **Lall Sanjaya and Wangwe, Samuel eds.** *Alternative Development Strategies in Sub-Saharan Africa*. London: Macmillan, 1992.

United Nations Development Programme (UNDP). *Human Development Report 1994.* New York & Oxford: Oxford University Press, 1994.

UNRISD. *States of Disarray: the Social Effects of Globalisation*, London: Banson, 1995.

van de Walle, Nicolas. "Review Essay: Adjustment Alternatives and Alternatives to Adjustment", *African Studies Review*, 1994; 37 (3), pp. 103-17.

F23 J16
514 L60

(Asia)

11

WOMEN WORKERS IN THE GLOBAL FACTORY:
Impact of Gender Power Asymmetries

Saud Choudhry
Trent University, Canada

This chapter will examine how the new international division of labor has impacted upon gender relations and the status of women in the Third World. Specifically, it will assess the claim that labor intensive, export-oriented industrialization has tended to marginalize women. Drawing on evidence from three countries with the longest experience with multinational manufacturing, I will demonstrate that the conventional wisdom is factually and analytically inadequate. The Duncan index of occupational segregation will be employed to demonstrate that in all three sampled countries, market forces are rapidly undermining gender-based tendencies towards social closure. This evidence lends credence to the neoclassical view that competitive pressures for profitability can be instrumental in eroding occupational differentiation between the genders.

As capital strives for more flexibility (Drache, 1991), a new division of labor is taking place across the globe creating what Poire and Sabel (1984) called the "second industrial divide". For poorer countries in the southern periphery, the latter is similar in significance to the industrial revolution as it features the steady shift of production facilities to the outer rims of civilization. More and more goods are thus manufactured in the new production centers of Asia, Africa and Latin America under direction from headquarters in the North. This is due to two factors: (a) innovations in transportation (*e.g.*, jet air-cargo carriers, containerized shipping, telecommunications *etc.*,) that have conquered long distances; and (b) to the deskilling of work (or the "massification of labor") through the technology for fragmenting the production process into a variety of component operations that can be performed across the planet. The result is the new global factory in which women widely participate. Whereever competitive conditions have created employment opportunities (as in manufacturing in the export platforms), it is women who have readily supplied cheap labor. They have been the cornerstone of labor intensive industrialization and the chief attraction for multinationals searching the globe for lower wages, as well as less stringent enforcement of labor legislation.

This paper will examine how the new international division of labor has impacted upon gender relations and the status of women in the Third World. Specifically, it will assess the feminist claim that women's paid employment in the global factory has reduced their economic status as more jobs have become "feminized"—*i.e.*, have become insecure, low paying and hold little or no advancement possibilities. In my mind, this is a rather dire assessment of the impact of Northern-based, transnational corporations (TNCs) on women workers of the LDCs. In reality, paid formal sector employment has been the catalyst for significant social changes. The economic independence that these jobs provide has for the first time given Third World women the ability to contribute to their families financially; the opportunity to delay marriages and child-bearing; even the means to end oppressive marital relationships. All these are emancipatory in nature and while acknowledging them, this paper will go even further. It will analyze occupational segregation in three NICs, using the Duncan dissimilarity index of occupational differentiation. The objective is to test the notion that gender subordination was a necessary condition for the success of export-oriented industrialization. The evidence will show that in the case of the sampled NICs, the conventional wisdom is factually and analytically inadequate.

The paper is organized into four sections. In the next section, I will review the extensive literature on women's work in the export factories. This is followed by the section that will discuss and analyze data from three NICs - Hong Kong, Singapore and South Korea - to evaluate the mainstream explanations of occupational segregation by gender. The penultimate section will employ the Duncan dissimilarity index to challenge the widely accepted stereotype of poverty-stricken Third World women suffering ruthless exploitation at the hands of the TNCs. Finally, the last section will provide a concluding assessment. While one may argue that the sampled countries are still a minority in the Third World, they were chosen because they are the ones that have the longest experience with multinational manufacturing. Their consequent economic transformation indicates what other LDCs can expect as multinational-led export manufacturing takes root in their own economies.

Feminist Research on Women's Involvement in Export Manufacturing

Since the mid-1970s, the problems facing women workers of the multinational factories have been a central preoccupation of two major forces within the women's movement: Women in Development (WID) and global feminism. At times these forces have interacted and in other instances proceeded independently, politicizing women's experience with globalization by focusing heavily on inequality: "inequality of access to power, to resources, to a human existence — in short, inequality in emancipation" (Schurmann, 1993). Their critique ranged from questioning the popular patriarchal and capitalistic notion that "women's main problem ... is one of insufficient participation in an otherwise benevolent process of growth and development" (Sen and Grown; 1987:15), to advocating a new ethical framework in which the development process should be placed. This impulse to re-define basic questions came from various directions: (a) feminists working on legal issues emphasized the importance of an awareness of all the sources of oppression: race, class, gender etc., and urged that these questions be addressed in relation to economics and development; (b) others argued that feminism is a holistic ideology that embraces the whole spectrum of political, economic and social ideologies and it is in this sense that it poses a serious challenge to traditional development theory and praxis. As the reality of women's lives in the Third World and the feminization of poverty in the North gained increased public attention, feminists quickly pointed out that there can be no real sexual equality when economic development is lopsided. In short, by the "1985 End of the Decade World Conference on Women" in Nairobi, the feminist critique ranged from advocating a new ethical framework in which the development process should be placed, to challenging both the concepts advanced by development researchers as well as their methods of gathering statistical data on which many development programmes are based.

While this paper cannot cover the entire body of this rich dialogue (and there is also no agreement on one feminist analysis of development), I will instead refer to one popular strand of the literature that focuses exclusively on women's involvement in export manufacturing. This area of feminist research is important as it gave voice to the complex and diverse realities of working women's lives in the Third World. But in the process it has also created the stereotypical view of young, single, female factory workers suffering long hours, low wages and insecure, unhealthy and unsafe working conditions in the multinational factories. These women are also exploited by their own families who claim a disproportionate share of their wages without according them any power or status within the household. In other words, working women suffer a "double oppression" (Elson and Pearson,

1981) - imperialist/capitalist exploitation at work and gender subordination at home - and as such benefit little from paid employment in the global factory.

Interestingly, this strand of feminist thought may have found an ally in the industrial North - a powerful coalition of industry, labor and local communities -all opposed to export manufacturing in the Third World. Outwardly their protectionist stance is cloaked in humanitarian rhetoric - the need to free women from exploitation in harsh factory environments where they face constant harassment by employers, supervisors and even the government; in reality, it is based on political and economic self-interest. Activists in the labor, feminist and church movements support protectionism in order to safeguard women's employment in labor-intensive, import-competing manufacturing in the industrial North; many businesses are similarly supportive since import restrictions support the monopolistic profits of inefficient domestic producers. A final accomplice in this schematic framework is Third World traditionalists and/or religious conservatives, who oppose women's employment in export factories because it gives them greater economic and hence personal freedom, thereby liberating them from patriarchal control. The final result is a "triple alliance" of powerful interests - patriarchal, capitalist and nationalist - in both developed and developing countries, which feeds and sustains the opposition to Third World women's paid employment in the export factories.

While acknowledging that there are situations which resemble this negative stereotype of women factory workers, many feminists forcefully argue that it is by no means the norm in all or even most of the Third World. True, wages and working conditions in the LDC export factories are often inferior to those in the developed countries, yet they are almost always superior compared to women's jobs in other sectors of the LDC economies. For instance, Lim (1990) found that Mexican women working in the "maquiladoras" typically earn at least the legal minimum wage and this places them in the top quartile of Mexico's national income distribution. In fact, the great discrepancy between the stereotype and the reality of women factory workers' lives may be attributed to the following reasons:

Firstly, the field is dominated by anthropologists, journalists and activist groups who often focus on extreme rather than representative situations (*e.g.*, Asian Women Workers Newsletter, Christian conference of Asia, Grossman 1979, Karl 1983). Dated information is widely used and hence errors of fact and omission abound. For instance, massive layoffs in the female-intensive, export industries of Malaysia and Singapore during the OPEC oil crisis of 1974-75, is commonly cited as evidence that TNCs relocating manufacturing in the LDCs are footloose. In fact recovery was remarkably swift and in Singapore the demand for labor has outstripped supply for a decade or more; Malaysia meets it labor shortages by drawing on unskilled workers from Indonesia and the Philippines (World Labor Report, 1993).

Secondly, few, if any, of these studies compare the circumstances of women workers in the export factories with their compatriots in other industries or occupations. Lim (1990) notes that while no more than 10 percent of the urban labor force in Bangkok and Manila earn the legal minimum wage, the same is paid by virtually all multinational export factories; in China's export platforms, wages are more than double their levels outside of these enclaves.

Thirdly, modern export factories not only generate more incomes, but shorter working hours and better working conditions compared to traditional occupations or unpaid family labor on the farm. This is because factory employment is more heavily regulated by governments, whereas 16-hour work days, seven days a week is commonplace in the latter.

Fourthly, the view that labor subordination was necessary for attracting TNC investment, which in turn fueled the momentum of export-oriented industrialization (EOI), is in many respects factually inaccurate. In Hong Kong, for instance, the authorities have always maintained worker's rights in terms of full freedom to strike and picket peacefully. Deyo (1989), a prominent proponent of the labor subordination hypothesis, concludes that East Asia does not support a supposed link between EOI and state repression of labor. Haggard (1990), well known for his position on 'development without democracy' in the NICs, takes a similar position.

It is for these reasons among others that the analysis and body of knowledge produced by this branch of the feminist movement has come under sustained attack from many Third World feminists. The latter have charged that this group is guilty of generalizing and extrapolating from its own Western experiences. In the process these women have projected their privileged identity as a referent to the rest of the world in culturally destructive ways. Hence a Third World or "indigenous feminism" has emerged, clearly distinct from this particular brand of Northern feminist research. A popular strand in this critique argues that these Northern representations of Third World women as the vulnerable, exploited, helpless "other", reflects an ethnocentrism that causes Western writers and activists to judge conditions in the Third World by Western standards[1]. Instead they ought to focus attention on the fact that in patriarchal LDC settings, women face such strong anti-female bias in intra-family resource distribution that their chances for survival are reduced. In South Asia, West Asia, North Africa and rural China, where classical patriarchy is at its strongest, one even encounters the systematic food deprivation of women vis-a-vis men (Dreze and Sen, 1989). In such restrictive circumstances, female industrial employment has often had immensely positive social consequences. For instance, Safa (1992) reports that women factory workers in export manufacturing in the Caribbean use their earnings to bargain for increased authority within the household; Ecevit's (1991) study found that Turkish wives had gained considerable decision-making authority as a result of their employment; a similar conclusion was recorded in a series of country studies edited by Bruce and Dwyer (1988).

Indigenous feminism thus concludes that women do well when given opportunities to be financially independent and to earn income, and that they are invariably better off in paid employment in EOI than in unpaid family labor. Its critique of the negative (but popular) feminist position is significant on two counts:

a. By focusing attention to local, spatially and culturally specific studies, it has largely abandoned the Northern fascination with global explanations of the subordination of women. Instead, it acknowledges the diversity of national and regional experiences and emphasizes the need to search for solutions, firmly grounded in the realities and experiences of women in the South.

b. It argues that the Northern feminists' negative perspective relies much too heavily on the operation of some sort of reserve army mechanism. While there is some scope for arguing along these lines, this explanation runs into difficulties when used to explain the observed rise in living standards in the sampled NICs. More appropriately, one should perhaps argue that the process of development changes the conditions under which labor is reproduced and as such, an increased amount or value of commodities becomes necessary to reproduce labor in the required quantity (and of the desired quality). One can then view this rise in the level of subsistence as an explanation for rising money wages in the NICs, thus enabling their workers to enjoy a higher standard of living. The attempt by Jencks (1975) to redefine subsistence in terms of necessary participation costs - which would explain why its level rises as the economy becomes more complex - is noteworthy in this respect.

Indigenous feminism is also interesting as it appears to highlight the evolutionary progression of communities, from hunting and gathering to agricultural and finally to industrial societies. Engel's (1884) referred to the transition to agrarian societies as the "world-historical defeat of the female sex" and Gerda Lerner (1986) referred to it as "the creation of patriarchy". With the rise of capitalism, Western Europe witnessed a decline in patriarchy as the same was replaced by other forms of gender inequality. In the view of indigenous feminism, a similar if not identical trajectory is also evident in parts of the Third World where female factory employment is widespread.

Occupational Segregation, Compensating Differentials and Discrimination by Gender

This section will introduce the reader to the data used to examine the adequacy of various theories of gender-based employment segregation. I used aggregate data reported in the *Year Book of Labor Statistics*, an annual ILO publication on employment statistics of some 180 countries, areas and territories. This is in contrast to earlier empirical work which was often based on standpoint feminism, focusing mainly on women's lived experiences in specific situations and locales. While the earlier approach was useful for formulating theory and expectations, it is inherently limited in its ability to test general theoretical propositions. The important methodological innovation of this paper is its reliance on aggregate national statistics. True, my use of aggregate data will result in the loss of detailed understanding of particular jobs and work situations. Yet this approach is followed because it provides a better understanding of the forces that operate across most jobs and workplaces. In the final analysis, this generalized knowledge will prove useful when assessing the impact of the global factory in diverse national and regional settings.

Table 1 focuses on occupational segregation along gender lines. The statistics indicate that all three NICs have performed remarkably well in terms of creating overall employment opportunities. Unemployment rates have generally been low in all three countries, with female unemployment rates falling to less than 2 percent by the end of the decade. The latter is all the more remarkable considering that it was achieved in the face of a rise in the economically active population.

The growth in manufacturing employment has helped maintain a high GDP growth rate in all three NICs. The increased labor force attachment of women alongside this rise in per capita GDP suggests (contrary to popular belief), that the economic necessity for women to work does not decrease with rising per capita income. Two factors may explain this apparent paradox. First, there is the subjective feeling of necessity linked to rising expectations as material prosperity increases. Many goods (*e.g.*, household appliances) which under poorer

Table 1: The Gender Gap as Reflected in Selected Labour Market Indices

| Country | Period | Economically Active Population (%) | | Open Unemployment (%) | | Distribution of the Sexes by Major Occupational Groups (%) | | | | | | | |
| | | | | | | Professional and Technical | | Administrative and Managerial | | Clerical | | Production-related workers, transport equipment operators and labourers | |
		Male	Female	Male	Female	Male	Female	Male	Female	Male	Female	Male	Female
Hong Kong	1981	62.1	37.2	3.9	3.4	59.36	40.64	88.23	11.77	49.24	50.76	65.41	34.59
	1985	61.9	37.4	3.8	3.3	57.16	42.84	89.61	10.39	41.81	58.19	68.28	31.72
	1989	62.0	37.6	1.1	1.1	56.42	43.58	85.87	14.13	37.31	62.69	74.74	25.26
Singapore	1980	59.2	33.0	2.9	3.5	61.05	38.95	85.84	14.16	37.30	62.70	68.51	31.49
	1985	59.8	34.3	4.2	4.1	61.55	38.45	80.13	19.87	47.90	52.10	76.40	23.60
	1989	59.6	37.8	2.3	1.9	60.69	39.31	75.50	24.50	28.73	71.27	70.40	29.60
South Korea	1981	47.2	28.6	5.7	2.5	68.89	31.11	98.04	1.06	66.92	33.68	73.32	26.68
	1985	46.3	29.3	5.0	2.4	64.48	35.52	95.87	4.13	65.41	34.59	72.42	27.58
	1989			3.0	1.8	59.47	40.53	95.55	4.45	61.05	38.95	68.97	31.08

Source: Year Book of Labour Statistics, ILO, Geneva, Switzerland. (Various issues)

circumstances were considered luxuries are now deemed necessities. While their ownership liberates women from time intensive household chores, they are also led into meeting the cost of such goods by undertaking paid outside work. Secondly, the rising level of female wages increases the opportunity cost of foregoing employment opportunities outside the home. All these explain the new and enlarged role played by women in the national economy and together they constitute the positive side of the picture depicted by Table 1.

The other side of the coin is the persistence of occupational segregation. The evidence clearly shows that in all three NICs, women's concentration is the greatest in the female ghettoes of low-skill, dead-end jobs, while male workers monopolize positions in the white collar aristocracy (administration and management). Discrimination is clearly at work here, but the popular justification for these disparities is the lesser labor force attachment of women. It is alleged that differing home responsibilities causes women to have more discontinuous work histories. Employers respond to this greater propensity of women to leave the work force, by investing less in their training and this in turn hinders their chances for promotion. This economically rational but discriminatory process leads to occupational segregation, wherein women choose jobs that require little firm-specific human capital and where there is relatively little atrophy of skills when not in use.

This is the well-publicized "statistical discrimination model" which sees employment segregation as the outcome of generally rational, if exaggerated, attempts by employers to reduce costs. Couched in these terms, it appears to be a problem of imperfect information, with employers unable to distinguish between those women who will remain on the job and those who will leave. But if discrimination were only a problem of imperfect information, it would be eroded fairly quickly by market forces. For instance, women who presumably know whether they will leave their employer to assume responsibilities at home could negotiate contingent claims contracts insuring employers against lost investments. Since the erosion is not rapid in reality and there is no compelling evidence that there are differences in training costs, a more parsimonious approach should focus on the real cause - gender power asymmetries - rather than on an economic rationalization of current discriminatory practices.

Sex-based Wage Differential

Male-female occupational attainment disparities have resulted in sharply different wages for men and women across the spectrum of wage labor. Although Table 2 indicates a clear improvement in the economic well-being of women wage earners over this ten year period, the pace of change has been quite slow in both Hong Kong and Singapore, though fairly rapid in South Korea. Earnings differentials are the least in Hong Kong whose figures indicate an apparent 20 percent penalty for being female in both the textile and electronic industries[2].

South Korea has the worst case of wage disparity by gender, but it is also the one that has recorded the greatest improvements on this front over the decade. While Singapore and South Korea still show a sizeable male-female wage disparity, the gap is only about 10 percent greater when compared to the developed Northern economies. Furthermore, this is only a crude indicator because once job characteristics and human capital differences are controlled, the North-South gap in gender disparity could turn out to be even smaller. This is why neoclassical economists employ the logic of the compensating differentials hypothesis, to argue that the wage gap may be attributed to the premium paid to males because of undesirable working conditions in their jobs. The implication is that the wage gap that flows from gender segregation is the consequence of genuine job differences[3]

The empirical support for the compensating differentials hypothesis is weak (see England *et al.*, 1988; Glass 1990) as most investigators report an "uncomfortable number" of exceptions to the predictions of this theory. In the present context, a fairer test of this premise would have to consider the widest array of job characteristics found in both male and female intensive occupations. Specifically, one would have to consider the effect of undesirable working conditions on wages, net of education, experience, responsibilities and other productivity related attributes - a highly detailed test that is beyond the scope of this paper. Hence, rather than testing the basic premises of the compensating differentials hypothesis, we will now concentrate on gender power asymmetries, a natural order inherent to the human condition, to explain existing wage disparities. The dominant view is that gender power asymmetries are the outcome of a culture of patriarchy, whose exclusionary policies ensure that the best positions are reserved for males, while females are relegated to a secondary and inferior position. The dominant males do not strive to monopolize all jobs; gender segregation only supplants total exclusion as the primary method for disadvantaging women in the labor force. As noted earlier, the WID movement attributes this subordination of women to the designs and practices of transnationals. Hence the widely held view that TNC-sponsored development is a contradictory process that liberates women through the provision of wage employment while at the same time marginalizes them.

Table 2: Earning Differentials Between Male and Female Workers by Industry

Country	Period	All Manufacturing Industries			Textiles			Footwear			Electronics			Professional & Scientific Measuring & Controlling Equipment		
		M	F	F/M (%)	M	F	F/M (%)	M	F	F/M (%)	M	F	F/M (%)	M	F	F/M (%)
Hong Kong[1]	1982	85.70	66.60	77.71	78.50	68.60	87.39	99.10	86.10	86.88	74.30	62.60	84.25	80.80	61.30	75.87
	1985	115.10	91.20	79.23	107.70	95.20	88.39	124.60	97.10	77.93	101.70	84.20	82.79	106.90	84.60	79.14
	1989	191.70	140.30	73.19	184.10	148.10	80.45	175.20	132.60	75.68	172.40	132.00	76.57	183.40	128.90	70.28
Singapore[2]	1986	1005.9	566.05	56.27	881.78	627.57	71.17				987.89	580.74	58.78	940.35	630.78	67.08
	1988	1118.1	652.39	58.35	970.72	751.07	77.37				1140	617.67	54.18	1056.7	715.02	67.67
	1989	1228.6	707.02	57.55	1021.5	785.10	76.86				1199.6	677.33	56.46	1175.1	799.79	68.06
South Korea[3]	1981	234.32	106.02	45.25	226.5	106.20	46.89	185.2	111.3	60.1	239.5	108.9	45.47	170	99.5	58.53
	1985	346.85	162.71	46.91	319.0	155.20	48.65	242.7	159.3	65.64	361.3	173.5	48.02	304.9	162.7	53.36
	1989	608.93	367.45	60.34	544.9	287.80	52.82	443.8	285.6	64.35	609.3	341.1	55.98	535.9	331.7	61.89

[1] daily earnings in HK$
[2] monthly earnings in Singapore$
[3] monthly earnings in '000 Won

Source: Year Book of Labour Statistics, ILO, Geneva, Switzerland. (Various issues)

In reality, women's wages and working conditions are set primarily by traditional patriarchal social relations that define the sexual division of labor within the family. The primary assumption here is that the labour supply of each family member is oriented towards the achievement of a certain standard of living over the family life cycle and the husband's commitment to the achievement of that target is the greatest. Hence men's higher wage demands reflect their family-related income commitment. Provided that the husband's wage covers the major part of the planned family income, the wife may be willing to accept a lower wage if her household responsibilities leave her with fewer alternative opportunities of topping up the family income to the desired level. In other words, women are available at lower wages than men not because they consider their income commitment as secondary, but because the sexual division of labour in the family prevents them from trading work effort and wage income along a conventional supply curve[4].

Hence it is traditional patriarchal social relations that relegate women to inferior positions in the labor market, which in turn makes them the preferred employees of multinational employers. In other works, the TNCs are following the path of least resistance by following existing labor market practices and while doing so, are guilty of *de facto* segregation, not *de jure* segregation[5]. In all fairness, they are certainly not the original perpetrators of occupational segregation or differential remuneration by gender.

The view that multinationals are only guilty of *de facto* segregation, may give rise to a false aura of total innocence. In reality, the multinationals have a vested interest in pursuing a path of least resistance. Beginning in the late 1960s, textiles gave way to consumer electronics and the semiconductor industry, as the principal items of export in all of the sampled NICs. But because of heavy research and development expenditures, as well as short product life cycles, manufacturers in these industries are compelled to produce the largest volumes at the lowest possible costs. Hence, they look for low cost women workers to forestall competition and recover investment before imitation or obsolescence of new products set in. In other words, women's comparative disadvantage in the labor market serves to enhance the comparative advantage of the TNCs producing for the world market.

In the end, multinational operations and hiring practices do play a role in the complex, diverse and multilayered realities of Third World women's lives. On the one hand, low-wage female employment in the export factories is the vehicle whereby capitalism and imperialism nurture and even reinforce patriarchal relations of production. But at the same time, wage employment contributes to greater gender equity by providing women with a greater range of life options - falling birth rates, a rise in the average age of first marriage and the gradual concentration of childbearing among women aged 25 and 30. With material prosperity, the supply and use of household appliances has increased[6] freeing women from domestic chores and thus making it possible for them to undertake paid outside employment. The end result is that the social environment is becoming transformed: full-time, lifelong work for women is rapidly becoming the established norm in the NICs and to this, family and social life is slowly learning to adapt itself.

Dissimilarity Indexes of Occupational Differentiation

While Table 1 indicates some progress in women's occupational attainment (*e.g.*, female managers increased by 3% in both South Korea and Hong Kong; by as much as 10% in Singapore), what cannot be discerned from these statistics is whether a new, but less obvious pattern of occupational segregation has emerged. Hence we need to focus on occupational distributions rather than wages in order to understand the mechanism behind falling labor market barriers between the sexes. This section will describe occupational differentiation along gender lines using the Duncan and Duncan dissimilarity measure of occupational segregation[7] (see Appendix for the mathematical formulation). The index ranges from 0 to 100 and its value stands for the proportion of men (or women) who have to change occupations in order to equalize the distribution of the sexes among occupations. To illustrate: say, all men and women are employed in just two occupations, teachers and clerks. Assume further that 10 percent of women are teachers and 90 percent are clerks, while the employed men are evenly split between the two occupations. The dissimilarity measure would then be:

$$\frac{1}{2} \left\{ \left|(0.10-0.50)\right| + \left|(0.90-0.50)\right| \right\} = 0.40$$

It therefore appears that 40 percent of either men or women would need to shift occupations in order to equalize the proportions of men and women employed as teachers and clerks.

An oft-cited limitation of the Duncan index is that problems arise when it is used to measure segregation over time. While changes in the relative size of the groups being compared does not affect the measure, changes in the number of occupations generally does. Hence, if an increase in the number of job titles over time only represents a finer definition of existing occupations, then the index may erroneously generate higher measures of segregation. It is for this reason that dissimilarity indexes, based on larger numbers of occupational descriptions of more recent years, will not be directly comparable to those calculated using the less refined job titles of an earlier era. Doing so will not only underestimate the level of segregation in earlier years but understate the decrease in segregation over time, as well.

The dissimilarity estimates reported below are however free from this weakness since the occupation categories used (obtained from the ILO Yearbook) do not change from one year to the next.

Table 3 presents dissimilarity measures calculated by using employment statistics reported in the ILO Yearbook. This source publishes data on employment, unemployment, hours of work, wages and consumer price indices drawn mainly from information sent to the ILO by national statistical services. For the dissimilarity indexes, I used absolute figures on the distribution of the employed by major divisions of economic activity—mining, manufacturing, utilities (electricity, gas and water), construction, trade-restaurants-hotels, transport-storage-

Table 3: Dissimilarity Indexes of Occupational Differentiation Between the Genders *(D,x 100)*

Country	1976	1979	1983	1988	1992
Hong Kong	27.05	27.2	20.7	15.2	9.9
Singapore	16.5	18.05	18.2	14.6	16.3
South Korea	10.0	13.2	14.3	14.7	17.0

source: *Year Book of Labor Statistics*, ILO, Geneva, Switzerland; various issues; see Appendix for methodology.

communications, financing-insurance-real estate-business services, community-social and personal services. These employment categories account for 90 percent or more of the urban work force in the sampled NICs. The clearest picture emerging from the estimates above is that in all three countries, the absolute level of occupational segregation is remarkably low. This implies that contrary to what Table 1 suggests, the various occupations are nearly gender-balanced. While Hong Kong's initial level of segregation was higher, the proportion of men (or women) required to change occupation in order to achieve a more symmetrical distribution of employment decreased considerably over the years. In all of the sampled NICs today, job segregation is so low that a proportionate representation of both sexes would entail a shuffling of less than 20 percent of the working population (male or female). In this respect all three NICs appear to fare better than many developed countries. For instance, Mary King (1992) quotes Andrea Beller's 1984 paper, one of the most rigorous analysis of gender segregation in the United States, which reports dissimilarity measures of between 68 in 1960 and 61 in 1981: King herself examined occupational differentiation along both race and gender lines from 1940 through 1980, and for 1988. Using a nationally representative sample compiled from the Public Use Micro-data Samples of the U.S. Census, she found that approximately two-thirds of men or women would have to change jobs to achieve complete gender integration.

The Duncan index is, however, an absolute measure that does not take into account the share of women in the total work force. As such the progress reported above may be less substantial than what a mere comparison of the values of the index over the years would indicate. For instance, the progress towards desegregation could be the result of the entry of men into feminized occupations without the converse being true. Hence, the need to decompose the recorded decline into two: (a) variations in the sex composition within occupations (the share effect); and (b) variations in the weights of occupations in total employment (the weight effect). The share effect reflects genuine changes in segregation, understood as the degree of sex-typing of occupations. The weight effect, on the other hand, reflects changes in the structure of employment. Decomposition into share and weight effects plus a residual will now be carried out for variations in the index of dissimilarity. The residual effect measures the interaction between the share and weight effects, and its interpretation is not always clear-cut (see Appendix). While decomposing the values of the segregation index in the table below, I will not attempt to define any statistical threshold of significance for either the share effect or the weight effect. This discussion is intended to simply investigate the foundations of the belief that the factors under consideration played a role significant enough to be detectable in the aggregate.

Hong Kong reported the steepest decline in segregation over the seven year period (1976-83) under investigation and to this, the share effect (i.e., an actual easing of sex-typing) made the greatest contribution. The sharp decline is not surprising if one distinguishes between the pre-oil and post-oil shock periods and examines their impact on the island colony. Hong Kong's unemployment rate reached a high of 9.1 percent in 1975 and this tapered off to less than 5 percent by 1980 (Asian Development Bank 1990). A supplementary explanation would be that the feminist wave of the seventies also played a role. It not only impacted upon attitudes but also succeeded in easing sex-typing in both quantitative and qualitative terms. However, as the initial degree of sex-typing was much higher in Hong Kong (compared to the other two NICs), even the steep decline reported above appears to constitute relatively slow progress. Both Singapore and South Korea, on the other hand, exhibit actual increases in their segregation indexes. However, when spread over the seven years under review, the increases (5.5 and 6.78 points respectively), does not in any way look all that remarkable.

In South Korea, a large part of the increase in the segregation index stemmed from the weight rather than the share component. This suggests that in South Korea, the effect of industrial restructuring over this time interval was the creation of a new layer of women's jobs, rather than a relaxation of segregation. In Singapore, the negative weight effect was largely offset by a positive share effect resulting in a net increase in segregation. The positive share effect between 1976 and 1983 is probably due to the much larger weight of substantially feminized service sector occupations, among those that recorded the greatest gains in the share of women (school teachers, clerical staff, shop assistants etc.,). While counter instances of women increasing their representation in male dominated occupations were also numerous over this time period, the net result suggests that the impact of these gains was mostly qualitative rather than quantitative.

Singapore's negative weight effect needs clarification. Late in 1978, the government realized that its industrial strategy had to forge a new path, in order to withstand competition from neighbors offering cheaper labor and equally attractive incentives to foreign capital. Accordingly, the city state embarked on the next stage of industrialization - one that emphasized capital-intensive, high-technology and high value added industries. This industrial transformation soon altered the nature and rates of women's economic participation in Singapore's multi-ethnic society[8]. The government's Labor Force Survey (1975, 1979) shows that while Chinese women traditionally had the highest rate of economic activity (21.8 percent in 1957 compared to 7 percent or less for Malays and Indians), the situation changed rapidly with economic restructuring. By 1979, the economic activity rates of the three major groups had leveled out to approximately 42 percent each; the proportions of Indian and Malay women in manufacturing jumped to 41.1 and 55.3 percent respectively (up from 18.9 and 31.2 percent in 1970). The structure of employment was rapidly changing because over this same period, Malay and Indian women experienced a corresponding decline in the proportion of their ranks in community, social and personal services. Additionally, the large-scale influx of Malay and Indian women into the manufacturing sector was not only due to the expansion of industrial employment but also because older Chinese women were moving into higher-paying, white collar jobs in commerce and the services. All this contributed to the negative weight effect seen in Table 4.

Table 4: Index of Dissimilarity and its Components of Change (1976-1983)

	ΔD$_t$×100 (1)+(2)+(3)	*W* *(1)*	*P* *(2)*	*R* *(3)*
Hong Kong	-23.1	-2.6	-11.4	-9.1
Singapore	5.5	-0.8	2	4.3
South Korea	6.78	5.4	0.8	0.58
Key: Δ = absolute variation W = weight effect		P = share effect R = residual effect		

source: Year Book of Labor Statistics, various issues; see Appendix for methodology.

In the final analysis, the dissimilarity indexes of Table 3 are only marginally affected by the decomposition exercise conducted above. Even after the corrections, the segregation levels remain remarkably small in all of the sampled NICs. This is not surprising considering the severe labor shortages that they all face. The 1993 World Labor Report put Hong Kong's shortage of professionals, managers and skilled workers at approximately 62,000 in 1990; the labor intensive textiles, footwear and garments industries in South Korea are reported to lack 20 to 30 percent of the workforce that they need; and in Singapore, the government has for years pursued a carefully controlled policy of bringing in foreign workers as needed and expelling them again when no longer required. It appears that in all three countries, market forces are helping to undermine male-female workplace inequalities. As the tenets of neoclassical economics would predict, acute labor shortages in these economies make for a highly competitive work environment and that in turn undermines gender and racial inequalities in the labor market. Firms in these high growth, dynamic settings are continually changing production processes, employees, capitalization patterns and competitive strategies. One implication of these attempts to maximize income is that employees are rewarded with wages and other benefits commensurate with their individual productivity. In such progressive settings, sexism begins to be seen as historical vestiges of alternative utilities, precapitalist social relations, short-term market imperfections and informational deficiencies. The evidence in tables 2, 3 and 4 suggests that in all of the three NICs, labor market mechanisms are already working towards this end. Workplace inequality is being obliterated as profit maximizing firms employ lower-priced female labor and in doing so, bid up their wages. Simultaneously, severe labor shortages provide women the opportunity to seek out nondiscriminating employers as well as the incentive to invest in the necessary human capital to compete for the best available jobs.

Conclusion

In surveying the relative positions of men and women in the three NICs, Tables 1 and 2 appeared to reinforce the popular view that globalization has produced a pattern of employment segregation by sex that produces additional gender inequalities, beyond that which can be explained by human capital differences. A very vocal strand in the contemporary women's rights movement attributes this to social closure processes that preserve the best positions for males (members of the dominant group), while those dominated (mainly women) are relegated to inferior positions in the job hierarchy. Ethnicity, race and religion are other group characteristics that form the basis of these exclusionary rules.

While acknowledging the existence of gender subordination in varying degrees, many Third World feminists are still supportive of the global factory, arguing that its jobs will eventually spell the demise of traditional patriarchy. Women's increased ability to assist their families financially, enhances their social standing and consequently their subjugation as women is undermined. All these are emancipatory in nature and fairly revolutionary in their implications.

Empirical analysis, based on the Duncan's dissimilarity index, in this chapter reinforced this more recent strand of feminist thought by demonstrating that in the sampled NICs, market forces are gradually undermining tendencies towards social closure. The remarkably small dissimilarity indices lend credence to the neoclassical view that gender-based processes of social closure are neither total nor permanent. Rather, market competition and pressures for profitability will undermine costly tastes for discrimination among employers, which in the long run will help eliminate segregation. True, discriminatory differences, however small, remain and this implies that there are some limitations to the success of the free market strategy in closing the gender gap. Still, the evidence suggests that it may be prudent to wait for discrimination to be gradually eroded by the imperative of market competition, rather than passing formal legislation seeking to diminish the foundations of segregation. After all, legislative manoeuvring of any kind may well bring about an elimination of the jobs themselves, given the great mobility of multinational capital and the ready availability of exploitable labor in other countries. This is certainly not warranted. As the late Mrs. Joan Robinson once said, a fate worse than being exploited by capitalists is not to be exploited at all.

Appendix

The Duncan and Duncan Measure of Segregation

Duncan and Duncan's Index of Dissimilarity is defined as $D_t = \left(\sum_i |u_{it} - f_{it}| \right) / 2$

where $f_{it} = F_{it} / \Sigma F_{it}$

F_{it} = number of females in occupation or sector i, year t

$u_{it} = U_{it} / \Sigma u_{it}$

U_{it} = number of males in occupation or sector i, year t

To isolate the weight, share and residual effects, D_t is first specified as

$$ D_t = \left(\sum_i |\eta_{it} Z_{it} - P_{it} \omega_{it}| \right) / 2 $$

where $P_{it} = F_{it} / (U_{it} + F_{it})$ is the share of women in occupation or sector i, year t;

$\eta_{it} = (1 - P_{it}) = u_{it} / (u_{it} + F_{it})$ is the share of men in occupation or sector i, year t;

$Z_{it} = (u_{it} + f_{it}) / \Sigma u_t$ is the weight of occupation or sector i, year t, in total male employment;

$\omega_{it} = (u_{it} + F_{it}) / \Sigma F_{it}$ is the weight of occupation or sector i, year t, in total female employment.

If Year 0 is taken as the standard, then $D_1 - D_0 = W_{1,0} + P_{1,0} + R_{1,0}$

where $W_{1,0} = (\Sigma |\eta_{i,0} Z_{i,1} - P_{i,0} \omega_{i,1}|)/2 - (\Sigma |\eta_{i,0} Z_{i,0} - P_{i,0} \omega_{i,0}|)/2$
is the weight effect;

$P_{1,0} = (\Sigma |\eta_{i,1} Z_{i,0} - P_{i,1} \omega_{i,0}|)/2 - (\Sigma |\eta_{i,0} Z_{i,0} - P_{i,0} \omega_{i,0}|)/2$
is the share effect; and

$R_{1,0} = (\Sigma |\eta_{i,1} Z_{i,1} - P_{i,1} \omega_{i,1}|)/2 - (\Sigma |\eta_{i,0} Z_{i,1} - P_{i,0} \omega_{i,1}|)/2$
$- (\Sigma |\eta_{i,0} Z_{i,0} - P_{i,0} \omega_{i,0}|)/2 + (\Sigma |\eta_{i,1} Z_{i,0} - P_{i,1} \omega_{i,0}|)/2$
is the residual or interaction effect.

Endnotes

1. In Bangladesh and other Islamic countries many western observers fixate on the practice of purdah (veil) or female seclusion as the main feature of women's disadvantage, whereas one should argue that grinding poverty is the primary constraining feature of local patriarchy amongst women.

2. The Hong Kong situation appears to be superior to that in the United States. Randall Filer (1989) found that in the United States median weekly earnings of full-time female workers had risen from 61 percent of those for men in 1978 to 71 percent of male earnings by 1987.

3. The idea that workers are paid extra compensation for labouring under unfavourable conditions originated with Adam Smith. In the Wealth of Nations, Smith takes the position that "the wages of labour vary with the ease or hardship, the cleanliness or dirtiness, the honourableness or dishonourableness of the employment".

4. This interpretation is derived from Classical and Marxist analyses of the labour market which holds that the long-term or natural wage level is determined by historical subsistence needs at the family level. Thus as long as married men remain the more committed participants in the work force, their wages will have to cover at least part of the subsistence of wives and other dependents, whose wages can consequently be lower.

5. *De jure* segregation refers to a situation where men and women are legally constrained to work at separate jobs; *de facto* refers to a situation where segregation results, not from edict, but from circumstance. De jure segregation is commonly seen as the consequence of evil intent, while the other is viewed as the innocent by-product of socio-economic forces.

6. Lim (1990) notes that in 1983, 96.2% of the households in Singapore owned a refrigerator, 95.9% a television set, 44.7% a washing machine, 12.8% a car and 17.5% a motorcycle.

7. Duncan and Duncan first proposed their index to measure racial segregation. Others have subsequently applied it to census data to measure sexual segregation.

8. Singapore's population is heterogenous: roughly 76 percent are Chinese, 15 percent Malay, 7 percent Indian and 2 percent Eurasian or of other ethnic groups.

References

Bruce, J., and Dwyer, D., eds., *Women of the Andes*, Ann Arbor, MI:University of Michigan Press, 1988.

Deyo, F. *Beyond the Economic Miracle: Labour Subordination in the New Asian*

Industrialism, Berkeley: University of California Press, 1989.

Drache, D. "The Systematic Search for Flexibility: National Competitiveness and New York Relations," in D. Drache and M.S. Gertler, eds., *The New Era of Global Competition*, Montreal and Kingston: McGill-Queen's University Press, 1991.

Dreze, J. and Sen, A. K. *Hunger and Public Action*, Oxford: Clarendon, 1989.

Duncan, O. and Duncan, B. "A Methodological Analysis of Segregation Indexes", *American Sociological Review*, April, 1955.

Ecevit, Y. "The Ideological Construction of Turkish Women Factory Workers," in N. Redcliff and M. T. Sinclair, eds., *Working Women : International Perspectives on Labour and Gender Ideology*, London and New York: Routledge, 1991.

Elson, D. and Pearson, R. "The Subordination of Women and the internationalisation of Factory Production," in Kate Young et al., eds., *Of Marriage and the Market: Women's Subordination in International Perspective,* London: CSE Books, 1981.

Engels, F. *The Origin of the Family, Private Property and ths State*, New York: International Publishers, 1975.

England, Paula, et al. "Explaining Occupational Sex Segregation and Wages: Findings From a Model With Fixed Effects," *American Sociological Review*, 1988, vol. 53, pp. 544-58..

Filer, R.. "Occupational Segregation, Compensating Differentials and Comparable Worth", in Robert T. Michael et al., eds., *Pay Equity: Empirical Enquiries,* Washington, D.C.:National Academy Press, 1989.

Glass, J. "The Impact of of Occupational Segregation on Working Conditions", *Social Forces*, 1990, vol. 68, pp. 779-96.

Grossman, Rachel. "Women's Place in the Integrated Circuit," *South-east Asia Chronicle, Pacific_Research*, 1979, vol. 9, pp. 5-6.

Haggard, S. *Pathways From the Periphery: Politics of Growth in the Newly Industrailising Countries,* Ithaca and New York: Cornell University Press, 1990.

Jencks, C. *Inequality; a Reassessment of the Effect of Family and Schooling in America*, Peregrine Books, Harmondsworth, 1975.

King, M. "Occupational Segregation by Race and Sex, 1940-88," *Monthly Labor Review*, April, 1992.

Lerner, G. *The Creation of Patriarchy*, New York: Oxford University Press, 1986.

Lim, L. "Women's Work in Export Factories: The Politics of a Cause," in I. Tinker ed., *Persistent_Inequalities: Women and World Development*, New York: Oxford University Press, 1990.

Poire, M.. and Sabel, C. *The Second Industrial Divide*, New York: Basic Books, Inc., 1984.

Safa, H. I. "Women, Production and Reproduction in Industrialism Capitalism: A Comparison of Brazilian and U.S. Factory Workers," in June Nash et al., eds., *Women , Men and the International_Division of Labour,* Albany: State University of New York Press, 1983.

Schurman, F. "Introduction: Development Theory in the 1990s," in Frans Schurman, ed., *Beyond the Impasse,* London: Zed Press, 1993.

Sen, G. and Grown,C. *Development, Crises and Alternative Visions,* New York: Monthly Review Press, 1985.

World Labour Report, ILO, Geneva, International Labour Office, 1993.

Year Book of Labour Statistics, ILO, Geneva, International Labour Office, 1989-90.

12

TECHNOLOGICAL CHANGE AND INTERNATIONAL ECONOMIC INSTITUTIONS[1]

Sylvia Ostry

Centre for International Studies, University of Toronto, Canada

Economic interdependence has increased sharply since the end of World War II when the architecture of international economic cooperation was constructed. The term globalization, first used in 1986, conveys the increasing linkages among countries, or <u>deeper integration</u> of the world economy, by trade, finance, direct investment and technology. This deeper integration is pushing trade policy more and more inside the border, blurring the lines between international and domestic policies and blurring the lines among the three engines of globalization, trade, investment and technology. These engines are largely embodied in the multinational enterprise (MNE), primarily in technology-intensive trade and services industries. This has raised the profile of technology issues in the international policy agenda. A new institution is not required, but the new WTO, and other multilateral fora such as the OECD, must launch new policy initiatives to prevent further high-tech friction.

Economic interdependence has increased sharply since the end of World War II when the architecture of international economic cooperation was constructed. The term globalization, first used in 1986, while never precisely defined is meant to convey the increasing linkages <u>among countries</u> or deeper integration of the <u>world economy</u> by trade, finance, direct investment and technology. Interdependence also involves an increasing interrelationship among major influences on the world economic system, with monetary policy affecting trade policy feeding back into monetary and fiscal policy. It is this continuing force of globalization and, of course, the end of the Cold War, that capture the essential and stark contrast between the environment that generated the impetus for the postwar institutions and the world of the 1990s and demands a rethinking of their *raison d'être*.

There has been a great outpouring of analysis on proposed reforms of the Bretton Woods institutions, the International Monetary Fund (IMF) and the World Bank.[2]   There's considerable irony in the fact that the new World Trade Organization (WTO), a descendant of the ill-fated International Trade Organization (ITO) which was never born, is the first construct in a new post cold war architecture of international cooperation.   Indeed, the Uruguay Round itself reflected, in the inclusion of "new issues" (such as trade in services, intellectual property and aspects of investment), the impact of globalization on the agenda of trade policy. The deeper integration of the world economy is pushing trade policy more and more inside the border, blurring the lines between international and domestic policies, and blurring the lines among the three engines of globalization, trade, investment and technology. The GATT reflected the postwar world inherited from the disastrous tariff wars of the 1930s: the prime focus of GATT negotiations was to reduce border barriers. The WTO's major focus in the future will be on "domestic" policies: for example domestic regulatory regimes; administrative law regimes; competition policy; foreign investment impediments and incentives; high-tech industrial policies, etc.

The multinational enterprise (MNE) is the main vehicle for transmission not only of investment but also of trade and technology. And the MNE is the main agent of globalization and the agenda of deeper integration. Indeed the surge in foreign direct investment in the second half of the 1980s, heavily concentrated in technology-intensive goods and services, was the prime factor in raising the profile of technological issues in policy debate.

The purpose of this Chapter is to highlight some of the technology policy issues. No new institution is needed to deal with the ongoing impact of technological change but the agendas of existing institutions should be adapted to the reflect the importance of the issue. Before turning to some suggestions in this regard, it is useful to review the main features of the intensification of globalization and deeper integration as they emerged in the 1980s.

Globalization and Deeper Integration in the 1980s

While the value of total production of industrial countries increased at a rate of about 9 percent a year on average over the past three decades, the value of the exports of these nations grew at an average rate of 12 percent. This steady increase in trade flows has been accompanied by a significant change in the <u>sectoral composition</u> of trade, from low-tech to medium and high-tech goods, especially in the developed economies. The share of low-technology goods in manufacturing exports declined from 45 percent in the mid 60s to less than 35 percent at the end of the 1980s. While data are very scarce, trade in commercial services also increased over the 1980s from a share of exports of 17 percent in 1986 to 21 percent in 1992.

As may be seen from Table 1, the U.S. postwar dominance in both medium-tech (capital intensive sectors such as autos and technology-intensive components and equipment) as well as high-tech has been increasingly challenged by Japan: and Europe even more so. Further, as is clear from Table 1, the real impact of the Japanese challenge over the 1970s and 1980s was rising import penetration rather than declining export share. But Japan's import share did not follow this trend. One consequence of *le défi Japanais* was a marked increase in international friction over the 1980s as well as changes in the domestic policies of the OECD countries (see below).

Another significant development linked with the growth of technology-intensive manufacturing has been the increase in intra industry trade (Table 2). This trade within the same broad industry or product group, stimulates competition and pressure for continuous innovation and is also an important channel for diffusion of technology embodied in sophisticated components and equipment. Foreign sourcing of such inputs increased rapidly in the 1980s in sectors whose products represented complex systems: automobiles, aerospace, communications, semiconductor equipment and computers.

Much of the intra industry trade in components and equipment takes place within the multinational firm. Unfortunately, little information is available on this important aspect of globalization except for some American data. It is estimated that in 1989 nearly 40 percent of U.S. merchandise exports and more than two-fifths of its merchandise imports were intrafirm transactions[3] The ratios for such transactions are highest in high-wage, technology-intensive sectors such as machinery, electronic equipment, and transportation equipment.

But these figures do not capture the full impact of MNEs on the global economy. The United Nations estimates that worldwide sales of foreign affiliates amounted to $5.2 trillions in 1993 as compared with $4.8 trillions for world exports of goods and services. These sales grew by 17.4% in the second half of the 1980s compared with 14.3% growth of exports, reflecting the investment surge of that period to which we now turn.[4]

Table 1: Export shares, revealed comparative advantage and import penetration in the developed economies 1970 and 1990

		Export Shares[1]		*RCA[2]*		*Import Penetration[3]*	
		1970	*1990*	*1970*	*1990*	*1970*	*1990*
United States	High Technology	31.1	26.3	1.54	1.51	4.2	18.4
	Medium Technology	21.7	15.4	1.07	0.89	5.6	18.5
	Low Technology	13.4	13.3	0.66	0.76	3.8	8.8
Japan	High Technology	13.2	21.1	1.20	1.41	5.2	5.4
	Medium Technology	8.5	16.9	.77	1.12	4.5	5.9
	Low Technology	13.2	7.1	1.19	0.47	3.0	6.6
Germany	High Technology	17.7	16.2	0.93	0.79	14.9	37.0
	Medium Technology	23.1	24.7	1.22	1.20	17.2	29.5
	Low Technology	15.0	17.9	0.79	0.87	11.1	20.9
France	High Technology	7.7	8.7	0.83	0.84	21.6	31.6
	Medium Technology	8.5	10.0	0.92	0.97	19.7	34.1
	Low Technology	10.7	12.1	1.15	1.18	10.7	21.4
United Kingdom	High Technology	10.5	10.2	1.01	1.16	17.4	42.4
	Medium Technology	11.9	8.5	1.14	0.96	n.a	39.4
	Low Technology	8.9	8.5	0.85	0.95	12.4	19.8
Italy	High Technology	5.5	5.1	0.75	0.59	16.2	22.8
	Medium Technology	7.1	7.7	0.97	0.89	23.6	28.9
	Low Technology	8.5	12.8	1.16	1.49	11.6	15.7
Canada	High Technology	3.9	2.8	0.54	0.55	42.2	63.4
	Medium Technology	8.9	5.9	1.22	1.14	42.9	53.3
	Low Technology	7.0	6.1	0.96	1.19	12.1	16.8

1. Share of OECD exports in each category.
2. Revealed Comparative Advantage is calculated as a country's exports in an industry divided by its total exports, normalized by the same ratio for the OECD countries.
3. Imports divided by total domestic demand (production plus imports less exports).
Source: OECD, Economic Surveys, United States 1993, Table 16, p. 87.

Table 2: Bilateral intra-industry trade indices[1], total products[2], G-7 Countries

		Japan	Germany	France	U.K.	Italy	Canada
United States	1970	32	44	52	52	34	63
	1980	31	48	59	55	42	71
	1990	48	64	69	63	56	71
Japan	1970		54	62	45	50	9
	1980		69	47	66	41	12
	1990		77	31	62	44	9
Germany	1970			72	77	55	16
	1980			83	59	54	24
	1990			88	76	66	31
France	1970				66	63	19
	1980				69	59	30
	1990				31	71	39
United Kingdom	1970					64	36
	1980					75	39
	1990					75	38
Italy	1970						14
	1980						22
	1990						24

1. Definition and Measurement: Intra industry trade (IIT) is a measure of two-way trade within the same industrial or product classification. An example of intra industry trade is where Japan exports laptop computers to the United States, while the US exports mainframe computers to Japan. For a particular product of industry I, IIT is defined as the value of total trade (X_i+M_i) remaining after subtraction of the absolute value of net exports or imports, $\left| X_i-M_i \right|$. In order to be able to compare between countries and industries, the measure is expressed as a percentage of each industry's combined exports and imports. A measure of inter industry trade is then expressed as $100[(X_i-M_i)/(X_i+M_i)]$ and the intra industry trade measure is given by $100[(1-(X_i-M_i)/(X_i+M_i)]$. The index varies between 0 and 100. If a country exports and imports roughly equal quantities of a certain product, the IIT index is high. If it is mainly one-way trade (whether exporting or importing), certain products, the IIT index is low. For aggregation purposes, the measure can be summed over many industries.

2. Figures are calculated from SITC Rev. 2, 3-digit product categories and are adjusted for overall trade imbalances.

Source: OECD, Industrial Policy in OECD Countries, Annual Review, 1992 Paris, pp. 209.

As Figure 1 demonstrates, after moderate growth in the 1970s and a slowdown in the first half of the 1980s a remarkable and unprecedented surge of FDI flows took place after 1985. Part of the "bulge" was due to one-off factors (e.g.

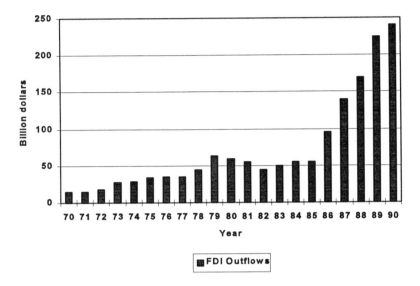

Figure 1: Foreign-direct-investment outflows, 1970-1990
Source: World Investment Report: Transnational Corporations and International Production, United Nations, 1993.

protectionist action, in Europe and the U.S., directed at Japan and the wide exchange rate savings of the decade) but the outflows also reflected the underlying structural changes described earlier. Growth of investment in the second half of the 80s averaged nearly 30 percent per year, four times the rate of world output and three times the rate of trade. Technology flows (as captured by the very inadequate measure of royalties and fees) also exploded, increasing from an annual growth rate of less than 0.1 to nearly 22 percent between the first and second half of the decade.[5]

Eighty percent of the flow of investment was controlled by MNEs from the Triad: the European Union (EU), the U.S. and Japan. Throughout the 1980s, the U.S. was the primary host country but for the first time in the postwar years Japan became the major source of FDI outflow. The stark contrast between Japanese outflows and inflows exacerbated the inherited asymmetry of inward and outward investment stocks between Japan and the rest of the OECD (see Table 3) and created another source of friction with the U.S. Since effective access to markets often involves an investment presence, especially in high-tech and services, impediments to investment will also act as impediments to trade and the acquisition of knowledge. This latter point requires further explanation.

It is well established in both the theoretical and empirical literature that foreign direct investment involves technology transfer to the host country. So the growing ubiquitousness of the MNE involves increasing diffusion of technology: globalization of investment means technoglobalism, a new term of the 1980s.

This technology transfer includes not just coded technological knowledge of new products and processes but also what economists call tacit knowledge, including, for example, new forms of coordination and control of production or new ideas in marketing: wetware is the new term, or all the ideas stored in the "wet" computer of the brain. But FDI is also a channel of knowledge acquisition and MNEs are increasingly aware of the need to set up early warning systems to detect technological threats from their competitors in host country markets, especially in advanced markets with strong technological and scientific capabilities. While there is considerable variation by industry and home country ownership and global R&D is not yet widespread, it seems likely to increase, albeit with some lag following the establishment of a foreign manufacturing base.[6] Technoglobalism is becoming a two way channel.

One manifestation of this new technoglobalism in the 1980s and 1990s was the enormous increase in strategic technology alliances which hardly existed in the 1970s. Figure 2 shows the surge in these new forms of investment (as they are sometimes termed) in the three most significant current technologies: information, biotechnology and new materials. These alliances take place in a wide variety of organizational modes: equity arrangements such as joint ventures; research corporations and minority investments; contractual joint development agreements; R&D contracts, etc. The basic reason for these alliances is an exchange of complementary assets. The costs of R&D and the widening range of technologies which feed innovation today means that few firms want to undertake the risk of development alone and thus seek partners to reduce cost and spread risk. Often these partners are competitors in final markets and so the alliance is risky as well -- one reason for a high failure rate reported in a number of case studies. Nonetheless the trend to strategic alliances shows no sign of abatement and is indeed accelerating.

Table 3: G-7, Inward and Outward stocks of FDI by Regions and Countries: 1980, 1985, 1990.
(millions of dollars and world shares).

	1980				1985				1990			
	Inward		Outward		Inward		Outward		Inward		Outward	
	$	%	$	%	$	%	$	%	$	%	$	%
United States	16918	8.6	21746	9.7	19022	8.4	8924	2.7	37213	6.4	28960	3.0
Canada	51681	26.4	22585	10.1	62438	27.7	38742	11.8	108051	18.7	74722	7.8
Japan	2979	1.5	36497	16.3	6397	2.8	83649	25.4	18432	3.2	310808	32.5
France	15477	7.9	12222	5.5	19196	8.5	20261	6.2	57791	10.0	84596	8.9
Germany	36630	18.7	43127	19.3	36930	16.4	59916	18.2	93456	16.1	155133	16.2
Italy	8892	4.5	6970	3.1	18875	8.4	16215	4.9	57983	10.0	26102	5.9
United Kingdom	63057	32.2	80785	36.1	62587	27.8	101236	30.8	205884	35.6	245069	25.7
Total	195634	100.0	223932	100.0	225445	100.0	328942	100.0	578810	100.0	955391	100.0

Source: Country tables, United Nations, World Investment Directory, Volume 3: Developed Countries, New York, 1993.

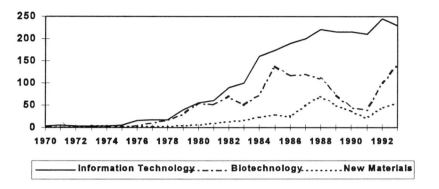

Figure 2:Growth of newly established strategic technology alliances in information technologies, biotechnology and new materials, 1970-1993
Source: Maastricht Research Institute on Innovation and Technology

As this review of the main features of globalization, and especially the intensification in the 1980s, demonstrates, increasingly fierce competition among the MNEs of the Triad created new strains among the major trading countries. One response was the implementation of domestic policies designed to foster innovation among domestic firms: the term technonationalism was invented as efforts were made to exclude or discriminate among foreign subsidiaries, i.e. to halt or slow the diffusion of knowledge across borders. On the international front a number of high-tech battles were fought, mostly between the U.S. and Japan (involving, for example, semiconductors; pharmaceuticals; government procurement for technologically advanced equipment; government standards for high-tech products, etc.) but also with Europe (for example Airbus subsidies; procurement of telecommunications equipment). While it is not necessary to detail these developments here[7], it is important to explain the linkage between the ongoing process of globalization and the emerging policy template of deeper integration if suggestions for new ways to tackle some of the issues relating to technological change are to have any relevance.

The New Policy Template of Deeper Integration

The growing interdependence among countries which began in the postwar period is the primary reason for the changing policy focus of deeper integration. Under U.S. leadership the postwar architecture of international institutions as well as the Marshall Plan and the reconstruction of the Japanese economy set in play a process which produced, by the early 1970s, a rough parity or convergence in living standards and overall technological capabilities among the OECD countries: convergence, by definition, involved the erosion of American postwar economic and technological dominance. The most fundamental consequence of the erosion of hegemony was the growing view in the U.S. that the trading system of the GATT was basically "unfair" because the U.S. market was structurally more open than that of other countries. This unfairness or asymmetry of access stemmed not primarily from transparent border barriers -- tariff or overt quotas -- but from a range of other domestic practices by foreign governments which had the effect of impeding access for American exports into these markets or, by the spillover effects of these policies into third country markets. The Tokyo Round of the 1970s reflected this American view of unfairness in its focus on domestic subsidies and the Common Agricultural Policy of the European Community.

The Tokyo Round was mainly a transatlantic negotiation. By the 1980s, the American view of asymmetry of access had shifted to Japan and one result was the high-tech battles just noted, reflecting the growing awareness of innovation as a source of competitiveness and an expanding definition of unfair impediments to access by trade and investment.

Another result was the long and difficult effort to launch the Uruguay Round. The agenda of The Uruguay Round included *inter alia* the unfinished business of the Tokyo Round (especially agriculture) but also a major transformation of the GATT system designed to restructure the scope of trading rules by including sectors such as services as well as intellectual property rights and investment. The original GATT covered only trade in goods and primary products. Trade in services would have been termed an oxymoron in 1950 and intellectual property rights were the domain of the World Intellectual Property Organization or WIPO. While the International Trade Organization (ITO) would have included investment, it never came into existence. But by the onset of the 1980s trade in services was growing much more rapidly than merchandise trade and the U.S. was the leading exporter by a considerable margin. The same lead status was true in investment and technology. Thus the basic structure of the GATT was "unfair" because it excluded sectors of fundamental importance to American comparative advantage in global markets and thus required rebalancing.

But rebalancing involved more than broadening the scope of GATT coverage. In the case of the new issues, border barriers were largely irrelevant. Barriers to access stemmed from domestic regulatory and legal regimes. In services, trade, investment and access to advanced information and communication technology are inextricably interwoven. The new issues of the Uruguay Round exemplify, in other words, the new policy template of deeper integration. Or at least the outline of that template: the full dimensions of the regime will only emerge over time.

Thus it can be argued that the decline of U.S. economic and technological hegemony was the most important factor behind the launch of the most significant multilateral negotiations since the founding of the GATT. But the Uruguay Round was not the only "defining event" of the new trade policy regime. The high tech battles, especially between the U.S. and Japan under the umbrella of U.S. unilateralism (Super 301 of the 1988 trade act), were of equal importance in establishing a new trade agenda which exemplified key characteristics of deeper integration, i.e. the linkage between effective access (by trade) and effective presence (by investment) and the focus on domestic regimes or even entire systems rather than border impediments. Indeed, at the end of the decade the bilateral negotiations termed the Structural Impediments Initiative (SII) covered a wide array of domestic policies from land use regulation and retail distribution regulation to broad framework policies such as competition policy as well as issues related to technology access. It is important to underline that the high-tech conflicts between the U.S. and Japan as well as SII also reflected a transformation of American trade policy in the 1980s from a single, overriding commitment to mutilateralism to a multi-track policy of multilateralism (the attempt to launch the Uruguay Round); bilateralism (the Canada-U.S. Free Trade Agreement); and unilateralism (the various forms of section 301 of the 1974 Trade Act and the Super 301 of the 1988 Trade Act).[8] These options as alternative or complementary routes to deeper integration remain part of U.S. trade policy today and are likely to remain so. We shall return to this issue in our discussion on policy in the WTO, below.

Finally, the globalization of the 1980s in itself was a force for a new trade agenda. One of the consequences of the growing role of the MNEs is pressure on governments to reduce transactions costs associated with different regulatory and legal regimes, i.e. pressure to harmonize different systems. And the significant role of the MNEs generates another impetus to the harmonization trend on the part of many host governments because more and more investment today is not tied to the location of natural resources or to supplying protected local markets and this invokes governmental fears of "footloose" firms or delocalization. Indeed liberalization of both trade and investment policies has led to increasing competition for investment and unilateral reduction of "hassle costs" for the entry of MNEs, especially in many non-OECD countries.

But the fear of footloose investment has also raised concerns in the advanced countries which could lead to new protectionist pressures. Thus it has been argued that with the narrowing of the margin of comparative advantage among MNEs from the OECD countries footloose firms create greater "volatility" in competitiveness and thus comparative advantage today is also far more volatile -- or knife-edged[9] -- than in the past when it was basically determined by fundamental factors related to resource endowment. The notion of knife-edged comparative advantage has provided additional impetus to policies designed to slow the diffusion of technology across borders and to enhance the innovation capacity of domestic MNEs. More broadly, the idea of "created" comparative advantage has generated an ongoing debate on the appropriate role for government S&T (science and technology) policy. While there is full agreement that government support of basic research is essential to build the knowledge base necessary to sustain technological change, there is less agreement on the role of government support for technological development which is closer to the market implementation or innovation end of the knowledge continuum. We shall return to this point in our discussion of policy proposals to which we now turn.

Technological Change and the Post Uruguay Policy Agenda

A -- perhaps even the -- major achievement of the Uruguay Round was the creation of a new institution, the WTO. The WTO turned the GATT from a trade agreement into a membership organization which brings together all the various pacts and codes and other arrangements that were negotiated by the GATT under one legal framework with a single, strong and effective dispute settlement mechanism. The creation of the WTO was not part of the agenda of the Round when it was launched in *Punta del Este* in September 1986. The Canadian proposal for the creation of a new institution was put forward in April 1990 and was unlikely to have succeeded without the strong support of the EU. The main reason for this change was growing concern about American unilateralism, a concern which has not abated since the debate in the U.S. over the WTO as a threat to sovereignty. Nor is American unilateralism the only challenge to the new liberalized regime. Rising structural unemployment in Europe has evoked demands for protection from unfair competition by low-wage labor in developing countries and calls for harmonization of labor standards to prevent "social dumping". And some environmental non-governmental organizations (NGOs) have argued for the use of trade measures to prevent "downward harmonization" or a "race to the bottom" of environmental standards.

Thus the completion of the Uruguay Round, designed to restore, renew, and redesign the rules-based multilateral system which had seriously eroded over the 1970s and 1980s represents only the first step in the process of renewed multilateralism. The completion of the Uruguay Round should be viewed as a necessary but not sufficient condition for a sustainable rules-based system. Bridging the gap between necessity and sufficiency will require undertaking a number of policy initiatives rather than following the usual tradition of heaving a sigh of relief and marking time until the launch of the next decennial round. Some examples of WTO policy possibilities related to technology issues will be discussed below.

But the WTO is not now and never will be the only game in town. The flexibility necessary to adopt trade policy to ongoing change which is a feature of the world today will require action in a number of fora, including regional arrangements like NAFTA or APEC, and the OECD, which played a major role in the preparation of the Uruguay Round with its work on agriculture and services. The OECD, unlike other international economic institutions, has an array of programmes in the innovation field and so is well-equipped to tackle some of the preparatory work for policy initiatives in the area of technology and some suggestions along these lines will also be proposed. But it is essential that all regional, plurilateral and bilateral agreements should be tabled in the WTO as part of an overall monitoring process. This would provide an opportunity for WTO members not only to keep abreast of policy evolution but also to discuss whether and how policies should be multilateralized and perhaps linked.

The need to enhance the adaptiveness of trade policy-making to continuing change in the international economy cannot be overemphasized. To avoid repeating errors of the past, the lessons of history should provide guidance. An appropriate motto for the Uruguay Round, which followed the GATT tradition of decennial negotiations, could be "too much (almost) too late." The new international regime housed in the WTO provides an <u>opportunity</u> for an "evolutionary" approach to negotiations by policy monitoring and discussion to provide the opportunity for mini-negotiations endorsed by WTO ministers who are required to meet every two years. But the key word is <u>opportunity</u>: none of this will automatically take place without leadership from member countries. The suggestions put forward here are simply examples of what might be done in a key area of globalization, i.e. technological change. The basic purpose of the suggestions is simply to initiate the evolutionary process of policy-making afforded by the success of the Uruguay Round.

Policy Options in the WTO

Three initiatives could be undertaken in the WTO to improve the Uruguay Round Agreements in items related to technological change. Since these three issues -- R&D subsidies; government procurement; and intellectual property rights -- will continue to generate disputes, especially among OECD countries, plurilateral or even bilateral agreements could be negotiated and then extended, on a voluntary (conditional MFN) basis to other members.

R&D Subsidies

Traditionally, the line taken by the U.S. government regarding what kinds of government R&D spending or subsidy were fair, and what kinds were not, tended to be relatively simple. Government support of "basic research" was completely fair. On the other hand government funding of industrial applied research and development, where the objective was to help firms create new commercial products and processes, most certainly was not fair. Of course governments could fund industrial R&D, if the objective were to create new products or technologies of use to the military. Commercial spillover from such projects was simply ignored. Also, government funding of applied research and development to improve agricultural technology was, somehow, quite acceptable. So also was, for a while at least, funding of R&D on nuclear power. But these complications tended to get pushed aside in statements of general principles. The essential position was that funding of basic research was fair, but that anything that subsidized commercial technological development was not.

There was a rather dramatic change in the American line that has occurred as the Clinton administration came to power. No longer was a sharp line drawn between basic research and applied. And support of industrial research and development no longer was a no-no, but rather a perfectly legitimate act of government. The consequence of these changes in the American viewpoint was a

Uruguay Round agreement where a "green light" is given for assistance for research activities conducted by firms or higher education or research establishments on a contract basis with firms if the assistance covers not more than 75 percent of the costs of industrial research or 50 percent of the costs of "pre-competitive development activity." The permissible costs are also detailed in the text as follows:

- personnel costs (researchers, technicians and other supporting staff employed exclusively in the research activity);
- costs of instruments, equipment, land and buildings used exclusively and permanently (except when disposed of on a commercial basis) for the research activity;
- costs of consultancy and equivalent services used exclusively for the research activity, including bought-in research, technical knowledge, patents, etc.;
- additional overhead costs incurred directly as a result of the research activity;
- other running costs (such as those of materials, supplies and the like), incurred directly as a result of the research activity.

Compared with the levels set in an earlier (1991) draft agreement, under the Uruguay Round Agreement, permissible levels of government subsidies were doubled for pre-competitive development activities and increased by half for "basic research" from those agreed in the earlier 1991 Draft Final Act endorsed by the previous administration. Indeed the adjective "basic" is not used and the definition of the activity was altered significantly to a more applied commercial orientation. In addition, the cut-off for activity which it is permissible for governments to fund has been expanded to include creation of the first non-commercial prototype. More specifically, the code defined research subsidies as follows:

- "the term 'industrial research' (formerly basic industrial research) means planned search or critical investigation aimed at discovery of new knowledge, with the objective that such knowledge may be useful in developing new products, processes or services, or in bringing about a significant improvement to existing products, processes or services.
- the term 'pre-competitive development activity' means the translation of industrial research findings into a plan, blueprint or design for new, modified or improved products, processes or services whether intended for sale or use, including the creation of a first prototype which would not be capable of commercial use. It may further include the conceptual formulation and design of products, processes or services alternatives and initial demonstration or pilot projects, provided that these same periodic alterations to existing products, production lines, manufacturing processes, services, and other on-going operations even though those alterations may represent improvements."

The agreement also provides a mechanism for securing "green light" status through a review by a Subsidies Committee after notification of a programme. Such notification is to be updated yearly and the entire provision is to be reviewed after five years.

It will be extremely difficult to get explicit, meaningful binding rules regarding government research subsidies. Indeed, the issue was so contentious even within the U.S. that it threatened to hold up confirmation of the entire Round. For one thing, differences across industries are so great that rules for one may make no sense for others. For another, "national security" can be used as a reason for avoiding discipline even though this is not explicitly recognized in the new WTO code. And, of course, governments differ with respect to their view on high tech industrial policy although these differences have narrowed with the changes initiated by the Clinton administration but may reemerge because of the Republican majority in the new Congress.

Thus to preclude disputes in this potentially fractious field a more precise and analytically rigorous agreement on definitions should be undertaken. The basis could be the definitions used in the OECD for its work on innovation policies. More specifically, for over thirty years the OECD Directorate for Science, Technology and Industry has developed and refined extremely detailed definitions to collect information on the measurement of human and financial resources devoted to R&D.[10] These same definitions are also used in some countries not only for analytical and evaluation purposes but also for income tax regulations. The OECD definitions and methodology should form the basis for an early WTO Subsidy Committee review and for the WTO dispute settlement procedure. Indeed, just as the Uruguay Round provides that science advisory groups may be called in disputes over the environment, it might be useful to consider an expert group on innovation policy issues should the need arise in the fractious area of R&D subsidies before a new agreement on definitions is achieved. While this proposal may not solve all the difficult and complex definitional issues, it would promote constructive, plurilateral debate and perhaps foster progress on eventual harmonization of subsidy practices while helping to constrain serious bilateral and unilateral destabilizing friction.

Government Procurement of High-Tech Goods

While the new Government Procurement Agreement (GPO) in the Uruguay Round was a major improvement over the Tokyo Round code and opened access to a broad range of government contracts, most of the commitments are based on reciprocity and do not apply to all signatories, i.e. the GPA is on a conditional MFN basis. But it provides a major opportunity for adding new members and thus for continuing expansion. Also the Uruguay Round agreement included a commitment for new negotiations on procurement to begin before the end of the decade.

Thus preparations could start now for a new approach to government procurement for high tech products on a plurilateral or even bilateral basis. The market-oriented sector-specific (MOSS) negotiations between the U.S. and Japan in the 1980s included a number of high-tech products such as medical equipment, pharmaceuticals, supercomputers and telecommunication equipment. Among the many areas of dispute, which essentially reflected fundamental differences in regulatory practices, was the issue of specification of the product. The American regulatory system focuses on performance norms and the Japanese system focuses on design specifications. Design specifications tend to be more intrusive and less transparent and therefore, the Americans argued, more subject to possible government-business "collusion."

Since these disputes were never really resolved and may well lead to more pressure for complete harmonization and/or pressure for market share arrangements a new initiative to lay the groundwork for negotiations in the WTO is well worth consideration. This initiative would involve an agreement among an interested group of countries to launch an internationally funded performance centre to develop technical standards for performance evaluation to be applied under the GPA for procurement of specified products. There are many precedents for adopting international product standards in the GATT code on technical barriers to trade. Further, in the U.S. the Sematech Consortium has provided a central funding and testing organization for performance specifications for semiconductor equipment which has lowered the costs of adoption by reducing duplication among manufacturers.[11] The new international performance centre should include government and business collaboration as well as funding, along the lines of Sematech or the EU's program of pre-normative research which deals with similar issues in the standards realm.

Intellectual Property Rights

The Uruguay Round made a major breakthrough by establishing comprehensive standards for domestic intellectual property laws and rigorous provisions for enforcement and dispute settlement. The inclusion of IPRs was strongly opposed by a number of developing countries not only because it would involve higher costs of technology acquisition but because it would limit the use of industrial policy instruments such as compulsory licensing or technology transfer conditions on foreign investment. The "north/south" disputes are likely to recur, especially over the enforcement provisions as the Chinese example illustrates. But there are also likely to be conflicts among some OECD countries and newly industrializing countries like Korea because the accord did not succeed in achieving harmonization of IPR regimes.

There are some good reasons for trying to make national intellectual property rights laws more consistent with each other. The most important one is that it would greatly simplify international business, and reduce transaction costs, if companies and other inventors were able to deal with one basic legal code, rather than a collection of codes with significant differences from country to country.

The categories "strong intellectual property rights" and "weak intellectual property rights" do not characterize adequately the prevailing differences across the industrialized nations in their property rights laws. The United States currently awards patents to "the first to invest", while all of the other major industrial nations award patents to "the first to file." In most of Europe, and in Japan, patent applications are made open to the public and other parties to get their evidence heard prior to decision. In some of Europe, and in Japan, there are provisions for compulsory licensing of patents under certain circumstances. In the United States compulsory licensing mainly exists as a remedy put forth after an antitrust case. The European nations distinguish inventions in terms of the inventive step involved, and grant stronger and longer patent protection for inventions that represent a large step forward, than for those that represent a small step. The United States has no such provisions. Patent lawyers tend to push the point of view that, absent strong patent protection, firms or private inventors would have no incentive to invent. In fact, however, there have been numerous studies indicating strongly that elimination of patent protection would have little effect on R&D in a large number of industries. Thus in industries like aircraft, aircraft engines, computers, semiconductors, and many others, it would appear that the natural lead time of an innovator is the principal reason that innovation pays, and the availability of patent protection does not add much. The industries producing fine chemical products, and in particular pharmaceuticals, are exceptions. Here patent protection almost surely is necessary for companies to have incentive to do R&D. It is not surprising, therefore, that representatives of these industries have been the strongest and most vocal advocates for strengthened intellectual property rights. But for many high tech industries patent protection is but a small part of the incentives that draw forth R&D aimed at creating new products and processes.

Of course a major facet of globalization is that lead times in many areas are shrinking, and the number of companies capable of imitating relatively quickly has grown. In particular, the number of countries housing technologically sophisticated companies has expanded greatly. Much of the friction relating to intellectual property rights is associated with the rise of new industrial powers. Thus American firms, who over the years have adopted a policy of not enforcing patents or cross-licensing them with their American peers, began to get upset when Japanese firms rose to prominence in their industries, clearly taking advantage of American creative technology. As Japan has moved to the forefront, and countries like Korea and Taiwan have begun to develop rapidly, Japanese firms which earlier were relatively passive about enforcing their intellectual property rights, have become more aggressive.

However, strong intellectual property rights in a field can cause difficulty for leading firms, as well as those aiming to catch up. In many technologies, the intellectual property rights associated with a broad process, or a broad product configuration, tend to be spread out among a number of companies. When patents are strongly enforced and costly to license, no company may be in a position to design and produce the best possible product without courting lawsuits. This is the reason why, in many industries, intellectual property rights have been shared, or not strongly enforced.

Thus, as noted, the growing importance in high technology industries of international trade, and multinational operation of firms, has significantly increased the transaction costs of dealing with a number of different national intellectual property rights systems. There is every reason to try to harmonize better. Another benefit of a new harmonization initiative would be that the negotiations would also provide an opportunity to discuss the new issues arising from the ongoing revolution of ICT as exemplified by the growing debate over the Internet and the protection of copyright. These formidable issues will not be easily resolved but they merit discussion in the WTO.

In the Uruguay Round, with the exception of intellectual protection of computer software, and semiconductor chip design, the negotiators did not succeed in achieving much in the way of harmonization. It is interesting, and noteworthy, that while the negotiators agreed that "copyright" is the way all nations should treat computer programs, in the United States many voices have been raised recently to the effect that copyright is a very awkward way of doing that job. Similarly, concerns have been expressed that the U.S. way of protecting integrated circuit design, which is implicitly accepted in the Uruguay agreement, won't do the appropriate job for very long. In short, not very much harmonization was achieved, and where there was agreement on a common standard, it is not at all clear that the right one was achieved.

Most of the issues impeding harmonization can be resolved in negotiations between the U.S. and Europe on the one hand, and the U.S. and Japan on the other hand. In many cases, the reforms ought to involve the U.S. law, rather than the law abroad. There are signs that U.S. policymakers are beginning to see it that way too. Thus the U.S. has made noises about adopting a "first to file" system. Particularly with the rise of patenting of computer software, there are many Americans arguing for opening up the patent application evaluation process in the United States, so that the U.S. would look more like Europe in that regard. And regarding software, and several other areas, a number of suggestions have been made that the Americans, like the Europeans and the Japanese, ought to adopt a compulsory licensing clause regarding patents that block the use of other patented technology.

Thus a new initiative for harmonization could proceed on the basis of bilateral, trilateral or plurilateral negotiation and then extended on a conditional MFN basis to other countries who agree to accept the standard. In this way, and also by fostering discussion on the impact of continuing technological change on IPRs, an evolutionary policy approach could be launched.

In addition to these three examples of policy initiatives to be undertaken in the WTO which could heighten the importance of understanding the pervasive influence of technological change in the international economy, there is scope for similar initiatives in the OECD. The first -- strategic dumping -- would also involve negotiations in the WTO and thus could establish a useful precedent for international institutional cooperation.

Policy Options in the OECD

Strategic Dumping

One of the issues which generated continuing friction between Japan and both the EU and the U.S. during the 1980s concerns "strategic dumping." The 1988 statement of Willy de Clerq, then head of the E.C.'s trade directorate, has often been cited:

"dumping is made possible only by market isolation in the exporting country, due primarily to such factors as high tariffs or non-tariff barriers and anticompetitive practices. This prevents the producers in the importing country from competing with the foreign supplier on his own ground while allowing him to attack their domestic market by sales which are often made at a loss, or are financed from the profits made from the sale of the same or different products in a protected domestic market."[12]

More technical expositions of a similar model have been elaborated in the analysis of the U.S. color television antitrust case in which Zenith sued Matsushita for predatory pricing.[13] Strategic dumping essentially involves subsidizing exports through higher home prices sustained by collusive price behavior and a protected home market. In industries with significant dynamic economies of scale, high fixed costs -- for example by coordinated R&D expenditure -- would serve to deter entry. Thus the essential dimensions of strategic dumping are the exporting country's trade policy and competition policy. The injury to the importing country's firms involves both restriction of exports and loss of dynamic efficiency gains (learning by doing) which may be cumulative and dispersed over a wide range of products.[14]

One option to deal with strategic dumping would be for the importing country to undertake a form of harassment as a policy of deterrent: strategic antidumping. This is likely to induce investment by the exporting firms into the importing country, as happened in autos and semiconductors during the 1980s, and thus creates another set of problems. Another possibility is domestic subsidy, which would require multilateral negotiations on a new subsidy code. A third option would be to tackle the root causes of the problem, the exporting country's trade and competition policy.

In order to remove the barriers to access into the exporter's market the first step to be undertaken in the appropriate Working Party in the OECD would be to agree to a list of industry characteristics; for example, degree of concentration as measured by exporting firms' share of home market; exporting firms' share of world market (which would affect alternative third country producers); extent and nature of barriers to entry of new firms or expansion of existing firms; degree of import penetration; prices in the exporting country's home market relative to prices elsewhere, etc. The purpose of selecting specific industries would be to focus proposed negotiations in the WTO on eliminating protection for sectors where strategic behavior is feasible. These are high tech industries, industries i.e. sectors with oligopolistic structures; high entry barriers; significant static and dynamic efficiencies; and dominance in global markets.

From this agreed industry list one could then assemble a group of products and for these compile a list of specific import barriers. This should be done in cooperation with the WTO secretariat. This would then form the basis for a "zero, for zero" negotiation, i.e. the removal of all border restraints on a reciprocal basis. The negotiations could begin with a small group of countries, including the U.S., EU and Japan, and then they could decide whether the agreement should be conditional or full MFN. If conditional, the agreement should be open to all countries willing to accede to the zero tariffs.

The removal of trade barriers will not, on its own, remove the threat of strategic dumping which also requires action on competition policy in the exporting market. But convergence, however desirable, will be a lengthy process, although talks in the OECD have been underway since 1992 and competition policy is now also on the agenda of the WTO for future negotiations. In the meantime, a strong case could be made that in the absence of a supranational authority, bilateral agreements to ensure a fair hearing of disputes over enforcement where there is a charge of spillover on the trade front might be contemplated. By means of transparency and international peer pressure, the process of convergence would well be speeded up. If this option is not pursued, extraterritoriality seems a likely alternative.[15]

Strategic Alliances in R&D

Another competition policy issue which has so clearly emerged over the 1980s is transnational mergers or, even more, transnational joint ventures in high tech sectors. Each of the national governments may not be concerned about potential abuse of dominant position in their own country or, indeed, each may hold different views on the matter. So disputes are likely to become more frequent. In any case, globalization logically requires a supranational authority and dispute settlement mechanism. The trend to global oligopolies in financial services, telecommunications and multimedia is already evident. A hard look at the global welfare implications -- the relationship between competition and innovation -- will be increasingly difficult for national governments who want a "piece of the action" in leading edge high tech sectors. Further, in many R&D alliances designed to internalize the inter-industry externalities (multimedia ventures, for example) disputes over a division of the benefits are increasingly likely and will involve a combination of competition and intellectual property issues. No international forum now exists to handle these disputes. A supranational competition policy body could, if required, have the right to establish advisory panels on intellectual property issues. In the absence of such a body, various proposals have emerged for interim bilateral or plurilateral agreements which are under discussion in the OECD and other fora such as the American Bar Association.

But policy initiatives related to global dominance, whether through mergers or alliances, are unlikely in the foreseeable future. For example, in the case of alliances, national governments have scarcely acknowledged the significance of their growth, especially in joint R&D arrangements. Yet the new feature of globalization is likely to accelerate not only within the OECD but more widely as new MNEs, for example the Overseas Chinese corporations, play a larger role in the international economy. A basic reason for lack of policy interest is that the information available on these alliances is woefully inadequate and since the data are sparse, the analysis essential for policy debate is very limited. Thus a high priority for the OECD should be to launch a project involving innovation policy experts and statistical agencies to explore avenues for data collection to expand the information on these transnational alliances, including information by sector and location; on form (e.g., equity or non-equity, etc.); as well as on the major objectives where specified by written agreements. This data base would provide the necessary input to a discussion of a number of issues related to competition policy and intellectual property as well as information on a significant new dimension of technoglobalism. The information would also be important for domestic policy, especially for smaller countries who are concerned about technology access and whose national firms lack the strategic assets essential to global partnering. The traditional channels of technology diffusion -- trade and investment -- have long been the focus of policy both in the GATT and the OECD. It's now necessary to look at this new feature of globalization, which, *inter alia*, also highlights the mismatch between the global economy and the policy architecture of the nation state and international institutions.

R&D Consortia

During the 1970s, as part of Japan's innovation policies designed to catch-up with the advanced industrialized countries and especially with the U.S., cooperative research programs were launched by the government to promote technological advance in the private sector. These joint government-private initiatives in cooperative research were aimed at "precompetitive generic technology" and were regarded by at least some observers as a successful strategy to encourage technological advance by encouraging the sharing of costs and risks in this "middle" territory of the innovation continuum between basic research and market application. During the 1980s, partly as a response to this Japanese policy "model", both the E.U. and the U.S. adopted research consortia as part of their broader innovation policy set.[16]

It seems likely that jointly funded research consortia will remain a standard feature of domestic high-tech policies in the OECD and will also be adopted in an increasing number of newly industrializing economies (NIEs). There are, however, no internationally agreed guidelines for these consortia governing the membership of foreign subsidiaries. Different practices in different countries have already created considerable friction, and since ongoing globalization will increase flows of foreign investment (including new forms such as strategic alliances) a harmonization of membership rules for consortia should be negotiated in the OECD as expeditiously as possible. The OECD practice of involving the NIEs in a number of working groups should be adopted in this case with a view to transferring to the WTO the agreed guidelines.

There are no formal conditions for participation in EU projects governed by the Commission Framework Program on technology projects. But membership in consortia are negotiated on a case-by-case basis and the "unofficial" conditions which broadly govern foreign subsidiary access to technology consortia are as follows:

- the research must be carried out in Europe
- therefore the firm must have R&D facilities in a member country
- the first commercial application of any technology emanating from the program must be carried out in Europe.

The same criteria appear to be applied in the Eureka program which is funded by national governments and the EU and is open to other Western European countries and not just EU members. A form of "conditional national treatment" also applies in the United Kingdom and Australia.

In the U.S. participation by foreign subsidiaries of multinationals is proscribed both in Sematech and in the "automobile partnership" launched by President Clinton in September 1993. Other government-sponsored technology programs do not prohibit foreign participation but condition such participation on reciprocity, i.e. on how U.S. companies are treated in the home country of the firm as well as other factors such as market access for U.S.-owned firms and protection of intellectual property rights, etc.[17] Thus the rise of the competitiveness concerns of the 1980s has led to the introduction of "conditional national treatment" for investment in a number of OECD countries. There is, however, no full inventory of these programmes and only very incomplete information on the nature of the conditions and how they are implemented.

By way of contrast, in Japan in recent years the shift to a more basic research orientation for consortia has also been accompanied by a move to encourage more international participation. Indeed the term technoglobalism was coined in Japan to signal this "new look". This has been widely criticized as more rhetoric than reality, especially by the U.S. Indeed such consortia are becoming less important in Japan than they were in the past and the bulk of Japanese R&D funding comes from the private sector. Nonetheless Japan is aware of growing criticism of the asymmetry of access for both investment and technology as compared with the U.S. and Europe.

Thus, in addition to the proposal on R&D subsidies in general, it is worthwhile trying to achieve a degree of harmonization regarding the rules for participation of foreign-owned firms in government subsidized research consortia. The first priority should be to develop a comprehensive inventory on the rules governing membership of foreign subsidiaries in government sponsored research consortia in OECD and the NIEs. This information would provide the basis for launching the discussion on a harmonization code. The issue of national security exemptions would have to be tackled since, as noted in the area of R&D subsidies more broadly, it provides an enormous "loophole", for escaping international discipline. If national security is an escape from rules for one country it will provide ammunition for an exemption for "strategic" technologies in some others.

It's open to debate where rules for foreign participation in research consortia should be treated as part of a new multilateral agreement on investment (MAI) in the OECD or as a separate "high tech" policy item. The likelihood of getting agreement on traditional national treatment by either the EU or the U.S. seems small so some limited form of conditionality might be necessary to achieve harmonized and transparent rules on membership. Because such rules can only be meaningful if full transparency on existing arrangements is achieved, the need to launch a notification procedure as quickly as possible is underlined. Finally, because more significant home and host countries for high tech FDI are outside the OECD, especially in East Asia, it is essential to transfer the discussions to the WTO as soon as possible.

International Cooperation in Basic Research: A Global Public Good

One of the negative spillovers of globalization and the increased rivalry among high-tech firms and among national governments concerned with "competitiveness" is that there seems to be an erosion of support of basic and long run research programmes, both private and public. While firms in high-technology industries are, in many cases, being forced to invest even more than they used to in product and process development, in order to stay ahead of or up with the pack, companies that used to support significant basic research seem to be withdrawing from that. And governments seem to be shifting the portfolios of research they support towards the areas and kinds of projects that promise short run and specific results, and away from fundamental research.

While the data are sketchy, a considerable evidence, however anecdotal, suggests that companies that used to invest heavily in long-run research, now are drawing back. A number of American companies who, during the period 1950-80, had significant basic research programs, have abandoned them, or have moved to make them more applied. While the case of AT&T is somewhat special, the shortening of time horizons and the associated erosion of basic research at Bell Labs may, over the long run, lead to a significant decline in the pace of major innovation in electronics. The collapse of RCA's basic laboratory and of Xerox Park are different in some respects, but part of the same story. IBM's troubles in being able to take advantage of what comes out of its Yorktown laboratories, almost surely will lead to major changes in what is done in those laboratories, perhaps at major costs to the evolution of computer technology.

The combination of very strong competition and diminished ability to prevent rivals from finding out what one is doing in research is a recipe for driving companies out of the basic research business. It clearly is happening in the United States.[18] It seems to be happening in Europe. Knowledgeable observers suggest that, while Japanese firms now are increasing their investments in basic and long-run research, the same problems that plagued American firms with such large investments may soon make Japanese firms think twice about the matter.

At the same time, the attention of governments has been drawn increasingly towards trying to help out their high-technology firms, and, as noted, a standard instrument is research support. For the most part governments have not gotten into funding commercial product development, but the industry research they do support tends to be focussed on achieving particular technological capabilities in a relatively short period of time, i.e. pre-competitive generic research is moving closer to the market phase of innovation. These new programs are not about basic and long-time horizon research.

In the United States at least, the government agencies that traditionally have supported basic research at universities have been under strong pressure from Congress, and recently from the Executive, to shift their funding more towards fields and projects where relatively clear and short-run commercial benefits can be seen. And universities, and government laboratories, are being strongly encouraged to get closer to industry. While there is less information about Europe, it appears that the same trends may be ongoing there.

More generally, there seems to be a Gresham's law at work, in which all the present inducements are for firms and governments and universities to shift away from basic and long-run research, and towards research that is closer to commercialization, and easier to appropriate. Thus far this problem largely has been in electronics, but there are indications that the same problem is arising in the chemical products industry.

The tendency of firms, and nations, in the name of competition, to focus their R&D where commercial payoffs are clear and short-run, is a strategy to minimize "spillover", to keep the payoffs "internal". But if all firms and countries do it, the result may be the slowing down of the rate at which new understandings that open up broad new technological prospects are won. Most of the analysis about competing industrial policies has focussed on the wastefulness that often is involved, and the international conflicts. Not much of the analysis has noted this other problem, which over the long run may be more serious.

This is a problem that calls for more coordination and cooperation among governments than has been given to it thus far. Once again the OECD should play a key role. First, the question should be put to member governments: is there evidence that corporations are shifting from basic and long run research, which they finance themselves? The hypothesis that this is an inevitable and durable aspect of the broader competition in high technology fields, because of the reduced ability of the companies that undertake and fund such work to take the lion's share of the benefits themselves, needs documenting by the OECD in its survey work on S&T indicators. Further, are governments responding by themselves shifting their research portfolios toward the applied and shorter run? If both these developments are widespread, then the consequences for global welfare should be spelled out. Finally, policy options should be explored including not only proposals for domestic S&T (i.e. more emphasis on basic and long run) but also for international research projects in both basic science and technologies applicable to global problems such as the environment.

With respect to international projects it would be useful to review recent experience in this field. The Japanese have initiated two international projects, one in biological science (the Human Frontiers Science project) and the other in pre-competitive research (the Intelligent Manufacturing System). Serious difficulties were encountered in the launch of both. This illustrates the need to develop new rules for international research governing issues such as sharing of costs and benefits and intellectual property rights. And the new rules should also include guidelines for evaluation.

Conclusions

This Chapter has stressed the importance of the globalization or deeper integration of the world economy as a prime force in shaping the policy agenda of the postwar institutions. The focus of the discussion was on the GATT and the new WTO, and in particular the impact of deeper integration in raising the profile of technological change as a prime engine of economic growth. This has generated an ongoing debate in the discipline of economics and, in part as a consequence, prompted a rethinking of domestic innovation policies. But there has been surprisingly little response in the international policy sphere. The purpose of this analysis, then, has been to highlight some of the policy issues stemming from the ongoing transformation of the global economy which is to a considerable degree fed and led by technological change and especially by the revolution in information and communication technology.

It is argued in this chapter that a policy response to deeper integration is urgent to ensure that the fruits of the Uruguay Round and other liberalizing trade initiatives are not dissipated. No new institution is required: in any case, grand designs for institutional reform are not on the "political radar screen" of any of today's heads of government. The alternative is not to do nothing, of course, but to launch with some urgency a number of specific and feasible policy initiatives in the OECD and the WTO designed both to stave off increasing friction as well as to begin an ongoing process of incremental change to achieve a new world trading system that fully matches the new world of deeper integration.

These policy initiatives cover trade policy issues such as R&D subsidies; government procurement; intellectual property rights and strategic dumping in high tech sectors. On the investment policy side a proposal is made with respect to R&D Consortia. And, finally, the fundamental issue of international cooperation in basic research is highlighted as an urgent policy need to enhance long-term global growth, the most basic and pervasive of international public goods.

Endnotes

1. This chapter is an abridged and updated version of my recently published Industry Canada Working Paper, no. 2, entitled Technological Change and International Economic Institutions, December, 1995.

2.. See, for example, Bretton Woods Commission, *Bretton Woods: Looking to the Future*, Commission Report and Conference Proceedings, Washington, D.C., July 20-22, 1994.

3.*Ibid.*, pp. 16-19.

4. UNCTAD, *World Investment Report*, 195, Table 1.1.

5. *Ibid.*

6. Ostry and Nelson, *Techno-Nationalism and Techno-Globalism*, Washington, D.C.: Brookings Institution, p.24.

7. *Ibid.*, Chapter 3 and references cited therein

8. See Thomas O. Bayard and Kimberly Ann Elliott, *Reciprocity and Retaliation in U.S. Trade Policy*, Institute for International Economics, Washington, D.C., September, 1994.
    The SII was, in point of fact, a substitute for Super 301. See Sylvia Ostry, *Who's on First: The World Trading System in the 21st Century,* University of Chicago Press, 1997, (forthcoming).

9. Jagdish Bhagwati, "Trade and Wages: Choosing Among Alternative Explanations," *Economic Policy Review*, January, 1995, Federal Reserve Bank of New York, pp. 44-45.

10. The *Frascati Manual*, developed by the OECD Directorate for Science, Technology, and Industry.

11. Peter Grindley, David Mowery, and Brian Silverman, "Sematech and Collaborative Research: Lessons in the Design of High-Technology Consortia," Journal of Policy Analysis and Management 13, Fall, 1994, pp. 723-58.

12. "Fair Practice Not Protectionism," *Financial Times*, November 21, 1988, p. 29.

13. F.M. Scherer, *International High-Technology Competition*, Harvard University Press, 1992, pp. 54-57.

14. Ostry and Nelson, *op.cit.*, p. 98.

15. In October 1994 the U.S. Justice Department and the Federal Trade Commission issued draft guidelines on enforcing U.S. antitrust laws internationally in cases where "anti-competitive conduct" by foreign firms affects U.S. trade. See *International Trade Reporter*, Washington, D.C., October 19, 1994, p. 1609.

16. For a comprehensive review of these and other policies see Richard R. Nelson (ed.), *National Innovation Systems*, New York, 1993.

17. Office of Technology Assessment (OTA), *Multinationals and the U.S. Technology Base*, Congress of the United States, Washington, D.C., 1994, pp. 32-39.

18. See, for example, "Research with a pinch of spice," Financial Times, August 20, 1996, p. 8.

References

Bayard, T. O. and Elliott, K. A. *Reciprocity and Retaliation in U.S. Trade Policy.* Washington, D.C.: Institute for International Economics, 1994.

Bhagwati, Jagdish. Trade and Wages: Choosing among Alternative Explanations. *Economic Policy Review,* January 1995, pp. 44-45.

Financial Times. "Fair Practice Not Protectionism." November 21, 1988, p. 29.

Financial Times. "Research with a pinch of spice." August 20, 1996, p. 8.

Grindley, P.; Mowery, D. and Silverman, B. Sematech and Collaborative Research: Lessons in the Design of High-Technology Consortia. *Journal of Policy Analysis and Management,* Fall 1994, 13, pp. 723-58.

International Trade Reporter. Washington, D.C., October 19, 1994, p. 1609.

Nelson, Richard R. (ed). *National Innovation Systems.* New York, 1993.

OECD. *Frascati Manual.* Paris: Directorate for Science, Technology and Industry.

Office of Technology Assessment (OTA). *.Multinationals and the U.S. Technology Base.* Washington, D.C.: Congress of the United States, 1994, pp. 32-39.

Ostry, Sylvia. *Who's on First: The World Trading System in the 21st Century.* Chicago: University of Chicago Press, 1997 (forthcoming).

_____. "Technological Change and International Economic Institutions," Industry Canada, Ottawa, Working Paper, no. 2, December 1995.

_____ and **Nelson, R. R.** *Techno-Nationalism and Techno-Globalism.* Washington, D.C.: Brookings Institution, 1995.

Scherer, F. M. *International High-Technology Competition.* Harvard University Press, 1992; 54-57.

United Nations. *World Investment Report, 1995.* New York: UNCTAD, 1995.

.

13

DEBT MANAGEMENT AND
STRUCTURAL ADJUSTMENT:
Neglected Issues
Kunibert Raffer
University of Vienna, Austria

In spite of innumerable publications on debt management, the literature has not given sufficient attention to the efficiency of debt managers - the Bretton Woods Institutions. Their advice exacerbated the debt problem starting well before 1982, though temporarily veiled by liquidity in the 1970s. The economic effects of contradictions and logical U-turns of debt management are easily forgotten. Research and political conclusions have been based on IBRD and IMF data, whose reliability must be questioned seriously. After showing that the evolution of multilateral debts is characterized by risk shifting and bad management, a viable alternative to their inefficient approach is presented.

Writing about the management of the debt crisis has developed into a formidable cottage industry during the last 15 years. It is all the more astonishing that some important problems of so-called "Structural Adjustment", the present method of debt management, have not received the attention they deserve. This paper will therefore focus on four crucial but neglected flaws of present debt management, rather than repeat broadly discussed points. All concern the fundamental problem of quality and efficiency.

First, it will be argued that the debt problem began long before the conventional date of August 1982. The debt crisis was foreseeable well before that year. This is important for the evaluation of the effectiveness of present debt management by the IBRD and the IMF, referred to as the Bretton Woods Institutions (BWIs) in the text below. *Second,* two fundamental logical inconsistencies and contradictions in their argumentation are documented. The paper will not go into details of Structural Adjustment, on which countless publications exist, but limit itself to two main assumptions of BWI-policies. *Third,* it will be shown that the reliability of BWI-statistics, on which research and policy advice are based, is highly doubtful. *Fourth*, the burden of multilateral debts, which has received some attention recently, mainly because of NGO pressure, will be touched upon. Finally, an economically sound solution will be briefly sketched.

The Real Beginnings of the Debt Crisis

The Pearson Report (Pearson et al, 1969, pp.153ff) prepared at the request of the president of the IBRD, already identified structural origins of the debt problem, and strongly recommended debt relief. It warned of "many serious difficulties" that could result from "very large scale lending", emphasizing that "The accumulation of excessive debts is usually the combined result of errors of borrower governments and their foreign creditors. Failures on the part of the debtors will be obvious. The responsibility of foreign creditors is rarely mentioned." (*ibid.*, p.156). Debt management had emphasized spending cuts and credit restrictions while neglecting the need to sustain sound development outlays.

Abbott (1972) saw the roots of the debt crisis in Sub-Saharan Africa in the 1960s, when foreign debts first began to accumulate faster than the growth of economies or foreign exchange earnings. Seeing insolvency rather than illiquidity as the problem, he proposed debt cancellation.

Accepting the need for debt alleviation the major creditors adopted the so-called Retroactive Terms Adjustment (RTA) in 1978, measures to provide debt relief and improve the net flow of bilateral official aid to Low Income Countries. Debts of these countries were mostly caused by official flows, including aid. One should mention the co-responsibility of official creditors, who decide and monitor where and how their money is spent. The programme's long-winded, clumsy name documents the creditors' desire to avoid the words debt relief or debt cancellation, not to mention insolvency. This steadfast refusal to recognize realities officially has remained the most important hindrance to proper debt management and to a viable solution of the crisis until the present day. The word insolvency remained ostracized until the first shock after the Mexican disaster in 1995, and creditor governments are still not willing to accept insolvency procedures as a solution to the debt problem.

Warnings against over-indebtedness were heard in Latin America as early as the late 1960s. Citing dramatic proportions of foreign public debts, Wionczek (1978, p.118) thought a debt crisis comparable to the 1930s was possible. A conference in Mexico City in October 1977 discussed solutions to the debt problem. G.K. Helleiner (1979) demanded rules for debt relief, including the reduction of present values of repayments. The IBRD's C.S. Hardy (1979, p.196) warned of debt problems, classifying refinancing as "not really a credible alternative". The coordinator of this conference, M.S. Wionczek (1979, p.93), explained the post-1977 wave of optimism in the face of a deteriorating situation: "in terms of institutional interests and social psychology rather than economic and financial analysis".

The BWIs themselves started Structural Adjustment well before 1982. According to *Finance & Development*, their official quarterly, the IMF started in Africa already after 1973 (Kanesa-Thasan, 1981). During this early phase, when the Fund was apparently glad to find clients, conditionality was considered lenient "in relation to the required adjustment effort" (*ibid.*, p.20). Adjustment programmes were initially planned for one year, apparently because of convenient accounting. In 1979 conditionality became stricter. 88 arrangements were approved by the IMF between January 1979 and December 1981, to support adjustment policies, particularly measures to reach a sustainable balance of payments position (Crockett, 1982). All countries asking for rescheduling in 1981 "had adopted an adjustment program" with the Fund when negotiating with their creditors (Nowzad, 1982, p.13).

Officially the IBRD started its involvement in programme lending in 1980, but it had previously exerted its influence in connection with projects. The Bank always used its leverage to support the IMF and its policy against resistance by Developing Countries (DCs).

The BWIs, particularly the IMF, did not arrive on the scene after August 1982 to solve a problem created by others, but they had been part of the process leading to it (cf. Raffer, 1994a). Their type of adjustment did not prevent the debt crisis. A critic might say that the first unsuccessful adjustment programmes existed before the official start of the debt crisis. The IMF might counter by pointing out that it did not have sufficient leverage before 1982 to force countries into necessary reforms. Naturally, this would be at odds with the claim that debtors themselves "own" programmes only "supported" by BWIs. The claim of country-"ownership" is heard more often recently than in the past, when more pride was expressed on how tightly DCs were controlled. Both official sources and publications by leading

BWI-staff show that countries do not "own" programmes (cf. Raffer, 1993). The issue of "ownership" is another peculiar feature of the BWIs. Depending on occasions and audiences these institutions either claim to be only supporting a country's own programme or to make a country adopt "sensible" policies. Finally, one would have to ask why programmes were financed if and when the IMF was aware that necessary reforms were not undertaken and the money could thus not be put to good use.

By calling 1982 the beginning of the debt crisis, a long and dismal record of ineffective debt management is forgotten. The BWIs have been consistently unable to restore the sustainable economic viability of debtor countries. 1982 is an important date with respect to BWI-influence on debtor economies. Any financial support to debtors has been made contingent on the "seal of approval" by the BWIs. Debt management by Bank and Fund has received unconditional support by their major shareholders, in spite of apparent and protracted lack of success. Gravest officially documented failures (e.g. by the internal Operations Evaluation Department or the Wapenhans Report) have not even made creditor countries dominating the BWIs by their voting majority question the effectiveness of the BWIs seriously, let alone demand appropriate reforms.

Illiquidity and Poverty - Two Fundamental Errors

Assessing the evolution of debts and the severity of the crisis after 1982, one must remember that the BWIs strongly encouraged DCs to borrow in international markets. Giving this advice, the BWIs are part of the problem. In spite of RTA, the Pearson Report and other explicit warnings quoted above, the fact that new loans were mostly used to service old ones on time during the last years before 1982, or their own macroeconomic interventions and adjustment programmes, the BWIs did not realize seriousness of the situation. It took them an embarrassingly long time to acknowledge the nature and the dimension of the debt problem, as can be proved by a host of evidence from their own publications. As late as 1982 a paper in their official quarterly allayed fears that private banks might not cover DC-deficits. These widespread concerns of "two years ago" had become unfounded "nowadays" (Nowzad 1982, p.14), although it could not be excluded that some groups of non-oil exporting DCs might not be able to borrow all the funds they might need in the future. Nowzad echoes the findings of an IMF working group on international capital markets published in *Finance & Development* of March 1981 in an unsigned article and as an *Occasional Paper*.

Even after August 1982 the BWIs thought the money market functioned well, seeing no signs of liquidity bottlenecks, nor of restrictions regarding the capital base of private banks limiting lending to DCs, which was supposed to continue on a large scale (Versluysen 1982). The Task Force on Non-Concessional Flows established by the BWIs in 1979 presented their findings in May 1982 (*ibid.*, p.33). Pointing out that the conclusions had been presented before the crisis and there was presently even less reason for optimism the author insisted that they did still hold (*ibid.*, p.34).

In spite of this embarrassing (now largely forgotten) record, the BWIs are now allowed to lecture on prudent borrowing. The *World Debt Tables 1992/93* (pp.10ff), e.g., explain that "the principal policy lesson of the debt crisis is that domestic resources and policy, not external finance per se are the key to economic development". The IBRD goes on drawing conclusions such as

"heavy reliance on external finance is a risky strategy because it increases vulnerability to adverse external development and their attendant long-term development impact ...
Prudent lending and borrowing policies should take into account the vulnerability to adverse external shocks. Current interest rates are a poor guide for external finance decisions. Seemingly cheap variable-rate loans may turn out to be expensive if interest rates increase. Negative terms of trade shocks may be permanent rather than transitory and merit adjustment rather than external finance.
In a solvency crisis, early recognition of solvency as the root cause and the need for a final settlement are important for minimizing the damage. ...protracted renegotiations and uncertainty damaged economic activity in debtor countries for several years ... It took too long to recognize that liquidity was the visible tip of the problem, but not its root." (*ibid.*, stress in o.)

Ahmed and Summers (1992, p.4) quantify the costs of delaying the recognition of the now generally acknowledged solvency crisis as "one decade" lost in development. This delay was caused by defenders of the so-called illiquidity theory in the 1980s, notably the IMF and the IBRD, positing that the debt crisis was a liquidity, not a solvency crisis. As most explicit advocates they supported this theory by overly optimistic forecasts "showing" that debtors would "grow out of" debts. In line with US policy they defended the view that debt reductions were unnecessary until the "Brady Plan" discarded it in 1989.

After defending the illiquidity theory for quite some time the BWIs simply chose to forget their own arguments and analyses. They also failed to remember that the policies advised to (or forced on) debtor countries by them were based on this error. In other words: their "advice" or - paraphrasing a sterner source - their "firmer understanding" (Stern, 1983) of monitoring has created economic and social damages in DCs for which the debtor countries, not the BWIs, had to pay, thus increasing debt burdens, not least by new multilateral loans necessary to finance rehabilitation measures. The Bank and the Fund gained financially from their own errors.

Poverty is another issue where the BWIs prefer to forget their own record completely (cf. Raffer, 1994a). During the McNamara years the IBRD advocated helping the poor, although with debatable results. As late as 1982, the conclusions of a working group on poverty demanding measures to alleviate the effects of Structural Adjustment on the poor were officially approved. But the tide turned quickly. The BWIs insisted that carrying on Structural Adjustment had positive impacts and was in the very interest of the poor, while special measures to protect them would be superfluous if not harmful. Emphasizing human needs might obstruct needed reforms.

Meanwhile, strong public pressure has changed the picture. Special pro-grammes to help those affected by Structural Adjustment are officially accepted again. It is argued that they would make Structural Adjustment more acceptable and thus more efficient - a point denied shortly before. Whatever they do, the BWIs claim to be "helping" the poor. In practice, though, little was changed and measures for the poor have largely remained lip service. Inconsistency occurred more in formulations than in practice.

If the BWIs are now right, this implies that their previous adjustment efforts were flawed and inefficient, causing damage to their clients. If they were right then, they are causing damage now. But no damage compensation has been paid. On the contrary, any damage resulting from errors of the BWIs has to be borne by their clients. Particularly, the IBRD is keen to stress that it has learned, but avoids specifying at whose cost.

Doubts on Debt Statistics and Their Use

To support the claim that their policies work, BWIs have repeatedly flashed countries as examples for successful policies. Statistically debatable groupings of adjusters and non-adjusters have repeatedly been compared without producing convincing statistical differences. Occasionally claims were made that the debt crisis was over for one region or the other. In the case of Africa, the famous statement "Recovery has begun" (IBRD & UNDP 1989, p.iii) had to be withdrawn quickly, quite rightly so, as present experience shows. In the case of Latin America, official optimism about renewed market access and claims that the debt crisis was overcome - often backed by the example of Mexico - was called into question by the Mexican crisis of 1994/5 and the $50 billion rescue package, which was required to defuse it. As in many other cases, the BWIs had not foreseen the crash of their model-debtor, a country which had implemented BWI-"recommendations" faithfully.

Although statistics provided by the BWIs are used by practically everyone working on debts, and by the institutions to support their conclusions, they have not received the scrutiny they deserve. Doing so questions both their reliability and casts further doubt on the efficiency of the BWIs as debt managers. This is an important point.

Raffer (1994b) showed that BWI-optimism with regard to Latin America before the Mexican crisis was not justified by their own data. In its *World Debt Tables 1992/93* the IBRD (WDT 1992, p.3), e.g., concluded with regard to "a number of" Latin American countries:

"With debt indicators now back to pre-1982 levels, most of these countries are emerging from the debt crisis, helped in some cases by the catalytic effects of reductions in their commercial bank debt."

Conventional indicators such as Debt Service Ratios (DSR; defined in Table 1) did indeed fall because Latin America's arrears increased steeply.

The IBRD's statement on debt indicators only holds for the region if one disregards arrears. This, however, is definitely wrong if one defines debt overhang as a situation where the debt burden is so disproportionately large that conceivable efforts to pay according to contract could not ameliorate the debtors situation. Growing arrears are certainly a clear indication of an overhang. If calculated as the relation between contractually due debt service and exports, Latin America's debt service ratio had deteriorated massively, while indicators using actual payments fell indeed to pre-1982 levels because of tolerated non-payment. Since the IBRD itself published the data on arrears allowing Raffer to re-calculate their indicators, the IBRD must have been aware of this precarious situation. Nevertheless, and in view of rapidly deteriorating balance of payments positions, the Bank stated that Latin America had dealt with its debt overhang (WDT, 1993, p.5). The IBRD took care to place caveats more visibly than in the case of Africa in 1989 - possibly a fine example of learning by doing - but optimism was prevailing. This sentiment was shared by the Fund and the Inter-American Development Bank. Private consultants acting this way would have been sued for damages - not unsuccessfully, as examples prove.

Table 1: Sub-Saharan Africa's Arrears and Debt Service 1980-1993

	1980	1986	1987	1988	1989	1990	1991	1992	1993 p
Debt- (DSR) and Interest-Service-Ratios (ISR) on Cash Base: *									
WDT 1993									
ISR	6.2	11.4	9.4	10.3	9.7	9.0	9.2	8.6	7.3
DSR	9.7	24.9	19.6	21.0	18.0	18.0	17.1	16.9	13.5
WDT 1992 **									
ISR	5.7	11.6	9.2	11.5	10.2	8.9	10.0	8.8	-
DSR	10.9	28.2	22.1	24.7	21.8	20.9	19.8	18.5	-
Contractual DSR and ISR: ***									
WDT 1993									
ISR_d	6.4	15.8	16.3	19.7	20.5	20.9	23.4	25.7	26.8
DSR_d	11.2	39.4	39.1	50.5	48.0	50.2	56.7	64.9	68.0
WDT 1992 **									
ISR_d	6.1	18.7	20.3	26.9	27.7	27.2	32.6	34.5	-
DSR_d	11.2	49.4	49.4	67.9	64.6	64.0	76.6	-	-

* DSR = Debt Service Ratio: (actual) total debt service/exports of goods and services as %;
ISR = Interest Service Ratio: (actual) interest payments/exports of goods and services as %;
** Data for 1992 are provisional estimates;   *** d indicates that payments contractually
  due (actual payments plus arrears) are used in the numerator;   p   projected.
Source: WDT 1992; 1993

Debt indicators for Africa, taken from two consecutive years of the IBRD's *World Debt Tables,* may illustrate the problem of reliability of BWI-data. Table 1 compares the figures for the same years with quite interesting results.

From one year to the next, debt indicators for Sub-Saharan Africa "improved" dramatically, but without any explanation unless one accepts the old adage of time as the great healer. The country grouping Sub-Saharan Africa had not been altered. DSR_d for 1993 was finally 77.6, definitely higher than the optimistic estimate. After two decades of IMF adjustment, Sub-Saharan Africa's arrears were projected to be roughly 5.5 times the amount of debt service actually paid in 1994 (WDT, 1994).

A comparison of time series of the ratio Total Debts/GDP published for

Latin America in the *World Debt Tables* shows great and unexplained differences of up to 10.1 percentage points for the same year. The ratios of external debt to GDP in the IMF's *World Economic Outlook* show a maximum difference of over 13 percentage points (cf. Raffer, 1994b.)

Chile represents one more illustration of the data problem. Its DSR improved dramatically from WDT 1992 to WDT 1993. For the year 1991 it "fell" from 33.9 to 23.1, although the country had no arrears. But Chile is remarkable in another respect too. During the 1980s when capital flight was - quite correctly - seen as a sign of wrong economic policies, statistics on Chile showed no capital flight and the country was presented as a model of sound economic policy by the BWIs. Nevertheless, Chile was able to benefit massively from returning flight capital as soon as repatriation became the touchstone of soundness, and Chile could again be presented as a model (cf. Raffer, 1994b). Questions regarding the seriousness of such arguments or such data have never been raised by the BWIs praising Chilean economic policies nor by creditor governments.

The Evolution of the Multilateral Debt Burden

During the 1970s commercial banks lent eagerly while multilateral lending declined. Commercial loans covered the structural problems identified in the 1960s. Political intervention to help commercial banks during the 1970s contributed to the growth of debts. After 1982, when commercial banks withdrew from the South, multilateral funds poured in, allowing commercial banks to receive higher (re)payments than otherwise possible. A remarkable shift in the structure of debts occurred. It deserves mentioning that the BWIs did not even criticize the practice of some private banks to force debtor governments to guarantee already insolvent private debts retroactively. They chose to ignore it. Although this ex post socialization made debt management more difficult the BWIs insisted on punctual service of these debts as well.

The substantial bail-out of private banks by multilaterals was aptly called an "implicit taxpayers' subsidy" by Jeffrey Sachs (1988). In a major process of risk-shifting, risk was reallocated to public multilaterals, increasing their share of debts substantially. This hardened conditions for debtors since multilaterals - in marked contrast to private banks - have always refused to reschedule or reduce their claims. A financial merry-go-round was started to keep up the pretense that multilaterals do not reschedule. Funds from the Bank were used to repay the IMF, allowing it in turn to lend again to the DCs, so that the IBRD's loan could be serviced "in time". OECD governments often participated as intermediary financiers. The whole bill had to be picked up by debtors. It must also be pointed out that official debts are not necessarily cheaper than private loans (cf. Raffer, 1994b).

In the 1990s another shift took place. New flows from new sources, namely bonds (as in the 1930s) and foreign direct investment poured into some DCs, allowing voluntary repayments to commercial banks and easy servicing of multilateral debts. Commercial banks themselves knew better than to put substantial sums of their own money into these countries again. Regulatory changes, relaxed quality guidelines and lowered minimum credit ratings induced institutional investors to place money there. Official optimism as well as interest rate differences helped to attract money until the Mexican crash. Risk was shifted again, this time away from mulitlaterals onto institutional investors and the public at large. Induced by regulatory changes and official optimism, they had replaced banks and international financial institutions to an extent that these "tens of millions of little-guy investors" (*Time*, 13 February 1995) were one, if not *the*, main argument for the new $50 billion bail-out in Mexico.

Many DCs, particularly the poorest, remain burdened by a high amount of multilateral debts, which they have to service with priority. Other creditors must wait and multilaterals receive the lion's share of debt service payments actually made by the poor DCs. At the end of 1993 they received more than half the payments made, a multiple of their share in total debts. 62 per cent of multilateral debts were owed to the BWIs.

The specific characteristic of multilateral debts is that creditors do not only lend, but have always influenced the way their resources are used on a massive scale. To the extent that clients do not see these operations as in their interest any longer - they do not "own" them. As DCs have to pay for BWI-errors this is hardly surprising. This victim-pays-principle is a unique arrangement, which cannot be justified by economic or legal reasoning (cf. Raffer, 1993). Under market conditions international firms do sue their consultants successfully in cases of wrong or negligent advice. Orange County sued Merill Lynch for $2 billion. Bank Austria sued Price Waterhouse for £147 million, arguing they had not checked Sovereign Leasing, a firm Bank Austria invested in, with sufficient care. Damage compensation is also awarded to private individuals in the Anglo-Saxon legal system if a bank goes beyond mere lending. A British couple borrowing money from Lloyds sued the bank successfully, because its manager had advised and encouraged them to renovate and sell a house at a profit. The High Court ruled that the manager should have pointed out the risks clearly and should have advised them to abandon the project. Because of its advice Lloyds had to pay damages when prices in the property market fell and the couple suffered a loss (*Financial Times*, 5 September 1995). If comparable standards were applied to the South there would be no problem of multilateral debts. At present multilateral institutions insist on full repayment, refusing to reschedule. Failures caused by their staffs have to be paid for by borrowers, who might get burdened with a further loan enabling them to repair the damage financed by the first. At a time when letting the market work by connecting decisions and risks is gaining popularity in the former Soviet Union, there is no reason why it should not become popular with multilateral creditors. Bringing the market to multilaterals would increase the quality of their programmes and projects considerably. The total and unjustified protection of the BWIs from legal and market consequences is one important factor explaining the present disaster. It defies both the very basic principle of the rule of law that anyone has to compensate damage done by him/her and the most basic principle of economics that those deciding must carry financial risks connected with their decisions. It is therefore mandatory that multilaterals, too, are finally subjected to these principles, having to pay for damages done by them and their staffs (cf. Raffer, 1993).

Present debt management makes the BWIs both judge and interested party. The most basic principles of the rule of law demand that this be changed. An impartial and independent third party is needed to supervise debt management and to award damage compensation where appropriate. The in-house Inspection Panel established recently by the IBRD, under pressure from the public and some of its own executive directors, does not go far enough, although it is a unique feature that should be copied by other multilaterals. Unfortunately the very first case made the IBRD look for ways to restrict access to the Panel in the future. (cf. Raffer and Singer). There is still a long way to go before the victims of development finance will be treated in the way transnational firms, counties or individuals within OECD countries have always been treated. As long as present BWI-impunity is preserved, no incentives to avoid failures exist.

Until September 1995, the BWIs denied officially that multilateral debts were a problem. Then, a leaked discussion document of the IBRD acknowledged for the first time that something had to be done about multilateral debt, since it is a heavy burden on many poor countries. A Multilateral Debt Facility was suggested and backed by the new president of the IBRD, James Wolfensohn, but internal opposition could not be overcome by the time of writing. The idea is simple: a fund financed by contributions from individual countries and from multilaterals themselves would pay off multilateral debts of eligible countries, thus maintaining the fiction that multilaterals do neither reschedule nor reduce debts. As creditor countries had to bail out multilaterals repeatedly in the past to keep this fiction "intact", the first part is not entirely new. The suggestion that multilaterals themselves should finance reductions of their own debts may be called new, although the IDA Debt Reduction Facility is already funded from the Bank's net income to reduce commercial debts. Making debt service of the IBRD's own loans easier implies an element of fungibility. The precise contribution by multilaterals to the new Facility remained unclear, although the IBRD expected a $850 million windfall surplus this year, which was seen as one source to finance the fund. According to *The Economist* (16 September 1995), many people within the BWIs still cling to the old idea that new money and growing out of debts are the best solutions. Considering that this has been practiced unsuccessfully for quite some time, this view is hard to understand. Establishing the Facility against this opposition, though not yet a solution, would already be a step in the right direction.

An International Chapter 9 Insolvency

The Mexican crisis once again underscored the need to find a permanent and viable solution to the debt problem. The idea of an international insolvency, proposed immediately after 1982, was revisited. Shortly after the Mexican crash, the Chairman of the Federal Reserve System, Alan Greenspan, suggested thinking about an international insolvency. The *Financial Times* reported that Treasury Secretary Robert Rubin said he carefully avoided the term "international bankruptcy court", but that some procedures to work out the debt obligations of debtors were needed. In an article in the *Wall Street Journal* of 10 April 1995, the Chairman of the House Banking and Financial Services Committee, Rep. Jim Leach of Iowa, recommended international insolvency proceedings: "What is needed today is a Chapter 11 (insolvency of firms) process for the global financial system, a technique to keep nation-states and their people from the impoverishing implications of insolvency." Mentioning the little known Chapter 9 proceedings for debtors with governmental powers briefly, he specifically pointed out its implicit understanding that local government must continue to function. The US Chapter 9 is therefore particularly well suited for sovereign debtors.

Chapter 9 regulates the insolvency of municipalities. Designed and used in the US for decades, this solution to the problems of debtors vested with governmental powers can be easily applied to sovereign lenders. Like all good insolvency laws it combines the need for a general framework with the flexibility necessary to deal fairly with individual debtors. Under its umbrella many proposals made so far can be accommodated. An international Chapter 9 has been advocated (Raffer, 1989) and elaborated in more detail elsewhere (Raffer, 1990). This paper confines itself to the essential elements of this solution.

In a Chapter 9 proceeding, US laws protects both the governmental powers of the debtor and individuals affected by the plan. Affected taxpayers as well as employees of the municipality have a right to be heard in defense of their interests. Creditors are to receive what can be "*reasonably expected*" from the debtor under given circumstances. The living standards of the municipality's residents are protected. Specifically, a decision in 1942 that the jurisdiction of the court depends on the city's volition, beyond which it cannot be extended, clearly demonstrates the appropriateness of Chapter 9 for sovereign debtors.

As no court in a creditor or debtor country is likely to be totally unbiased, the role of the court would have to be taken by international arbitrators, as it is usual in international law. Each side (creditors/debtor) nominates the same number of persons, who elect one more person to chair them, so that an uneven number of arbitrators results. This council would have to mediate between debtor and creditors, to chair and support negotiations by advice, to provide adequate possibilities for those affected to be heard, and - if necessary - to decide what should be done. Also, it should monitor the implementation of economic restructuring as contained in the plan. Unless one breaks one of the most elementary principles of the rule of law, the BWIs do not qualify for this task: they are both creditors themselves and controlled by voting majorities of creditor countries.

People affected by the solution could be represented by organizations speaking on their behalf, such as trade unions or employees' associations - like in a US Chapter 9 case - or international organisations,(e.g. UNICEF, religious or non-religious NOGS, and grassroots organizations of the poor).

Debt service payments have to be brought in line with the debtor's capacity to earn foreign exchange. Where the removal of protectionist barriers can be expected to lead to higher export revenues, a trade-off between more repayments and less protection or higher debt reduction without reduced protection is necessary.

No doubt there exists a need for reform within debtor countries too. These reforms, monitored by the council of arbitrators, should adjust the debtor to the real international environment, not to a textbook illusion of "free markets". Realistic strategies have to drop the BWIs' predilection for one-sided liberalization by those countries that can be forced to do so. Import substitution should be encouraged where economically viable, to form the basis of future economic diversification. Monitoring by the arbitrators, agreed upon in the plan, could help to overcome the problem of petrifying protection. Temporary protection should allow domestic industries to compete with imports, and should be reduced as domestic industries become more efficient. Looking at successful East Asian economies could provide useful insights into how to implement economic interventions.

Finally official creditors, including multilateral institutions, must be treated in the same way as commercial banks during an insolvency. This is particularly so as they - in contrast to commercial banks - have routinely taken decisions on how their loans were to be used. As argued above, it is the most basic precondition for the functioning of the market mechanism that economic decisions must be accompanied by (co)responsibility: whoever takes entrepreneurial decisions must also carry entrepreneurial risks. If this link is severed - as it was in Centrally Planned Economies - market efficiency is severely disturbed.

For an international Chapter 9 a symmetrical treatment of all creditors follows convincingly. It is a matter of fairness to debtors as well as to other creditors. Multilateral institutions must not be treated more favorably. Debt reduction must be uniform; the same percentage must be deducted from all debts. In poor African countries, where multilaterals account for a relatively large share of debts (without being financially accountable), equal treatment of all creditors has important effects on the debt burden and is particularly justified. Symmetrical treatment in an insolvency could be the way how the BWIs are held financially accountable. Compensation for damages done within projects, where determining faults and errors is much easier - which has nothing to do with insolvency, but is an issue in its own right - would reduce the debt burden further.

Only after removing the oppressive debt overhang can long term plans to develop poor countries be expected to be successful. Nevertheless, creditor governments are still not prepared to realize this idea. Instead of some form of international insolvency, the G-7 meeting (1995) in Halifax chose to strengthen the IMF. The real reasons for the reluctance to adopt a proper solution are difficult to fathom. Clearly, moral hazard is not among them. It is proved wrong by every insolvency case, as well as by the historical experience of present creditor countries themselves, most notably Germany, which got a *de facto* insolvency in 1953. As long as the big moral hazard of the present perverted incentive system allowing the BWIs to gain from their own failures at the expense of the poor is not even noticed by OECD governments, it is impossible to believe their moral arguments.

Economic analysis would suggest that the overexposure of the BWIs, which resulted from the bail-outs of the 1980s, might make OECD governments unwilling to embrace a sound solution. If multilaterals were to pay for their failures - as has been usual for anyone outside former communist economies - capital presently on call might have to be recalled. Under present budgetary restrictions, this would not be welcomed by the main BWI-shareholders. By allowing multilaterals to go on muddling through these payments can be postponed or avoided, even though debt management does not produce sustainable recovery. Furthermore, determining debt reductions politically gives creditors influence - in contrast to international insolvency, an economic solution based on debtors' abilities to pay and on the principle of treating all debtors equally. Logically these could be two reasons why the debt crisis is still dragging on. If they are, they should not justify further muddling through at the expense of Southern economies and the world's poorest.

References

Abbott, George C. "Aid and Indebtedness - A Proposal." *National Westminster Bank Review* May 1972: pp. 55-67

Ahmed, M. and Summers, L. "Zehn Jahre Schuldenkrise - eine Bilanz." *Finanzierung & Ent-wicklung* 1992, 29 (3), pp. 2-5

Crockett, Andrew. "Issues in the use of Fund resources." *Finance & Development* 1982, 19 (2), pp. 10-15

Hardy, Chandra S. "Commercial Bank Lending to Developing Countries: Supply Constraints." *World Development* 1979; 7, pp. 189-97

Helleiner, GK. "Relief and Reform in Third World Debt." *World Development* 1979, 7, pp. 113-24

IBRD & UNDP. *Africa's Adjustment with Growth in the 1980s.* Washington DC: IBRD, 1989.

Kanesa-Thasan, S. "The Fund and adjustment policies in Africa." *Finance & Development* 1981, 18 (3), pp. 20-24

Nowzad, Bahram. "Debt in developing countries: some issues for the 1980s." *Finance & Development* 1982, 19 (1), pp. 13-16

Pearson, Lester B. et al. *Partners in Development: Report of the Commission on International Development.* New York: Praeger, 1969.

Raffer, Kunibert. "International Debts: A Crisis for Whom?," in *Economic Development and World Debt*, H. W. Singer and S. Sharma, eds. (Papers of a Conference at Zagreb, 1987), Basingstoke: Macmillan, 1989.

_____. "Applying Chapter 9 Insolvency to International Debts: An Economically Efficient Solution with a Human Face." *World Development* 1990, 18, pp. 301-13

_____. "International financial institutions and accountability: the need for drastic change," in S. M. Murshed, K. Raffer, eds. *Trade, Transfers and Development, Problems and Prospects for the Twenty-First Century*, Aldershot: E.Elgar, 1993

_____. "'Structural Adjustment', Liberalisation, and Poverty," *Journal für Entwicklungspolitik*, 1994a, 10, pp. 431-40

_____. "Is the Debt Crisis Largely Over? - A Critical Look at the Data of International Financial Institutions", paper presented at the DSA Annual Conference, Lancaster 1994b (forthcoming in R. M. Auty and J. Toye, eds. *Challenging Orthodoxies*, Basingstoke: Macmillan).

_____ **and Singer H. W.** *The Foreign Aid Business: Economic Assistance and Development Co-operation*, Aldershot: E.Elgar (in print)

Sachs, Jeffrey. New approaches to the Latin American debt crisis. Paper prepared for the Harvard Symposion on New Approaches to the Debt Crisis, 1988 September 22 - 23

Stern, Ernest. "World Bank Financing and Structural Adjustment." in John Williamson, ed. *IMF Conditionality*. Washington DC: Institute of International Finance & MIT Press, 1983.

Versluysen, Eugene L. "Der Kapitaltransfer in Entwicklungsländer zu Marktbedingungen." *Finanzierung & Entwicklung*, 1982, 19 (4), pp. 33-36

World Debt Tables. Washington DC: IBRD, various years [WDT 1993-94 quoted, e.g., WDT 1993]

Wionczek, Miguel S. "El endeudamiento público externo y los cambios sectoriales en la inversión privada extranjera de América Latina," in H. Jaguaribe, A. Ferrer, M. S. Wionczek and T. Dos Santos, *La dependencia político-económica de América Latina.* Mexico: SXXI (10th ed), 1978.

Wionczek, Miguel S. "Editor's introduction." *World Development* 1979 ,7, pp. 91-94

14

NAFTA AND LABOR: *A Global Strategy for the Global Economy*

Esmail Hossein-zadeh

Drake University, USA

This study argues that in challenging the corporate free trade agenda the labor must put forth its own agenda, one that will go beyond the type of "buy American" slogans. A positive left-labor agenda must emphasize, among other things, the importance of a long-term international labor strategy based on worker-to-worker or union-to-union links. Such a strategy would replace the current downward competition between workers in the three (and hopefully all) countries with coordinated bargaining and joint policies for mutual interests and problem-solving.

The North American Free Trade Agreement (NAFTA) generated an almost unprecedented debate over the effects of the treaty on employment, income distribution, and the environment. As its proponents touted NAFTA as the cure-all for the 1990s and beyond, its opponents condemned it as hazardous to U.S. jobs, wages, working conditions and the environment. While some NAFTA opponents sought to defeat the deal, others tried to amend it with "codes of conduct" for transnational corporations.

This study seeks to show that while the free traders' defense of NAFTA clearly stemmed from a staunch devotion to the free reign of capital, most of the labor arguments against it simply echoed the arguments of protectionist politicians and business leaders, and were therefore both misguided and misleading. While the strategy of imposing "codes of conduct" on transnational corporations was (and remains) wishful thinking so long as such safeguard measures are not enforced, that of "just say no to NAFTA" was clearly deceptive. It was deceptive on two accounts. First, it implicitly assumed that capital flight and plant relocation would stop if NAFTA was formally defeated. Second, by heightening the international labor competition and magnifying the likely impact of lower Mexican wages on U.S. unemployment, it diverted attention from the major source of unemployment: the systemic tendency for labor to be constantly replaced with machine.

Whether top labor leaders' NAFTA strategies stemmed from sincere misconceptions or from populist sentiments and short-term "political correctness" is not the issue here. The claim this study will make is that while nationalist and/or protectionist policies such as "buy American" may be pleasing to populist sentiments, such policies are in the long run damning to the interests of labor. I shall therefore argue that, in challenging the multinational corporations' free trade agenda, labor must put forth its own agenda; a positive agenda whose aim would be to influence, shape and, ultimately, lead the world economy. Such a strategy would aim at (a) eliminating or reducing international labor rivalry by taking the necessary steps toward the establishment of wage parity within the same company and the same trade, subject to the cost of living and productivity in each country; and (b) establishing independent labor, community, and environmental organizations that would monitor the implementation process of NAFTA's "safeguard" measures. A strategy of this sort would replace the current downward competition between workers in the three (and ultimately all) countries with coordinated bargaining and joint policies for mutual interests and problem-solving—just as the GATT, WTO (World Trade Organization), the World Bank, and other international organizations are constantly seeking solutions for the problems facing international capital.

What is NAFTA All About?

In the history of capitalism, the state's "visible hand" has always played a crucial role in facilitating the operation of Adam Smith's "invisible hand." The state played an important role in the early stages of the development of capitalism in the West. It contributed to the establishment of the general conditions for capitalist accumulation and development by facilitating the separation of the worker from the means of production (through the enclosure of common lands, for example), by encouraging the free movement of labor and capital through the modification of existing settlement and welfare laws, by eliminating internal obstacles to exchange such as tolls and tariffs, by standardizing currency and exchange, developing new modes of credit formation, and so on.

State intervention in other forms such as subsidization, the underwriting of risk, protection from foreign competition, and penetration into foreign markets through wars or coercion has been of vital importance to the accumulation and expansion of Western capitalism. To use James Dickinson's words, "socialization of losses, privatization of profits, stabilization of the business environment at home and abroad—these functions summarize the role of the state" under capitalism (1981, 25; see also Dobb, 1963; de Brunhoff, 1978; O'Conner, 1973; Szymansky, 1978).

Transnational economic agencies such as IMF, the World Bank, and GATT can be better understood in light of this history and its underlying philosophy. NAFTA too is more easily comprehensible in this context: it represents, in its most recent form, the evolving agenda of capital-state collaboration; a form that is more suitable to the current needs of international capital. Although NAFTA is framed in ideologically laden terms such as "free trade agreement," free trade is not the main thrust of the treaty. In fact, free trade in the usual or traditional sense, i.e., in the sense of reducing or eliminating tariff barriers, has largely been accomplished as a result of GATT-sponsored trade negotiations. Tariff rates on industrial products have been reduced in the last 25 years from an average of 40-45 percent to an average of 5-8 percent. With few exceptions, Mexico has accordingly reduced or eliminated most of its tariff barriers since joining GATT in 1986.

Flawed Arguments Against NAFTA

A logical, first step deterrent to multinational corporations' blackmailing strategies, and their actual export of jobs, would be to remove the lures that induce plant relocation. Making labor costs of production comparable within the three countries would be crucial for this purpose. This would entail taking the necessary steps toward the establishment of wage parity within the same company and the same trade, subject to the cost of living and productivity in each country. Envision, for a moment, a scenario in which the top leaders of organized labor in the three countries broke ranks with their respective countries' ruling classes and came up with the positive response of cross-border unionization and trinational working class collaboration in order to eliminate or reduce labor costs as a factor in international labor competition . This would immediately take political initiative from the likes of Ross Perot and other self-styled capitalist allies of labor, and drastically change the course of debate over NAFTA.

Some may view this suggestion as unrealistic. But the rapid internationalization of production, technology, and information is increasingly creating favorable conditions for such an alternative. The evolving internationalization of capital and integration of world markets is pulling the workers of the world together to an unprecedented extent. "More and more workers around the globe not only work for the same 1,000 or so dominant multinational corporations (MNCs) or their contractors," as Kim Moody points out, "but are linked in common production or service delivery system" (1994, 5). In fact, the ideological and economic offensive of neo-liberalism since the early 1980s has already prompted the emergence of a number of transnational grassroots coalition networks of unionists, environmentalists, women and other citizen activists (Brecher/Costello, 1994; Moody/McGinn, 1992; Krimerman/Lindenfeld, 1992; Bello, et al., 1994; Danaher, 1994; for example). These include the formation of a new global labor organization, International Center for Trade Union Rights (ICTUR), which has established National Committees in 23 countries covering Europe, Africa, Asia, America and Australia. In the defense and extension of the rights of trade unions around the world, "the work of these Committees is complemented by a network of international correspondents including journalists, lawyers, trade union leaders and academics" (*International Union Rights*, Vol. 1, Issue 6, p. 24).

While not widespread, these initial transnational coalition networks of grassroots indicate, if only in faint outlines, that the potential for cross-border solidarity networking and organizing from "below" is real if cultural and political obstacles can be overcome. Experience shows that organizing strategies of this type could be formulated not by lobbying politicians—though this may at times be necessary—but by initiating transnational unionization and working class solidarity; not by heightening inter-labor competition, but by eliminating it. It only makes sense that as trade, investment, and business organizations become global so should labor organizations. There is absolutely nothing radical about workers wanting to eliminate labor costs as a factor in competition. Nor is such an idea very new. Over a century ago, a group of British trade unionists—including a painter, joiner, bookbinder, carpenter, and shoe-maker—sent a letter to their French counterparts in which they suggested establishing an international "fraternity of peoples" in order to reduce international labor rivalry:

A fraternity of peoples is highly necessary for the cause of labor, for we find that whenever we attempt to better our social conditions by reducing the hours of toil, or by raising the price of labor, our employers threaten us with bringing over Frenchmen, Germans, Belgians and others to do our work at a reduced rate of wages.... This has been done not from any desire of our continental brethren to injure us, but through a want of regular and systematic communication between the industrious classes of all countries, which we hope to see speedily effected, as our principle is to bring up the wages of the ill-paid to as near a level as possible with that of those who are better remunerated, and not allow our employers to play us off one against the other, and so drag us down to the lowest possible condition, suitable to their avaricious bargaining (Waterman, 1988, 22-23).

Unfortunately, with few exceptions, the top U.S. labor bureaucracy during the NAFTA debate, while giving lip service to workers' interests, fell in line with the protectionist/nationalist faction of the capitalist class, and pursued policies of "buy American," or "just say no to NAFTA"—and if these failed, try to amend NAFTA with "codes of conduct" for transnational corporations. While a code of conduct for big business is desirable, and the fight on the legislative front to establish labor and environmental safeguards is important, such safeguard measures are worthless in the absence of enforcement mechanisms and institutions. Experience shows that corporations routinely disregard environmental and labor rights not only in Mexico but also in the Unites States and Canada. And if these fundamental rights are easily disregarded on a national level, assuring them would be all the more difficult on an international level. Reporting on "NAFTA's Progress" on the occasion of its ratification anniversary, *The Economist* recently wrote that the treaty's labor and environmental side-agreements constituted a "grand fiasco" (February 18, 1995, p. 24).

An obvious weakness of the "buy American" policy is that, while heightening international labor competition, it accepts the primacy of the needs of (national) capital, thereby making labor hostage to capital's exigencies. (This point is further elaborated in the next section) Furthermore, the "buy American" slogan provided the NAFTA proponents with the opportunity to argue that while this may save some jobs in import-related industries it will hurt jobs in export industries. In fact, arguments of this type helped the NAFTA champions to define the entire agenda of national debate over the treaty on the basis of "pains" versus "gains" of the deal in terms of employment, wages, trade, and so on. The debate was therefore reduced to a battle of hypothetical statistics, often highly exaggerated on both sides.

For political expediency, proponents of NAFTA usually prefaced their defense of the treaty by briefly acknowledging that NAFTA might cause "some initial, temporary pains" such as loss of "some low-skilled" jobs, but they quickly moved on to discussion of its "far reaching gains": that it would boost U.S. exports, hence export-based and high-skilled jobs; that the loss to some U.S. workers would be balanced by gains to Mexican workers; and that the decline in some U.S. wages would be more than offset by lower prices, hence higher purchasing power of the dollar.

A logical response to this argument would be something along these lines; granted. NAFTA will probably be a shot in the arm for the U.S. economy, and benefits may then spill over into various sectors of society. But there is nothing new or surprising here. Heightening labor rivalry and lowering wages have always been a boon to capital, which might then incidentally help the economic situation for a while. But this would only be a temporary, trickle-down gain, and would come to an end as soon as the expansionary cycle turns into another contractionary cycle. Once again, we will face an economic slow down and a rise in unemployment—ad infinitum along this cyclical path, the familiar path of business cycles.

Arguments such as this would have greatly narrowed the maneuvering space of the treaty's champions and effectively undermined their game of NAFTA's "pains vs. gains." Acknowledgment of undeniable properties of market mechanism could therefore help avoid the fruitless war of hypothetical statistics on the "pains" and "gains" of the deal and focus the debate, instead, on issues of democracy and sovereignty, of social services and development strategies, and of education, health care, and environmental needs and concerns of communities. By ignoring the ABCs of a market economy and insisting that NAFTA would have no positive impact on the U.S. economy, its opponents inadvertently helped the arguments of its proponents appear reasonable while weakening the arguments of U.S. labor in the national debate over the issue.

Opponents of NAFTA invested a lot of time and resources on trying to formally defeat the deal. Because ratification of the treaty further aggravated the unemployment fears of U.S. unions, their support of this strategy is understandable. No doubt, the fight against the agreement on formal grounds was necessary. But to pin too much hope on the formal decision on the treaty by making it a make-or-break decision is questionable. While NAFTA will serve to accelerate the process of market integration and its disruptive effects, the fact remains that the agreement is primarily a formalization and culmination of this process rather than its initiator. Again, this is no reason for not fighting the deal on the legislative front; the point, rather, is not limiting the fight to this front. The labor bureaucracy could take advantage of the widespread debate that NAFTA generated, and use it as a national forum for articulating an affirmative working class alternative.

Commenting on how the national debate over the deal could serve as a "catalyst" for cross-border labor solidarity, David Brooks, Director of the Mexico-U.S. Dialogos Program, wrote, "This is an extraordinary moment in history: as our governments have opened trinational negotiations from 'above,' they inadvertently opened a space 'below'—a space that scarcely existed before" (1992, 96).

The fears and the costs of losing jobs under a market economy, especially in a period of "streamlining" and plant closing, are real and strong. While competition from low wage Mexican workers heightened these worries for the U.S. labor, exaggeration of such legitimate concerns during the national debate over NAFTA ran the risk of diverting attention from the major, systemic source of unemployment under capitalism: the secular and/or systemic tendency to constantly replace labor with machine, or to create a "reserve army of the unemployed," as Karl Marx put it. The fundamental laws of demand and supply of labor under capitalism are determined by the market's ability to constantly produce a reserve army of labor, a "surplus population":

The greater the social wealth, the functioning capital, the extent and energy of its growth...the greater is the industrial army...The relative mass of the industrial reserve army increases therefore with the potential energy of wealth. But the greater this reserve army in proportion to the active labor-army, the greater is the mass of a consolidated surplus population...This is the absolute general law of capitalist accumulation. Like all other laws it is modified in its working by many circumstances (*Capital*, Vol. 1, Moscow, n.d., 592-93).

This surely sheds light on the relationship between the steady rise of unemployment in major industrial countries and technological development in those countries (the official unemployment figure for the 24 industrialized countries of the OECD now stands at 36 millions). It is the competitive pressure from the reserve army of the unemployed that explains the limited resistance from the unions to employers' economic rollback and "downsizing" schemes of the recent past. This also explains the steady decline in the size and the bargaining power of the unions since the early 1970s in major industrialized countries. Pressure of losing jobs to the mass of the unemployed has been key to capital's successful introduction of "management-by-stress" methods throughout North America. This pressure has been greatly intensified by the unfortunate international labor rivalry brought about by global capital mobility and its ability to transfer production or service operations to cheap-labor sites in the less developed area of the world. Under these circumstances trade unionism and politics "as usual" will continue to lose force as means of defending workers' economic rights.

Checking Capitalism's Logic

It follows from the preceding that the reserve army of the unemployed and international labor rivalry will continue to grow unless the logic that governs the demand and supply of labor under capitalism is checked. What is needed to reverse the decline of labor and the balance of class forces is a new type of union strategy and a new labor movement.

International Unionism

A first logical step in this direction would be the organization of international trade unions. If, at an earlier stage of capitalist development, "workers of the world unite" seemed an impossible dream articulated by labor's prophets, Karl Marx and Frederick Engels, internationalization of capital has now made that dream an urgent necessity. As capital and labor are the cornerstones of capitalist production, their respective organizations and institutions evolve more or less apace, over time and space. Thus, when capitalist production was local, so was labor: carpenters, shoemakers, bricklayers, and other craftsmen organized primarily in their local communities. But as capitalist production became national, so did trade unions. Now that capitalist production has become global, labor organizations too need to become international in order to safeguard their rights.

True, transition of labor organizations from the national to an international level is much more difficult than one that would evolve within national boundaries. While objective conditions—internationalization of production, communication, transportation and the like—are increasingly becoming conducive to cross-border contacts and solidarity, the capitalist nation state has erected all kinds of political and cultural prejudices and barriers in the way of such contacts.

Despite these barriers, official international trade union organizations have already come to existence; they are called international trade secretariats (ITS's). They include, for example, the International Union of Food and Allied Workers (IUF) and the International Metalworkers Federation (IMF), with similar organizations for public employees, chemical workers, communications workers, etc. These are worldwide organizations to which the relevant national unions in each country can affiliate. ITS's have at times conducted effective international solidarity campaigns, such as the IUF's support of the Guatemalan Coca Cola workers' strike in 1984-85. Because the ITS's are based on national unions, however, they are leadership-to-leadership organizations bound by the politics and bureaucracy of their affiliates. They could play a role in getting affiliates to coordinate their bargaining internationally, but have not yet done so. Furthermore, local unions only have access to the ITS's through their national leaderships.

While international trade union bureaucracies, like their national affiliates, have so far pursued policies that favor collaboration with the ruling powers in their respective countries, and thus only partially served the long term interests of rank and file workers, the very fact that international labor networks and institutions already exist denotes an important step forward in the history of the working class. For it is much easier to dismantle the structures and practices that insure the power of bureaucratic labor leaders—through a political reform movement initiated from below, for example—and to redirect the services and facilities of the international labor institutions so they serve the interests of labor, than to establish such institutions from scratch. (For a critical evaluation of international trade union bureaucracies see Thompson and Larson, 1978; Sims, 1992; Waterman, 1988; MacShane, 1992; Fraser, 1991).

A retarding factor in the effectiveness of the official international labor organizations to defend the interests of their members has been the business unionist policies of the labor bureaucracy in major industrialized countries, especially in the U.S., that accept the primacy of capital's needs and, therefore, advocate collaboration with the capitalist class on a national(ist) basis. With some exceptions, the leaders of organized labor in these countries have played a dual role. On the one hand, using labor leverage, they have at times defended trade unions' economic interests within the nation state; on the other, they have at other times rallied workers to the side of business in its search for market and investment opportunities abroad. Without this support, wars of an imperialist nature fought over global markets and resources—especially the two world wars of this century—would have been impossible.

Organized labor in major industrialized countries, particularly in the Unites States, has been haunted by this experience. As Walden Bello points out, "The extreme international mobility of corporate capital coupled with the largely self-imposed national limits on labor organizing by the Northern labor unions (except when this served Washington's Cold War political objectives) was a deadly formula that brought organized labor to its knees as corporate capital, virtually unopposed, transferred manufacturing jobs from the North to cheap-labor sites in the Third World" (1994, 114). While many in the "northern" labor leadership continue to pursue the ideas and practices of national business unionism, there are signs of growing internationalist consciousness in the grassroots. Reflecting the changing views of the many rank and file union members in the United States, David Johnson, an organizer for the United Electrical Workers, recently wrote:

The response of the labor movement [to NAFTA] has been terrible. We have the equivalent of a cancer, and there's an attempt to put a band-aid on it. Some unions are still talking about "buying American." The problem with buying American, the problem with protectionism, is that it doesn't address who the enemies are. It is not the workers in Mexico who decide to move these plants down there....Another response of the labor movement is what I call "solidarity by resolution." Trade unions get together, sometimes in a beautiful resort in a nice hotel, and they pass a lot of nice resolutions that say things like, "Workers have to stick together," and "By god its long past time we did something about it." I think we've all seen those resolutions and probably written some of them, and I know we've voted for some of them. It's our opinion in the UE that the time is really over for that stuff. A few years ago, maybe, we had the luxury of playing around with that stuff. It's time now to get beyond that. (1993, 8).

Expressing frustration with the official AFL-CIO policy, Johnson continues:

With very few exceptions, the U.S. labor movement has a well-deserved reputation, not only in Mexico but throughout Latin America and through much of the world, of racism, of paternalism, of interference in their national sovereignty. Workers in Latin America have not forgotten the role of the international arms of the AFL-CIO, with their friends in the CIA. This is a terrible legacy we have to overcome if we're going to build up real solidarity across the borders, and it needs to be said right out that we're starting from way back. (Ibid., 9).

While not widespread, the dissenting views among labor ranks are not exceptional either. The fact that during the national debate over NAFTA dozens of independent labor and other grassroots' organizations sprang up across the U.S., Mexico, and Canada in opposition to the treaty is a clear indication of the changing views. These organizations, with their often meager resources, were able to establish cross-border contacts with their counterparts, exchange ideas on issues of international unionization such as wage and benefits coordination and, in a small number of cases, succeeded in organizing labor unions in U.S.-owned plants operating in Mexico. Examples of these initiatives include the IBT Local 912/Green Giant solidarity caravan, the UE-FAT (Mexican Authentic Workers' Front) Strategic Alliance, and the AFL-CIO-backed Coalition for Justice in Maquiladoras. Less official transnational solidarity organizations such as Labor Notes and the Transnational Information Exchange succeeded in establishing trinational exchanges and meetings of auto, telecommunications, and garment workers. Similarly, solidarity tours by members of the Ford Workers Democratic Movement of Mexico and by telecommunications workers, teachers, and others have taken place in the last few years. The formation of the North American Worker-to-Worker Network in 1992, which includes both labor and community organizations, has been another important step toward strengthening this new form of internationalist organizing.[1]

Beyond Unions: A New Labor Movement

Crucial as they are in the struggle for labor rights (i.e., the right to organize, the right to strike, and the right to bargain collectively), trade unions have their limitations in the fight against the vagaries of a market economy: unemployment, alienation, and poverty. To begin with, they encompass only a small portion of the working class, usually the more skilled and better paid layers. Secondly, trade unionist politics is usually limited to economic demands such as wages and working conditions. While critical to the economic welfare of union members, broader social issues such as democracy, equality, universal health and education, and environmental concerns remain outside the purview of trade union politics.

Thirdly, to the extent that trade unions defend the economic interests of the working class, their bargaining power is limited by a number of factors. One such factor, as discussed earlier, is the market's tendency (and capability) to create a "reserve army" of the unemployed which severely limits the unions' power to bargain with the employers. The second factor is workers' dependence on the requirements of capital accumulation. Since wages and profits share the economic surplus, increases in the share of wages cut down on profits and investment[2], and result in a slackening of growth and a rise in unemployment. As the late Stephen Hymer put it, "this makes the working class a hostage to the capitalist class on whom they depend for capital accumulation and to whom they must provide incentives in the form of profits and accumulation of capital" (1979, 269). A third factor that limits the bargaining position of the national union is the fact that investment, production, and competition now take place on an international level. Labor is therefore constrained in its defense of wages and employment by the threat of international capital flight and relocation. Even if we assume that international plant relocation is somehow successfully blocked by a country's unions and their allies, the dilemma for national labor remains that any national policy to increase (or maintain) employment and wages will undermine a country's position within the competitive world market, thereby further threatening wages and employment. In fact, even if a socio-political movement representing the poor and the working class came to power, it would face this dilemma. If it tries to break out of the global market, it will face capital flight, economic sabotage, currency depreciation, balance of payment difficulties, and economic collapse. The recent experiences of Nicaragua, Granada, France, and Cuba, among others, testify to this, and clearly show that, as Karl Marx concluded long ago from his study of human history, individual countries cannot break out of the grip of world capitalism.

Therefore, the solution to the vagaries of a market economy lies with the transformation of the transnational, not just the national, economy. Fighting against the ills of the market system—unemployment, poverty, environmental degradation, and the like—is crucial to labor and other social layers suffering from them. But it makes little sense to fight symptoms without challenging the system that produces them.

Many would argue that these are not propitious times to speak of radical alternatives to capitalism. Admittedly, global circumstances appear to support such arguments. The rise in the reserve army of the unemployed and international labor rivalry, combined with the monetarist/austerity offensive of neo-liberalism on a global level, have thrown the working class on the defensive. The steady drift of the European socialist, social-democratic, and communist parties toward the U.S.-type market economies and the erosion of their traditional ideology, power, and prestige have led to workers' confusion there. The collapse of the Soviet Union, however much some socialists have always distanced themselves from that system, haunts the specter of socialism, and is likely to do so for some time to come. These have led to workers' and leftists' disorientation globally.

None of these, however, mean that there is no way out of the status quo. Capitalism is not only "destructive;" it is also "regenerative," as Karl Marx put it in his discussion of the impact of capitalism on colonies and other less-developed areas. As it captures world markets, universalizes the reign of capital, and disrupts living conditions for many, it simultaneously sows the seeds of its own transformation. On the one hand, it creates common problems and shared concerns for the majority of the world population; on the other, it creates the conditions and the technology that facilitate communication and cooperation among this majority of world citizens for joint actions and alternative solutions. When this majority will come to the realization and determination to actually appropriate and utilize the existing technology for a better organization and management of the world economy, no one can tell. But the potential and the trajectory of global socio-economic developments point in that direction. The distance between now and then, between our immediate frustrations and the superior but elusive civilization of our desire, can be traversed only if we take the necessary steps toward that end.

As noted earlier, hopeful signs have already emerged that the global economic rollback policies of neo-liberalism have begun to awaken the grassroots and working people everywhere. The result has been a widespread but little-recognized resistance to these policies. Zapatistas' uprisings in the Chiapas, women's riots in the oil belt Nigeria, and the urban riots in downtown Los Angeles, Caracas, or Sao Paulo all represent one thing: poor people's response to the neo-librettists' economic austerity programs. But the grassroots' response to the economic rollback has been more than just rebelling against it; those resisting are also initiating positive alternatives to it. These include employee-owned and operated enterprises, community-based development projects, workers' and women's cooperatives, and demands for a new world bank and a new United Nations. These initiatives have led to a series of international solidarity networks of trade unionists, environmentalists, women, consumer advocates, and other citizen activists (Turner, 1994; Daly/Cobb, 1994; Krimmerman/Lindfeld, 1992; Falk, 1992; Shuman, 1994).

On the intellectual front too the hope and the promise of a superior civilization to capitalism have not died with the demise of the Soviet Union. While it is disappointing—and not only to its most ardent supporters—that the social experiment that began with the 1917 Bolshevik Revolution has failed, that failure, combined with the brutal offensive of "triumphant" capitalism in recent years, has spurred creative rethinking and critical debate on the nature and the future of capitalism (Cowling/Sugden, 1994; Silber, 1994; Roosevelt/Belkin, 1994; Wofsy, 1995; Albert/Hahnel, 1991; Kotz, 1992; Bello, 1994; Laibman, 1992a & 1992b; Epstein et al. 1993; for example).

Transforming the world economy in the interests of the majority of the people is, of course, not easy. It certainly cannot be brought about in one jump or an overnight uprising. It can come about only as the cumulative outcome of many steps along the path of a long and difficult journey of continuous social and economic change. If the ideal society in which we would all like to live is called Socialism with a capital S (or communism, as Karl Marx put it), achievement of that Socialism would evolve out of a series of socialism's, with small initial letters, along the transitional path—a series of ongoing experiments and struggles to constantly rectify the damage wrought by the existing social order. Nobody can tell a priori how long or what form the transitional steps or stages may take; nor would such speculation be very useful. It is clear, however, that to change the world economy in the interests of the majority of its inhabitants, labor needs a new politics and new organizations to articulate the struggle for change.

Many radicals have dropped class politics at exactly the moment it is needed most. Rosa Luxemburg's conviction that socialism is the only alternative to capitalist barbarism is as relevant today as when she expressed it, during the carnage of Wold War I. Barbarism stares us in the eye in many disguised forms. Yet, much of the left these days shy away from using words such as class struggle, organization, or the crucial role of labor for social and economic change. "It is fashionable these days," as Walden Bello puts it, "to describe the desired alternatives [to capitalism] as an equitable, democratic, and ecologically sustainable social and economic organization. But once one begins to attempt to spell out the concrete implications of this abstract ideal, one cannot avoid describing a system of social relations that checks or restrains the devastating logic of capitalism.... Whatever one wishes to call it [the alternative to capitalism], conscious cooperative organization must supplant both blind competition and monopolistic collusion as the strategic principle of production and exchange if the economy is brought back to its appropriate relationship to the community" (1994, 112-113).

To help initiate change in this direction, labor needs its own independent political organization(s) and its own class presence to influence the evolving one-world economy. As David Riehle recently put it, in an article on the occasion of a Labor Party Advocates convention in Chicago, a viable independent labor organization will be (or is) one that "advances the idea that workers should represent themselves, that workers would be candidates for public office, that the working class itself can provide the solutions to the permanent crisis of present society—a party that can mobilize the broadest sectors of society in struggle for those objectives" (1993, 13).

It is true that in the older industrialized countries the percentage of the labor force working in large manufacturing and mining enterprises has declined, compared to those working in the so-called service industries. But this is no more than diversification of the work force that follows diversification of technology and economic activity, and the conclusion that it represents a decline in the overall weight or importance of the working class is unwarranted. The type of one's work uniform, the color of a wage earner's collar, or whether one's pay is called wage or salary does not make him/her more or less of a worker than other wage earners. In fact, statistics on wage and benefits of the work force clearly show that, on the average, the so-called white collar workers are paid less and are much less secure economically than the traditional industrial/manufacturing workers. Growth of the service industries also means growth of minimum wage/no benefits workers. Concentration of large numbers of workers in telecommunications, transport, banks, hospitals, energy sector, and the like can today paralyze the capitalist economy even more effectively than their "blue-collar" counterparts in the manufacturing sector. Furthermore, "professionals" and salaried employees such as teachers, engineers, physicians, and even middle and lower level managers are increasingly becoming wage workers, and are thus ruled by the supply and demand forces of the labor market. The tendency for wage work to become the dominant or universal form of work means that, overall, the ranks of the working class are expanding, not contracting, despite the relative decline in manufacturing employment (Braverman, 1974; Schor, 1992; Yates, 1994; for example).

More numerous and capable than ever before, the working class can influence, shape, and ultimately lead the world economy if it takes on the challenge (a) on an international level, and (b) in the context of broader coalitions and alliances with other social groups also struggling for equity, environmental protection, and human rights. This requires a new labor movement with independent politics and organization(s). Whatever the new labor organization is called (call it a party, a labor coalition, or anything you like), it has to be different not only from the U.S. business union model but also from the social democratic model of Europe, trade unions + party. It can certainly learn from models of labor movement in Latin America and South Africa where unions, grassroots' parties, and community-based organizations (frequently led by women) increasingly function as arms of a single working class movement (Moody, 1994). This means that the new labor movement/organization has to represent the interests of the entire working class—not just organized industrial labor, nor only its singular economic interests. It must further aim at defending the interests of all those who challenge the logic of the profit-driven market mechanism. As Susan George, of the Transnational Institute, recently pointed out:

If the labour movement stays separate from all the other progressive forces in the world, we will be picked off one by one. There are tremendous opportunities for building alliances with environmentalists, with church groups, with development organizations. There is a whole host of people out there, but one has to go about building those alliances consciously. That does not mean you have to give up your own identity. That does not mean you have to agree on every issue, but it does mean that if we are going to beat this free market, competitive economy we have to re-group our forces. It is curious that the majority in the world is losing by this system and yet we do not seem to be able to unite and make our own political points (1994, 12).

The inadequacies and limitations of the existing major trade unions do not mean that a new independent labor organization should (or can afford to) bypass labor unions. Such a labor organization will have to grow out of, but go beyond, the existing labor institutions; it must expand its horizons from the industrial or trade level to the national level, and from purely economic to political action. In other words, it can no longer confine itself to the fight for wages but must fight for an equitable share of the aggregate economic surplus, a fair distribution and reasonable allocation of national income. As was pointed out earlier, these objectives cannot be truly achieved within a national framework, since no nation alone—perhaps with the exception of the United States, and even that is doubtful—is able to break the grip of world capitalism. Therefore, new, independent labor organizations of various countries must also shift their horizons from the national to the world level, to international solidarity and international coordination of policy and action.

As noted earlier, the road to a social structure not regulated by capitalist profitability is a long and tortuous one; it cannot be traveled in one jump, but rather through a series of transitional steps and stages. Only through a careful and timely formulation of transitional programs and demands—demands which must in part stem from the needs of the mass of the disaffected, and which therefore will draw the widest possible array of allies into the ranks of labor—can a bridge be built between the present and such a society. While the exact nature of transitional demands will depend on the concrete conditions of many specific movements along the way of this long struggle, the following seem to be some of the most appropriate demands for the present time.

1. The right to employment for all those able to work. Employers, their ideological allies, and their representatives in government will obviously cry out at this demand that "there are simply not enough jobs." The labor   coalition can then respond by raising the following demand.

2. A sliding scale of working hours. This means that the new international labor movement/coalition should correlate the length of the work week to labor productivity so that, as productivity rises, the number of working   hours   will automatically fall, and no jobs will be lost. If it takes less time to produce the same commodities, we should all work less rather than   eliminating some people's jobs. There is absolutely nothing outlandish or   radical about this demand; it only makes sense.

But capital has its own logic, and in the last half century or so, just the opposite has taken place in the United States: people are working longer hours as labor productivity has been steadily going up. A recent study by Professor Juliet Schor of Harvard University (1991) shows that productivity in the United States has risen about 2.7 times since WW II. If the gains in productivity had been directed into decreasing the work week, Professor Schor observes, the amount of labor time required to maintain a constant standard of living would have declined to 20 hours per week. Instead, both men and women now devote more time to combined market and non-market labor than they did nearly 25 years ago.

3. A sliding scale, or indexing, of wages. This means adjusting wages to the rate of inflation so that workers' purchasing power and their standard of living will not fall as the prices rise. Closely related to this demand is the demand that the share of wages as a percentage of national income should not fall relative to the share of profit, rent, or interest. Studies of income distribution in the U.S. show, for example, that the relative share of interest earners as a percentage of national income has been rising much faster than the share of wage earners in the post-WW II period (Hixson, 1991, 199-210). Interestingly, some labor activists have recently begun to question this lop-sided trend of income distribution. Addressing the Labor Education Conference on the theme "Labor and Politics" in Toledo, Ohio, 10 December 1994, Bob Wages, the president of Oil, Chemical and Atomic Workers stated:

What's happened over the course of the past 30 years? In 1954 when the Internal Revenue Code was adopted, the tax code in this country, it was split roughly in the following way: large corporations and the rich assumed about two-thirds of the federal tax burden; one-third fell upon the poor and the working class. Now that burden has shifted. Now the working class and the poor pay two-thirds of the burden, and Corporate America complains about welfare (1995, 26).

4. The right to a decent standard of living for all; that is, nobody should fall below the officially-defined poverty line.

5. The right to a guaranteed universal, single-payer type health care system.

These and other demands such as the right to education, the right to pollution-free air and water, and the right to equal treatment of men and women regardless of gender and sexual preferences are certain to rally diverse segments of society behind the labor coalition, and thus help end the absolute rule of capital.[3]

Many people would view these proposals as unrealistic. What they mean by this is that these demands cannot be realized under the present socio-economic and political structure. And they are right. But, as this structure is reorganized, many of the currently "impossible" alternatives will become possible. There is definitely no dearth of material resources for this purpose, certainly not in the U.S. and other industrialized countries. What is lacking is the political will and/or capacity to reorient the society's priorities and reallocate its resources. The realizability of these proposals, ultimately, comes down to the relationship of social forces and the balance of class struggle.

Others might reject these demands on philosophical grounds: that in the great contest between capitalism and socialism, capitalism has decisively triumphed, that the rules and the laws of market mechanism are eternal, and that, therefore, any talk of socialism or proletarian internationalism is anachronistic and/or passé. Let us examine these contentions more closely.

Prospects for International Labor Solidarity

Internationalism is not a dogma invented by Marx and Engels but a recognition of the laws of capitalist development, of the laws of the accumulation of capital as "self-expanding value" that is blind to physical/geographical borders. The need and the call for international labor solidarity stems from a recognition of this process, a recognition that if not labor, then capital is going to rule the world, as is presently the case.

A comparison between the early stages of the development of capitalism on a national level and its subsequent expansion to international level is instructive. In its early stages of development, capitalism consolidated and centralized all the petty states, principalities, and feudal domains into nation states in order to create a broader arena for the development of productive forces. Today a similar consolidation of markets is taking place on an international level. Just as in the early stages of capitalism, nation states facilitated consolidation of national markets by establishing national currencies, national business laws, national tax laws, and the like, today they perform a similar task through international agencies such as IMF, the World Bank, GATT, NAFTA, and now the World Trade Organization (WTO).

Labor organizations too need to move from national to international arena—just as they moved from the local and/or craft level of early capitalism to the national level of today. The fact that earlier attempts at international labor solidarity failed by no means signals the end of the necessity of that solidarity—the growth of labor organizations has almost always lagged behind that of capitalist ones. Nor does it, therefore, detract in any way from the validity of the Marxian theory of proletarian internationalism. As a science, Marxism will have to deal with new developments by advances in its theory. But only the doctrinaire can perceive a crisis of Marxism and a doom of international labor solidarity from the unsuccessful international labor experiences of the past, or from the failure of economic planning experiments in the former U.S.S.R. and its allies. From a Marxian perspective of history, the collapse of the Soviet system should have come as no surprise; on the contrary, the demise of that system gives striking confirmation to the scientific validity and continued relevance of Marxist theory. A crucial factor in Marx's view of the viability of a socialist society is its achievement to a higher productivity of labor than under capitalism. Without this condition, and without democratic decision making, revolutionary expropriation of the means of production and their placement at the disposal of the state would be, according to this view, a dramatic event without a future as these revolutionary gains would sooner or later succumb to the more competitive capitalist market forces (*Critique of the Gotha program*, *The German Ideology*, *The Civil War in France*, for example). In the absence of these two key conditions, the collapse of the Soviet-type economies was inevitable.[4]

Those who refer to a crisis of Marxism and the "end of history" see the conjunctural deviations of actual developments from theory, and an altering of conditions, as a loss of the general explanatory power of the theory. Some of the general conditions that have contributed to the failure of past efforts at international labor cooperation are: the prematurity of some of those efforts, including perhaps that of the First International; the corruption and/or ideological bankruptcy of the leadership of the working class; the successful promotion of the ideology of nation state and/or nationalism; the divisive atmosphere of the Cold War era; and, perhaps most importantly, the immediate post-WW II economic boom in the United States, which afforded the working class there a decent standard of living, thereby fostering a policy of cooperation with the capitalist class at home and a cavalier attitude toward workers abroad. Whatever the reason(s), the fact is that most of these conditions have changed, or are changing, and new conditions that will prepare and/or favor international labor collaboration are replacing them—euphoric celebrations of the "triumph" of capitalism and the apparent confusion of the working class notwithstanding.

Chief among the emerging new conditions is the change in the U.S. international economic position and, with it , in the traditional labor strategies in the face of globalization of production. Until the early 1970s, the Unites States was the major world supplier of manufactured products. Furthermore, those products were largely produced at home, by U.S. workers. As long as the U.S. produced at home and sold abroad, its workers did not have to compete with those of other countries. It should therefore not be surprising that, during that era, the AFL-CIO pursued a policy of free trade and shunned international labor cooperation as these served its (temporary) economic interests.[5] World economic integration and globalization of production have changed this. Workers in the United States are beginning to realize that they can no longer afford to shun workers in other countries as this would be leaving corporations free to play them off against workers in low-wage parts of the world.

While the new world economic situation has led to a shift in the official labor strategy from the active pursuit of free trade to the current policy of protectionism, many in the labor ranks question the efficacy and the wisdom of this policy; instead, they suggest positive alternatives based on international labor cooperation that would eliminate labor costs as a factor in competition. Shoots of a new labor politics in the labor ranks and in the independent unions are reflected in both domestic and international labor strategies of recent years. New labor strategies in the domestic front include union reform activities, cross-union solidarity actions/organizations, community-based labor organizations, and efforts to build a labor party. At the international level, the new ideas and strategies are reflected in worker-to-worker exchanges, cross-border organizing, support for international labor rights, international strike support, contacts with workers in the NICs and Third World countries, and enhanced labor communications.[6]

Globalization of production, technology, and information have created not only favorable conditions for labor internationalism but also for other grassroots movements which are likewise challenging capitalist regulation of our lives, and are therefor potential allies of labor if labor would seriously address their concerns. Though little-recognized by official accounts and rarely mentioned in national headlines, these parallel international coalition networks are quite diverse and very extensive. They represent grassroots' response to the global corporate agenda: they signify efforts at saving jobs, preserving small farms, stopping toxic dumping, winning labor rights, preventing privatizations, fighting for provision of basic needs, and the like. In short, they represent "an unanticipated and often unrecognized backlash" to the globalization of capital, as Brecher and Costello put it (1994, 83).[7]

Almost all of these organizations have at least an office and a telephone in at least one country. Fax machines and computer networks are also increasingly emerging as instant means of communications between these international groups. The daunting experience and the frightful prospects of international labor rivalry has lately prompted some labor activists and independent unions to establish computer networks with these organization in an effort to broaden their social base. For example, the LaborNet, the computer network of the Institute for Global Communications, "ties into other 'Nets' dedicated to social movements like the environmental movement, peace movement,..." (Ibid., 160). Labor communications expert Peter Waterman has called this international computer networking of diverse social groups dedicated to fighting the global economic rollback of neo-liberalism a "communications internationalism," and suggested that perhaps it can be called a "Fifth International" (1992).

It is true that despite their significant growth in recent years, these grassroots groups are highly fragmented, and their resistance to corporate "lean" production and austerity policies is almost entirely defensive. To the impatient radicals, who are eager to see all their desired social changes take place in their own life time, this is frustrating. This feeling of disappointment is understandable because it is easy to focus on the individual droplets without seeing the wave/cascade that those droplets can generate. The fragmented and the defensive status of labor and other grassroots' coalition networks does not detract from the importance of the potential and the opportunities that these movements represent for social and economic change in the interests of the majority of world population. They show how globalization of capital can create globalization of resistance movements, and are therefore reasons for hope and optimism. This is why I think the defeatist conclusion in the face of the current celebrations of the "triumph" of capitalism and the "end of history" is wrong. The task of those who are convinced that capitalism is not the ideal summit of human history is therefore not to wring their hands but to dust off their clothes and go to work.

Endnotes

1. Labor and other grassroots' international coalition networks/organizations that have developed during the last several years are too numerous and their activities are too extensive to be cited here.

A few good sources (among many) on these organizations and their activities are: Moody, 1994; Moody & Mcginn, 1992; Brecher & Costello, 1994; Brecher & Costello, 1991; Amalgamated Clothing and Textile Workers Union's (ACTWU) "annotated Bibliography on NAFTA (Draft Copy)," 1993; the "Resources" section of *Labor Notes*, various issues of the last three years; Krimerman & Lindenfeld, 1992; Prasnikar, 1991; Shuman, 1994; Bello et al., 1994.

2. During periods of expansionary cycles and a labor shortage, a rise in the overall surplus can afford an increase in the shares of both wages and profits--like the immediate post-WW II period in the U.S. But increasing automation and internationalization of capital are making a repeat of that experience highly unlikely.

3. Among the many labor advocates who have written on these strategies and demands, the term "transitional demands" is most closely associated with Leon Trotsky's name who systematically formulated these strategies in his *The Transitional Program for Socialist Revolution* (New York: Pathfinder Press, 1977); see also Weitzman (1984); and Gorz (1967).

4. Evidence shows that prominent Bolshevik leaders such as Lenin and Trotsky occasionally spoke of the ominous likelihood of the failure of their revolution in the absence of the revolutionary outbursts in advanced capitalist countries. For example, in "A Letter to American Workers," dated 20 August 1918, Lenin wrote: "We are now as if in a beleaguered fortress until other detachments of the international socialist revolution come to our rescue.... We know that help from you, comrades American workers, will probably not come soon.... We know that the European proletarian revolution also may not blaze forth during the next few weeks.... We stake our chances on the inevitability of the international revolution.... We know that circumstances brought to the fore our Russian detachment of the socialist proletariat, not by virtues of our merits, but due to the particular backwardness of Russia, and that before the outburst of the international revolution there may be several defeats of separate revolutions." (in Mason, D. & Smith, J. eds., *Lenin's Impact on the United States*. New York: NWR Publications, Inc., 1970). Leon Trotsky likewise predicted (in his well-known *The Revolution Betrayed*) the possibility of restoration of capitalism in the Soviet Union if the more advanced economies remained capitalist.

5. Interestingly, architects of the U.S. labor's foreign policy during the Cold War regarded themselves as internationalists--anti-communist internationalists. They cooperated closely with the CIA to break left-led strikes (for example in France in 1949) and overthrow leftist governments (for example in Guatemala in 1954). *Business Week* described the AFL-CIO's global operations, such as its International Affairs Department in Washington and its American Institute for Free Labor Development in Latin America, as "labor's own version of the Central Intelligence Agency--a trade union network existing in all parts of the world." (*Business Week*, May 15, 1966; as quoted in Brecher/Costello, 1994, 150; and in Sims, 1992).

6. Due to space constraint, these new labor ideas, strategies, and movements cannot be discussed here. But I hope readers interested in more information on these fascinating new developments will benefit from consulting the reference sources provided in footnote 1 above and footnote 7 below.

7. A full account of international coalitions of grassroots groups is beyond the scope of this study. A brief tour through some computer networks (the worldwide web of the internet, for example) shows hundreds of such groups, despite the fact that only a fraction of them are connected with computer

networks. (See also the following: Shuman, 1994; Danaher, 1994; Turner, 1994; Waterman, 1992; Bello, et al. 1994).

References

Albert, M. and Hahnel, R. *The Political Economy of Participatory Economics.* NJ: Princeton University Press, 1991.

Ashworth, L. M. "The North American Free Trade Agreement: A Pearl of What Price?" *Durell Journal of Money and Banking*, Summer 1993, pp. 26-32.

Babson, S. "The Multinational Corporation and Labor," *Review of Radical Political Economics*, Summer 1973, (1), pp. 19-36.

Bello, W. et al. *Dark Victory.* Pluto Press with Food First and Transnational Institute, 1994.

Bernard, E. "Remarks on the North American Free Trade Agreement," *Bulletin In Defense of Marxism*, January 1994, (112), 3 & 31.

Braverman, H. *Labor and Monopoly Capital.* New York and London: Monthly Review Press, 1974.

Brecher, J. "The Stupid Economy," *Z Magazine*, April 1993, pp. 29-34.

Brecher, J. and Costello, T. *Global Village vs. Global Pillage: A One-World Strategy for Labor.* Washington, DC: International Labor Rights Education and Research Fund, 1991.

_____. *Global Village or Global Pillage: Economic Reconstruction From the Bottom Up.* Boston, MA: South End Press, 1994.

Brooks, D. "The Search for Counterparts: A labor-community agenda must cross borders as well," *Labor Research Review*, Fall 1992, (19), pp. 83-96.

Cowling, K. and Sugden, R. *Beyond Capitalism: Toward a New World Economic Order.* NY: St. Martin's Press, 1994.

Daly, H.E. and Cobb, J.B. *For the Common Good: Redirecting the Economy toward Community, the Environment, and a Sustainable Future* (second ed.), Boston: Beacon Press, 1994.

Danaher, K. (ed.), *50 Years is Enough: The Case Against the World Bank and the International Monetary Fund.* Boston, MA: South End Press, 1994.

De Brunhoff, S. *The State, Capital and Economic Policy* . London: Pluto Press, 1978.

Dentzer, S. "The Pains and Gains of Trade," *U.S. News & World Report*, September 28, 1992, pp. 62-69.

Dickinson, J. "State and Economy in the Arab Middle East: Some Theoretical and Empirical Observations," *Arab Studies Quarterly,* 1981, 5 (1), pp. 22-50.

Dobb, M. *Studies in the Development of Capitalism.* New York: International Publishers, 1963.

Dornbusch, R. "Why the U.S. Needs to Nail Down NAFTA," *Business Week,* April 26, 1993, pp. 18.

Elson, D. "The Brandt Report: a Programme for Survival?" *Capital and Class*, 1982, (16), pp. 110-127.

Enderwick, P. *Multinational Business and Labor.* London: Groom Helm, 1985.

Epstein, G.; Graham, J. and Nembhard, J. (eds.), *Creating a New World Economy.* Philadelphia: Temple University Press, 1993.

Falk, R. *Explorations at the Edge of Time.* Philadelphia: Temple University Press, 1992.

Faux J. & Rothstein, R. "Fast Track, Fast Shuffle," (briefing paper), Washington, DC: Economic Policy Institute, 1992.

Fraser, D. *Labor Will Rule: Hillman and the rise of American Labor.* New York: The Free Press, 1991.

Geoghegan, T. *Which Side Are You On?* New York: Farrar, Straus & Giroux, 1991.

George, S. "The New World Order: Development or Exploitation," *International Union Rights,* 1994, 1(6), pp. 10-12.

Gorz, A. *Strategy for Labor; a radical proposal* . Boston: Beacon Press, 1967.

Haworth, N. and Ramsay, H. "Workers of the World Unite," in R. Southall, ed., *Third World Trade Unions and the Changing International Division of Labor.* London: Zed Books, 1986.

Hixson, W. *A Matter of Interest: Reexamining Money, Debt, and Real Economic Growth.* Westport, Connecticut & London: Praeger, 1991.

Hufbauer, G. C. & Schott, J. J. *NAFTA: An Assessment* . Washington, DC: Institute for International Economics, 1993.

Hymer, S. *The Multinational Corporation: A Radical Approach* . Cambridge, MA: Cambridge University Press, 1979.

Jenkins, R. *Transnational Corporations and Uneven Development*. London and New York: Methuen, 1987.

Johnson, D. "U.S., Mexican Unions Are Teaming Up To Organize," *Labor Notes*, September 1993, (174), pp. 8-9.

Kotz, David. "The Transformation of the Economic Reform Process in the USSR," *Review of Radical Political Economics, 1992*, 44(4), pp. 14-34.

Krimerman, L. and Lindenfeld, F. *When Workers Decide: Workplace Democracy Takes Root in North America*. Philadelphia, PA & Gabriola Island, BC: New Society Publishers, 1992.

LaBotz, D. *A Troublemakers Handbook: How to Fight Back Where You Work—and Win*. Detroit, MI: Labor Education & Research Project, 1991.

Laibman, D. *Value, Technical Change, and Crisis*. Armonk, NY & London, England: M.E. Sharpe, 1992.

_____. "Market and Plan: The Evolution of Socialist Structure in History and Theory," *Science & Society*, Spring 1992, 56 (1), pp. 60-92.

Levinson, C. *International Trade Unionism*. London: George Allen & Unwin, 1972.

Lovell, F. "Union Activists Assess Prospects for Labor Party," *Bulletin in Defense of Marxism*, February 1995, (122).

MacEwan, A. "Technical Options and Free Trade Agreements," *Science & Society*, Spring 1995, 59(1), pp. 9-37.

_____. "The New Evangelists: Preaching that old-time religion," *Dollars & Sense*, November 1991, pp. 6-9.

MacShane, D. *International Labor and the Origins of the Cold War*. Oxford: Clarendon Press, 1992.

Miller, T. "Surveys Highlight Union Leadership in Crisis," *Independent Politics*, March-April 1995.

Moody, K. "Meaning of new World Trade Organization: Are Transnationals Taking Over the World?" *Independent Politics*, March/April 1995, pp. 20-21.

Moody, K. 1994. "Pulled Apart, Pushed Together: The North American Working Class & the Labor Movement in the U.S.," Unpublished paper, 1994.

Moody, K. and McGinn, M. *Unions and Free Trade: Solidarity vs. Competition.* Detroit: Labor Notes Books, 1992.

_____. "From the Yukon to the Yucatan," *Dollars & Sense*, November 1991, pp. 10-12.

Nove, A. *The Economics of Feasible Socialism Revisited.* London: Routledge, 1991.

O'Connor, J. *The Fiscal Crisis of the State.* New York: ST. Martin's Press, 1973.

Olle, W. and Schoeller, W. "World Market Competition and Restrictions Upon International Trade Union Policies," *Capital and Class*, 1977, (2).

Prasniker, J. *Workers' Participation and Self-Management in Developing Countries.* Boulder/San Francisco/Oxford: Westview Press, 1991.

Ranney, D. C. "NAFTA and the New Transnational Corporate Agenda," *Review of Radical Political Economics*, Winter 1993, 25(4), pp. 1-13.

Riehle, D. "Labor Party Advocates Gather in Chicago Consider Call for Convention of a U.S. Labor Party," *Bulletin In Defense of Marxism*, November-December 1993, (111), pp. 12-13.

Roosevelt, F. and Belkin, D. (eds.), *Why Market Socialism? Voices From Dissent.* Armonk, NY & London: M.E. Sharpe, 1994.

Schor, J. *The Overworked American.* Basic Books, 1992.

Seidman, G. "Facing the New International Context of Development," in Jeremy Brecher, John Brown Childs, and Jill Cutler, eds., *Global visions: Beyond the New World Order.* Boston, MA: South End Press, 1993.

Shuman, M. *Towards a Global Village: International Community Development Initiatives.* London & Boulder, CO: Pluto Press, 1994.

Silber, Irwin. *Socialism: What Went Wrong?* London & Boulder, Colorado: Pluto Press, 1994.

Sims, B. *Workers of the World Undermined: American Labor's Role in U.S. Foreign Policy.*

Boston: South End Press, 1992.

Slaughter, J. "Long-Anticipated Next Step: Advocates to Launch Labor Party," *Labor Notes*, March 1995, (192).

Szymansky, A. *The Capitalist State and the Politics of Class* . Cambridge, MA: Wintrop Publishers,1978.

Thompson, D. and Larson, R. *Where were you, brother? An account of trade union imperialism.* London: War on Want, 1978.

Turner, T.E. *Arise Ye Mighty People*! Trenton, NJ: Africa World Press, 1994.

Wages, B. "We Have to Form Our Own Independent Political Party—With an Agenda that Makes Sense for Working Men and Women," *Bulletin in Defense of Marxism*, February 1995, (122), pp. 26-27.

Waterman, P. (ed.), *The Old Internationalism and the New.* The Hague: International Labor Education, Research and Information Foundation, 1988.

_____. "International Labor Communication by Computer: The Fifth International?" Working Paper Series No. 129. The Hague: Institute of Social Studies, 1992.

Weitzman, M. *The Share Economy* . Harvard University Press, 1984.

West, J. "Trumka Wins Rank & File Election," *Labor Notes*, May 1995, (194).

Wilson, R. "Jobs with Justice Takes On Newt's Contract," *Labor Notes*, May 1995, (194).

Wofsy, L. *Looking for the Future.* Oakland, CA: I W Rose Press, 1995.

Yates, M. *Longer Hours, Fewer Jobs.* NY: Monthly Review Press, 1994.

15

GLOBALIZATION AND DEVELOPMENT:*Facing the Challenges*

Brigitte Lévy[1]
University of Ottawa, Canada

Most countries around the world now favor stable macro-economic management, outward-oriented trade and investment policies, and an increased role for markets and the private sector. This paper explores the dominant capitalism paradigm and its recent effects on globalization and on the reliance on economic achievements. It also raises questions about the legitimacy of the global pattern of development and investigates the compatibility of new concepts such as sustainable development and old ones such as maximizing economic growth.

There is an ongoing debate over the nature and scope of the transformation of the global economy. Globalization is the increasing internationalization of the production, distribution, and marketing of goods and services. In the global process, both the economic and social dimensions of globalization are conceptually unified. The term indeed involves a wide variety of political, sociological, environmental and economic trends (Harris, 1993). The effect of globalization in recent years has been a considerable reduction in the capacity of nation-states to control their national economies, which are more influenced by supranational institutions and trade agreements such as the IMF, the World Bank, the coalitions for economic exchange among countries, and the GATT-WTO than they are by internal economic levers.

The economic decision-making process illustrates a partial transfer of authority and power from national bodies to international bodies. This trend is not limited to the economic sphere. Nation-states are under increasingly strong pressure to harmonize a wide variety of laws and policies, such as pollution standards and labor legislation, with those of other nation-states (Savoie, 1994).

At the same time, there is a lack of international leadership which might be attributed to the fear of the leaders of nation-states, including super-powers, to lose key elements of their national sovereignty.

The list of problems facing the world is huge. There is a lack of leadership on the international scene and no single superpower is capable today of handling strategic issues related to trade, the transition to free market ideology, economic crises, wars or ethnic conflicts, environmental degradation, and poverty alleviation. International organizations cannot easily cope with any one of these critical issues. The UN is showing definite signs of stress in dealing with regional political conflicts. The IMF, the World Bank and the WTO are far from capable of coping with the spectrum of economic and financial problems, old and new. Unfortunately no coordination mechanisms exist among international organizations and dialogue does not take place easily among them. Given the changes taking place in the world economy, political leaders must be prepared to question the working of their own institutions and to reform them. On the global scale, decision makers will have to define the operational terms and conditions of the new world order and solve conflicts that emerge between nations, regions and firms.

Globalization has disrupted longstanding patterns of social relationships and is paving the way for worldwide economic restructuring. Since the late 1950s, and accelerating rapidly in the 1980s and 1990s, industrial production has shifted from the advanced industrial countries of western Europe and the United States, to Japan, then to the Asian newly industrialized countries (NICs). Hong Kong, Taiwan, South Korea and Singapore were the first countries to witness the shift of the manufacturing base. This shift has been accompanied by a tremendous expansion of trade flows and foreign direct investment (FDI). Transnational corporations (TNCs) have been responsible for a strong surge in FDI since the mid-1980s. Between 1985 and 1990, FDI grew at four times the rate of the world output and nearly three times the rate of trade flows. TNCs from the Triad (the European Community, now the European Union [EU], the U.S. and Japan) controlled 80% of FDI. At the beginning of the 1990s, the total amount of FDI owned by TNCs was $1.9 trillion, six times their net worth in 1979. Those flows of FDI, along with the activities of TNCs, demonstrate the degree to which the world has become interdependent and integrated.

The effects of globalization and economic restructuring are calling into question old notions of development and progress. At the end of World War II, we saw the emergence of the United Nations and other international organizations designed to make the world more peaceful and to help poorer countries climb the development ladder. Economic gains and humanitarian objectives were both pursued through various programs and initiatives. Today, globalization, regionalization (the formation of trade blocs) and the activities of TNCs are salient characteristic features of the development process. The nation-state has been a less significant economic actor and the TNCs have become more powerful actors that base decisions primarily on profit-making criteria. This leaves certain countries and regions of the world behind. Globalization of the economy and all of the other factors contributing to the restructuring of the social political and economic environment are changing the ways of governing in a climate of economic interdependence. Globalization forces a rethinking of the role of the nation-state and the way international institutions function, and requires a capacity to adjust to rapid changes in the world economy.

This paper will explore the dynamics of globalization and its effects on world development. Particular attention will be given to the question of sustainable development. Exploring these issues will help explain widening gaps in incomes between and within countries. The new economic paradigm must contain elements of reform that cover many aspects of the world trade system. Questions of ethics, gender, equity, environmental consciousness, poverty eradication, and a genuine search for a new "sustainable" world order are critical to the present and future development needs of society.

The New Global Economic Environment

Globalization, along with regionalization, worldwide lowering of tariffs through the GATT, rising levels of international competition, and new technologies and innovations in production and management, have been the driving forces of change around the world. Driven by heightened global competition and the availability of new technology, the structure of production and employment is changing dramatically in the 1990s and is affecting competitiveness, employment patterns, populations, and economic and welfare systems.

Population trends and employment patterns are particularly important issues. Almost six billion people live in the world today, three-quarters of them in developing countries. These countries vary greatly in geographical size, in levels of development, and in economic, political and social structures. Their population growth rates have no historical precedent. As population has more than doubled since the middle of the century, so too has per capita income. From 1984 to 1994 alone, the growth in output of goods and services totaled more than $4 trillion - more than from the beginning of civilization until 1950 (Brown, Lenssen, Kane, 1995).

Cities are places where jobs are created and lost and where new skills and interests are pursued. Many cities, however, are showing signs of environmental decay, shortfall of basic services, overcrowding, and increased crime rates. Many rural people, particularly those in the developing world, have moved to cities where production takes place. According to UN estimates, about 45% of the world's population are urban dwellers, and by 2025, that proportion will probably exceed 60%. In 2015, Tokyo will likely remain the world's largest "urban agglomeration", with an expected population of 28.7 million (compared with 26.5 million in 1994). Bombay's population is forecast to reach 27.4 million in 2015, nearly double its 1994 total. New York, currently the world's second largest city, with 16 million people, is expected to be overtaken by Sao Paulo, Mexico City, Shanghai, Beijing, Jakarta, Lagos, and Karachi. According to the most recent UN projections, by 2050, global population is forecast to rise given present trends to at least 7.9 billion, and could reach between 10 and 12 billion. The fastest population growth will occur in the cities of the developing world.

TNCs are the primary actors directing export-led industrialization strategies since countries encourage the investment of foreign capital. The establishment of export-processing zones (EPZs) has been an important feature of the globalization process. It has enabled to accommodate TNCs transfers of production/assembly process to take advantage of cheap labor and other sources of competitive advantage. Bina and Davis (1996) argue that the mission of globalization is not to go after the cheap labor *per se*, but to engage in a global fashion in cheapening the labor power through technological change. Very often, this strategy has increased human migration to urban centers and has exacerbated environmental problems. Given the nature of this process of capital and trade flows, it is necessary to understand the relation between human activities, production, the environment, and the growing worldwide urban crisis.

In the last forty years, the internationalization of economic activities has given rise to new patterns of trade and investment. These patterns have far-reaching implications for nation-states and for the international division of labor. By 2010, developing countries' share of world trade could account for almost half, with China, India and Indonesia potentially holding the greatest purchasing power (World Bank, 1995). Increased prosperity in some developing countries is expected to create demand for exports of capital goods and consumer products. By

2010, according to World Bank predictions, more than one billion consumers in developing countries could have per capita incomes higher than those of Greece and Spain today and the volume of developing countries' imports could grow faster than those of industrialized countries. Several key issues remain.

Will all developing countries benefit equally from that pattern of trade? A look at FDI trends reveals that developing countries' share of total FDI is rising. According to UNCTAD (1995), FDI in developing countries reached a record $80 billion in 1994, or nearly 40% of total overseas investment flows of an estimated $204 billion. However, 80% of all FDI going to developing countries accrues to just 10 countries, nearly all of them in Asia and Latin America. China alone accounted for half this amount in 1993 when, with $27.5 billion, it was the world's single largest recipient of FDI. UNCTAD attributes the shifting pattern of FDI to strong growth in recipient countries, the liberalization of investment rules, privatization, and the continuous search by TNCs for new markets and cost-efficient production. The World Bank's 1995 World Development Report raises questions about the feasible ways to prepare workers for membership in a global labor market. That question is likely to top the international policy-making agenda in years to come. The International Labor Organization (ILO), in its first global job survey, World Employment 1995, estimates that of the world's labor force of about 2.5 billion people, about 30% are unemployed. The ILO reports double-digit unemployment in Canada, Australia, many European countries, and in several other industrialized nations. This has given rise to new names of poverty - "social exclusion" in Europe or "growth" of an underclass in the U.S.

Will global trade support sustainable development? Policy makers must concern themselves not solely with trade, but also with all the ways in which TNCs gain access to market. To continue functioning within the predominant capitalist paradigm, a social charter and a social clause applicable to TNCs must be introduced within international and national institutions. Can the capitalist paradigm survive in a new world where the goal will be a genuine search for sustainable development? How far can it go to adapt itself to the new realities of the next decade? Those are the challenges of globalization.

The world will also face intensified friction and protectionist demands as industries in industrialized countries adjust to stiffer competition from developing economies. Such competition may spread to services, given that technology enables many services, such as order-processing and even research, to be carried out in countries with low labor costs. A major change in world trade over the years has been the steady decline in the importance of primary products, with a particularly sharp drop since the mid-1980s. This decline is considerable, ranging from two-thirds of the total at the beginning of the century to less than one-third today. Biotechnology has encouraged the range of substitutes for natural products, from synthetic fibers to coffee substitutes. Industrialized countries, with their relatively large dominance in food exports and in manufactured products, continue to supply 80% of all manufactured goods and 40% of all primary products entering world trade, while NICs have improved their competitive positions in world markets, and LDCs are not likely to improve their positions in such a system of uneven distribution.

The Uruguay Round of the GATT, ratified in 1994, paved the way for reductions in trade barriers beginning in 1995. Expanded trade is expected to add billions of dollars per year to the global economy - up to $275 billion over ten years. However, the fruits of this expansion will not be shared equally. Industrial nations will reap some 65-85% of the projected gains to the detriment of the developing world. According to the most recent estimates by the United Nations Conference on Trade and Development (UNCTAD), the world's poorest countries may lose between $300 million and $600 million per year in reduced exports and increased food imports as a consequence of the Uruguay Round. LDCs find it difficult to compete with industrialized countries that are subsidizing their growers and are using capital intensive models of production. Though LDCs' losses are small in a global context, they can account for up to 50% of a country's exports. These losses can, therefore, have serious consequences for the countries concerned. Africa is projected to lose more than $2 billion as its exports lose preferential access to European markets and its agricultural imports rise in price. Per capita income in Africa and many other regions will likely be lower in 2000 than in 1980 (World Bank, 1995).

Much has changed in the global economic environment in recent years. There have been tremendous changes in the direction, size and owners of FDI. Among the main patterns to be considered is a need for a deeper analysis of regional economic integration processes, communication and information technology advancement, and shifts in economic strength between countries and regional areas. The activities of TNCs in the manufacturing and service sectors dominate urban employment in both the developed and developing world. According to one estimate (UNCTAD, 1994), there are now 150 million people working, directly and indirectly, for TNCs; these people represent 20% of employment in the non-agricultural sector. Countries that attract a greater volume of FDI, therefore, stand a better chance of achieving a high rate of growth and international competitiveness.

The globalization of national economies results not only in the loss and gaining of jobs, but also in the shifting of the location of work. The first response of industrialized countries to the complexities of the global economy has often been regional. The North American Free Trade Agreement (NAFTA), the EU, and hopes of further regional integration in Asia are the focus of most trade policy debates in many countries.

Implementation of the NAFTA in 1994 has boosted North American trade significantly. At the Miami Summit in December 1994, leaders throughout the Americas agreed to establish a Free Trade Area, covering 850 million people and, by 2005, possessing $13 trillion in purchasing power. In Europe, a process of "widening" and "deepening" is still going on, despite difficulties of implementing the European Monetary Union portion of the Maastricht Treaty and problems integrating former Eastern European countries. In the Pacific Rim region, members of the Asia Pacific Economic Cooperation (APEC) agreed to work toward establishing a free trade zone by 2020. Most of the increase in APEC's share of world export has been generated over the last decade by Asian nations.

Trade, Development and Global Economic Management

The liberalization of international trade and capital movements opens the possibility of worldwide growth, according to the prevalent neoclassical theory. With worldwide growth, employment creation and poverty alleviation should result. However, adjustment processes taking place in all countries can marginalize segments of society, particularly the poorest ones. One major drawback to automatic economic adjustment to free trade is the lack of understanding of social processes. Greater social justice will not automatically result from trade liberalization; the social dimension of globalization must be addressed.

In 1994 and 1995, the anniversaries of a number of international organizations and movements were celebrated. Some institutions have been around for thirty years (the Group of 77 and UNCTAD), and others for fifty years (the UN, the Bretton Woods institutions, the World Bank, the IMF, and the GATT). These institutions have played a major political and economic role over the years, but today their organizational structure and processes as a system of agencies in the new world order is being increasingly questioned.

On one hand, there is a need for some sort of international governance to coordinate policies and regulate growing problems. On the other hand, national governments want to assert their sovereignty. Miller (1995) suggests that critics, who are concerned about global well-being over the long-term, struggle politically to take some power away from the national business and political players who act on the basis of short-term horizons, and, at the same time, to shift such power to agencies of international governance. This would likely imply changes in the present organizational and policy features of the international, financial and development institutions so as to establish, enforce and monitor "rules" for global trade and capital flows as prevailed from 1945-1970. The question remains; if a new Bretton Woods Agreement is indeed the answer to the search for a more equitable and less volatile pattern of development, where will the leadership required to implement it come from?

The world has changed from a bi-polar world, which set out two main models of political and economic development, capitalist and centrally planned, to a global capitalist world. Liberalism is regarded worldwide as a consensus and its motto of "good governance" from an economic and political perspective is hoped to be achieved. Free market ideology and human rights issues are at the forefront of economic and political analysis. Nevertheless, in the 1990s, all countries are facing development problems.

Both rich and poor countries constitute a single world system and human development is a challenge for world society. The distinction between North and South, and between East and West is eroding. Some would argue that the old stereotypes of North and South have no meaning anymore, largely due to globalization. Others, however, will suggest that the concept of North-South, the privileged versus the disadvantaged, remains as valid as ever (Hansenne, 1994). Even if some of the developing countries of the 1960s have become major economic powers since the 1980s, many others are still lagging behind, while the affluent North is facing increasing poverty, formerly associated with the South.

The South that now stands to face the 21st century is vastly different from the South of the 1960s. The East Asian component is already assuming the role of the engine of development for its Asian neighbors and for the world economy as a whole. The economic success of Japan and other Asian NICs in adopting modern technology and conquering world markets is changing international trade patterns and development issues. The economic recession in Europe and the U.S. is also a sign that the world economy is going through a period of adjustment.

Current and continuing changes in the global political, economic and ecological spheres are challenging prevailing views on the world trading system. Todaro (1995) reminds us that throughout the 1950s and for most of the 1960s, the development economics literature centered around one or more variants of the neoclassical "linear stages" paradigm. Development was viewed as a series of stages through which all economies must proceed, albeit at varying rates of progress depending on factors such as resource endowments and rates of savings and investment. However, those models could not adequately deal with the ubiquitous phenomena of rising unemployment, growing inequality and deepening rural poverty in almost every country of the developing world. This paradigm influenced a large number of economists who became responsible for the economic policies of international and national institutions, and governments in developing countries.

Consequently, the immediate post-World War II period is referred to as a paradigmac phase where the orthodox paradigm emerged and reigned over weaker alternative paradigms (Billet, 1993). The scientific community embraced the orthodox paradigm and the modernization theory as its main approaches to economic growth and development in the LDCs. Modernization theorists attribute the lack of economic development in the LDCs to the relatively low level of capital available. This led developing countries with lower levels of domestic savings to have higher levels of foreign aid and FDI. The dominant forms of external capital available are official development assistance (ODA), external debt and FDI. Therefore many governments of LDCs have been actively seeking international financial linkages through international institutions (IMF, World Bank), and FDI of multinational corporations. Although LDCs are wary of high levels of FDI and external debt that are perceived to decrease national sovereignty, both are often viewed as remedies.

By the mid-1980s, it was clear that a reformulated approach to the balance of payments and debt difficulties of developing countries was not working. Current account deficits had been reduced and debt brought temporarily under control within the debtor nations, but this occurred at the cost of large declines in investment, imports and per capita income. The prospects for future growth were compromised for these countries and their ability to service their debts was undermined. The export sector of the industrialized countries was also affected. A new formula of "adjustment-with-growth" was initiated by James Baker, U.S. Secretary of the Treasury, in October 1985 and became known as the Baker Plan. Technically speaking, the Baker Plan does not contain a formula for solving the debt crisis, but it did reveal a welcome recognition that some corrective and preventive action needed to be taken as the debt burden mounted with no prospect of reversing this worrisome trend that threatened creditor banks (Miller, 1986).

Political science literature has begun to deal with the political dimensions of adjustment (Nelson, 1990), including the need to look at power relations and to redirect public resources to the poor. The view emerged that adjustment could negatively affect women, vulnerable community groups and non-governmental organizations (NGOs). The mid-1980s viewed adjustment-with-growth, democracy and the involvement of the poorest segments of societies as a new panacea for development. Empowerment of women and minority groups became a new subject of discourse. These adjustment policies challenge neither the international division of labor nor the production-distribution-consumption model.

Some economists have tried to provide a different framework for dealing with development issues through radical paradigms which view developing countries as beset by political and economic problems and trapped by dependency relationships with industrialized countries. Many scholarly works, such as those by dependency theorists, are an extension of Marxist thinking. Underdevelopment is primarily attributed to the evolution of a highly unequal international capitalist system. Much of the developing world's poverty is also attributed to the policies of the northern hemisphere and their extension to small but powerful elites in the South. Dos Santos (1971), Gunder Frank (1967) and Prebish (1971) argue that underdevelopment is a consequence of dependent colonialism which causes LDCs to be both backward and exploited.

In the 1970s, economic development was redefined to place poverty reduction higher on the scale of objectives within the context of a growing economy (Chenery et al., 1971). But, although a few LDCs, particularly the Asian NICs, have experienced high growth rates of per capita income and reduced poverty since the 1960s-1980s, the majority showed little or no improvement in employment, equality or the real incomes of the poorest segments of their population, even though their national incomes were growing.

There is a fundamental dichotomy between the neoclassical paradigm and the so-called radical paradigm. The power structures of the actors involved in these two paradigms are quite different, as are their views of development. Under the radical paradigm, interdependence between rich and poor countries is unequal. During the last two decades, the radical approach itself has undergone a fundamental transformation, sweeping aside both the dependency theory and orthodox economics alike. The most compelling approach to result from all this is the theory of "internationalization of capital" and its many variants (Palloix, 1975; Cypher, 1979; Bina and Yaghmaian, 1991; Bina and Davis, 1996). According to this theory, the economic and social dimensions of globalization are conceptually unified.

Some authors have celebrated the victory of the ideals of capitalism (Fukuyama, 1993) whereas others (Hobsbawm, 1994) are warning us of the forces of the techno-scientific economy that threaten to destroy the environment and structure of human society. Kennedy (1993) sees a central paradox at work in the new international order in which the nation-state is surrendering more of its sovereign powers, yet in which nationalist sentiment is on the rise. Kennedy raises many complex questions about issues ranging from job creation to human rights. The answers to these questions do not necessarily imply more interventionism or some kind of utopian world government, Kennedy suggests. Rather, what is required is an attitudinal change by national governments; the change would demand a restructuring that would make these institutions more effective.

Rethinking the UN has involved institutes and governments, all of whose leaders and spokespersons say they want to debate and implement programs of reform. This is understandable given that the major concern of the UN 50 years ago was rebuilding nation-states destroyed by two world wars and preparing colonial territories for statehood. The existence of states was affirmed and the idea that the global community might be faced with collapsed states in the future was not anticipated. As well, the possibility that environmental damage and the depletion of natural resources might weaken societies was not on the agenda a half-century ago.

So far, the UN has provided a forum for mediation between the superpowers. The latest report (1995) submitted to Secretary-General Boutros-Ghali proposes changes to make the UN more effective. Among areas of consideration are the Security Council, which no longer reflects the world, the addition of permanent members (Japan, Germany, India or Brazil or the EU), the dropping of some Permanent Members (Britain and France), and changing the veto system. A standing army could become part of the UN to be sent to areas of crisis immediately, rather than waiting for individual members to respond. Peacekeeping and peace enforcement will depend on defined guidelines of intervention. Another suggestion is that economic and social councils oversee all organizations, including the World Bank, to set goals and streamline their functions.

From the start, the UN was a vision of a better, more just and equal world. Its Charter pledges that member nations will promote higher standards of living, full employment, and economic and social progress. Sadly, as previously noted, the rate of development has not been equal in all countries. Most of Africa is becoming the symbol of worldwide demographic, environmental and societal stress while some Asian NICs are highly successful economically.

In strictly economic terms, "development" for the past decade has meant the capacity of a national economy, whose initial economic condition has been more or less static for a long time, to generate and sustain an annual increase in its gross national product (GNP) at rates of 5 to 7% or more. The 1960s and 1970s were dubbed the "Development Decades" by a UN resolution, and development was seen largely as the attainment of a 6% annual target growth rate of GNP. The rate of growth of per capita GNP has also been a common economic measure to take into account a nation's ability to expand its output faster than the rate of population growth. Within such a limited framework, Asian developing nations are particularly vibrant, averaging more than 8% growth in the 1990s. Despite the success of the NICs, Asia is still struggling to alleviate poverty. Of the more than one billion poor people in the developing world, about 800 million live in Asia and about 500 million of them are considered to live in absolute poverty (Asian Development Bank, 1994).

Development cannot be viewed as a strictly aggregate economic phenomenon. And indeed, new indexes are being used today by international institutions to reflect changes in social institutions and social values given the multidimensional process of development. Since 1993, new initiatives for development projects have been adopted by international institutions. The World Bank encourages a greater local participation in all stages of development projects. The IMF stimulates a wave of privatization in which the private sector objectives must take into account social goals and environmental constraints. TNCs are encouraged to become more socially integrated with their host countries. This process might provide a better framework for development, but it raises issues related to national sovereignty.

Sustainable Development: Turning a Concept Into Reality

Sustainable development is still a concept that has galvanized the energies of those seeking to find solutions to environmental, social, political and economic problems. It reflects the global popular concern about the well-advertised threats to the world development pattern. Its acceptance as a meaningful slogan reflects the world's need for a new paradigm, a new conceptual framework that will bring with it constructive reforms for the renewal of society.

Sustainable development is defined as development that meets the needs of the present without compromising the ability of future generations to meet their own needs. The needs of the world's poor and the idea of limitations imposed by the state of technology and by social organization on the environment's ability to meet present and future needs, are two key concepts of sustainable development. According to that definition, the Brundtland Commission (WCED, 1987) notes seven strategic imperatives to pursue: reviving growth; changing the quality of growth; meeting essential needs for jobs, food, energy, water, and sanitation; ensuring a sustainable population level; conserving and enhancing the resource base; reorienting technology and managing risk; and merging environment and economics in decision-making.

Table 1 illustrates the complexities involved in dealing with the concept of sustainability. The rows show the types of sustainability, and the columns the influences of those types. The sustainability of economic growth would therefore be considered across the second row, with environmental influences (e.g. resource depletion) in cell A, economic influences (e.g. inflation and balance of payments) in cell B, and social influences (e.g. social cohesion) in cell C. The importance for sustainability of ethical influences is reflected in the first column. Relevant influences in cell E could be of concern for future generations or for non-human life; in cell F, they could be attitudes to poverty and income distribution.

Social sustainability refers to a society's ability to maintain, on the one hand, the necessary means of wealth creation to reproduce itself and, on the other, a shared sense of social purpose to foster social integration and cohesion. In such a context, having a sustainable economy is not only fundamental, but also a question of culture and values. Within such a context, social sustainability is likely to be a necessary condition for the widespread commitment and involvement that *Agenda 21* sees as necessary for the achievement of sustainable development.

Table 1: Types of Sustainability and their Interactions

Types of Sustainability	Influences on Sustainability			
	Ethical	Environmental	Economic	Social
Environmental	E		D	
Economic		A	B	C
Social	F			

Source: Ravaioli, Carla, *Economists and the Environment*, Zed Books, London and New Jersey, 1995, p. 188.

Decision makers face increasing levels of political, economic and ecological interdependence. Environmental disasters are presumed to result from the failure of decision makers to link activities in one field of action, such as industrial development, with effects on another field, such as fisheries. Therefore, the environmental repercussions of trade and development policies must be addressed in ways that are consistent with the continued promotion of sustainable development (rhetoric or reality?).

Environmental sustainability may always be considered desirable, but economic and social sustainability do not have such a bright prospect. For example, in many countries, structural unemployment is showing signs of continuing. In developing countries, the complexity and linkages between issues of population, youth and unemployment are of great concern. By the year 2000, 700 million jobs will have to be created in those countries to absorb new entrants into the job market. The experience in developed countries since the 1960s demonstrates that failure to create the necessary jobs will contribute to social discontent, which could trigger conflict.

Despite the fact that poverty alleviation is a central objective of development and a key concern for environment policies, poverty is showing signs of continuing. Poverty reflects both societal and global inequalities in the distribution of political and economic assets. To alleviate poverty, encourage worldwide economic growth and institutional and policy reforms, financial and technological resources must be transferred from industrialized countries to developing countries. Trade liberalization can be an important component of progress toward sustainable development for all countries. It may also be a component of the failure to maintain environmental quality. Therefore, trade policies that respect environmental and social policy goals should be a primary objective of national governments and policy makers in international institutions.

The ethics of sustainability will determine where the responsibility for promoting trade and environmental sustainability lies. This responsibility will also have to be enforced. In April 1994, when the Morocco Agreement of the Uruguay Round of the GATT negotiations was signed, the proposed WTO was given a program of future work, including a framework for approaching trade and environmental issues. The environment is likely to be an important component of future regional trade agreements between northern and southern countries. It is already a major component of NAFTA, which seems to be more environmentally friendly than the GATT given that the preamble to the main agreement explicitly recognizes the concept of sustainable development.

Increasing economic openness, both multilaterally and regionally, has given rise to concerns about detrimental effects on the environment. The debate about trade and the environment is not new, but it is intensifying. The OECD (1994) points out that the emphasis given to sustainable development, combined with more universal interest in outward-oriented development strategies, has linked the issue of longer-term growth with trade and the environment.[2] Galbraith (1995) states that "With the exception of the risk of nuclear war, the question of the environment is the most serious problem in the world." Analysis from the environmental commissions of the UN, the World Bank and the OECD states that if production continues at the present rate, the risk to the environment will reach unsustainable levels. This possibility gives rise to questions about the ability of market mechanisms alone to address environmental problems. National and international government regulations must, therefore, be in place to protect the environment. An international institution dealing specifically with environmental issues may help to harmonize efforts developed by individual countries.

Sustainable development has emerged as a key objective of the GATT and now of the WTO, NAFTA and the EU. Expanded trade is seen as a powerful means to this end, but there are fears that expanded trade will lead to environmental damage. Therefore, profound changes in world economic and environmental relations are needed to achieve a balanced relationship between trade and sustainable development.

Economic growth and the search for competitiveness continue to be the main objective for governments and enterprises. It is more important to increase GDP by 3 or 4% and be on the competitive edge than to try to work toward social justice. Somehow, decision makers refuse to accept that the system of the distribution of wealth must change. Issues of domestic production, international trade and government finance are integral to discussion of sustainable social development in relation to their impact on social and economic processes at national and international levels. After more than a decade of structural adjustment program initiatives supported by the World Bank, there have been few improvements in the economic performance of many low-income developing countries. Those adjustment policies have failed to have as central goals the reduction of poverty, direct support for environmentally positive policy or support of sustainable development (Singh et al., 1995). However, some new attitudes have emerged lately.

A collective responsibility of all humankind, a change in values, and perhaps a cultural revolution are all required to make the world a more just society. This seems to be an impossible dream, but as stated in *Uncommon Opportunities. An Agenda for Peace and Equitable Development* (1994): "The advance guard of those who have already achieved high levels of prosperity in both the industrial and developing countries have a special responsibility to assist the rest of the humanity to do so as well... A world in which 20% of the population enjoy 84% of the income, while another 20% struggle for survival on a mere 1.4%, can never provide a secure and sustainable way of life for humankind."

The same report makes the following recommendations:

- UN restructuring;
- establishing a global cooperative security system;
- setting a peace dividend to reduce global defense spending;
- implementing a universal ban on the possession of nuclear weapons;
- working toward full employment;
- creating one billion jobs in developing countries;
- developing a global employment program;
- creating an international sustainable development force for food deficit regions;
- adopting model district programs in many countries;
- eliminating crop losses in Russia and the other republics of the former Soviet Union;
- designing an institutional development framework for economic transitions;
- developing a global education program;
- implementing a plan for debt alleviation;

- developing a comprehensive, human-centered theory of development;
- practicing tolerance, diversity;
- reducing small arms proliferation.

The challenge is to address how these bench-marks are to be achieved. Given the current political and economic situation, there is a case for agnosticism when dealing with the above issues. Since the 1980s, LDCs have undergone profound economic and policy changes. Trade reforms have been implemented worldwide and policy changes have been brought about by regional and multilateral integration. Many countries have liberalized their trade regimes, reduced import tariffs and eliminated non-tariff barriers to trade. Liberalization processes are taking place in Asia and have been accompanied by the so-called economic miracle of the Asian NICs. Latin American countries are also on the path toward liberalization and economic integration with the U.S. and Canada. However, the sustainability of reforms, particularly their impact on social welfare, is still unclear.

Development is embodied in the globalization process, therefore economic interactions between countries and regions, and political struggles between rival nations or groups of nations are part of the development process. It is within this context that development must be pursued. To be successful, genuine development must last. Therefore, sustainability, self-reliance, and independence are essential to effective development. The Rio Global Summit in 1992 emphasized the extent of the conflict between the world's contradictory priorities of environment and development. Sustainable development became the theoretical answer to those conflicting priorities, but so far there is still no consensus on how it can be attained. There is some resistance to interpreting the changed world economy as a new system, although modified versions of existing analytical tools can be used to understand new economic realities.

Traditional political economy approaches should be rethought. The focus should be on the poor, on the importance of global economic inequalities, and on the need to implement strategies to deal with urgent issues such as overpopulation and the environment. Rules of ethics for policy making in nation-states and in TNCs must play a key role in the search for a more balanced way of development. It might be difficult, if not impossible, to maximize all values of social, natural and human development simultaneously and globally. Some basic assumptions of the capitalist dominant paradigm will have to be challenged. Free trade does not benefit all countries and partners to the same extent. The pursuit of individual interest does not necessarily lead to collective interest. Issues of world consumption and exploitation of labor (e.g. child labor, poor wages, and unsafe environmental standards of production) on a global scale are fundamental.

Conclusion

This paper has examined globalization patterns and development processes. In doing so, it has referred to the dominant capitalist paradigm and has questioned the legitimacy of such a concept toward the search for sustainable development. Solutions to common worldwide problems must restore a balance between economic growth and social development.

The main challenge of the 21st century will be to find the leadership required to achieve global welfare. If in such a search the capitalist paradigm does not provide the answer, there is a risk of being left with no direction in the absence of political leadership. If the capitalist paradigm continues to predominate, there is still the risk that the goal of abolishing poverty will not be present. Capitalism still lacks a comprehensive framework for moral ethics; the emphasis on the individual interest is not properly balanced by social welfare.

Endnotes

1. The author would like to thank Robert deCotret, Morris Miller and an anonymous reviewer for their helpful comments.

2. This study, entitled *A Survey of Trade and Environment Nexus: Global Dimensions*, surveys the literature dealing with the ongoing debate about trade and environment.

References

Asian Development Bank. *Annual Report*, Hong Kong: Golden Cup Printing Co. Ltd., 1994.

Billet, B. L. *Modernization Theory and Economic Development, Discontent in the Developing World*, London: Praeger, 1993.

Bina, C. and Davis, C. "Wage Labor and Global Capital: Global Competition and Universalization of Labor Movement," in C. Bina; L. Cléments and C. Davis , eds., *Beyond Survival: Wage Labor in the Late Twentieth Century*, Armonks N.Y.: M.E. Sharpe, 1996.

Bina, C. and Yaghmaian, B. "Post-war Global Accumulation and the Transnationalization of Capital," *Capital and Class*, 1991, No. 43, pp. 107-130.

Brown, L. R.; Lenssen, N. and Kane, H. *Vital Signs 1995. The Trends That Are Shaping our Future*, W. W. Norton & Company, Inc., Worldwatch Institute, 1995.

Chenery, H. B., et al. *Studies in Development Planning*, Cambridge: Harvard University Press, 1971.

Corniea, Giovanni Andrea; Jolly, Richard and Stewart, Frances. *Adjustment with a Human Face: Protecting the Vulnerable and Promoting Growth*, Oxford: Clarendon Press, 1987.

Cypher, J. "The Internationalization of Capital and the Transformation of Social Formations," *Review of Radical Political Economics*, 1979, Vol. 11, No. 4.

Dos, Santos T. "The Structure of Dependence," in K.T. Kan and Donald C. Hodges, eds., *Readings in U.S. Imperialism*, Boston: Extending Horizons, 1971, pp. 225-236.

Friedman, J. *Empowerment: The Politics of Alternative Development*, Cambridge: Blackwell, 1992.

Fukuyama, F. *The End of History and the Last Man*, New York: Avon Books, 1993.

Galbraith, J. K. *in* Carla Ravaioli, ed., *Economist and the Environment*, London: Zed Books, 1995.

Gunder, Frank A. *Capitalism and Underdevelopment in Latin America*, New York: Monthly Review Press, 1967.

Haggard, S. *Developing Nations and the Politics of Global Integration*, Washington, D.C.: The Brookings Institution, 1995.

Hansenne, M. "UNCTAD in the Changing World," *Development and International Cooperation*, 1994, Volume X, Number 19, pp. 27-38.

Harris, Richard G. "Globalization, trade and Income," *Canadian Journal of Economics*, 1993, XXVI, pp. 755-776.

Hobsbawm, Eric J. *Ages of Extremes: The Short Twentieth Century, 1914-1994*, London, Michael Joseph, 1994.

International Labor Organization, *World Employment 1995 Report*, Geneva: ILO, 1995.

International Monetary Fund. *World Economic Outlook*, Washington, DC: IMF, 1995.

Kennedy, Paul M. *Preparing for the Twenty-First Century*, New York: Random House, 1993.

Miller, Moris. "The Folly of Demonology," Program of Research in International Management and Economy, Faculty of Administration, University of Ottawa, Working Paper 95-02, January 1995.

_____. *Coping Is Not Enough! The International Debt Crisis and the Roles of the World Banks and the International Monetary Fund*, Homewood, Illinois: Dow Jones-Irwin Inc., 1986.

Nelson, Joan M. *Economic Crisis and Policy Choice: The Politics of Adjustment in the Third World*, Princeton, N.J.: Princeton University Press, 1990.

Organization for Economic Cooperation and Development. *The OECD Jobs Study: Facts, Analysis, Strategies*, Paris: OECD, 1994.

_____. *A Survey of the Trade and Environment Nexus: Global Dimensions*, OECD Economic Studies, 1994, No. 23, pp. 167-192.

Palloix, C. "The Internationalization of Capital and the Circuits of Social Capital," in H. Radice ,ed., *International Firm and Modern Imperialism*, Penguin, 1975.

Prebish, R. *Change and Development - Latin America's Great Task*, Report submitted to the Inter-American Development Bank, New York: Praeger, 1971.

Ravaioli, Carla. *Economics and the Environment*, London: Zed Books, 1995.

Report of the International Commission on Peace and Food. *Uncommon Opportunities. An Agenda for Peace and Equitable Development*, London: Zed Books, 1994.

Savoie, Donald J. *Globalization and Governance*, Canadian Centre for Management Development, Research Paper No. 12, November 1994.

Singh, N. C.; Titi, V. and Strickland, R. *Sustainable Development and the World Summit for Social Development*, International Institute for Sustainable Development (IISD), 1995.

Todaro, M. P. *Reflections on Economic Development*, Brookfield, USA: Edward Elgar Publishing Limited, 1995.

UNCTAD. *World Investment Report 1994: Transnational Corporations, Employment and the Workplace*, United Nations, New York and Geneva, 1994.

_____. *Trends in Foreign Direct Investment*, United Nations, New York and Geneva, 1995.

WCED (World Commission on Environment and Development). *Our Common Future* (The Brundtland Report), Oxford: Oxford University Press, 1987.

World Bank. *Global Economic Prospects and the Developing Countries*, Washington, DC: The World Bank, 1995.

_____. *Workers in an Integrating World*, World Development Report 1995, Washington, DC: The World Bank, 1995.

INDEX

CONTRIBUTORS

Francis Adams is Assistant Professor of Political Science, Old Dominion University; former Assistant Professor of Politics at Itahaca College. His recent research works includes *From Economic Nationalism to Neo-Liberalism: A Comparative Analysis of Foreign Economic Policy-Making in Venezuela and Jamaica.* He is currently editing *Globalization and the Dilemmas of the State in the South* (with Gupta and Mengisteab).

Dwight W. Adamson is Associate Professor of Economics, South Dakota State University; former Assistant Professor at Northern State University. He is a specialist on the union effects and international trade effects on the labor market, and has published several scholarly papers in leading economics journals.

Cyrus Bina is Director of the Center of Unified, Global, and Applied Research and a Lead Faculty for Research and Honors Program at the University of Redlands; former Fellow and Research Associate at Harvard University. He is the author of *The Economics of the Oil Crisis* and several scholarly papers,and a coeditor of *Modern Capitalism and Islamic Ideology in Iran* and *Beyond Survival: Wage labor in the Twentieth Century,*.

Saud A. Choudhry is Associate Professor of Economics, Trent University; former Assistant Professor at the Universities of Winnipeg and Manitoba. He has published several scholarly papers in leading economics journals and books in the fields of development, public finance and family economics.

Satya Dev Gupta is Professor of Economics at St. Thomas of University. Formerly, he has held teaching positions at McGill University, University of Toronto, University of the West Indies and University of Delhi. He has been Visiting Scholar at the Economics Research Unit, University of Pennsylvania. He has published several scholarly papers in the areas of international economics, regional economics, public finance and applied econometrics. He has authored *The World Zinc Industry* and has recently edited the three volume set on globalization and development: *Globalization, Growth and Sustainability, Dynamics of Globalization and Development*, and *Political Economy of Globalization*. He is currently editing *Globalization and the Dilemmas of the State in the South* (with Adams and Mengisteab).

Esmail Hossein-zadeh is Associate Professor of Economics at Drake University. His research work is in the field of international economics, development and political economy. He is the author of *Soviet Theory of Non-Capitalist Development.*

Tim Koechlin is Associate Professor of Economics at Skidmore College. He has published several scholarly papers in the areas of international investment, capital mobility, the North American Free Trade Agreement, economic integration and other topics. He has also published opinion pieces in the *Boston Globe* and other papers, and he has been interviewed about NAFTA by National Public Radio, *The NewYork Times* and the *Los Angeles Times.*

Brigitte Lévy is an Associate Professor of International Business (Faculty of administration) at the University of Ottawa. She has published *L 'économie Indienne: Stratégie de développement, Les Affaires internationales: l 'économieconfrontée aux faits* and *L 'enterprise, économie et gestion* and a number of scholarly papers in the area of international trade and development strategies. She is co-editor of the Canadian Journal of Development Studies. She has been consultant to the Economic Development Institute of the World Bank.

Sandra MacLean is a Doctoral Fellow, Centre for Foreign Policy Studies, Dalhousie University. She has published several papers in the areas of international political economy, democratization and civil society.

S. Mansoob Murshed is Lecturer in the Department of European Studies at the University of Bradford. He has published *Economic Aspects of North South Interaction* and several scholarly papers in the areas of international economics, environment and principal-agent models.

Deepak Nayyar is Professor of Economics at the Centre for Economic Studies and Planning, Jawaharlal Nehru University, New Delhi. He was the President of the Indian Economic Association (1995). Formerly, he has taught at the University of Sussex and the Indian Institute of Management, Calcutta. He has also served as Chief Economic Advisor to the Government of India and Secretary in the Ministry of Finance. He has authored *India's Exports and Export Policies, Migration, Remittances and Capital flows: The Indian Experience,* and *Economic Liberalization in India,* and has edited *Economic Relations between Socialist Countries and the Third World* and *Industrial Growth and Stagnation*: The Debate in India. He has also published several articles in leading economics journals.

Sylvia Ostry is Chairman, Centre of International Studies, University of Toronto and Chancellor, University of Waterloo. She has held a number of positions in the Federal Government of Canada and several national and international organizations. Some of her former positions include Deputy Minister, Chairman of the Economic council of Canada, Head of the Economics and Statistics Department of the OECD in Paris and Volvo Distinguished Visiting Fellow, Council on Foreign Relations, New York. She has received 17 honorary degrees from universities in Canada and abroad and, in 1987, received the outstanding Achievement Award of the Government of Canada. She has authored and edited several books and scholarly papers. Her most recent publications (1995-97) include *Technonationalism and Technoglobalism: Conflict and Cooperation* (with Richard Nelson), *Rethinking Federalism: Citizens, Markets and Governments in a Changing World*, and *Who's on First? The Post Coldwar Trading System*.

Mark D. Partridge is Assistant Professor of Economics, St. Claud State University. He has published several scholarly papers in leading economics journals in the area of the international trades effects on regional, national and international labor markets

Kunibert Raffer is Associate Professor of Economics at the University of Vienna. He has published *Unequal Exchange and the Evolution of World System*, *The Foreign Aid Business: Economic Assistance and Development Cooperation* (with H.W. Singer) and *Market Forces and World Development* and several scholarly papers in leading journals in the fields international trade, aid and debts.

Timothy M. Shaw is Professor of Political Science and Director of Centre for Foreign Policy Studies at Dalhousie University. He is editor of *International Political Economy Series* published by Macmillian. He has authored and edited several books and scholarly papers in the field of third world development, especially PE and FP in Africa and Southeast Asia. His recent publications include *Reformism and Revisionism in Africa's Political Economy in the 1990s* and *The South at the End of the Twentieth-Century*.

Brigitte Unger is Assistant Professor of Economics at Vienna University of Economics and Business Administration. Her former positions include Joseph Schumpeter Professor at Harvard University and Erwin Schroedinger Fellow and Maria Schaumayer Fellow at Stanford University. She has published *Convergence or Diversity? International and Economic Policy response* (with Frans van Waarden) and several scholarly papers. She is currently working on *Institutional*

Convergence? (ed. with Frans van Waarden) and *Internationalization and Economic Policy Making: How much Room for Manoevre is Left?*.

Beth V. Yarbrough is Professor of Economics at Amherst College. She has been Visiting Scholar in Economics, University of California at Berkeley and Visiting Scholar in Political Science at Stanford University. She has co-authored (with R. Yarbrough) *Cooperation and Governance in International Trade: The Strategic Organizational Approach* and *The World Economy: Trade and Finance* and has published several scholarly papers.

Robert M. Yarbrough is an Adjunct Associate Professor of Economics at Amherst College. He has been Visiting Scholar in Economics, University of California at Berkeley and Visiting Scholar in Political Science at Stanford University. He has co-authored (with B. Yarbrough) *Cooperation and Governance in International Trade: The Strategic Organizational Approach* and *The World Economy: Trade and Finance* and has published several scholarly papers.